www.wadsworth.com

wadsworth.com is the World Wide Web site for Wadsworth and is your direct source to dozens of online resources.

At *wadsworth.com* you can find out about supplements, demonstration software, and student resources. You can also send email to many of our authors and preview new publications and exciting new technologies.

wadsworth.com
Changing the way the world learns ®

Beyond Sovereignty

Issues for a Global Agenda

Second Edition

Maryann Cusimano Love
The Catholic University of America

THOMSON
™
WADSWORTH

Australia • Canada • Mexico • Singapore • Spain
United Kingdom • United States

THOMSON
WADSWORTH

Executive Editor: David Tatom
Assistant Editor: Heather Hogan
Editorial Assistant: Dianna Long
Marketing Manager: Janise Fry
Advertising Project Manager: Brian Chaffee
Print/Media Buyer: Barbara Britton
Permissions Editor: Elizabeth Zuber
Production, Copyediting, Illustration, &
*   Composition:* Summerlight Creative
Text Designer: Paul Lacy
Text & Cover Printer: Transcontinental–
    Louiseville, Quebec

Cover Designer: Jeanette Barber
Cover Image: AFP Photo/Jewel Samad

In Dhaka, Bangladesh, a child shows a banner as others hold black flags during a demonstration on September 14, 2001, protesting the terrorist attacks against the United States. More than 100 men, women, and children took part in the demonstration to pay their respects for the 50 Bangladeshis who were among the more than 2,000 people killed when two hijacked planes were flown into the twin towers of the World Trade Center in New York.

For more information about our products, contact us at:
Thomson Learning Academic Resource Center
1-800-423-0563

For permission to use material from this text, contact us by:
Phone: 1-800-730-2214 **Fax:** 1-800-730-2215
Web: http://www.thomsonrights.com

Wadsworth/Thomson Learning
10 Davis Drive
Belmont, CA 94002-3098
USA

Asia
Thomson Learning
5 Shenton Way #01-01
UIC Building
Singapore 068808

Australia
Nelson Thomson Learning
102 Dodds Street
South Melbourne, Victoria 3205
Australia

Canada
Nelson Thomson Learning
1120 Birchmount Road
Toronto, Ontario M1K 5G4
Canada

Europe/Middle East/Africa
Thomson Learning
High Holborn House
50/51 Bedford Row
London WC1R 4LR
United Kingdom

Latin America
Thomson Learning
Seneca, 53
Colonia Polanco
11560 Mexico D.F.
Mexico

Spain
Paraninfo Thomson Learning
Calle/Magallanes, 25
28015 Madrid, Spain

ISBN 0-534-60893-0

In memory of

Francis Cusimano, S.J.,

who taught me Africa was only as far away
as your uncle's smile, and that we can imagine and create
a better globalization for our future.

Contents

About the Editor

Maryann Cusimano Love is an associate professor of politics at the Catholic University of America in Washington, D.C., and a member of the Council on Foreign Relations and the International Policy Committee for the US Conference of Catholic Bishops. She teaches graduate and undergraduate courses on international relations and US foreign policy at both Catholic University and the Pentagon. She is also author of *Unplugging the Cold War Machine: Globalization and US Foreign Policy* (Sage Publications, 2002) and a children's book, *You Are My I Love You*. She holds a B.A. degree from St. Joseph's University in Philadelphia, an M.A. degree from the University of Texas, and a Ph.D. from Johns Hopkins University.

About the Contributors

Christopher A. Corpora is a research analyst for the US Department of Defense and a Ph.D. candidate in the School of International Service at American University in Washington, D.C. He is the author of many professional and scholarly publications and is currently conducting research and writing on transnational organized crime in the former Yugoslav republics. All statements associated herein with Mr. Corpora are his own and do not reflect the official positions of the US government or Department of Defense.

Maria Green Cowles is an assistant professor at American University. She is coeditor of *Transforming Europe: Europeanization and Domestic Change* (Cornell University Press, 2001) and *The State of the European Union,* Vol. 5 (Oxford University Press, 2001). She is the author of numerous articles and book chapters on the European Union's effects on domestic institutions, the role of multinational firms in EU policy making, and the influence of transnational and global business organizations in global regulatory and governance matters. She is a former vice chair of the European Union Studies Association.

Martha Crenshaw is John E. Andrus Professor of Government at Wesleyan University, where she has taught international politics and foreign policy, including a course on terrorism, since 1974. Her research has produced many publications, beginning in 1972 with an article titled "The Concept of Revolutionary Terrorism" in the *Journal of Conflict Resolution*. She is the author of *Revolutionary Terrorism: The FLN in Algeria, 1954-1962* as well as *Terrorism and International Cooperation*, and she edited the books *Terrorism, Legitimacy, and Power* and *Terrorism in Context*.

Stephen Flynn is a senior fellow with the National Security Studies Program at the Council on Foreign Relations, headquartered in New York City. Currently he is directing a multiyear project, "Protecting the Homeland: Rethinking the Role of Border Controls." He has served in the White House Military Office during the George H.W. Bush administration and as a director for global issues on the National Security Council staff during the Clinton administration. He is author of several articles and book chapters on border control, homeland security, the illicit drug trade, and transportation security, including "American the Vulnerable" in *Foreign Affairs* (Jan.–Feb. 2002) and "The Unguarded America" in *How Did This Happen?* A career Coast Guard officer, Commander Flynn is a 1982 graduate of the US Coast Guard Academy and has served twice in command at sea. He received a M.A.L.D. and Ph.D. in 1990 and 1991 from the Fletcher School of Law and Diplomacy, Tufts University.

James L. Ford recently retired from the Department of Energy, where he held various senior executive positions in the Office of Nonproliferation and National Security. He is currently working as a private consultant in the nuclear nonproliferation field. He is the coauthor of *Controlling Threats to Nuclear Security* and the author of two monographs: *Nuclear Smuggling: How Serious a Threat* and *Radiological Dispersal Devices: Assessing the Transnational Threat* (all from National Defense University Press, Washington, D.C.). He holds B.A. and M.A. degrees from Louisiana State University, and a second M.A. from the University of Kansas.

Vicki L. Golich is professor of political science at California State University, San Marcos. She is the coauthor of two environmental politics cases— on debt-for-nature swaps and acid rain negotiations—as well as lead author of articles on global environmental management issues. She is active in the governance of the environmental politics sections of both the International

Studies Association and the American Political Science Association. She holds an A.B. in Diplomacy and World Affairs from Occidental College, an M.A. from California State University—Fullerton, and a Ph.D. in International Relations from the University of Southern California. She is also a master case teacher and author of *The ABCs of Case Teaching*.

Hal Kane is a writer and consultant in San Francisco and a senior fellow at Redefining Progress, a public policy think tank. He is author or coauthor of more than ten books about international environmental issues, hunger, and economic development, many of them written for the Worldwatch Institute in Washington, D.C. His most recent book is *Triumph of the Mundane: The Unseen Trends that Shape Our Lives and Our Environment* (Island Press, 2000). He holds his M.A. degree from Johns Hopkins University School of Advanced International Studies.

Rensselaer W. Lee is president of Global Advisory Services in McLean, Virginia, and author of *Smuggling Armageddon: The Nuclear Black Market in the Former Soviet Union and Europe* (St. Martin's, 1999). He currently is working as a consultant for the Congressional Research Service on terrorism, drugs, and homeland security issues.

Richard A. Love is an attorney and senior analyst at Science Applications International Corporation in McLean, Virginia, where he has served as a legal and policy consultant for the White House and the Departments of State, Defense, and Justice. He teaches graduate courses in international law and national security policy at Catholic University in Washington, D.C., and has authored many academic articles and book chapters on globalization, technology, and law and corporate responsibility. He holds a B.A. in history and International Relations from the University of Virginia, a J.D. in Law and Economics from George Mason University, and an LL.M. in International Law from American University, and he is working on his SJD in International Law. He is currently working on the Financial Crimes and Money Laundering Project at the Brookings Institution.

John T. Picarelli is an analyst at the Transnational Crime and Corruption Center and a Ph.D. candidate at the School of International Service—both at American University. He has studied the topics of transnational organized crime, terrorism, and information technology since 1995 and has published widely in academic and policy journals. He holds a B.A. from the University of Delaware and an M.A. from the Graduate School of Public and International Affairs at the University of Pittsburgh.

Dennis Pirages is Harrison Professor of International Environmental Policy at the University of Maryland, College Park. He is the author or editor of several books on international relations and environmental politics, including *Building Sustainable Societies* (M. E. Sharpe, 1996), *Transformations in the Global Political Economy* (St. Martin's, 1990), and *Global Technopolitics* (Brooks/Cole, 1989). Dr. Pirages holds a Ph.D. in political science from Stanford University.

Paul Runci is a researcher with the Global Climate Change Group of the Pacific Northwest National Laboratory in Washington, D.C. He is also a Ph.D. candidate in the Department of Government and Politics at the University of Maryland, College Park.

Louise Shelley is a professor in the Department of Justice, Law, and Society and the School of International Service at American University. She is founder and director of the Transnational Crime and Corruption Center (TraCCC), a center devoted to teaching, research and training, and public outreach on these issues. She is the recipient of Guggenheim, NEH, and Kennan Institute grants and received a MacArthur grant to establish the Russian Organized Crime Study Centers. Professor Shelley is the author of *Policing Soviet Society* (Routledge, 1996), *Lawyers in Soviet Worklife,* and *Crime and Modernization* and numerous articles and book chapters on all aspects of transnational crime and corruption.

Preface

The first edition of *Beyond Sovereignty* argued that world politics had changed: Nonstate actors operating across international borders were increasingly important; globalization carried unintended consequences (including terrorism) to which even strong states were vulnerable; countries cannot manage pressing global problems alone; and sovereign, military responses are less effective ways to manage global issues. Developments since the first edition reinforce these themes.

The events of September 11 hit home professionally and personally. I teach at the Pentagon every Tuesday through Catholic University's graduate program in international affairs for military officers and government employees. At 9:30 A.M. on September 11, a dead car battery kept me out of harm's way. My students were in the Pentagon offices that were hit. They lost co-workers and offices (including our class materials and books), but they escaped. Except for that day, we continued to meet every week—on the site where 189 people had died, past the emergency vehicles (modified golf carts marked with medical Red Cross symbols) that lined the hallways outside our classroom with stretchers and body bags ready for the next attack, and past the crayon drawings on the walls from grade schools all over the country, "Our hearts are with you. Hope you find your friends. Be strong. You are in our prayers." Like the experiences of colleagues who teach in Ramallah and Beirut, the semester was an interesting experience in teaching about terrorism and global problems at the site of a terrorist attack, during a war against nonstate actors, and with students who were all under attack and charged with carrying out the US military response. As students replaced their copies of *Beyond Sovereignty: Issues for a Global Agenda* burned in the fire (one student recovered a smoke- and water-damaged copy from the FBI evidence team), they encouraged me to quickly produce a second edition. One student, an army chaplain, argued it was our moral responsibility to get information out to the public that could help people to understand what had happened and put events into the context of the challenges of globalization.

I did not need much convincing. For the past three years, colleague and contributor Stephen Flynn had led, and I had participated in, a Council on Foreign Relations project on Homeland Security. We briefed policy makers; government officials in the national security bureaucracy; Congressional representatives; and business, civic, and academic leaders in Washington, D.C., New York, Miami, Houston, Los Angeles, Ottawa (Canada), Port of Spain (Trinidad), and Kingston (Jamaica). We warned of the vulnerabilities of the global trade and transportation infrastructure to exploitation by terrorists and criminals. My "stump speech" line was, "Terrorists and tourists alike use the same global infrastructure." We told leaders the question was not whether an attack would occur, but when.

Our briefings were met with either sympathy or skepticism. The sympathetic said they agreed but were powerless to change the allocation of resources to better respond. The only new security initiative being funded by the United States was missile defense. The Clinton administration had increased anti- and counterterrorism measures, but scandals dissipated any political capital to do more, and the Bush administration favored unilateral rather than multilateral approaches to security. The sympathetic in business argued that they could not convince their shareholders or CEOs to reallocate resources to public security functions. The skeptics argued that if terrorism was such a clear and present danger, then why did only nineteen Americans die in the year 2000 from terrorist attacks? Business leaders in particular argued that the problems, while interesting, were really not their concern. In their view, counterterrorism was the government's job—specifically, the job of the military and law enforcement. We countered that trade and transportation infrastructure are largely privately owned and operated. Government cannot protect critical infrastructure without information, assistance, and cooperation from the private sector.

Since September 11, many of our proposals are being considered (with some adopted) by governments and businesses. However, the status quo is a powerful force, and there is still a disconnect in policy, academic, and public discussions in thinking about global problems. Discussions of global problems, state sovereignty, and globalization too quickly degenerate into either–or, all-or-nothing debates. Advocates of globalization oversell it in their zeal to convert opponents. According to many representatives of international financial institutions, governments, and businesses, globalization promotes progress, life, liberty, and the pursuit of happiness, everything that is good about the enlightenment tradition. Critics respond by over-demonizing globalization. From poverty to injustice to exploitation and environmental degradation, there is no evil in the world that cannot be traced to globalization. Clearly, good and evil existed long before globalization. But in the marketing attempts to persuade converts and win the media public relations battle, careful thought too often loses out. For the past several years, I have been working with various religious groups and nongovernmental organizations on projects that examine the ethical implications of globalization and ways to reform globalization to be more in line with important societal values. But even among ethicists and religious leaders with nuanced and sophisticated understandings of good and evil, the same either–or debates often prevail. The same goes for discussions of the future of sovereignty. Some argue globalization means the sovereign state is dead, while others argue that nothing has changed.

Beyond Sovereignty takes a different approach. We argue that globalization (the interdependent infrastructure of global open economies, societies, and technologies) brings both promise and problems. We cannot get one without the other. Societies pursue policies of economic and political liberalization in order to achieve peace and prosperity only to find they are increasingly vulnerable to a host of global problems that use the same global infrastructure. To create a more just and sustainable globalization, transsovereign problems must be recognized, understood, and carefully managed.

The same logic applies to the future of sovereign states. States do not sign up for globalization policies in order to put themselves out of business. Yet attempts to mitigate global problems produce unintended side effects; sovereignty is changing. Even the most powerful states in the system are increasingly affected by nonstate actors and global problems they cannot solve alone. To maintain legitimacy, domestic and international law, order, peace, and justice, states must become increasingly skilled in coordinating efforts with other states and a host of nonstate actors locally and internationally. Failure to manage global issues further undermines sovereignty. But efforts to solve global problems also must go beyond sovereignty.

Our choices are not between a globalization that puts profits before people or no globalization at all. Similarly, our choices are not between autonomous sovereign states as they existed in 1648 or no sovereign states at all. The world is more complex and adaptive than that. We can imagine globalization without exploitation, and sovereignty with social responsibility acting in concert with nonstate institutions. Imagination is the first step in creation.

The silver lining of the September 11 attacks and the subsequent "war on terrorism" attempts to counter the problems of global terrorism, refugees, nuclear smuggling, crime, and disease may be a greater understanding that no one is immune or invulnerable to global problems and that no one can solve these problems alone. Our hope lies in adapting new systems to coordinate actions across a wide variety of actors and to develop better ways to work together. Because our problems cross state borders and include states and nonstate actors, the public and private sectors, so must our solutions.

Beyond Sovereignty: Issues for a Global Agenda begins with an outline of the debates over globalization; the rise of transsovereign problems and open markets, open societies, and open economies; a historical description of sovereignty; and a review of current theories about whether sovereignty is receding or changing or remaining as powerful as ever. The chapters that follow, written by noted academics and expert practitioners, consider various global issues; their connections with globalization's open economies, societies, and technologies; and potential policy solutions. Chapters describe the changing roles of nonstate actors, including intergovernmental organizations (IGOs), nongovernmental organizations (NGOs), and multinational corporations (MNCs). To manage global issues, institutions must change. Global changes move quickly, while institutions change slowly, creating a variety of institutional gaps. Obstacles and the promise of institutional change are then discussed. The concluding chapter reviews the various policy proposals to combat global issues. Some of the prescriptions focus on the state as savior. Others regard states as ill-equipped to manage global issues and instead suggest that private or nonstate actors intercede. Other proposals suggest that some combination of state and nonstate activities manage global issues. The volume then returns to the theoretical arguments about the future of sovereignty. Do the preceding chapters support or challenge the various theories on the future of the state? If sovereignty has not yet been dethroned by some competing organizational form, does that mean that it remains unchanged and unscathed by current developments?

Beyond Sovereignty is written with students in introductory courses in international relations, US foreign policy, global issues, and globalization in mind. *Beyond Sovereignty* differs from other issue texts. The chapters were written explicitly for this volume. Each chapter addresses the common themes of globalization, the rise of nonstate actors, and the effects on sovereignty, and each proposes potential solutions to pressing global issues. The issues are not presented in an ad hoc, disconnected fashion, as occurs with many issues texts that present descriptive accounts (usually reprinted from journals) without providing the theoretical or historical context that unites current challenges. Instead, readers are offered an understanding of how these issues intersect, why they are on the rise simultaneously, the origins of these issues, and the theoretical and practical problems in policy solutions. Too often, political science books present the problems and criticisms of current policy without presenting alternatives. These books do not meet our moral responsibilities as citizens, students, and scholars not only to describe problems but also to propose possible solutions. In contrast, *Beyond Sovereignty* describes both global problems and possible solutions.

The second edition's chapters are briefer and more on point than those of the first edition, with new chapters on terrorism, the environment, cyberthreats, transnational crime, IGOs, MNCs, and NGOs. Each chapter begins with new and brief minicase examples to launch exploration and discussion of the materials. All chapters were revised in light of new twists in the globalization debates, new data, and the events of September 11. The second edition includes more discussions of developing countries', women's, constructivist, and normative perspectives.

This book benefited from conversations and input from many individuals, although any errors or omissions are purely my own. Discussions with Drs. Richard Love, Stephen Flynn, and Deborah Gerner encouraged me to go forward with the second edition. Meetings with policy makers and bishops from Latin America, Canada, and the United States on humanizing globalization helped convince me of the need for this book and the importance of its thesis. Discussions with colleagues James Rosenau and James Goldgier of George Washington University, Anne Florini and P. J. Simmons of the Carnegie Endowment for International Peace, Virginia Haufler of the University of Maryland, and Wolfgang Reinicke of the World Bank cross-fertilized ideas and encouraged me to proceed. Many thanks go to the volume contributors who worked with great speed under a tight deadline to produce a quality edition. My undergraduate and graduate students at the Catholic University of America and the Pentagon, especially Nate Frier, David Caldwell, Lance Moore, Greg Brady, Klaus Schmidt, Karen Kwiatkowski, Erin Ennis, Steve Lemons, Paul Sunwabe, Audrey Ammons, James Herrera, Michelle Boomgaard, Jennifer Jaskel, and Emily Levasseur provided lively discussions. The editorial and production staff at Wadsworth, especially Executive Editor David Tatom, Assistant Editor Heather Hogan, and book producer S.M. Summerlight were strongly committed to fast-tracking a September 11 second edition. The manuscript was also helped by the reviewer comments of Lowell Barrington, Marquette University; Deborah J. Gerner, University of Kansas; Darren Hawkins, Brigham Young University; Stacy D. VanDeveer, University of New Hampshire; Joseph Lepgold, Georgetown University; and Thomas Volgy, University of Arizona.

Last, but not least, my husband, family, and friends—especially at St. Aloyius Gonzaga Parish, the Center for International Social Development at Catholic University, Women in International Security, and the Jesuit order—buoyed my spirits and kept me sane throughout. A portion of the proceeds from this book will go to the Francis Cusimano S. J. Scholarship Fund to support the education of children in Nigeria.

Maryann Cusimano Love
The Catholic University of America
Washington, D.C.
July 2002

CHAPTER ONE

Global Problems, Global Solutions

Maryann Cusimano Love

> We have entered the third millennium through a gate of fire. If today, after the horror of 11 September, we see better, and we see further we will realize that humanity is indivisible. New threats make no distinction between races, nations or regions . . . wealth or status. A deeper awareness of the bonds that bind us all in pain as in prosperity has gripped us.
>
> —UN Secretary-General Kofi Annan, accepting the Nobel Prize for Peace, December 10, 2001

On September 11, 2001, the world witnessed a fiery and fatal demonstration of global issues that move beyond sovereignty. Nonstate actors used nonmilitary means to attack primarily nongovernment targets. Nineteen terrorists who represented no state inflicted massive casualties and approximately 3,000 deaths against citizens from the most powerful state in the international system as well as from 80 other countries. They used commercial airlines, the tools of transportation and commerce, to attack, and chose as their primary targets the twin towers of the World Trade Center, symbols of global capitalism. Members of the al Qaeda terrorist network, the presumed perpetrators, operate across sovereign borders through cells in an estimated 50 countries. The suicide bombers were Saudis and Egyptians who had been living in the United States, trained in Afghanistan, and organized and financed in Germany, England, and Spain with information and money sent to them from companies, nongovernmental organizations (NGOs), and individuals around the world. The al Qaeda financial network drew from the diamond trade in Sierra Leone and the heroin trade in Afghanistan, effectively linking the terrorist network with global crime and drug trafficking networks. The hijackers exploited the very global transportation, communication, and economic systems they protested—and which they believed carry undue and unwanted US and Western influence around the world. Their high visibility attacks were planned to maximize global media exposure.

After September 11, airlines increased security. NGOs addressed the flows of refugees fleeing the fighting in Afghanistan. The banking and financial communities increased their efforts to curtail money laundering. Osama bin Laden videotaped messages that were broadcast to his followers by the global media. Pharmaceutical companies decided how much of the antibiotic Cipro to produce and at what price, and doctors and hospitals worked to try to diagnose and halt the spread of anthrax infections. None of these important global responses is captured by the traditional view of International Relations as the activities of states.

This book investigates global issues that move beyond sovereignty in both the nature of problems and solutions. As one UN official observed, "Disease and pollution cross borders without passports."[1] Borders are more permeable, and threats are decentralized, fast, fungible, and fluid. How can transsovereign issues be tackled in a system that is based on sovereignty? How does globalization facilitate both global problems and attempts to manage them? How do the debates over globalization frame our understanding of these issues? We describe the rising importance of nonstate actors and global issues, and the challenges to changing institutions. Finally, the volume reviews various theories on the status and future of sovereignty, and assesses where sovereignty is heading.

Transsovereign problems are the downsides of globalization. Globalization is the fast, interdependent spread of open society, open economy, and open technology infrastructures. Globalization is not new, but the speed, reach, intensity, cost, and impacts of the current period of globalization are. Earlier periods of globalization moved trade, missionaries, and colonizers far more slowly with the speed of frigates. Now people and products cross borders in hours. Ideas and capital move around the globe at the touch of a keystroke. Transsovereign problems are "problems [that] transcend state boundaries in ways over which states have little control and which cannot be solved by individual state actions alone."[2] Nonstate actors are important players both in creating and managing global issues—from legal groups such as NGOs, intergovernmental organizations (IGOs), and multinational corporations (MNCs) to illicit groups such as international crime cartels and terrorist organizations. The rise of transsovereign problems is made possible by the very changes that have been facilitated andcelebrated by many policy makers: the rise of democracies and liberal, capitalist economies, and advances in technology, transportation, and communication. Thus, the rise of transsovereign problems is full of irony. It is physically difficult to limit the flow of particular peoples and goods at a time when technological, market, and societal forces make such movement easier than ever before.

Although globalization did not create transsovereign problems, it has facilitated and intensified them. For example, although terrorism existed long before, the modern period of globalization certainly facilitates the work of terrorist groups such as al Qaeda.[3] Open economies, societies, and technologies gave al Qaeda the opportunity to take its complaints to a global stage, to act at a distance cheaply, to perpetrate greater casualties using global technologies, and to elicit greater fear by playing in front of cameras and satellites that broadcast its members' actions instantly and globally. Globalization gives breakdowns in state authority and capacity and transsovereign problems greater reach, speed, intensity, and impact.

Sovereignty is the form of political organization that has dominated the international system since the Treaty of Westphalia in 1648. Sovereign states have exclusive and final jurisdiction over territory, as well as the resources and populations that lie within such territory. A system based on sovereignty is one that acknowledges only one political authority over a particular territory and looks to that authority as the final arbiter to solve problems that occur within its borders. Sovereign states have four characteristics, three of which are negotiable: territory, population, a government with control over the territory and population, and international recognition. In practice, only international recognition is non-negotiable. If a political entity has territory, population, and a government but lacks international recognition, then it is not considered a sovereign state; the Palestinian Authority is one example. Once a state is internationally recognized, such as Somalia, it does not matter if it lacks a government with the ability to control the territory and population, if territory is contested, or if population varies widely (because of large refugee flows, for example).

Although many policy makers and journalists (and sometimes even scholars) use the term *transnational* in discussing such problems, this volume will instead use the more accurate term *transsovereign* problems or global issues. The term *nation* is not synonymous with the term *sovereign state*. A nation is a group with a common cultural, linguistic, ethnic, racial, or religious identity—such as the Sioux nation of the US plains or the Moluccans in Northern Europe. A sovereign state or country, however, is an internationally recognized unit of political authority over a given territory, such as the United States of America or the Netherlands. National boundaries— where various ethnic or linguistic groups are located—often do not coincide with sovereign state boundaries. For example, the Basques live on either side of the border between Spain and France, and the Kurds live in the region straddling Iraq and Turkey. By some counts, more than 8,000 national groups exist—but only 189 sovereign states.[4] The distinction is not just academic. Each year, tens of thousands of people die trying to make their nations into states. This volume uses the terms *transsovereign* or *global* to keep clear the distinction between sovereign states and national groups.

Twentieth-century international relations were epic battles of behemoth states, a century of "heroic warfare" among strong, competing states—for example, World Wars I and II and the Cold War. In contrast, the twenty-first century is marked by "postheroic warfare."[5] Conflicts now come not from battles among strong states but from the problems posed by nonstate actors and weak or disintegrating states ("Humpty Dumpty wars" in which all the king's forces and men may not be able to put fractured states back together again). Although global issues move beyond sovereignty, the machinery we have to manage these problems is still wired for the sovereign, often state-to-state, military confrontations of a bygone era. Within two months, the US government responded to the September 11 terrorist attacks with a military attack on the Taliban government in Afghanistan not only because it was sheltering Osama bin Laden, but also because this is what the US government knows how to do: fight other states. It is difficult to attack an unknown, moving target, a nonstate actor with no known address.

The post–Cold War era is witness to the collapse of many weak states that had previously been kept afloat by Cold War aid and alliances.[6] These same trends of open societies, open economies, and open technologies can further erode already weak state institutions in many quasi-states, pushing them closer to collapse. Failed states provide a natural breeding ground for transsovereign problems such as terrorism, international criminal activity, flows of refugees, the spread of contagious disease, and trafficking in drugs and nuclear materials. Failed states also attract the relief and development efforts of NGOs and IGOs. In a world primarily organized around state sovereignty, world politics practitioners are challenged by a double bind. How can transsovereign issues be dealt with effectively in a world of sovereign states? Simultaneously, how can democratization and economic liberalization be promoted in ways that do not undermine already fragile state institutions to the point of collapse, thus increasing the spread and intensity of transsovereign problems?

GLOBAL PROBLEMS AND THE GLOBALIZATION DEBATES

Globalization creates a world of paradox. Global transportation, communication, and economic interdependence make possible the vision of a closer human family. A million people cross an international border every day. Terrorists and dangerous microbes, however, use the same global infrastructure that tourists do. Although capital flows of $2 trillion cross borders each day, most poor people and poor countries see little of it. Building the global infrastructure of open economies, technologies, and societies creates great benefits, but globalization also carries significant costs that are often not equitably dispersed, especially to the world's poor.

Some scholars[7] and advocates argue that globalization is a means to bring peoples and cultures together; route tyrannical governments; easily and cheaply spread information, ideas, capital, and commerce; and transfer more power than ever before to civil society and networked individuals.[8] For advocates such as McDonald's, Nike, other international businesses, the International Monetary Fund (IMF), the World Bank, and government officials in developed countries, curtailing globalization would be immoral. Global poverty is a problem—and globalization is the key to solving it. The world's most impoverished countries are those that are least globalized.

Other scholars and critics, however, see globalization as neoimperialism wearing Bill Gates's face and Mickey Mouse's ears, extending the web of global capitalism's exploitation of women, minorities, the poor, and developing regions. It fouls ecosystems, displaces local cultures and traditions, mandates worship at the altar of rampant consumer capitalism, and deepens the divide (digital and otherwise) between the global haves and have-nots.[9] Opposition to globalization comes from many different camps, but critics share a common view that globalization puts profits before people. Globalization benefits a few at the top and in the West at the expense of the rest. Environmental, human rights, and labor advocates charge that globalization brings a race to the bottom in human rights and environmental standards as businesses extend their reach to benefit the corporate bottom line. Local laws and control may be sacrificed to international regimes that are controlled by a few powerful states or corporations. These regimes are not democratic, representative, or transparent. Critics see globalization as a new form of imperialism—whether corporate, cultural, or US or Western—that is immoral and unjust. Liberal consumer advocates such as Ralph Nader, conservative protectionists such as the Peronistas in Argentina and Patrick Buchanan in the United States, radicals such as Osama bin Laden and al Qaeda, and anticorporate activists such as anti-McDonald's farmer Jose Bove in France have little in common other than their opposition to globalization. For these opponents, the biggest question is how to stop globalization and the harms that come from it.

Opponents and advocates see globalization differently in part because the costs and benefits of globalization are asymmetrically distributed rather than shared equally. Capitalism is criticized for disparities between rich and poor in terms of income, political power, participation, and opportunities. In parallel, the worldwide spread and intensification of capitalism that globalization represents is criticized for exacerbating capitalism's excesses and exporting the resulting problems to the entire world. For example, before the latest phase of globalization, the disparity between the richest and poorest quintiles of the earth's population was 30 to 1. In 1997, the richest 20 percent were 74 times richer than the world's poorest 20 percent. The wealth of the world's three richest individuals surpasses the combined gross domestic product (GDP) of all the world's underdeveloped countries (with their 600 million inhabitants).[10] Although global population growth certainly plays a part, 100 million more people now live in poverty than in the early 1990s.[11] Of the 6 billion people now on the planet, 3 billion live on less than $2 a day, and 1.3 billion live on less than $1 per day.[12] Sixty countries are poorer than they were in the early 1980s, and 80 countries are poorer than they were in the early 1990s.[13] Critics say globalization widens the gap between rich and poor. Advocates say the lack of globalization causes such poverty.

Wealth is only one indicator of global asymmetries. Decisions about globalization are made in corporate boardrooms and state capitals generally in economically developed states. Toxic waste from developed countries, however, is shipped to the world's poorest communities as some corporations exploit regions where environmental legislation or enforcement is weak. Most foreign direct investment and corporate shareholder profits go to developed states. "Controlling for the opening of both China and the former Soviet bloc, which attracted almost no investment before 1985, the share of foreign direct investment going to the developing world actually dropped" from 1985 to 1995.[14] Globalization's costs and benefits are unequally distributed, with poor people and poor countries too often not participating in the full benefits that globalization may bring. Maximizing the benefits of globalization while minimizing or managing the challenges is difficult because the institution we generally task with managing global problems—the sovereign state—cannot do the job alone.

Most of the clashes between globalization's proponents and skeptics are peaceful, carried out in op-ed pages, in consumer boycotts, and on the floors of parliaments. However, even before September 11, violence was increasing in debates about globalization. Ninety-three people were wounded and one killed protesting the "Group of Eight" (G-8) meeting of leaders of the world's richest economies in Genoa, Italy, in July 2001. Nigerians who were protesting the activities of Shell Oil in their country were killed in the mid-1990s. As globalization is embraced by more governments around the world, frustrations are also rising. Tensions rise as opponents are shut out of the boardrooms in businesses, international organizations, and governments where crucial decisions are made about the pace and nature of globalization. Nearly all global skeptics decried the September 11 attacks, but the attacks were visual metaphors for some elements of the debate. Planes piloted by hijackers from the developing world attacked symbols of international corporate wealth and control and US military power.

This book takes a third way in this debate: Globalization is neither inherently good nor evil—but both. Terrorists and tourists alike use the same global infrastructure. Transsovereign problems are the unintended side effects of globalization. As globalization advances, so will both opposition to globalization and its unintended adverse effects. To better harness and spread the benefits of globalization, we must take these adverse effects and the ethics of globalization seriously and work to better contain globalization's challenges. Failure to do so will risk more days like September 11 as vulnerability to problems and the intensity of opposition increase simultaneously.

As the sides become polarized, this third way is often overlooked. Proponents do not adequately recognize globalization's failures, while opponents do not fully recognize its benefits. Some proponents argue that the way to address global inequities and poverty is more globalization more quickly—and full speed ahead. Some opponents argue that attempts to lessen globalization's downsides are misplaced. Creating a kinder, gentler "globalization with a human face"[15] allows unjust systems to persist longer rather than allowing them to fall from the weight of their problems. Ironically, opponents to globalization use the tools of globalization (global media and the Internet, for example) to organize, mobilize, and publicize their opposition to globalization. And proponents of globalization use the arguments of opponents who are concerned with serious poverty and environmental problems to justify more globalization, arguing that only greater globalization will increase living standards and eventually leave more disposable income to address environmental problems. Too often both sides talk past each other. The same is true in the sovereignty debates. Some argue sovereignty is dead, while others argue it remains unchanged. This book takes the third approach: Sovereignty remains but is changing in important ways.

Understanding pressing global issues means understanding that globalization creates both benefits and challenges that states cannot control or solve alone. Because the problems go beyond sovereignty, so must the solutions. But going beyond sovereignty to manage global problems also carries unintended consequences for the state. The growth of the private sector, often with the aid of deliberate policy choices by states (political, economic, and technologic liberalization) now often dwarfs the capacity of the public sector, even in the strongest states. In their attempts to manage pressing global problems, states contract out and form networks and alliances with the private sector (NGOs and MNCs) and with other states and multilateral organizations (IGOs). States enter into these partnerships voluntarily, expecting help in managing global problems. Yet in doing so, states unintentionally lose some autonomy, authority, and legitimacy as they acknowledge their incapacity to solve problems alone and the rising capacity of other actors.

THE DIFFICULTIES IN ADDRESSING TRANSSOVEREIGN PROBLEMS

Transsovereign problems are difficult to solve for many reasons. First, states and the private sector have to figure out how to control or contain them without moving to close off economies, societies, or technologies. Second, because their very nature precludes unilateral solutions, transsovereign problems are harder to tackle because they require the cooperation of a greater number of actors. Third, they are complex because they entail both state and nonstate actors, which creates coordination problems. Effective action requires complex coordination among states, NGOs, IGOs, MNCs, and other nonstate actors. These groups have different interests, capabilities, and constituencies. As more groups attempt to coordinate action, more opportunities are created for policy to go awry. As a British minister for the environment explained,

> We face new dilemmas—of problems that cross boundaries, of issues that no single government can control, of shared risk. Nowhere is this collectivity more true than with the environment. Pollution, global warming, ozone depletion, and loss of species do not respect borders. . . . Globalization—in the form of increasing trade, the communications revolution, and increasing cultural exchanges—means that . . . governments have less influence over activities and economic sectors that were formerly under their control. . . . Some people refer to the effect this has on governments as "loss of agency." But the need for intervention in the public interest has not diminished—it is just that the locus has changed. Activities that were formerly national are now international, but the institutional capacity to deal with them has yet to evolve . . . we must manage the changing responsibilities of governments, business and civil society, forming new partnerships, learning from each other, finding new ways of harnessing the expertise and legitimate concerns and aspirations of each.[16]

Fourth, transsovereign problems are challenging because they often take place in the economic and social spheres, where the arm of liberal capitalist states has the shortest reach. Fifth, addressing global issues is difficult because these problems blur the borders between domestic and foreign policy. As domestic constituencies become mobilized over transsovereign issues, policy makers find their tasks complicated because they must address and coordinate the interests of additional groups. Domestic labor, environmental, and industry groups mobilize for international discussions of acid rain, for example. Politics does not stop at the water's edge. Efforts to manage global issues may stumble over contentious and unsettled domestic policy debates. For example, Brazilian government policies toward global warming involve discussions of the rights of indigenous peoples and the private industries that cut, burn, and develop the rain forests.

As a US State Department official described it, transsovereign issues signal a fundamental change in foreign policy:

> Foreign policy as we have known it is dead . . . because it is no longer foreign. The world has invaded us and we have invaded it. . . . The distinctions between domestic and foreign are gone. Look at the issues: The . . . fight against drugs and crime has major international components. Our stolen cars end up in El Salvador or Guatemala, or Poland. Our drugs come from Peru or Pakistan or Burma or elsewhere and transit almost anywhere. Crime cartels spread tentacles from Nigeria or Russia or Columbia. Today it is inconceivable to consider a coordinated attack on crime without working a part of the strategy in the international arena. . . . International terrorism has reached our shores. . . . We cannot deal with the threats to our environment, to assaults on biodiversity with domestic policy. Ozone layer depletion and global warming cannot be addressed by domestic environmental regulations alone. Over and over again we find issues that are domestic in consequence but international in scope. These are the consuming issues of the twenty-first century.[17]

Transsovereign problems also can be difficult for states to address because of institutional gaps (these are discussed more fully in Chapter 13). Existing institutions were not created to handle these problems, and they may be slow to change, resist taking on new functions that may divert resources from their traditional missions, and have difficulties coordinating with other institutions. Finally, contracting out or cooperating with the private sector and multilateral organizations to combat or contain global problems may unintentionally further undermine sovereignty.

YESTERDAY: WHERE SOVEREIGNTY CAME FROM

The international system has not always been organized around sovereignty. Prior to the Treaty of Westphalia in 1648, there were overlapping jurisdictions of political authority with no clear hierarchy or pecking order among them. In this feudal system, claims to authority were diffuse, decentralized, and based on personal ties rather than territory. Medieval subjects faced simultaneous and competing claims for allegiance to the pope, the king or emperor, the bishop, and local feudal princes, dukes, counts, lords, and so on.[18] Taxes and military service could be required of a person from several different authorities within the same territory. A person's bonds to an authority figure were based on personal ties and agreements, and "political authority was treated as a private possession."[19] This made secession problematic because contractual obligations might not survive a person's death.

Rather than land, authority claims were based on the divine—on spiritual connections or on the legitimacy of lineage to the Church (and in the days before the Reformation, that meant the Roman Catholic Church). Secular and spiritual authority were intertwined. Kings were anointed with holy insignia (for example, British monarchs took the title "Defender of the Faith"), emperors were crowned as "servants of the apostles," and popes and bishops needed the support of nonclerical leaders to gain and retain power. Both the Church and the Holy Roman Empire sought to fill the vacuum left by the fall of the Roman Empire and made universal claims of authority. People, not territory, were the primary objects of rule, and "rule was per definition spiritual" rather than spatial.[20] In the struggle between the papacy and the Holy Roman Empire for control, both institutions were weakened in ways that helped new forms of political organization to emerge.

There were many reasons why the feudal system declined and the sovereign state emerged. According to scholar Hendrik Spruyt, the rise of long-distance trade in the late Middle Ages created both a new merchant class of elites and the need for a new political system that could better accommodate the mercantilist economic system. The Church was against the exchange and loan of money and the taking of oaths, but currency and contracts were crucial to long-distance trade. Trade also required more precise and consistent measurements of time, weights, jurisdiction, and private property. As Spruyt notes,

> [t]he result of this economic dynamism was that a social group, the town dwellers, came into existence with new sources of revenue and power, which did not fit the old feudal order. This new social group had various incentives to search for political allies who were willing to

change the existing order. The new trading and commercial classes of the towns could not settle into the straightjacket of the feudal order, and the towns became a chief agent in its final disruption. . . . Business activity could not be organized according to the . . . system of personal bonds. . . . Contracts could not depend on the initiating actors. Sometimes these contracts might have to carry through beyond the death of the original contractors.[21]

The rise of a new economic system with its own needs, however, was not enough to bring about the rise of the sovereign state. The currency of other ideas aided the development of the concept of sovereignty. Martin Luther and the Protestant Reformation, Henry VIII and his Anglican separatists, the rise of scientific knowledge and explorations of the non-European world, along with the new merchant elites, challenged the authority and legitimacy of the Church in Rome. Roman ideas of property rights—which stressed exclusive control over territory—also were on the rise.[22] Ideas of individual autonomy and freedom from outside interference, later captured by Immanuel Kant, were important in the development of sovereignty.[23] Nicholas Onuf cites three conceptual crucial antecedents to the genesis of sovereignty: *majestas,* or that institutions inspire respect; *potestas imperiandi,* or the ability to coerce and enforce rules; and the Protestant idea of stewardship, or rule on behalf of the citizens of the body politic, not the personal rule of the Middle Ages.[24]

Besides conceptual changes, sovereignty also emerged because of changes in practical political balances. Sovereign states were more effective and efficient at waging war and conducting trade than were competing political organizations.[25] Elites who benefited from the new form of organization sought to delegitimize actors who were not like them (who were not organized as sovereign states) by excluding them from the international system.

Other forms of political organization competed with the sovereign state to succeed the feudal system: the city-state, the urban league, and the empire. Hendrik Spruyt believes that the sovereign state eventually won out for three main reasons. First, states were better able to extract resources and rationalize their economies than were other forms of political organization. Second, states were more efficient and effective than were medieval forms of organization, especially at being able to "speak with one voice" and make the external commitments necessary to the new trading system. And third, social choice and institutional mimicry meant that sovereign states selected out and delegitimized other actors who were not sovereign states.[26]

Out of these changes in economics, political balances, and conceptual frameworks came the eventual acceptance of the sovereign state. Authority was now based on exclusive jurisdiction over territory. Identity became based on geography: You were where you lived—a citizen of French territory, not primarily a member of the Holy Roman Empire or the community of Christians or the Celtic or Norman clans.

In theory, the sovereign state had a monopoly on the legitimate use of force within a territory. Sovereignty was reciprocal. One state recognized the others' exclusive jurisdictions over their territories and the populations and resources that resided on their lands; in return, they recognized that state's exclusive jurisdiction over its territory and everything on its land.[27] From the beginning, sovereignty was based on a social compact. Sovereignty never meant that all states had equal power or resources—some had vast lands, populations, and resources, while the capabilities of other states were meager. But sovereignty meant that only other sovereigns had legal standing in international agreements. States were the main unit of the international system.

From its origins in Europe, the idea and practice of sovereignty spread around the globe as Europeans conquered and carved up the planet into colonial territories. Sovereignty (with its territorial limits) came into conflict with the unlimited, universal Chinese, Japanese, and Ottoman empires, but eventually sovereignty came to dominate worldwide, whether by force or accession. When European colonies became independent after World War II and later when the Soviet bloc disintegrated between 1989 and 1991, the political units that emerged sought sovereign statehood, not recognition of other forms of political organization.

Sovereignty is an equalizing concept. Internally, governments organize themselves in whatever fashion they choose: monarchy, republican constitutional parliamentary system, autocracy, theocracy, and so on. Externally, however, all a state needs is international recognition as a sovereign state.

TODAY: SOVEREIGNTY CHALLENGED

The modern international system is built on the foundation of sovereignty. Today, sovereignty is under siege. There have always been weak states, and distinctions between the theory and the practice of sovereignty, yet both *de jure* and *de facto* sovereignty are now under assault more than ever. The sovereign state will likely continue to be the main unit in the international system for some time, but the operation and legitimacy of sovereignty are being undermined by both external and internal dynamics.

The principle of sovereignty is under siege by those who contend that in grave humanitarian crises the international community (of NGOs, IGOs, and states) has a right to intervene to aid citizens who are not being protected by the state. In Somalia, Bosnia, and Rwanda, the international community intervened in the internal affairs of states to distribute aid directly to individuals in times of grave humanitarian crisis without either the invitation or consent of the sovereignties involved. In the past, only sovereign states, not individuals, had standing in international law; within sovereign borders, a polity could do whatever it pleased with its citizens, even if that meant abusing their human rights or neglecting basic human needs.

Now such thinking is changing among some observers. As Kofi Annan, Secretary-General of the United Nations, said in his speech accepting the Nobel Prize, "In the 21st century I believe the mission of the United Nations will be defined by a new, more profound awareness of the sanctity and dignity of every human life. . . . This will require us to look beyond the framework of sovereign states. . . ."[28] These are strong words from the director of an organization founded on the principle of sovereign states and constituted solely of sovereign states as voting members.

The *Wall Street Journal* editorialized in a similar vein, saying that sovereignty is not an absolute right because starvation and wanton killing are "everybody's business," and that in cases such as Somalia or Rwanda, "any absolute principle of nonintervention becomes a cruel abstraction indeed."[29] Editorial writers at the *Economist* agreed, noting that we

> are increasingly concerned not just to see countries well governed but also to ensure that the world is not irreparably damaged—whether by global warming, by the loss of species, by famine or by war. . . .
> Increasingly, world opinion, when confronted by television pictures of genocide or starvation is unimpressed by those who say "We cannot get involved. National sovereignty must be respected.". . . National sovereignty be damned.[30]

Principles of sovereignty took centuries to become established and are not in danger of dissolving any time soon. However, perhaps we ought to take notice anytime the more liberal Kofi Annan and the conservative *Wall Street Journal* and *Economist* agree that the principle of sovereignty is challenged, and that individuals in need might seek international redress if states are unable or unwilling to carry out basic duties to their citizens.

Sovereignty not only is being challenged in theory, but also is under siege in practice. Sovereignty is challenged externally by the globalizing dynamics of open markets, open societies, and open technologies, which make the borders of even strong states permeable by outside forces. Sovereignty is also under siege internally from the rise of internal conflicts and subnational movements, as well as from the reinforcing crises of economic development (resource scarcity, environmental degradation, population growth) that undermine the international and internal legitimacy on which sovereignty stands. Both of these dynamics have led to a growing number of collapsed and collapsing states. But even the strongest states in the system cannot effectively manage global issues alone.

In his book *Collapsed States,* I. William Zartman notes that half the states in Africa may be in serious or maximum "danger of collapse, if not already gone."[31] Not coincidentally, Africa has the most wars of any continent on the planet, with the majority of the deadliest major armed conflicts on the globe taking place there today. All but two major armed conflicts are internal conflicts,[32] showing that sovereign states beyond Africa are feeling the effects of substate challenges.

When sovereign states collapse, the international system feels the shock waves. A state is in a process of collapse when its institutions and leaders lose control of political and economic space. When state authorities can no longer provide security, law and order, an economic infrastructure, or other services for citizens, then government retracts and the countryside is left on its own. Political space broadens as outside actors usurp (as in Lebanon) and intervene (as IGOs and NGOs enter to provide relief services necessitated by state breakdown). Economic space contracts as the informal economy takes over beyond state control, and as localities resort to barter, as occurred in Somalia.[33] In the power vacuum left by state collapse, transsovereign problems thrive. For example, as al Qaeda fighters were pushed out of Afghanistan, they moved to Sudan, Somalia, and Yemen—other areas where state control is weak.

When states implode, more than the residents are affected. In an interdependent world, the event can hurt distant international actors. Refugee flows, disease, terrorism, crime, drug smuggling, ethnic conflict, and civil war all thrive as the state recedes and often spread beyond borders. NGOs, IGOs, and criminal organizations are all drawn to collapsed states, whether to help restore law and order or to exploit its absence.

Robert Jackson, in his book *Quasi-States,* notes that the international system used to be based primarily on "positive sovereignty," the actual, empirical ability of a state to control its political and economic space, to "provide political goods for its citizens . . . the sociological, economic, technological, psychological, and similar wherewithal to declare, implement, and enforce public policy both domestically and internationally."[34] Weak states existed, but not for long, as it was considered perfectly legitimate for an outside power to conquer and absorb a weak state. The "old sovereignty game" recognized but did not protect weak sovereignties. They were vulnerable links in the international system's food chain. Their digestion by more powerful states was internationally sanctioned behavior.

This changed with the rise of Woodrow Wilson's idea of self-determination, with the discrediting of the concept of "salt-water colonialism"[35] and the end of colonial empires, and with the rise of democracy. The "new sovereignty game," Jackson contends, is increasingly based on "negative sovereignty," the formal-legal entitlement to freedom from outside interference and the *de jure* norm of nonintervention.[36] Thus, the current norms and practices of the international system create conditions that allow weak, ineffectual quasi-states to exist.

Sovereignty is under siege from internal pressures and conflicts that weaken state institutions. Many states in the developing world are undergoing related crises of poverty, environmental degradation, and internal conflict. Gross national product (GNP) per capita in Africa, for example, has stagnated or declined since the 1970s, and per capita grain production is lower than it was in 1950.[37] Population continues to increase, intensifying environmental degradation as trees are felled, topsoil is eroded, water supplies become fouled, and air is polluted in a desperate attempt to provide economic sustenance for the growing population.[38] The opportunity for conflict among societal groups increases as resources shrink.

Reinforcing economic and political crises are not restricted to Africa. GNP in the former Soviet states fell by as much as 30 percent after the

Cold War, while major armed conflicts in the region quadrupled.[39] Pressure on (and disillusionment with) fragile state institutions grows, as the state fails to break (or contributes to) the scarcity cycle, and as the chasm between the lesser developed and the developed states grows. States that are confronted with reinforcing crises can "harden," resorting to increased repression in an attempt to establish control.[40] Repressive tactics are costly, however. Civil institutions of the state atrophy (and economic and social performance often suffer) as power and resources concentrate in the military and police. State legitimacy and authority is further undermined, and opposition increases with the increase in repressive tactics.

The result is not just a crisis of a particular regime but of the sovereign state itself. Any regime that wins power will face extremely denigrated (to nonexistent) state institutions and societal bases of state power. Thus, the related crises of poverty and internal conflict undermine the foundations of sovereign power. Many areas of Afghanistan respond entirely to tribal and local authorities, not the sovereign state. After decades of warfare, arms are widespread, leaving the state with nothing close to a monopoly on the use of force. As NGOs, IGOs, and states aid Afghanistan's post-Taliban transition, many worry not only about the capacity of any new government, but also whether the area is governable.

Sovereignty also is undermined by external trends that have been heralded since the end of the Cold War: the opening of societies, economies, and technologies. Strong states are not immune to the problems of globalization, as shown by the events of September 11. Developing states are also caught in a bind. Leaders are attracted to the prospect of wealth promised by democracy, capitalism, and technology (which can strengthen the state), yet they fear the loss of control and the decentralization of power that these processes entail (which can weaken the state). Capitalism, democracy, and technology can devolve power away from central state institutions and undermine the state's ability to control its borders.[41] Many developing states desire international capital and jobs, but the process of liberalizing economic and political systems can be quite destabilizing. Citizen demands on government cannot wait until new institutions are built and put into place, so developing states are in the challenging position of trying to modernize and democratize their institutions as these same institutions try to solve critical problems. As Jack Snyder and Edward Mansfield describe the dangers of democratization, it is like changing the steering wheel while driving the car.[42]

The end of the superpower conflict has also increased the pressure on many weak states. More states compete for decreased overseas development assistance. The standard of living has dropped precipitously in many states that had received Cold War assistance, such as Cuba and North Korea (where famine has been a problem in recent years). The underlying in-effectiveness of state political and economic institutions becomes clear without the mask of Cold War aid and alliances. The authority and legiti-macy of the state suffer because the state cannot meet citizen expectations, and living standards decline.

It is not just the case, as Max Singer and Aaron Wildavsky argue, that the post–Cold War world is increasingly segregated into two zones—peace and turmoil—with a widening gap between the advanced capitalist democra-cies and the underdeveloped nondemocratic states. According to Singer and Wildavsky, the stabilizing solution to this dilemma was the advancement of democratization, economic liberalization, and development so that more states would move from the "zone of turmoil" to the "zone of peace."[43]

It is not that simple. Democratization and economic liberalization can undermine already fragile state institutions. During the transition period, attempts to establish open societies and markets can further move a weak state into the zone of turmoil. Even in peaceful and prosperous market democracies, terrorists fly planes into buildings. Singer and Wildavsky might have argued that the zone of peace (even with its problems of drugs and crime) is preferable to the zone of turmoil (with its starvation and war), but surely their argument needs qualification—at least to check the expectations of fledgling democracies. Singer and Wildavsky's zone of peace is not the promised land. Democratization and economic liberalization carry their own costs in terms of transsovereign problems. Even strong, wealthy states with healthy internal institutions cannot unilaterally defeat global problems.

Open Economies

Developed countries have long histories of promoting international trade and global capitalist economic systems, sometimes even through force, while also trying to protect some domestic markets from international competition. Squabbles with the Barbary pirates, who were supported by the pasha of Tripoli (present-day Libya—even in the 1790s, the United States had poor relations with Libya because of a form of state-sponsored terrorism), led to the formation of the US Navy and the beginnings of the president's ability to commit troops abroad without a formal declaration of war by Congress, in this case in order to protect commercial shipping engaged in trade. US tensions with China and Japan in the nineteenth and twentieth centuries concerned the opening of Asian markets to US goods.

European imperialism in Asia, Africa, and the Americas also served commercial interests. From the trade in spices, slaves, and rum to the extraction of precious metals, foreign commerce drove earlier periods of globalization. US imperialism in Latin America and the Pacific was also conducted in the name of promoting trade and opening commerce. The American empire— in the form of US protectorates in Puerto Rico, Guam, Samoa, and Hawaii, among others—was acquired largely to assist US commercial interests in their efforts to expand foreign trade. The United States forcibly created the country of Panama (by seizing territory from Colombia) in order to build the Panama Canal to facilitate trade. Military intervention in Guatemala in 1954 was done largely to protect the interests of the United Fruit Company. As one US trade official argued, "For most of America's history, foreign policy has reflected an obsession with open markets for American business. . . . Business expansion abroad was often seen as an extension of the American frontier, part of the nation's manifest destiny."[44]

Given these ties between colonialism and free market economics, it is no wonder that many citizens in developing countries are suspicious of globalization and the spread of international trade and capitalist systems. Many question just how "free" trade is among unequal trading partners and how "open" developed economies are to the goods (especially agricultural products) of lesser developed countries. Developed countries retain protectionist obstacles to the products in which developing countries enjoy comparative advantage. Some see free trade and monetary policies as neo-imperialism, with multinational corporations and international economic organizations such as the IMF and World Trade Organization (WTO) now infringing on the sovereignty of developing states in place of the colonial armies of a previous era. Trade ministers in developed countries counter that open markets, for all their imperfections, perform better than do state controlled markets.

The Cold War was caused in part by this clash between state and market economies, with the United States opposed to the Soviets closing Eastern European markets to Western goods and trade. During the Cold War, many

19

in the West believed that the superior economic performance of capitalist, free market systems would eventually bring state controlled, communist economic systems to their knees. George Kennan presciently predicted that the demise of the Soviet sphere would come about not through the external military confrontation of a globalized and militarized US containment policy, which the United States could not afford, but through the West's building of strong, internal open societies and open markets. Eventually, the Soviet bloc would be "unable to stand the comparison":[45]

> If economic recovery could be brought about and public confidence restored in Western Europe—if Western Europe, in other words, could be made the home of a vigorous, prosperous and forward-looking civilization—the communist regime in Eastern Europe ... would never be able to stand the comparison, and the spectacle of a happier and more successful life just across the fence ... would be bound in the end to have a disintegrating and eroding effect on the communist world.[46]

This thesis appeared to be confirmed at the Cold War's end. The Marshall Plan and forty-five years of a concerted policy of building open economic and political institutions in Western Europe succeeded in rebuilding a continent destroyed by war. Such rebuilding never took place in much of Eastern Europe. Eventually, even the top leaders of the Soviet Union were forced to admit that their economic system was in need of reform when Gorbachev came to power in the 1980s.

Gorbachev's reforms began as attempts to improve the productivity and efficiency of the state controlled economy: cutting down on vodka abuse on the job, decreasing bureaucratic red tape, and increasing worker and industry accountability. Quickly, these internal attempts to reform and strengthen the communist system unleashed massive dissatisfaction with the existing system. Gorbachev's reforms tapped into consumer and social unrest over shortages and poor economic performance (for example, exploding television sets in Moscow were a common cause of hospital emergency room visits), including the Chernobyl nuclear disaster. The legitimacy of the communist model was undermined, accelerating the pace of Gorbachev's initially modest reforms into the eventual overthrow of the entire system.[47] Gorbachev soon learned (what the Chinese are now grappling with) that it is difficult to uncork just a little economic freedom.

With the demise of communist regimes in Eastern Europe and the former Soviet Union, and with the demise of state controlled economies and authoritarian regimes in Latin America, many in the West assumed that it had won the Cold War's economic battle. As Paul Krugman put it, "Governments that had spent half a century pursuing statist, protectionist policies suddenly got free market religion. It was . . . the dawn of a new golden age for global capitalism." In addition, there

> was a sea change in the intellectual Zeitgeist: the almost universal acceptance, by governments and markets alike, of a new view about what it takes to develop. This view has come to be widely known as the "Washington Consensus.". . . It is the belief that . . . free markets and sound money [are] the key to economic development. Liberalize trade, privatize state enterprises, balance the budget, peg the exchange rate, and one will have laid the foundations for an economic takeoff.[48]

Of course, while many states "talk the talk" of capitalism, "free market religion" has not been established universally. Corruption is a huge obstacle to economic development around the world. According to a World Bank study, "40% of customs authorities in Latin America admitted to paying substantial bribes to get their jobs."[49] Property rights remain poorly defined and protected in many parts of the world. Many countries, such as Mexico, are privatizing state owned industries, but the process is vulnerable to distortion by corruption as the transition to free market economies is ongoing. This is the case in Eastern Europe, where formerly communist states are constructing the institutions that support free markets, such as laws that allow and protect the private ownership of property, stock exchanges, and laws that govern investment. There are still some states, such as North Korea, with closed economies. Others—such as Vietnam, Cuba, and China—are trying to attract foreign capital and investment and encourage some privatization of the economy, but the central government still owns and plays a key role in many industries. Developed countries retain popular, protectionist, agriculture subsidies and restrictions on certain foreign products. The Asian financial flu in the late 1990s and the collapse of Argentina's economy have led many observers to question the desirability of interconnected economies built on a "one-size-fits-all" Western model.

Yet for all the challenges facing economic liberalization, John Ikenberry contends that the triumph of Western policies of economic openness is so thorough that we often forget that "America is not adrift in uncharted seas. It is at the center of a world of its own making."[50] This US and Western dominance of international economic regimes is precisely the point that draws concern from many people around the world. The European Union (EU), WTO, IMF, and World Bank were all created by the United States and its developed allies. Developing countries often have little say in the rules and regimes that govern the global economy. For example, until recently, the WTO's rules favored Western pharmaceutical companies that were interested in protecting their patents and profits over developing countries that were interested in producing cheaper generic AIDS drugs to fight a pressing public health crisis. Regardless of the specific conditions in their own countries and economies, developing countries often find that relations with developed countries and access to international loans and aid are contingent on progress in privatization and liberal economic reform.[51]

However, even though open economies often perform better than their state-run counterparts, they also carry costs.[52] Resentment over a widening gulf between rich and poor states and developed countries' dominance of the global economy leads to increasingly violent protests of globalization. The transition to capitalist economic structures also can destabilize states. Argentina's economic difficulties led to five governments in four weeks in early 2002. Furthermore, instability provides openings for organized crime to step into the vacuum, as has occurred in Russia. The old order has been pulled down, but new laws and institutions that support free market economies are still being built, and much turmoil can result in the interim. Decreased regulation and increased transborder trade decreases the opportunities for shipments to be searched or monitored. Thus, states lose significant control over their borders, one of the hallmarks of sovereignty.

"Dirty money" follows many of the same paths as "clean money." The same emerging global financial infrastructure useful to legal businesses also increases the opportunity and ease of conducting and covering illicit economic activities, such as the smuggling of narcotics and nuclear materials. Profits from illicit activities can be hidden in legal investments, sprinkled into front companies, bank accounts, and small investments across a range of industries and states. With the Internet and e-cash, the money trail can move quickly and be erased as investments can be changed and moved with a keystroke. Attempts to freeze and seize the monies of terrorist organizations show how difficult it can be to track and stop illicit cash in interdependent economies.

Open economies also decentralize power as more and more actors have autonomous economic power and the central government loses its ability to control economic activities in a global marketplace. Microsoft founder Bill Gates's annual income is more than the annual GNP of many states. The income of prominent drug lords often overwhelms and distorts the legal economy in a state and becomes difficult for it to control or regulate.

Open Societies

Francis Fukuyama argues that the end of the Cold War also signaled the end of history, by which he means that "a remarkable consensus concerning the legitimacy of liberal democracy as a system of government has emerged throughout the world, as it conquered rival ideologies like hereditary monarchy, fascism, and most recently communism."[53] Although liberal democracy has not triumphed and may never in all areas of the globe, Fukuyama contends that the twentieth century has been marked by great battles of competing ideologies, and that now no alternative universal ideology of consequence exists to challenge liberal democracy. Liberal democracy "gives fullest scope" to satisfying "all three parts of the soul [desire, reason, and spirit] simultaneously."[54]

Fukuyama's thesis may be increasingly challenged by the ideas of some Islamic extremist groups that are intent on challenging Western government forms and promoting fundamentalist Islamic rule. Yet even analysts less optimistic about the liberal democratic form agree that we "are currently witnessing the fourth historical wave of democratization . . . more global in its reach . . . affecting far more countries and more thorough than its predecessors."[55] Democracy is not new and has been around in one form or another since the ancient Greeks. What is new, however, is the number of states that are turning to representative government forms with free multiparty elections and the protection of individual and minority rights including free speech and free press, freedom of association, freedom of movement, and freedom of religion. For the first time in history, a majority of states are either democracies or in transition to democracy.

In the first wave of democratization in the 1800s, universal suffrage was extended in states that were committed to democratic principles so that more than white male property owners could vote. This movement toward democracy ended as monarchies and authoritarian rulers sought to reestablish control in many states after the "springtime of freedom" in Europe in 1848–49. Although the first wave expanded democracy within societies and sought to spread democracy in Western Europe and North America, these same states were involved simultaneously in carving up the non-Western world into colonial empires in profoundly nondemocratic ways.

The second wave of democratization occurred with and in the aftermath of World War I as many states believed that autocracies were more to blame for starting the war than were democratic states. However, many of the democracies established after World War I were weak, such as the Weimar Republic, and many of these states reverted to authoritarianism as fascism swept the globe.

The third wave of democratization occurred with World War II as colonial powers were no longer able or willing to hold onto their overseas possessions, and a tidal wave of decolonization swept the globe. The number of independent states tripled from 1945 to 1979, and many of these former colonies turned to democratic government forms. Once again, however, this wave of democratization was followed by reversals. After historic initial democratic elections, many leaders would not hand over power to others, barring further elections. This pattern was pernicious in Africa. Ironically, the Cold War also caused some democratic backsliding, as the United States and the West supported noncommunist but nondemocratic regimes. "By some counts, one-third of the globe's democracies had fallen under authoritarian rule by the late 1970s,"[56] as personal rule, military rule, or single party autocracy replaced democratic political participation and institutions in developing states. Even though there were reverses, with each wave the number of democracies overall increased, as states such as India joined and stayed in the community of democracies.

The fourth wave of democratization differs from previous eras in two important respects. First, it was not the result of a single external event such as World War I or II. Although the end of the Soviet empire led many Eastern European states into the democratic experiment, other states such as Portugal, Spain, and South Africa turned to democracy for reasons other than (and prior to) the end of the Cold War.

Second, the most recent wave of democratization differs from its predecessors in scope and intensity. More states on more continents are becoming more democratic than ever before. This wave is not restricted to Europe or to former colonial empires, and this wave is more intensive, entailing a restructuring of political and economic institutions.

While the fate of these newly emerging democracies is by no means secure, the fourth wave of democratization has advantages that previous movements could not claim. The simultaneous trends of open markets and open technologies support and facilitate political openings. Previous reformers did not have CNN looking in and immediately reporting advances or backsliding to an international audience. Previous reformers also did not have to liberalize political institutions as a prerequisite to receiving international capital investments, whether from international lending institutions such as the World Bank or IMF or from private investors who believe the rule of law as practiced in democratic societies secures a better business environment. The growth of civil society internationally may also help solidify the current wave of democratization.

More than a decade ago, policy makers and scholars thought such extensive opportunities for democratization were unlikely. The opening of societies may lend itself to more open economic systems as people with some say in their political futures tend to desire openness in their economic futures as well.[57] Of course, movement toward open societies is not complete. Some states such as China are trying to open their economic systems to achieve prosperity and development without allowing significant political freedoms. Many states, particularly in Africa and the Middle East, retain authoritarian political systems.

Democracy is spreading for several reasons (of course, there are significant disagreements over how best to promote democracy in practice). Global media and cheap and ready access to information technology can help democratization. Democracies are more likely to have free market and free trade capitalist economies (encouraged by international financial institutions) and to have more prosperity and better records of economic development. Democratic protections of property rights and individual liberties provide a rule of law that fosters a more stable investment and business climate and better protects the larger number of citizens now traveling abroad and taking advantage of more advanced transportation and communication links. Perhaps most important, developed democracies tend not to go to war with one another.[58] Democracies are not more peaceful overall. They tend to go to war with nondemocracies, and the transition period of democratization can be wrought with conflict. But the empirical record of democracies not warring with other democracies is strong.

However, democratization carries costs. Transitions to democracy can be destabilizing in the short run, as "[d]emocratization typically creates a syndrome of weak central authority, unstable domestic coalitions, and high-energy mass politics."[59] If privatization and liberalization of the economy are occurring simultaneously with democratization efforts (as is often the case), then corrupt powerful corporate or criminal organizations may gain assets and influence before the civic institutions of public control and accountability are established (many observers argue that this has occurred in Nigeria, Russia, Ukraine, Tajikistan, Uzbekistan, Kazakhstan, etc.). Any one of these transitions would be highly complex and destabilizing for a society. The simultaneous and often sudden overlapping of these transitions only increases the level of difficulty for polities and increases the pressures for fragmentation that can undermine states.

Open Technologies

Developed countries tend to be enamored with technological advances, and it is easy to understand why. Cellular phones connect areas that are difficult to link by landlines in places such as Hong Kong and Israel. Technology made possible the settlement of the American continent and still undergirds the US military's preeminent position in the world today.

Americans own more computers and televisions than the citizens of any other country,[60] and the United States has the most Internet users by far: 168 million (China and Britain are second with 33 million each; Germany has 26 million, Japan 22 million, South Korea 16.7 million, Canada 14 million, and Italy and France 11 million each).[61] US scientists, industry, and government invented the computer and developed the Internet.

The "information revolution" is profoundly changing the way all states do their business: "Today all of humankind is linked by almost instantaneous communications. There is no corner of the globe that is not accessible to us, or us to them. Marshall McLuhan's global village is upon us with profound consequences . . . a market crash in Hong Kong is felt immediately by pensioners in Dubuque (Iowa)."[62]

Technological advances have been dramatically spurred by advances in computers. The first modern computer, developed in 1946 to calculate firing trajectories for artillery shells, "could execute the then-astonishing number of 5,000 arithmetic operations per second . . . weighed 30 tons, filled an enormous room at the University of Pennsylvania, consumed 150,000 watts of power, and used 18,000 vacuum tubes."[63] (The term "bugs in the system" literally referred to insects in these huge machines that interfered with operations.) Today, a Pentium chip is built on a thumbnail-sized piece of silicon, and laptop computers are smaller than briefcases, weigh less than four pounds, and can execute more than 200 million instructions per second.[64]

Many theorists argue that technology drives globalization and that the digital divide between rich and poor countries has kept the world's poor from enjoying the benefits of globalization. Computers, faxes, cell phones, and air travel have shrunk the planet and made sovereign borders less important for economic transactions. Television, radio, video cameras, and computers have made sovereign authorities less able to control the flow of information and ideas and thus made authoritarian control more expensive and difficult to maintain. Anyone with a concealed handheld video camera can record government abuses and instantly transmit these images via the Internet to place international pressure on the offending regime. Technology, in essence, undermined sovereign authority, decentralized power, and opened markets and societies.[65]

To some extent, this presents a "chicken-or-egg" question. Although technology may in some sense "drive" the process of globalization, technological advances do not occur in an economic or political vacuum. Sustained political and investment decisions drive technological advances. Scientists did not suddenly develop powerful supercomputers, tiny microchips, and fiberoptic telecommunications links by accident. These advancements came about through sustained investment, political and social policies that harnessed resources in pursuit of technological progress and innovation as tools to advance economic and political goals. The first mainframe computer and the Internet were developed by the US Department of Defense working in close connection with universities.

Causality flows in all directions, but together the trends of open economies, open societies, and open markets substantially reinforce each other. When combined, they equal more than the sum of their parts.

Technological advances facilitate the opening of markets and of societies, and vice versa.

However, like their counterparts, open technologies also undermine sovereignty and make transsovereign challenges possible. Technology moves legal and illegal information, people, and goods more quickly and efficiently than ever before across borders without the consent or even knowledge of sovereign authorities. Human smugglers use cell phones, e-cash, laptops, the Internet, and encryption software to track and direct their "product" flow.

Noting that globalization has downsides does not mean that sovereignty is dead or that state controlled economies and authoritarian societies free of advanced technologies would be beneficial. Human history is the unfolding story of numerous and varying social organizing frameworks. The sovereign state has had a good, 350-year run as an organizing unit. Although it is in no imminent danger of disappearing, we cannot expect that the sovereign state will be in the form we know it 350 years from now. For globalization to be both sustainable and just, its costs must be clearly understood and addressed. Sovereignty and globalization carry many benefits, but there is nothing sacrosanct about either.

TOMORROW: DEBATES
ABOUT THE FUTURE OF SOVEREIGNTY

There are three main views about the future of sovereignty. According to the first view, we are witnessing the end of the state. The second view argues that the sovereign state continues to be an important actor on the world scene, especially in the military security realm, but that the state is increasingly losing power to markets and nonstate actors. The third view argues that states are still the primary actors in international politics, and other actors (NGOs, IGOs, MNCs) exist and operate only as much as allowed by states.

The first view contends that sovereign states are a "nostalgic fiction" in the global economy. According to Kenichi Ohmae, states "are little more than bit actors." Decisions over investments, production, and exchange rates "are made elsewhere by individuals and institutions over which they have little practical control." National labels are becoming meaningless. Is a Toyota made in Mississippi a Japanese car? This does not mean that international politics will now be marked by the "clash of civilizations" or cultures, as Samuel Huntington contends. "There are now tens of millions of teenagers around the world who, having been raised in a multimedia-rich environment, have a lot more in common with each other than they do with members of older generations in their own cultures." States are losing their relevance to respond to economic bumps in the road, and so regions are becoming more important. Although it may still be politically correct to talk about states as the important actors, "it is a bald-faced economic lie."[66]

The second view sees the state retreating as its functions change.[67] Today, either other actors are increasingly filling these functions or no one fills them. For example, Susan Strange discusses ten important functions or authorities claimed by states that are on the decline. First, the state is responsible for defending national territory against foreign invasion, but in developed countries the threat of foreign invasion is declining or minimal, thereby eroding this source of state authority. Second, the state is responsible for maintaining the value of its currency, but inflation in one country can spread to others, revealing that this responsibility is now a more collective one. Third, the state used to choose the appropriate form of economic development, but open economies now allow market pressures from the IMF, World Bank, and private investors to limit state choice and force convergence on a narrow range of development models (the "Washington Consensus"). Fourth, the state used to be responsible for correcting the booms and busts of market economies through state spending to infuse money into public works or other state enterprises. Franklin Delano Roosevelt fought the Great Depression in the 1930s in the United States by initiating large public works projects, building national parks, the Tennessee Valley Authority dams, and highways and bridges to put people back to work and get the economy moving again. But this option is no longer open to governments, given the market pressures to keep government spending at a minimum. Fifth, states used to provide a social safety net for those who were least able to survive in a market economy by providing assistance to the very old and young, sick, disabled, and unemployed. Today, market pressures are leading states to cut back on their social welfare benefits and protective regulations. Sixth, states used to have the ability to set appropriate tax rates to pay for government public works or social benefits spending. Today, all states are pressured by international market forces to keep tax rates to a minimum, thereby limiting their autonomy and authority to raise funds. Seventh, states used to have great autonomy in control over foreign trade, especially imports. Today, government intervention can only affect the margins because most of the decisions that concern trade flows are the "aggregate result of multiple corporate decisions."[68] Strong international market forces pressure governments to reduce obstacles to cross-border trade.

Eighth, governments used to take responsibility for building the economic infrastructure of the state "from ports and roads to posts and telegraphs. . . . Even where governments, as in the United States, looked to private enterprise to find the necessary capital, they never hesitated in revising the laws on landed property so that landowners could not easily obstruct the infrastructural investment."[69] Today, public utilities are being privatized, and the key infrastructure needed in modern economies are communications technologies, most of which do not depend on government's control over territory. Infrastructure development decisions are being made in corporate boardrooms, not state offices. Eastern European states are being integrated into the modern telecommunications grid not by governments primarily, but by private corporations that recognize the profit margins that are available to the corporation that gets there first. States may have built the infrastructure of highways, but firms and private actors are building and extending the information superhighways.

Ninth, states used to be able to create or allow public or private monopolies to dominate the local market, but today international market pressures impose greater costs on state governments that try to maintain monopolies. Finally, states used to entertain one "special kind of monopoly—that of the legitimate use of violence against the citizen or any group of citizens."[70] Now, the globalization of the arms trade and easy access to technology make the means of violence more readily available to nonstate actors. Strong and weak states alike are losing their monopolies on force—as evidenced by the chemical attack on the Japanese subway and the destruction of the World Trade Center in the United States.

In essence, we are witnessing the incredibly shrinking state. States continue to exist, but their powers are not as extensive as they used to be, and other actors take or share power with states over key functions or sectors. The result is "a ramshackle assembly of conflicting sources of authority" in which individuals' loyalties and identities will not necessarily lie with the sovereign state but are spread among professions, civic groups, ethnic ties, firms, etc., just as state power is becoming diffused.[71] As more power shifts away from states and toward markets, accountability and democracy may decrease because corporate leaders are not subject to democratic accountability and market forces cannot be voted upon.

Other theorists agree that we are in a period of transition or turbulence[72] in which the sovereign state is increasingly under challenge but not obsolete yet because alternatives to sovereignty have not established themselves. James Rosenau argues that not just markets but also increasingly skilled individuals are driving the changes. He believes access to the Internet, to personal computers, faxes, jet planes, etc., have led to a "skill revolution." People who are plugged in have become better able to assess, compare, and contrast large amounts of data; are more sophisticated in critiquing the information provided to them by states and in seeking alternative information; and are better able to articulate and mobilize around goals. "It is unimaginable that people have not learned and become more complex in order to adapt to an increasingly complicated world."[73] In an evolutionary way, people are adapting to changes in their environment. "People have become increasingly competent in assessing where they fit in international affairs and how their behavior can be aggregated into significant outcomes."[74] Thus, the globalization of democratization is no accident, because the telecommunications revolution that is fueling the skills revolution is global. A people plugged in is a people empowered to bring about change, to end apartheid in South Africa, to tear down the Berlin Wall and the communist empire, and to challenge the dictatorship in Tiananmen Square. Rosenau believes the skills revolution makes governments more responsive to citizens' needs and more democratic, whereas Strange and others believe that increased market and corporate power reduces democracy and accountability.

Because of the digital divide, the rate of change is not uniform. But even though "the information-rich are getting richer at a quicker rate than the information-poor, the trend line is conceived to slope in the same upward direction for both groups."[75] Even citizens in lesser developed countries (where poverty and repressive regimes may limit access to technology) are becoming more skillful. For example, Haitians demonstrating in 1994 to turn back the USS Harlan County from intervening and Iranians denouncing US support of the shah of Iran in 1979, carried signs in English and timed their protests to appear on the US evening news broadcasts. As people become more skillful, they also become less deferential. Traditionally, state legitimacy and compliance

> derived from constitutional and legal sources. Under these circumstances individuals were habituated to compliance with the directives issued by higher authorities. They did what they were told to do because . . . that is what one did. As a consequence, authority structures remained in place for decades even centuries as people unquestioningly yielded to the dictates of governments.[76]

Today, because of the skills revolution, a pervasive "authority crisis" exists as people are increasingly inclined to question authority and have the means to do so. Legitimacy now derives not from tradition but from performance. States are no longer the only key actors, and they must manage and compete with a variety of organizations. Sovereignty continues to limp along—not because of its strength, but more by default because none of these new organizations has yet delivered a knockout blow.

Another cut at this second view is that sovereignty is losing its identification with territory. Richard Rosecrance argues, "In economies where capital, labor, and information are mobile and have risen to predominance, no land fetish remains. Developed countries would rather plumb the world market than acquire territory. The virtual state—a state that has downsized its territorially based production capability—is the logical consequence of this emancipation from the land."[77] By shedding outmoded functions to nonstate actors and by downsizing territory, states are adapting their logic to market forces. When the Treaty of Westphalia was signed, the economic system was mercantilist and land based. Wealth and power depended on the control of land, access to raw materials, and control of the means of production. In a world of slow-moving ships and horseback messengers, capital and labor were fixed in place, not mobile. Increasing power meant increasing land, and thus the European colonial empires were born. It is no accident that under this economic system, the political organization that developed—sovereignty—directly correlated authority to territory. But now the economy has changed, and states are changing to reflect the new reality. The new economic system is based on information, technology, and services—none of which depends on the control of land.

In a world of open borders and economic flows—and people who have access to computers, faxes, phones, the Internet, e-cash, and other advanced technologies—the means of production, capital, and labor are mobile. States have access to raw materials through trade, not conquest. Thus, for states with modern, information-based economies such as Japan, territory is not the source of their power, so conflict over territory becomes passé. For states with less developed economies that are still land based (and primarily dependent on natural resource extraction or agricultural exports), territory will not become passé and may still be a source of conflict. A population explosion might make land important again. But these trends are not sustainable in the long term because land does not produce a better return than knowledge, so states with lots of land (such as Russia) may not be especially powerful in the new economy. Knowledge allows more extraction and more efficient and effective utilization of resources. States recognize the success of "virtual" states such as Japan and will try to emulate them and thus develop modern economies that are less shackled to land.

The virtual state no longer commands resources as it did in the mercantilist yesteryear. It negotiates, deriving its power from direct foreign investment, an educated workforce, and market savvy, not from military superiority or control over territory. This brings a crisis for democratic politics as states lose some of their autonomy over electing and enforcing policy to unelected, nonstate actors. Citizens can, however, vote with their feet if they are unimpressed by their state's performance.[78]

The final view argues that nothing fundamental has changed. Stephen Krasner argues that weak states have always existed, and that sovereignty has always been "organized hypocrisy," challenged in theory and practice.[79] But even examples of problematic sovereignty only show how embedded the concept of sovereignty is.[80] It continues to be our default assumption. Changes in the environment do not readily or easily translate into institutional changes. Sovereign states persist over time, even when their functions are not in sync with a changed international environment because of vertical and horizontal linkages:

> Vertical depth refers to the extent to which the institutional structure defines the individual actors. Breadth refers to the number of links that a particular activity has with other activities, to the number of

changes that would have to be made if a particular form of activity were altered. . . . With regard to both breadth and depth, sovereign states have become increasingly formidable institutions. They influence the self-image of those individuals within their territory through the concept of citizenship, as well as by exercising control, to one degree or another, over powerful instruments of socialization. With regard to breadth, states are the most densely linked institutions in the contemporary world. Change the nature of states and virtually everything else in human society would also have to be changed. Hence, even though environmental incentives have dramatically changed since the establishment of the state system in the seventeenth century, there is little reason to believe that it will be easy to replace sovereign states with some alternative structure for organizing human political life.[81]

Despite interdependence, weak states, and compromised or problematic sovereignty, the sovereign state is not retreating. The costs of changing to an alternative system would be prohibitive, and people cannot conceive of a plausible alternative to sovereignty.

Others in this school of thought argue that no such fundamental change away from sovereignty is imminent because existing states have little incentive to alter the system. States are the gatekeepers to the international system, so it is difficult for actors other than states to be accorded equal participation in that system. The growth of the European Union is providing an alternative model to traditional sovereignty, but there are few other serious challengers to sovereign arrangements. Hendrik Spruyt argues that, for sovereignty to be replaced, there must be competition among alternative models of organization—as there was at sovereignty's initiation after competition with the urban league and city-state. If anything, sovereignty is becoming more entrenched because ethnic and nationalist challenges to sovereignty reinforce the state as a prize worth fighting for. Although sovereignty is not the optimal institutional arrangement, new institutional challengers have not yet arisen. Sovereignty took centuries to emerge, Spruyt argues. It is too early to declare its demise.

Another perspective argues there is no such thing as globalization, only Americanization. Kenneth Waltz contends that we are witnessing the advance of one incredibly powerful state—the United States—rather than the retreat of the state.[82] This third viewpoint paraphrases Mark Twain's famous observation by noting that the territorial state is being "buried too soon." William O'Neill believes that challenges to the existing sovereign state do not mean its death but that "pride of place [will go] to whatever authorities are able to organize and maintain superior armed force. This implies that their requiem for the Westphalian state is premature. So far, no promising alternative to the territorial organization of armed force has even begun to emerge."[83] To this, the other schools of thought argue "Yes, but so what?" If state military power is less able to prevail against nonstate threats in an interdependent world, then the state may retain coercive powers that are less and less useful. The state still exists but is more compromised in its ability to act in the economic and social spheres that increasingly affect citizens' everyday lives.

Mapping out these debates in the scholarly literature helps establish questions to consider in reading the chapters of this book. Do transsovereign problems challenge not only the interests of states (as the traditional realist International Relations theory stipulates) but also the very architecture of states? How can transsovereign problems be dealt with in a system of sovereign states? Do the responses to transsovereign problems (greater reliance on NGOs or IGOs, for example) undermine sovereignty? Are alternatives to sovereignty evolving as people struggle to respond to transsovereign problems? Or is the state becoming more entrenched as people rely on old responses to combat new threats?

THE NEW SECURITY DILEMMA

Security has been the dominant realm of sovereign states, but even this is changing. Weakened sovereignty and transsovereign challenges create a new security dilemma. In previous eras, threats came from strong states. The "old security dilemma" was how one state could contain another strong state without provoking counteractions on the other side that would make the state stronger. This spiral of insecurity was often cited in arms races, the outbreak of World War I, and the Cold War. The temptation was to over-respond and appear offensive, thus triggering a heightened response from opponents that further decreased one's own security. In a self-help international system of strong sovereign states, how could a state provide for its own military security against another state without setting off a self-defeating spiral of counteractions by other states?

But if the old security dilemma was how states could protect against strong states without making them stronger, then the new security dilemma is how to protect against transsovereign challenges and the implosion of weak states without taking actions that make weak states weaker and transsovereign problems more severe. Globalization plus weak states and transsovereign problems equals the new security dilemma. Globalization gives breakdowns in state authority and capacity and transsovereign problems greater reach, speed, intensity, and impact. Borders are more permeable, and threats are decentralized, fast, fungible, and fluid. The post–Cold War security dilemma is how to respond to the problems of weak states and nonstate threats without making these problems worse. Responding with the predominant tool of the old security dilemma—military force—may not be effective. For example, using force may make terrorist organizations stronger because they can appeal to messianic visions and have heightened international importance. Failure to respond to nonmilitary threats, however, allows these problems to grow until they present a threat of violence and instability that cannot easily be met by force. As HIV and AIDS spread throughout sub-Saharan Africa, millions of orphans (especially boys) live in gangs on the streets, supported by begging and crime and without socialization into families or community values. Although these growing numbers of hardened throwaway children pose real threats to security, military forces can do little to prevent the spread of HIV and AIDS or care for orphans.

The new security dilemma requires both creation of more powerful nonmilitary tools (including more effective involvement of the private sector), and the retooling of military forces to meet nonstate threats. This presents a challenge even for the world's most powerful military. Although the US military fought nonstate actors in Vietnam and Lebanon, these efforts did not go well. Many states faced with military defeat, such as Germany after World War I, go back to the drawing board to learn how to better equip, train, and organize forces to win the types of battles they lost. The United States did the opposite. Rather than resolving to learn how to better fight nonstate actors after Vietnam and Lebanon (and make appropriate changes in strategy, equipment, training, and organization), the United States instead devised the Weinberger doctrine (never involve US troops in those types of conflicts) and the Powell corollary (send in one-size-fits-all overwhelming force to respond to any situation—which created problems in Somalia).[84] Before September 11, the United States tried to avoid the wars it was least equipped to fight and to fight new threats with old Cold War doctrines and force structures.[85] But even if doctrine, organization, training, and equipment priorities are changed to better prepare for the type of conflict that now predominates, military force is just not sufficient to combat global problems, which often stem from economic or other causes. Threats are decentralized, as are the resources needed for the fight, which are not primarily military. We must go beyond the military tools of sovereignty to contain security dilemmas that go beyond sovereignty. Realizing this, militaries are increasingly reaching out to the private sector to help manage pressing security problems. The British government debates hiring mercenaries. The US government enlists the private sector in the war on terrorism. When the strongest military in the strongest state needs the private sector to help manage security problems (traditionally, the state's strong suit), then sovereignty is changing.

ENDNOTES

1. Gillian Sorensen, *The United Nations and Civil Societies: Redefining the Partnership for the 21st Century.* Keynote address to Women in International Security summer symposium, Washington, DC, June 15, 1998.
2. Donald Snow and Eugene Brown, *Beyond the Water's Edge* (New York: St. Martin's Press, 1997).
3. Maryann Cusimano Love, "Globalization, Ethics, and the War on Terrorism," *Notre Dame Journal of Ethics, Law, and Public Policy* (special "Violence in America" edition, 2002), 65–80; Maryann Cusimano Love, "Morality Matters: Ethics and Power Politics in the War on Terrorism," *Georgetown Journal of International Affairs* (Summer–Fall 2002): 7–16.
4. Ernest Gellner, "Nations and Nationalism," in Richard Betts (Ed.), *Conflict after the Cold War: Arguments on the Causes of War and Peace* (New York: Macmillan, 1994), 286.
5. Edward Luttwak, "Toward Post-Heroic Warfare," *Foreign Affairs* 74 (May–June 1995): 109–122; Francis Fukuyama, *The End of History and the Last Man* (New York: Free Press, 1992).
6. I. William Zartman, *Collapsed States* (Boulder, CO: Lynne Rienner, 1995); Robert Jackson, *Quasi-States: Sovereignty, International Relations, and the Third World* (New York: Cambridge University Press, 1990); Maryann K. Cusimano, "The New Containment Doctrine," in *Unplugging the Cold War Machine* (Thousand Oaks, CA: Sage, 2002); Gerald B. Helman and Steven R. Ratner, "Saving Failed States," *Foreign Policy* (Winter 1992–1993): 3–20; Alex Rondos, "The Collapsing State and International Security," in Janne E. Nolan (Ed.), *Global Engagement* (Washington, DC: Brookings Institution, 1994), 481–503; Ted Robert Gurr, "The State Failure Project" (available at <www.bsos.umd.edu/cidcm/inscr/stfail/>); James C. Clad, "Old World Disorders," in Brad Roberts (Ed.), *U.S. Security in an Uncertain Era* (Cambridge: MIT Press, 1993);

Chester Crocker, "The Global Law and Order Deficit: Is the West Ready to Police the World's Bad Neighborhoods?" *Washington Post,* Dec. 20, 1992, p. C1; Michael Brown, "Introduction," *The International Dimensions of Internal Conflict* (Cambridge: MIT Press, 1996); Pauline H. Baker and John A. Ausink, "State Collapse and Ethnic Violence: Toward a Predictive Model," *Parameters* (Spring 1996): 19–31.

7. The following remarks are taken from Maryann Cusimano Love, "Globalization: A Virtue or a Vice," Chapter 5 in Siamack Shojai (Ed.), *Globalization: A Virtue or A Vice?* (New York: Praeger, 2002).

8. John Micklethwait and Adrian Wooldridge, *A Future Perfect: The Challenge and Hidden Promise of Globalization* (New York: Random House, 2000); Thomas Friedman, *The Lexus and the Olive Tree* (New York: Farrar, Straus, & Giroux, 1999).

9. Robin Broad (Ed.), *Global Backlash* (Lanham, MD: Rowman & Littlefield, 2002); Joseph E. Stiglitz, *Globalization and Its Discontents* (New York: Norton, 2002); Noreena Hertz, *The Silent Takeover: Global Capitalism and the Death of Democracy* (New York: Simon & Schuster, 2002); James H. Mittelman, *The Globalization Syndrome: Transformation and Resistance* (Princeton, NJ: Princeton University Press, 2000); Dani Rodrik, *Has Globalization Gone Too Far?* (Washington, DC: Institute for International Economics, 1997); Benjamin R. Barber, *Jihad vs. McWorld: How Globalism and Tribalism Are Reshaping the World* (New York: Ballantine Books, 1995); Hans-Henrik Holm and Georg Sorensen, *Whose World Order?* (Boulder, CO: Westview Press, 1995).

10. United Nations Development Program, *Globalization with a Human Face* (New York: United Nations, 1999).

11. James Wolfensohn, *Coalitions for Change: Address to the Board of Governors* (Washington, DC: September 28, 1999), 3. Wolfensohn is president of the World Bank.

12. Ibid., 6.

13. Mark Malloch Brown, "Forward," United Nations Development Program, *Human Development Report 1999.*

14. Wolfgang Reinicke, "Global Public Policy," *Foreign Affairs* (Nov.–Dec. 1997), 128.

15. United Nations Development Program, *Globalization with a Human Face* (New York: United Nations, 1999).

16. Michael Meacher (UK minister for the environment), speech at the Royal Society of Arts, April 1998.

17. L. Craig Johnstone, *Strategic Planning and International Affairs in the 21st Century.* Address to the Conference Series on International Affairs in the 21st Century, US Department of State, Washington, DC, Nov. 18, 1997.

18. F. H. Hinsley, *Sovereignty* (London: C. A. Watts, 1966). The Treaty of Westphalia is a commonly used if somewhat controversial marker for a historical process that took centuries. Scholars such as Bruce Bueno de Mesquita claim that the move toward sovereignty actually came much earlier, while others such as Stephen Krasner point out that even after Westphalia there were struggles between religious and secular leaders and contested and overlapping authority claims.

19. Hendrik Spruyt, *The Sovereign State and Its Competitors* (Princeton, NJ: Princeton University Press, 1996), 40.

20. Ibid., 47.

21. Ibid., 62, 75.

22. Friedrich Kratochwil, "Sovereignty as Dominium: Is There a Right of Humanitarian Intervention?" in Gene M. Lyons and Michael Mastanduno (Eds.), *Beyond Westphalia:*

State Sovereignty and International Intervention (Baltimore: Johns Hopkins University Press, 1995), 21–42.

23. Nicholas Onuf, "Intervention for the Common Good," in *Beyond Westphalia,* 43–58.

24. Ibid.; Nicholas Onuf, "Sovereignty: Outline of a Conceptual History," *Alternatives* 16 (1991): 425–446.

25. Charles Tilly, *The Formation of National States in Western Europe* (Princeton, NJ: Princeton University Press, 1975).

26. Spruyt, *The Sovereign State and Its Competitors.*

27. Michael Ross Fowler and Julie Marie Bunck, *Law, Power, and the Sovereign State: The Evolution and Application of the Concept of Sovereignty* (University Park: Pennsylvania State University Press, 1995), 5–6.

28. UN Secretary-General Kofi Annan, Nobel Prize for Peace acceptance speech, Dec. 10, 2001; International Commission on Intervention and State Sovereignty, *The Responsibility to Protect* (Ottawa, Canada: International Development Research Centre, 2001) available at <http://www.iciss-ciise.gc.ca/pdfs/Commission-Report.pdf>.

29. "Everybody's Business," *Wall Street Journal,* Aug. 24, 1992, p. A8.

30. "New Ways to Run the World," *Economist* (Nov. 5, 1991): 11.

31. Zartman, *Collapsed States,* 3.

32. Stockholm International Peace Research Institute (SIPRI), "Major Armed Conflict," *SIPRI Yearbook 2001;* available at <http://projects.sipri.se/conflictstudy/MajorArmedConflicts.html>.

33. Zartman, *Collapsed States,* 1–11. State collapse is more than a succession struggle over which group will control the levers of state—it is the failure of function of those very state institutions. Although groups may be involved in leadership contests, state collapse continues no matter who wins the helm, because state authority, legitimacy, and competence have badly disintegrated. States that have protracted or persistent leadership battles are vulnerable to state collapse as state institutions atrophy during continued warfare and as the legitimacy and authority enjoyed by these institutions is undermined by the conflict. *Civil war* and *state collapse* are not synonymous terms. Internal war can occur in states that are not in the process or in danger of collapse—as in Britain and Israel. More rarely, states can collapse without violence—as in the breakup of Czechoslovakia. Not surprisingly, however, state collapse is highly correlated with internal violence, which can weaken state institutions and precede and contribute to state collapse. Alternatively, state collapse can provide the opportunity for groups to use violence as they try to assert authority in the power vacuum left by state failure. See also Gerald B. Helman and Steven R. Ratner, "Saving Failed States," *Foreign Policy* (Winter 1992–1993): 3–20; Alex Rondos, "The Collapsing State and International Security," in *Global Engagement,* 481–503; Gurr, "The State Failure Project"; James C. Clad, "Old World Disorders," in *U.S. Security in an Uncertain Era,* 181–188; Robert D. Kaplan, "The Coming Anarchy," *Atlantic Monthly* (February 1994): 44–76; and Jackson, *Quasi-States.*

34. Jackson, *Quasi-States,* 29.

35. Morton Halperin, *Self-Determination in the New World Order* (Washington, DC: Carnegie Endowment for International Peace, 1992).

36. Jackson, *Quasi-States,* 27.

37. Hal Kane, *The Hour of Departure: Forces That Create Refugees and Migrants* (Washington, DC: Worldwatch Paper, 1995), 10–17.

38. Ibid.

39. SIPRI, *SIPRI Yearbook 1995* (New York: Oxford University Press, 1995), 23–24.

40. Zartman, *Collapsed States,* 7–10.

41. Terry Lynn Karl and Philippe C. Schmitter, "Democratization around the Globe: Opportunities and Risks," in *World Security: Challenges for a New Century,* 43–62; Robert Rothstein, "Democracy, Conflict, and Development in the Third World," in Brad Roberts (Ed.), *U.S. Foreign Policy after the Cold War* (Cambridge: MIT Press, 1992), 271–291; Roberts, "Democracy and World Order," in *U.S. Foreign Policy after the Cold War,* 293–307.

42. Edward D. Mansfield and Jack Snyder, "Democratization and War," *Foreign Affairs* (May–June 1995): 79–97.

43. Max Singer and Aaron Wildavsky, *The Real World Order: Zones of Peace and Zones of Turmoil* (Chatham, NJ: Chatham House, 1993).

44. Jeffrey E. Garten, "Business and Foreign Policy," *Foreign Affairs* (May–June 1997): 68.

45. George Kennan, "Moscow Embassy Telegram #511:'The Long Telegram,' February 22, 1946," *Foreign Relations of the United States: 1946,* Vol. I, 696–709.

46. George Kennan, 1948, as quoted in John Lewis Gaddis, *Strategies of Containment* (New York: Oxford, 1982), 45.

47. Jessica Tuchman Matthews, "Lessons of Chernobyl," *Washington Post,* April 1996; "Sunshine and Shadow: The CIA and the Soviet Economy," John F. Kennedy School of Government case program.

48. Paul Krugman, "Dutch Tulips and Emerging Markets," *Foreign Affairs* (July–Aug. 1995): 28–43.

49. Stephen E. Flynn, *Globalization and Eroding Border Control: Developing a New US–Caribbean Regime to Meet the Challenge.* Paper prepared for the Council on Foreign Relations Homeland Security Group, Dante B. Fascall North-South Center, University of Miami, Florida, Nov. 17, 1999.

50. John Ikenberry, "The Myth of Post–Cold War Chaos," *Foreign Affairs* (May–June 1997): 91.

51. Paul W. Schroeder, "The New World Order: A Historical Perspective," in Brad Roberts (Ed.), *Order and Disorder after the Cold War* (Cambridge: MIT Press, 1996), 367–386; John Stremlau, "Antidote to Anarchy," in Roberts (Ed.), *Order and Disorder after the Cold War,* 397–412.

52. John Lewis Gaddis, "Toward the Post Cold War World," in Steven L. Speigel and David J. Pervin (Eds.), *At Issue: Politics in the World Arena* (New York: St. Martin's Press, 1994), 27–42. Clearly, many more costs have been attributed to global economies than those discussed here. These include exploitation of labor (John Sweeney, Address to the Bishops of Latin America, Canada and the United States on Humanizing the Global Economy, Washington, DC, Catholic University of America, Jan. 31, 2002; Vatican Special Advisor to the International Labor Organization Fr. Dominique Peccoud, S.J., Address to the Bishops of Latin America, Canada and the United States on Humanizing the Global Economy, Washington, DC, Catholic University of America, Jan. 31, 2002); the exploitation (even the apartheid) of the developing South by the developed North (Richard Falk, "Democratizing, Internationalizing, and Globalizing," in Yoshikazu Sakamoto (Ed.), *Global Transformation: Challenges to the State System* [Tokyo: United Nations University Press, 1994], 475–502); and environmental degra-

dation and endangerment of indigenous peoples and their civilizations (Falk, "Democratizing, Internationalizing, and Globalizing," 475–502).

53. Francis Fukuyama, *The End of History and the Last Man* (New York: The Free Press, 1992), xi.

54. Ibid., 337.

55. Terry Lynn Karl and Philippe C. Schmitter, "Democratization around the Globe: Opportunities and Risks," in *World Security: Challenges for a New Century,* 43–44. This description of the four waves of democratization is based on Karl and Schmitter's work. It should be noted that some theorists, such as Samuel Huntington, merge waves one and two into an overly long and undifferentiated category and thus count only three waves of democratization.

56. Ibid., 60.

57. This has been a problematic point for states such as Singapore, which have tried to open up free market, capitalist economic systems while restricting political participation and democratic political reforms.

58. Michael Doyle, "Liberalism and World Politics," in *Conflict after the Cold War,* 263–279.

59. Mansfield and Snyder, "Democratization and War," 88.

60. Daniel F. Burton, Jr., "The Brave New Wired World," *Foreign Policy* (Spring 1997): 32.

61. Global Users Online, Jan. 17, 2002: <http://cyberatlas.internet.com/big_picture/geographics/article/0,1323,5911_151151,00.html>; see also NUA at <http://www.nua.ie/surveys/how_many_online/>.

62. Johnstone, *Strategic Planning and International Affairs in the 21st Century.*

63. Burton, "The Brave New Wired World," 26.

64. Ibid.

65. Gaddis, "Toward the Post Cold War World," 27–42.

66. Kenichi Ohmae, *The End of the Nation State: The Rise of Regional Economies* (New York: Free Press, 1995).

67. Susan Strange, *The Retreat of the State: The Diffusion of Power in the World Economy* (Cambridge, UK: Cambridge University Press, 1996), 189.

68. Ibid., 78.

69. Ibid., 79.

70. Ibid., 81.

71. Ibid., 77, 199.

72. James N. Rosenau, "Sovereignty in a Turbulent World," in Gene M. Lyons and Michael Mastanduno (Eds.), *Beyond Westphalia? State Sovereignty and International Intervention* (Baltimore: Johns Hopkins University Press, 1995), 193; James N. Rosenau, *Turbulence in World Politics* (Princeton, NJ: Princeton University Press, 1990).

73. James N. Rosenau and W. Michael Fagen, "A New Dynamism in World Politics: Increasingly Skillful Individuals?" *International Studies Quarterly,* 41 (Dec. 1997): 660. Although he does not draw this comparison, Rosenau's arguments dovetail those of Neil Postman in *Amusing Ourselves to Death,* in which he maintains that the media technologies available to a generation affect not just the mode of their public discourse but also its content, as well as the way they think about and interact with the world. Postman sees the move to a visual era as negative, reducing public discourse to sound bites, whereas Rosenau points up the positive effects that a skills revolution can have on political outcomes and dismembering repressive regimes.

74. Rosenau, "Sovereignty in a Turbulent World," 204.

75. Ibid., 206–207; Rosenau, *Turbulence in World Politics,* 90–113.

76. Rosenau, "Sovereignty in a Turbulent World," 206–207; Rosenau, *Turbulence in World Politics,* 90–113.

77. Richard Rosecrance, *The Rise of the Virtual State: Wealth and Power in the Coming Century* (New York: Basic Books, 2000); and "The Rise of the Virtual State," *Foreign Affairs* (July–Aug. 1996): 59–60.

78. Ibid., 59–61.

79. Stephen D. Krasner, *Sovereignty: Organized Hypocrisy* (Princeton, NJ: Princeton University Press, 1999).

80. Stephen D. Krasner, *Problematic Sovereignty: Contested Rules and Political Possibilities* (New York: Columbia University Press, 2001).

81. Stephen D. Krasner, "Sovereignty: An Institutional Perspective," *Comparative Political Studies* 21 (April 1988): 74.

82. Kenneth Waltz, "Globalization and Governance," *PS: Political Science & Politics* (Dec. 1999): 693–700.

83. William H. McNeill, "Territorial States Buried Too Soon," *Mershon International Studies Review* 41 (1997): 269.

84. The real problem of US military intervention in Somalia was created by this inflexible attachment to the outdated doctrine of "overwhelming force." By deploying a large military footprint of more than 20,000 troops, the United States was forced to enter through the port of Mogadishu, the only area with an adequate infrastructure for such a large troop commitment as well as the only area where General Mohammad Farrah Aidid's forces were strong. This increased Aidid's importance and gave him an easy veto over the operation. If a smaller and more flexible US force had entered through the south, it would have met far less resistance. The large US force appeared imperialistic and created greater resistance rather than greater acquiescence.

85. Andrew J. Bacevich, "The Limits of Orthodoxy: The Use of Force after the Cold War," in Aspen Strategy Group, *The United States and the Use of Force in the Post-Cold War Era* (Washington, DC: Brookings Institution, 1995), 171–190.

CHAPTER TWO

Intergovernmental Organizations and Transsovereign Problems

The New Battleground*

Maria Green Cowles

Withstanding tear gas, rubber pellets and nightsticks, thousands of protesters faced down the World Trade Organization and police in Seattle yesterday, forcing authorities to order a curfew and call out the National Guard. . . . Protesters forced cancellation of the WTO's opening ceremonies yesterday morning at the Paramount Theater and for much of the day faced down outnumbered police on streets littered with the refuse of chaos: protest signs, spent tear-gas canisters and broken glass. . . . Delegates from 135 countries were prevented from attending meetings . . . in the morning, but business proceedings were held in the afternoon as police squeezed delegates through lines of protesters to the Washington State Convention and Trade Center. . . .

It began when a small group of self-styled anarchists started throwing bottles at police, and used hammers and crowbars to shatter store windows. . . . [Protesters] then set trash containers and protest signs afire. King County deputies responded by lobbing in a dozen tear-gas grenades. . . . Windows were broken at the Bank of America . . . as well as at Starbucks, Washington Mutual Bank, Warner Bros., Banana Republic, Nordstrom, FAO Schwarz and McDonald's. A red "A"—the symbol for anarchy—was spray-painted on some buildings. On another downtown building, someone painted in black, "We are winning, don't forget."[1]

Intergovernmental organizations (IGOs) are increasingly in the spotlight, but difficult to define. Some scholars view intergovernmental organizations such as the United Nations as vestiges of the nation-state system.[2] Others

*Special thanks goes to Stephanie Curtis for her research support. I also thank Tammi Gutner and Maryann Cusimano Love for their comments and suggestions.

recognize the same IGOs as actors who increasingly operate in an independent manner in the world today.[3] Some policy makers identify intergovernmental organizations such as the World Bank, International Monetary Fund (IMF), and World Trade Organization (WTO) as important forces in promoting economic development throughout the world. Yet numerous nongovernmental organizations (NGOs) regard these organizations as a means for the wealthy North to continue to dominate the economies, despoil the environment, and denigrate the cultures of the Global South.

There is much on which to disagree when defining and analyzing IGOs. They have been called the "ugly ducklings" of international relations studies, in part because they are misconstrued and do not fit easily into our understanding of how the international system of states functions.[4] But supporters and detractors of IGOs may agree on one point: It is increasingly difficult to discuss transsovereign problems today without any mention of IGOs. It is inconceivable, for example, to address the refugee situation in collapsed states such as Rwanda without reference to the UN High Commissioner for Refugees. It is rather difficult to understand the effects of international financial flows on East Asian countries without citing the policies of the IMF. Moreover, it is unimaginable to contemplate the rebuilding of war-torn countries such as Bosnia without citing the "blue helmets"—the UN peacekeepers. Ugly ducklings or not, IGOs serve and will continue to serve an important function in a world where problems can no longer be addressed by individual member states. They have also become one focal point for competing views on how these transsovereign problems should be addressed.

This chapter explores the changing nature of IGOs and the challenges they confront, as well as their prospects for the future in the governance of the international system. The next two sections define IGOs, examine their rise in the twentieth century, and then highlight some of the key challenges they face in this increasingly interdependent world. The chapter then examines four key IGOs in greater detail: the United Nations, the International Monetary Fund, the World Trade Organization, and the European Union. The chapter concludes with prescriptions for and reflections on the future of IGOs.

INTERGOVERNMENTAL ORGANIZATIONS: AN INTRODUCTION

Intergovernmental organizations are organizations whose members are state governments. In many respects, IGOs are creatures of the twentieth century. Their roots, however, can be traced back to basic ideas and practices that promote international cooperation and stem from diplomacy, rules of warfare, and international law in preceding centuries.

Today, there are more than 300 formal IGOs—that is, organizations that are permanent and have a secretariat to carry out functions, a voluntary membership, and a specific structure.[5] Many of the "classic" institutions are formal intergovernmental institutions: the United Nations, the International Monetary Fund (IMF), the Organization for Economic Cooperation and Development (OECD), the World Trade Organization (WTO), and the World Health Organization (WHO). Another 200 to 700 informal IGOs lack permanent bureaucracy and structure but function nonetheless to promote cooperation among governments.[6] An example of an informal IGO would be the Group of Eight (G-8). Its members—the large industrialized states of Canada, France, Germany, Italy, Japan, Russia, the United Kingdom, and the United States—regularly meet in an attempt to coordinate economic policies.

Intergovernmental organizations also differ significantly in terms of their scope and purpose. IGOs can be global, regional, and even bilateral in scope. At the same time, the organizations may hold broad, overarching purposes or more specific technical ones. The United Nations is an example of a global organization with a broad mandate. By contrast, the Universal Postal Union (UPU)—the world's second oldest international organization (established in 1874)—is a global organization (189 member countries) with a technical focus. The UPU sets the rules for international mail exchange and makes recommendations for improving the quality of mail services around the world.

The European Union (EU), comprising 15 Western European nations, is arguably the most important regional intergovernmental organization. Moreover, the EU covers a broad range of activities, including agricultural policy, commercial policy, competition policy, currency, customs union, and an embryonic foreign and defense policy. Some scholars argue that the EU, with its strong supranational bureaucracy and multilevel system of governance, should no longer be classified as a traditional international organization. Other regional organizations include the Association of South East Asian Nations (ASEAN), Mercosur, and the newly created African Union.

There are differing views of the relationship between states and IGOs in the international system. Some scholars believe that IGOs are created to serve the interests of states and to encourage cooperation among states by reducing transaction costs—the costs of making and enforcing agreements.[7] As such, IGOs are designed to reflect the wishes of the most powerful nation-states. If an IGO does not effectively champion the interests of these countries, then the countries can pick and choose other intergovernmental organizations to suit their purposes. Thus, IGOs themselves have minimal influence on—and do not challenge the sovereignty of—the member states that formed them.[8]

Other scholars disagree. They point out that the purpose of IGOs is not merely to represent states' interests or reduce transaction costs. IGOs "may be created not for what they do but for what they are for, what they represent symbolically and the values they embody."[9] Although states may still be the dominant actors within IGOs, they do not dictate the behavior of the organization. Many IGOs can and do exercise power autonomously, notably in the areas of human rights and refugees. They are purposive actors that can develop their own agendas, rules, and norms. Thus, states may choose one IGO over another not because one organization serves its interests better than another, but because some organizations are more adept at creating, developing, and implementing policies than intergovernmental bargaining alone.[10]

Globalization processes, it is argued, bring greater autonomy to IGOs because they offer IGOs more tools at their disposal.[11] IGOs may be better positioned than states to respond to the challenges of open societies, open economies, and open technologies and the resulting call for greater international cooperation. Understanding the effects of globalization on the rise and development of IGOs is the point to which we turn next.

THE RISE OF IGOS: THE RESPONSE TO GLOBALIZATION

Intergovernmental organizations increasingly became visible and important global actors in the twentieth century, particularly after World War II. Since 1945, the number of IGOs has increased fivefold. The creation of several institutions in the 1943–45 period—the IMF, World Bank, and United Nations—promised to usher in a new era of international cooperation and dialogue in the aftermath of the Second World War. However, the advent of the Cold War and the growing geopolitical concerns of the United States and the Soviet Union dampened any expectations that these organizations would rival powerful states for global leadership. IGOs often found themselves part of the Cold War battlefield. Superpower conflicts soon politicized programs that originated from the World Health Organization, the Universal Telecommunications Union (UTU), and the International Atomic Energy Agency.[12] Even UNICEF, the UN International Children's Education Fund, was tainted in the process.

At the same time, decolonization in the 1960s and 1970s produced new tensions within IGOs as the number of newly independent states increased. Many of these new countries did not cast their votes along the lines of their Western counterparts. Soon, certain organizations became forums for highlighting the differences in North–South conflicts. The Group of Seventy-Seven (G-77), for example, was established in 1964 at the end of the first session of the UN Conference on Trade and Development (or UNCTAD, as it is more commonly known). As part of its mandate, the G-77 sought to improve the terms of trade between industrialized northern and poorer southern countries.

Because of these Cold War and North–South tensions, countries such as the United States grew increasingly distrustful of key IGOs that were purportedly designed to promote international cooperation. According to Daniel Moynihan, a former US representative there, the United Nations itself had become "a dangerous place."[13]

IGOs created during this period, however, were still relevant. The North Atlantic Treaty Organization (NATO) and its Eastern bloc counterpart, the Warsaw Pact, proved to be powerful organizations. The creation of the Organization of Petroleum Exporting Countries in 1960 also demonstrated how an IGO could influence international economic and political relations. If anything, the oil crisis and growing environmental awareness in the 1970s brought home all too clearly to some countries the need to cooperate in international forums.[14]

The fall of the Berlin Wall signaled the end of paralysis within many IGOs. When President George H.W. Bush called for a "new world order" that emphasized multilateral cooperation in solving global issues, institutions such as the United Nations stood poised to gain further prominence in international affairs. The initial euphoria over this new world order was short-lived, however, with failed UN peacekeeping missions in Bosnia, Rwanda, and Somalia.[15] Although the new world order held promise for some IGOs, it threatened the existence of others. NATO, for example, found itself lacking a central purpose, and it had to reinvent itself. The Warsaw Pact, on the other hand, collapsed with the fall of the Berlin Wall.

The end of the Cold War and the emergence of what Thomas Friedman has called the "turbo-charged" era of globalization[16] have infused many IGOs with new life, new roles, and newfound influence. The opening of societies, for example, has led to greater roles for IGOs. The breakup of the Soviet Union and the democratic developments in Central and Eastern European states have provided new members and new agendas for organizations such as the Council of Europe and the Organization for Security and Cooperation in Europe. The new wave of democratization has also meant a growing role for IGOs in election monitoring around the world.

The opening of economies has also empowered IGOs as people and governments call for greater regulation of the world economy and rules for international investment and finance. The "seal of approval" of the IMF, for example, became even more vital for governments that wished to attract greater foreign investment.[17] The IMF was thus able to set down rules and conditions that governments were required to meet to receive the organization's blessing and funding. Although no sovereign government was forced to accede to these conditions, many accepted IMF recommendations that called for restructured government agencies, reprioritized government programs, and restricted government practices.

Globalization and the opening of technologies have also increased the number and types of parties who are interested in international policy making. This, in turn, has empowered international organizations. For example, people can now follow international political activities on a real-time basis over the Internet and buy and sell foreign countries' bonds in online trading. They are thus given greater incentive to follow and affect international policy making by working alone or within NGOs to make their interests known and heard. Moreover, states must now consider these domestic political actors in their foreign policy calculus.[18] In this respect, globalization empowers more actors who, in turn, limit the policy choices of individual states and encourage them to cooperate in international policy making.

Many IGOs have sought to take advantage of these globalization trends to attain greater autonomy and influence in global affairs. They have reached out to domestic organizations while building their own transnational coalitions with NGOs to promote agendas that, at times, contradict those of member states. The United Nations, for example, allied itself with the International Campaign to Ban Landmines.

It would be a mistake, however, to assume that the opening of societies, economies, and technologies solely supports IGOs that are dedicated to promoting these new globalization trends. Paradoxically, globalization also strengthens certain international organizations as bulwarks *against* globalization. On the one hand, the European Union advocates the opening of economies through the single market program, which was designed to remove barriers to trade among the fifteen member states. At the same time, however, the EU espouses policies that effectively seek to limit or counter globalization forces. The creation of the European currency, the Euro, was not merely designed to integrate European economies more effectively. It was also promoted as a means to challenge the US dollar in global finance. The rise of Mercosur, the "Common Market of the South," is another example of a regional IGO that both welcomes the opening of economies and seeks to contain them. Mercosur countries, for example, have created their own customs union and signed a free trade agreement with the European Union, which has resulted in a significant increase in trade between the two regions. On the other hand, in the midst of the Argentinean financial crisis in January 2002, Argentinean President Eduardo Duhalde announced that his country would join with Brazil to promote the creation of a Mercosur currency that would challenge the strength of the dollar.

Globalization, therefore, has led to the rise of IGOs that both promote and resist the opening of societies, economies, and technologies. Globalization has also prompted many new challenges to the roles, effectiveness, and legitimacy of IGOs in the world today.

CHALLENGES TO INTERGOVERNMENTAL ORGANIZATIONS: PROBLEMS, PERFORMANCE, AND PERCEPTIONS

The challenges faced by IGOs can be placed in three broad yet interrelated categories: the number and nature of today's problems, the emphasis on IGO performance, and the perceptions of IGO legitimacy, transparency, and fairness.

The Number and Nature of Problems

The past three decades have seen an explosion in the number of both transsovereign issues and demands for international policy coordination. According to some observers, the opening of societies, economies, and technologies has created a more informed population that calls on states to undertake greater international problem solving and global public policy making.[19] With President George H.W. Bush's appeal for a new world order, there was the expectation that transsovereign issues would increasingly be addressed in the multilateral forums of IGOs.

Flying in the face of these expectations, however, is the problem of "mandate congestion" and what Oran Young calls the growing "gap between the demand for governance and the supply of governance at the international level."[20] For example, many countries now demand that the United Nations assume more peacekeeping operations—without any significant increase in funding or meaningful revisions of the rules of engagement. Simply put, IGOs are asked to put more and more on their agendas without necessarily having the proper means to address these expanding issues.

It is not only the demand that has changed, but also the nature of the problems themselves. The United Nations' founders assumed that it would address interstate disputes, but most wars today are the result of intrastate conflict. The recent wars in Rwanda, Bosnia, Kosovo, and Afghanistan have all resulted from intrastate issues, although there were outside influences in each case. Today, the United Nations finds itself addressing not only refugee, human rights, health, and environmental matters in the aftermath of intrastate conflict but also the prospects of "state building."[21] Often, the United Nations is charged with rebuilding the administrative, political, judicial, and economic structure of these collapsed states.[22] Such failed states form the core of today's security dilemma and now dominate the agendas of many IGOs.

Performance

Of course, it is difficult for IGOs to perform and address these new and varied problems without the necessary financial and leadership support. This point was made to the United States more than once after it fell more than $1.5 billion behind in dues to the United Nations. Critics of US foreign policy have charged that by withholding funds and refusing to support specific programs, the United States has set up IGOs for failure.

Others, notably certain members of the US Congress, have maintained that many traditional IGOs have not adequately responded internally to the changed international agenda. Just as the private sector needs to restructure itself in light of economic trends, so too must IGO bureaucracies reform and transform themselves to better address today's political and economic environment. The United Nations in particular has come under considerable criticism for its bloated bureaucracy.

Some organizations have succeeded in "reinventing" themselves and their purposes in the post–Cold War, globalizing world. For example, although still not "lean and mean" as bureaucracies go, NATO has been successful in redefining its mission. Similarly, the IMF has shifted dramatically from being a short-term balance-of-payments provider to a major supplier of liquidity in times of global financial crisis. The International Telecommunications Union (ITU)—the oldest IGO (created in 1865)—has developed into a significantly streamlined organization by ridding itself of obsolete departments.

Over the years, some countries have decided to sidestep "ineffective" organizations and create their own "shadow institutions" or informal sessions where problems and issues can be addressed. Critics argue, for example, that the G-7 meetings were designed for the wealthiest countries to create a united front on issues that will later be discussed in other organizations. These critics also charge that these same countries move important issues such as the Code of Conduct for Multinationals and the Multilateral Agreement on Investment (MAI) to rich countries' "clubs" such as the Organization for Economic Cooperation and Development instead of addressing them solely in the United Nations.[23] The result, according to some critics, is a "crisis of multilateralism."[24]

To shore up support and improve both their autonomy and performance, many IGOs have brought in NGOs and built transnational coalitions around key agenda items. These "born-again institutions" are often infused with new life and influence as a result.[25] Yet the coalitions themselves can hinder an IGO's performance if it is "captured" by an NGO, which is a common phenomenon in domestic policy making of member states. Determining the proper role for NGOs in organizations that comprise nation-states is problematic. The participation of NGOs can lead to perception problems for the organization.

Perception

Perceptions—whether based on truth or fiction—can have considerable consequences for IGOs. Many NGOs and developing countries view the OECD as a tool of rich countries and big businesses setting their international agendas. The OECD's failed behind-the-scenes meetings to develop an MAI with representatives of multinational corporations are cited as a classic case of this collusion. Other critics charge that certain organizations, including programs within the United Nations, are being run by zealous NGOs that have developed their own global public policy fiefdoms. Government officials at the 1992 UN Conference on the Environment and Development in Rio de Janeiro, for example, found themselves surrounded by 1,500 NGOs accredited to the conference. In the final days, the officials opted to work behind closed doors to escape the NGOs and complete the work at hand.[26]

Of course, some critics will never be placated, and certain perceptions will never die. For example, the World Health Organization under the leadership of Gro Bruntland has been hailed for its progressive approach to eradicating disease. According to Bruntland, a key to the WHO's success has been forging partnerships with both NGOs and multinational corporations (MNCs) to carry out these global public policies. Nonetheless, certain NGOs have argued that the WHO's reputation and prestige will forever be tainted because of its working relationships with the multinational firms.[27]

Relations with NGOs and MNCs aside, arguably the most important challenge to IGOs today involves the perception of legitimacy. For too many IGOs, the democratic deficit and lack of transparency are at the core of this problem. As IGOs address more and more transsovereign issues, they are taking actions that have far-reaching implications for millions of people. The role of the IMF in the Asian financial crisis led to Asian governments making important decisions on employment, taxation, environmental, and even health policies. It also influenced massive protests in the streets of South Korea and the downfall of the political leadership in Indonesia. The IMF was criticized for both the policies undertaken and how these issues were decided in the first place. Managing the IMF is a technocratic elite that meets and consults with high government officials from its membership. Members of civil society are rarely involved in these discussions. Little, if any, democratic accountability or control is exercised over the IMF. This democratic deficit is compounded by the lack of transparency. More often than not, key negotiations in the IMF, the WTO, and other IGOs are made behind closed doors. How decisions are made, who makes them and for what reasons are rarely disclosed—much to the dissatisfaction of many citizens, NGOs, and even MNCs. Whether these IGOs have or should have this authority is controversial. Whether these IGOs are the legitimate decision makers in sovereign states is contested. In short, there is a crisis of legitimacy.

THE IGOS: EXAMPLES OF GLOBAL GOVERNANCE

Four key IGOs will now be examined in greater detail: the United Nations, the International Monetary Fund, the World Trade Organization, and the European Union.

The United Nations

Established by 51 countries in 1945, the United Nations now boasts a membership of 189 countries. The organization has six main bodies: the General Assembly, the Security Council, the Economic and Social Council, the Trusteeship Council, the Secretariat, and the International Court of Justice. The UN Charter identifies four main purposes for the organization: "to maintain international peace and security, to develop friendly relations among nations, to cooperate in solving international problems and in promoting respect for human rights, and to be a centre for harmonizing the actions of nations."[28] These objectives result in a rather broad mandate. During the 2000–01 session, for example, the General Assembly debated more than 170 different topics, including "globalization, nuclear disarmament, development, protection of the environment, and consolidation of new democracies."[29]

The United Nations also has several independent organizations, special programs, and funds that make up what is known as the UN family or UN system. For example, the Office of the UN High Commissioner for Refugees (UNHCR) and UNICEF are UN programs with separate government bodies, budgets, and secretariats that also are linked to the UN system.[30] The International Monetary Fund, the World Bank Group, and specialized agencies such as the World Health Organization and Universal Postal Union are all linked to the United Nations through cooperative technical agreements but are autonomous organizations in practice.

The United Nations is recognized as a provider of "international public goods," including international air traffic control, telecommunications and posts, humanitarian relief for refugees and victims of natural disasters, and protection of the environmental commons.[31] In recent years, it has been heralded as a promoter of "human security"—protecting states and individuals from danger and promoting individuals' political, social, and economic human rights.[32] Since they were first deployed in 1948, UN peacekeepers have taken part in fifty-four operations and were awarded the 1988 Nobel Prize for Peace.[33] Moreover, the United Nations has established international tribunals to prosecute individuals accused of war crimes and genocide in Rwanda and the former Yugoslavia. The United Nations protects more than 22 million refugees each year, buys half of the world's children's vaccines, and champions human rights around the globe.[34]

Despite these successes, critics charge that the United Nations is in need of serious reform. Several reform plans have been suggested in recent years.[35] The demand for reform is not novel, however, as various groups have called for significant changes to the organization since its inception.[36]

One set of critics has charged that the United Nations is a bloated, unruly bureaucracy. US critics in particular advocate "results-oriented" changes to the organization. Their solution is a fundamental overhaul that would include cutting unneeded or unnecessary programs and slimming the ranks of the bureaucrats. These critics argue that instead of being an organization that tries to cover everything under its broad mandate, the United Nations should focus on "global problems that nobody else can tackle" such as refugees and peacekeeping.[37] For example, although the United Nations devotes most of its time to development issues, it provides only 5 percent of the development aid to poorer regions of the world. The rest of this aid comes from private corporations, states, and NGOs.[38]

In response to these critics, Kofi Annan, the current and well-respected Secretary-General, has promoted several changes within the organization. His job, however, has not been easy. As an article in the *Economist* noted,

[t]he job of secretary-general at the United Nations is not unlike that of a medieval pope. In one sense, you are the leader of Christendom. Yet, at the same time, your power is limited: you have no battalions of your own (all those peacekeeping troops are only on loan); your own organisation is a hotchpotch of feuding bishoprics, most of whom feel more loyalty to temporal rules than to you; and you are normally broke.[39]

It is difficult not only to reform the United Nations, but also to find consensus on what these reforms should be. Not everyone agrees with the US results-oriented proposals. Nor do they trust the intentions of US congressional leaders such as Sen. Jesse Helms of North Carolina, one of the leaders of the UN reform efforts. Indeed, some US enemies and allies alike have viewed American calls for reforming the United Nations as an excuse for not paying US dues in the past. They "doubt that America really wants to see a more efficient [United Nations]—just a smaller one."[40]

It can also be argued, however, that if the United Nations is significantly reformed, then it would still face a lack of support and funding in key areas such as peacekeeping. There is little backing, for example, for a UN proposal to create a small standing army to bring peacekeepers to trouble spots immediately instead of wrangling with member states over troop numbers, contributions, and commands. Although this could render the body more effective in one of its core functions, it is unlikely that many key states would give the United Nations something as symbolic of sovereignty as an army. Nor would countries such as the United States allow any of its own troops to operate under a UN commander.

Similar problems arise when proposals are made to bring UN contributions and restructuring in line with today's political and economic realities. In 2000, the United States was the largest contributor to the UN regular budget, contributing 25 percent of the budget while representing more than 20 percent of world GDP. Japan, Germany, and France are the next largest contributors, providing 18, 9.6, and 6.5 percent of the UN regular budget while representing 8.3, 4.8, and 3.5 percent of world GDP, respectively.[41] In terms of overall contributions to UN programs, Japan and Germany are the largest contributors, yet neither serves as a permanent member of the UN Security Council.[42] On the other hand, China, a UN

Security Council member, contributes only 0.9 percent of the regular budget while representing 11.3 percent of global GDP. Successfully pressuring China to contribute significantly more to the UN budget, however, is just as unlikely as reforming the permanent membership of the Security Council. In recent years, calls have been made to expand the Security Council so that it better reflects the current configuration of power in the world by including countries such as Japan and Germany. Many UN member countries also believe that the Security Council should be more representative of other regions of the world by permanently including countries such as Brazil, Nigeria, and India. The current permanent members, however, are reluctant to revamp the body out of concern that such revisions would reduce their own powers.

Reform of the United Nations is particularly challenging because it "is a universal organisation that has to reflect its members' wishes."[43] On the one hand, many countries from the Global South do not want to see development programs cut, no matter what the argument. They are also reluctant to support any efficiency reforms that might undercut their own voices in the UN system. On the other hand, large member states who hold important positions in the Security Council are unlikely to accept reforms that challenge their strength in the organization. Of course, criticizing the United Nations as a whole is also problematic because many programs and units are seen as doing well. Proponents of reform need to take care when calling for certain measures across the board. In the end, whatever the case may be, UN reform is likely to be a slow, gradual process.

The International Monetary Fund

Since its conception in 1944, the IMF has lent hundreds of billions of dollars to countries in need of economic assistance. The charter of the IMF, and that of its sister organization, the World Bank, were formulated during a three week conference held in Bretton Woods, New Hampshire. Both organizations and their respective organs are commonly referred to as the Bretton Woods system. The World Bank was tasked with postwar reconstruction. The IMF's mandate was to promote international monetary cooperation through exchange rate stability and to facilitate the expansion of international trade by addressing balance of payment problems among the initial twenty-nine member countries.

In recent decades, IMF members have significantly expanded the IGO's mandate. As national economies have grown increasingly integrated, the global economy has become considerably more complex. The introduction of new technologies, coupled with a staggering increase in private capital flows and international transactions, has required organizations such as the IMF to broaden its functions.

The collapse of the gold standard in 1971, and the subsequent switch to floating exchange rates, for example, forced the organization to seek out a new *raison d'être*. Beginning with the debt crisis in Mexico and other Latin American countries in the 1980s, IMF members discovered a new and important role for the IGO in the international system. In addition to offering financial support and credit, the IMF began providing fiscal and monetary advice to governments and local economists. The organization increased its monitoring activities and vastly expanded the scope of conditions attached to the aid packages. In exchange for IMF loans, for instance, the fund demanded that politicians make specific macroeconomic policy changes to improve the economic health of their countries.

Later economic crises in the former Soviet bloc countries and in Southeast Asia triggered an even greater expansion in the functions and monetary support of the IMF. For example, in 1997 the fund was called on to aid the struggling economies of South Korea, Thailand, and Indonesia. The South Korean package alone amounted to $57 billion. The IMF "bailouts"—as some have termed the action—"provided enough credit to prevent formal government defaults and maintain future access to capital markets."[44] Had the IMF not intervened, the future of the Asian economies could have been even more precarious. In addition to constructing aid packages intended to avoid liquidity crunches, the IMF has begun providing loans to developing countries to assist with poverty alleviation and good governance programs. Consequently, the IMF has grown increasingly involved in the political realm of certain countries.

Despite continual requests for its assistance, the IMF has received its share of criticisms.[45] Critics, for example, have found fault with the clandestine workings of the organization. Most of the fund's activities "are shrouded in secrecy, and even when it releases statements or documents to the public, it tends to hide behind a smoke screen of technical jargon."[46] The secrecy surrounding the organization translates into a lack of transparency and accountability. IMF country documents and annual economic surveys remain private. As a consequence, its warnings and speculations about weak economies fail to reach the same international bankers and investors that the organization later bails out. Various reform agendas have sought to redress the problem of transparency through requests for increased public input and scrutiny, an independent evaluation board, and an overall demystifying of the fund.[47]

A second set of IMF criticisms is directed at the fund's country prescriptions for economic recovery. According to Joseph Stiglitz, a former chief economist and vice-president of the World Bank, during the Asian crisis the IMF delivered the "same medication for each ailing nation that showed up on its doorstep . . . even as evidence of the policy's failure mounted."[48] Moreover, the IMF attempted to temper the Asian financial crisis with a set of austerity measures similar to those prescribed to the Latin American governments in the 1980s—even though the reasons behind the Asian crisis were far different from those in Latin America. Critics argue that behind these poor prescriptions lay a group of inadequate economists who "are more likely to have firsthand knowledge of [a country's] five-star hotels" than of its social, political, and cultural makeup.[49]

Finally, more liberal critics claim that the IMF's policies "are a not-so-thinly disguised wedge for capital interests."[50] The fund has been criticized for being divided between the strong, Western economies and the poorer, developing member countries. Because the major economic powers are rarely forced to borrow from the IMF, they fail to foresee problems with continual expansion of the IMF's power and role.

To address the organization's many criticisms, critics have offered three broadly defined sets of reform proposals: abolishing the fund, significantly restructuring it, and scaling back its role to the original Bretton Woods mandate. Of course, selecting any one of these reforms would placate some groups and anger others. As Devesh Kapur joked, "If the IMF had a dollar for every criticism of its purpose and role by the Right, the Left, and the Center, it would perhaps never again have to approach its shareholders for more money to sustain its operations."[51]

The World Trade Organization

The primary purpose of the WTO is to facilitate free trade through trade agreements and negotiations, trade dispute settlements, assistance to developing countries on trade matters, and cooperation with other IGOs on international trade matters. One hundred and forty-four countries, accounting for more than 97 percent of world trade, represent the WTO membership.[52]

The WTO is the youngest of the major IGOs. It also is an example of an informal institution or regime that developed into a formal inter-governmental organization. WTO agreements are based on those of its predecessor, the General Agreement on Tariffs and Trade (GATT) (1947–1994), a one-time "temporary" agreement that became increasingly institutionalized over the years. Whereas the GATT focused solely on the trading of goods, the WTO agreements also include agreements on the trading of certain services (General Agreement on Trade in Services, or GATS) and the protection of intellectual property rights (Trade Related Intellectual Property Rights, or TRIPS). When creating the WTO, these future members also established the Dispute Settle Understanding (DSU), a specific process that encourages countries to settle trade disputes through consultation or, if that fails, to bring the disputes before a specially appointed panel of experts for a ruling. Through the DSU, the WTO "has profoundly changed the nature of trade disputes" by ending a country's ability to retaliate unilaterally against another country with sanctions and various protectionist policies.[53] Under the dispute settlement rules, a country that is found to have violated its WTO commitments must either change its domestic law, regulation, or practice, or accept retaliatory trade sanctions to compensate for the aggrieved parties' losses.

A look at the WTO's membership and the list of applicant countries clearly shows that governments believe the WTO is an important inter-governmental organization that must be joined. The recent accession of China to the WTO is a case in point. China's communist leaders participated in fifteen years of multilateral and bilateral negotiations with WTO members, and the country is apparently willing to adopt more market oriented laws and trade practices to meet WTO requirements—a sign of the WTO's success.

Yet the WTO is also one of the most controversial IGOs. Forty thousand activists and union members protested the organization and its free trade agenda at the December 1999 WTO ministerial meeting in Seattle, Washington. The result was the infamous "Battle in Seattle" highlighted in the opening of this chapter.

Perhaps one reason why the WTO is so controversial is that people from every part of the political spectrum can find fault with it. Problems of perception challenge the WTO's governance in global trade matters today. In the United States, some conservatives are wary of the organization because they believe it takes away US sovereignty through the voting procedures and the DSU. Unlike with the IMF and its weighted vote system, the United States is a coequal in the organization: Its vote counts the same as that of Jamaica. Moreover, under the DSU, the United States can no longer respond unilaterally to trade problems and instead must bring its grievances to the Dispute Settlement Body (DSB). Of course, the United States has been the target of other countries' grievances in the WTO process and has "lost" some of these cases.

On the other hand, protesters on the left of the political spectrum deride the IGO because the WTO focuses exclusively on trade issues and not on environmental and labor concerns. Accordingly, this results in a "race to the bottom"—the idea that countries and companies in the name of trade competition will push for lower and lower environmental and labor regulations. They often cite the classic tuna–dolphin ruling that occurred under the old GATT dispute settlement process. In that case, Mexico brought a grievance against the United States for banning the importation of tuna caught with purse seine nets that were deemed unsafe for dolphins.[54] When Mexico won the case, environmentalists in the United States and elsewhere viewed this ruling as a dangerous case of free trade trumping environmental concerns.

Still another category of protesters is from the developing countries. They argue that the WTO is biased toward wealthy countries and their multinational corporations. They point out that the United States and Europe pushed the developing world to accept new trade rules on services and intellectual property rights—areas where the Global North has the comparative advantage. Yet the United States and European Union were unwilling to quickly lift restrictions on textile imports or, in the case of the EU, end agricultural subsidy programs—two sectors where the Global South is more competitive. At the same time, the developing countries question the intentions of US labor and environmental activists. Requiring all WTO members to adhere to stricter labor and environmental standards would raise the costs of production in the Global South—and thus keep more jobs in the United States. The developing countries' other complaint concerns the rules and informal procedures that preclude developing countries from actively and effectively participating in negotiations. For example, unlike the United States and EU, the developing countries do not have the staff or resources to participate in complex multiple negotiations simultaneously. Thus, they are either railroaded through the process or forced to delay the process through vetoes or other tactics.[55]

The most telling criticism of the WTO, however, is its perceived lack of democratic accountability and transparency. The *Economist* magazine explained the perception in the following way:

> According to sceptics, the WTO takes powers away from elected governments and grants them to faceless bureaucrats . . . The WTO is a kind of embryonic world government, but with none of the checks and balances that true democratic government requires. In short, it is an embryonic world tyranny. That is why, in the view of many sceptics, it is the most dangerous of all the institutions of globalisation.[56]

The WTO secretariat with its 500-person staff in Geneva is not to blame for this perception. It is the member states themselves who conduct the trade negotiations, insist that they take place behind closed doors, and maintain that the deliberations of the DSB remain secret.[57]

The WTO and its membership has succeeded in moving on since the infamous Seattle ministerial meeting. At the Doha, Qatar, ministerial in fall 2001, members agreed to relaunch another round of trade liberalization. Yet the issue of WTO reform remains. Activists argue that the WTO's legitimacy has been so eroded that if reform is not carried out quickly and dramatically, the intergovernmental organization will "implode on itself."[58] Indeed, WTO Director-General Mike Moore has also suggested that failure to reform the WTO would condemn the organization "to a long period of irrelevance."[59] Issues surrounding the WTO's transparency need to be addressed sooner rather than later.

The European Union

The European Union is a classic example of a regional (as opposed to global) intergovernmental organization.[60] Since its creation as the European Coal and Steel Community in the early 1950s, the EU has emerged as an

61

important actor on the regional and global stage. Today, the EU represents 15 countries and nearly 378 million people, and it boasts a $7.8 trillion gross domestic product.[61]

The EU distinguishes itself from other IGOs in an important way. Member states "pool" their sovereignty within the EU. In effect, they share or grant part of their sovereignty to the EU itself in particular policy areas. For example, in January 2002, the twelve participating members of "Euroland" replaced their national currencies with a European currency, the Euro. Instead of twelve central banks making decisions, a single European Central Bank now oversees such monetary policy in Europe. Denmark, Sweden, and the United Kingdom opted not to adopt the Euro. Given the success of the European currency, however, most analysts believe these countries will join Euroland within the next decade.

Membership in the European Union also requires significant conformity to the *acquis communautaire*—the policies, rules, and regulations that form the legal and political basis for the European Union. EU law must be transposed into national law, so the five candidate countries that will likely join the union in the next few years—Cyprus, the Czech Republic, Hungary, Poland, and Slovenia—are currently rewriting their environmental, consumer protection, competition policy, and other laws and policies to conform with the *acquis*.

The EU is also different from other IGOs in terms of the powers granted to its supranational bodies: the European Commission, the European Parliament, and the European Court of Justice. Located in Brussels, the European Commission is the policy making body that initiates legislation primarily in economic matters and oversees the implementation of various EU-wide policies and programs, among other duties. It is the European Commission, for example, that represents the European Union in trade negotiations with the United States and in the WTO.

The European Parliament (EP) has evolved from a relatively weak assembly to a body whose voting power is equal to that of the member states in several policy areas. Scholars who study the EP argue that it is more powerful than many national parliaments in Europe.[62] The European Court of Justice (ECJ), however, is arguably the most powerful supranational body in the European Union. Today, ECJ rulings have precedence over national law in matters pertaining to EU treaties and secondary legislation. Moreover, national courts in EU member states may refer questions on particular cases to the ECJ to determine how the European law should be applied at the national level.

EU member states have not relinquished sovereign authority in all policy areas, however. In most matters pertaining to Justice and Home Affairs (JHA) (border controls, visas, immigration, and terrorism) and Common Foreign and Security Policy (CFSP) (including an embryonic military force), members retain their right of policy initiation and individual veto. Nonetheless, the countries pass important JHA legislation that is binding on the membership. In matters of CFSP, member states seek common positions and appointed a "High Representative" or "Mr. CFSP" to officially present EU policy on foreign and security policy matters to the outside world.

There is considerable debate over the autonomy of the European Union versus that of its member states.[63] The EU's distinctive traits have led some scholars to refer to it as a "multilevel system of governance" in which certain activities or forms of governance are carried out at the supranational level, others at the national level, and still others at the subnational or regional levels. Indeed, several scholars have argued that the EU should no longer be treated as an IGO but as a "polity."[64] Thus, instead of using international relations theory to explain member state cooperation, these scholars maintain that comparative politics theory can better explain how the EU functions. As noted above, for example, the European Parliament's powers can be judged by comparing the EP to other national assemblies. Similarly, the European Central Bank's role and functions can be ascertained by comparing it to other central banking systems.

Like other IGOs, however, the European Union faces many interrelated challenges. Perhaps the most fundamental is the perceived "democratic deficit" or what some term the "legitimacy deficit" of the European Union. Over a fifty-year period, the European Union developed from a small coal and steel community to today's complex organization. During this time, political elites generally encouraged EU expansion and allowed the EU institutions to define their scope, methods, and functions—all while the mass public remained largely unaware of these developments.[65] The 1992 Danish referendum on the Maastricht Treaty, in which the Danish people voted against the expansion of EU powers, signaled the end to this permissive consensus. Public opinion polls revealed that Danes and other Europeans were increasingly wary of decisions made by unknown "Eurocrats" in Brussels (the EU capital) on such matters ranging from the

size of apples to the elimination of national currencies. Government leaders who in the past found it easy to blame Brussels for forcing change on
national policies now struggled to explain the functioning and relevance of
the EU to their citizens. In recent years, member states and EU institutions
alike have sought to better clarify their policy decisions. For example, a
major sustained publicity campaign accompanied the introduction of the
Euro as a currency in 1999 and as legal tender in 2002. Recently, calls have
been made for the creation of a European constitution to replace the
hodgepodge of treaties and to spell out the roles and functions of EU institutions and member states.

The transparency of the European Union is a related problem. Critics
have long complained, for example, that the Brussels machinery is too
complex and obtuse to allow observers and lobbyists alike to track EU legislation. To successfully influence legislation in the early draft stages, for
example, one had to develop an extensive intelligence network to monitor
European Commission activities.[66] The body has endeavored to make its
machinery more transparent by providing organization charts, listing contact numbers of key personnel, and issuing status reports on various pieces
of legislation on its official Web site. More recently, the European
Commission issued a governance paper that suggested reforms in policy
making and decision making that would render the EU legislative process
more efficient, open, and timely.

Compared to the European Commission, efforts by the Council of
Ministers—the member states—to address the perceived democratic deficit
have been less impressive. The key decision making body of the European
Union still does not publish the voting records of its members. Major
newspapers have sued the council to make its meeting and voting records
more public—with little effect to date. Thus, the EU member states, not the
supranational institutions, have perhaps the biggest step to take to open up
their decision making processes and thus address the democratic deficit.

Reform of EU institutions is linked to legitimacy and transparency concerns. In 1999, the European Commission resigned *en masse* for perceived
mismanagement problems. Individual commissioners were alleged to have
improperly hired friends and relatives and misappropriated funds. For years,
the European Commission doled out management positions according to
an unofficial quota to ensure the representation of all member states. As a
result of the 1999 debacle, the European Commission has undergone and

continues to pursue significant institutional reforms, including the establishment of a promotion process based on meritocracy instead of national quotas. The European Parliament, however, whose scrutiny of the European Commission led to the 1999 resignation, has yet to embrace such reform. EP members, for example, enjoy a questionable salaries and expenses system that has not helped their reputation in the polls.[67] The fact that the 626-member European Parliament continues to meet in three different places—Brussels, Strasbourg, and Luxembourg—only reinforces the perception of an institution out of touch with its public.

The need to address these challenges of legitimacy, transparency, and reform are all the more important with the EU's pending enlargement. EU institution and member state officials alike are concerned with the governability of the union once new members join. At the same time, the fact that these countries—as well as many other European countries—want to join the EU despite these challenges suggests that one need not be too pessimistic regarding the organization's future. If anything, the EU now serves as an entity to be emulated by other regional groups in the world. There have been close consultations between EU and Mercosur officials, for example, in discussing the latter's development in South America. Even the nascent African Union—formerly the Organization of African Unity—is modeled after the EU to one day include a central bank, court, and parliament.[68]

PRESCRIPTIONS

Globalization has infused new life and purpose into IGOs. Far from being the ugly ducklings of the past, IGOs are now center stage in addressing the most important transsovereign issues of the day. Yet globalization has also prompted increasing criticism of IGOs. Individuals and NGOs increasingly question not only IGO policies but also the legitimacy of the IGOs themselves. The WTO Battle in Seattle, the debates over the United Nations on the US Senate floor, and the IMF and World Bank protests around the world have become modern-day battlefields for the future of these organizations. To remain relevant, IGOs and their members must address three core issues: reform, transparency, and legitimacy.

Reforming IGOs is not a question, but a necessity. As companies and countries adjust to globalization pressures, so too must IGOs. Many IGOs are not organized effectively to deal with today's transsovereign issues. Parts of the United Nations are prime candidates for reform because of bloated bureaucracies and poor management. However, reformers must take care to embrace efficiency without compromising the overarching values of the organization. For some countries, assessing the United Nations' performance solely in terms of an Anglo-Saxon measure of effectiveness is not appropriate. Different countries have different expectations regarding the United Nations. For some, the organization's primary role has been and still should be as a venue where dialogue can take place and where countries are treated as independent and equal—at least in the General Assembly meetings. To reform the United Nations or any other IGO, reformers need to find a balance.[69]

Transparency is the second core issue. The WTO, for example, touts the benefits of free and open markets. The IMF demands that states develop free and open financial systems. The EU requires open borders and the free movement of goods, services, people, and capital. Yet all three organizations fail to practice what they preach—conducting their primary decision making sessions in secrecy, behind closed doors. Who is making the decisions, why, and under what circumstances? Protesters argue that they have a right to know. Transparency allows for greater scrutiny of IGOs and "provides the basis for a highly democratic, albeit nonelectoral, system of transnational governance based on the growing strength of global civil society."[70]

Legitimacy is arguably the most important concern facing IGOs—in a sense, the umbrella issue under which all other concerns can be found. For example, whether an IGO is reforming or transparent will affect the public's determination of its legitimacy. Relations with NGOs, fairness, and adequate resources are three key factors that play an important role in enhancing the public and political support for IGOs. Today, IGOs seek to enhance their legitimacy by building coalitions and networks with NGOs and MNCs. Positive examples of such cooperation abound—from the WHO's compact with MNCs to eradicate disease to the United Nations' alliance with the International Campaign to Ban Landmines. Relations between IGOs, NGOs, and MNCs, however, must be developed carefully to ensure that IGOs are not beholden to or co-opted by particular groups or interests.[71] Failure to do so would result in the demise of the very legitimacy IGOs sought to enhance in the first place.

IGOs—including their members—must also seek to enhance fairness as a means to promote their policies. Who does the IGO represent? Western protesters in Seattle maintained that the WTO favored MNCs at the expense of the environment and laborers. At the same time, poor countries argued that the IMF, WTO, and other economic organizations were biased toward the richer North. Of course, schisms between rich and poor countries, environmentalists and economists are not new. Today, however, IGO policies that fail to consider these tensions are ripe for failure.

Providing adequate resources—funding, staff, and political support—is also critical to ensuring the future health and legitimacy of IGOs. Today, IGOs serve as primary, if not *the* primary, entities responsible for addressing the economic, political, and cultural fallout of failed states. They are the guardians of refugees, the lenders of last resort, and, in some cases, the bulwarks against the excesses of globalization. Yet they are often not given the resources to carry out these important policies in the most effective manner. Although critics and member states may complain about ill-advised programs, they often need not look beyond their own pocketbooks for the reason why an IGO has not fully fleshed out an issue.

Of course, critics, protestors, and battlefields are not going away anytime soon—nor should they. At the same time, member states recognize that they are ill-equipped to address today's transsovereign problems. Thus, IGOs are likely to persist. Addressing the core issues of reform, transparency, and legitimacy would ensure that they are here to stay and better poised to manage future transsovereign problems.

ENDNOTES

1. Scott Sunde, "Chaos Closes Downtown," *Seattle Post-Intelligencer,* Dec. 1, 1999; available at <http://seattlepi.nwsource.com/local/prot01.shtml>.
2. A. LeRoy Bennett and James K. Oliver, *International Organizations: Principles and Issues* (7th ed.) (Upper Saddle River, NJ: Prentice Hall, 2002), 3.
3. Michael N. Barnett and Martha Finnemore, "The Politics, Power, and Pathologies of International Organizations," *International Organization,* 53(4): 699–732; Bob Reinalda and Bertjan Verbeek, *Autonomous Policy Making by International Organizations* (New York: Routledge, 1998).
4. Clive Archer, *International Organizations* (London: Allen & Unwin, 1983).
5. Bennett and Oliver, *International Organizations,* 2.

6. The actual number of international organizations varies widely depending on various scholars' definitions of organizations and institutions. Keohane, for example, suggests there are currently more than 1,000 international institutions (Robert O. Keohane, "International Institutions: Can Interdependence Work?" *Foreign Policy* [Spring 1998]: 82–94). The term *regime* is yet another word used to describe these informal institutions. See Stephen D. Krasner, "Structural Causes and Regime Consequences: Regimes as Intervening Variables," *International Organization,* 36(2): 185.

7. Keohane, "International Institutions," 86.

8. John J. Mearsheimer, "The False Promise of International Institutions," *International Security,* 19(3): 5–49.

9. Barnett and Finnemore, "Politics, Power, and Pathologies," 703. See also Reinalda and Verbeek, *Autonomous Policy Making.*

10. Reinalda and Verbeek, *Autonomous Policy Making,* 5.

11. Bertjan Verbeek, "International Organizations: The Ugly Duckling of International Relations Theory?" in Reinalda and Verbeek, *Autonomous Policy Making,* 25

12. Ibid., 17.

13. Keohane, "International Institutions," 84.

14. Ibid.

15. Oran R. Young, "Governance without Government," in *Governance in World Affairs* (Ithaca, NY: Cornell University Press, 1999), 1.

16. Thomas Friedman, *The Lexus and the Olive Tree* (New York: Farrar, Straus & Giroux, 2000).

17. Jessica T. Mathews, "Power Shift," *Foreign Affairs* (Jan.–Feb. 1997): 58.

18. Reinalda and Verbeek, *Autonomous Policy Making,* 6–7.

19. Wolfgang Reinicke, "The Other World Wide Web: Global Public Policy," *Foreign Policy* (Winter 1999–2000): 44–57.

20. Oran R. Young, "Governance without Government," in *Governance in World Affairs* (Ithaca, NY: Cornell University Press, 1999), 2.

21. Donald C. F. Daniel and Bradd C. Hayes (Eds.), *Beyond Traditional Peacekeeping* (New York: St. Martin's, 1995); Lori Fisler Damrosch (Ed.), *Enforcing Restraint: Collective Intervention in Internal Conflicts* (New York: Council on Foreign Relations, 1993).

22. Bruce Russett, "Ten Balances for Weighing UN Reform Proposals," *Political Science Quarterly,* 111(2): 262.

23. Steve Kobrin, "The MAI and the Clash of Globalizations," *Foreign Policy* (Fall 1998): 97–109. As Kobrin notes, NGOs were largely responsible for stopping the MAI negotiations in the OECD. Today, the issue is headed for the WTO.

24. Martina Metzger and Birgit Reichenstein (Eds.), *Challenges for International Organizations in the 21st Century: Essays in Honor of Klaus Hufner* (New York: St. Martin's Press, 2000), viii.

25. Mathews, "Power Shift," 50–66.

26. P. J. Simmons, "Learning to Live with NGOs," *Foreign Policy* (Fall 1998): 5–6; available online at <www.ceip.org/files/Publications/simmfp.asp?from=pubtopic>.

27. CorpWatch, "UN and Corporations Fact Sheet, March 2001"; available at <www.corpwatch.org/press/PPF.jsp?articleid=928>.

28. "The UN in Brief"; available at <www.un.org/Overview/brief.html>.

29. Ibid.

30. Ibid.

31. David Held, Anthony McGrew, David Goldblatt, and Jonathan Perraton, *Global Transformations: Politics, Economics, and Culture* (Stanford: Stanford University Press, 1999).

32. Russett, "Ten Balances," 260.

33. UN Secretaries-General Dag Hammarskjöld and Kofi Annan were also given the Nobel award in 1961 and 2001, respectively. Annan's prize was shared with the United Nations. The UNHCR and UNICEF have also been recipients of the Nobel Prize for Peace.

34. "Reforming the United Nations: Pope Kofi's Unruly Flock," *Economist* (Aug. 8, 1998): 19.

35. Major reform plans include Erskine Childers with Brian Urquhart, *Renewing the United Nations System* (Uppsala, Sweden: Dag Hammarskjöld Foundation, 1994); South Commission, *Reforming the United Nations: A View from the South* (Geneva: South Centre, 1995); Commission on Global Governance, *Our Global Neighborhood* (New York: Oxford University Press, 1995); Independent Working Group on the Future of the United Nations, *The United Nations in Its Second Half-Century* (New York: Ford Foundation, 1995).

36. See, for example, Ronald I. Meltzer, "Restructuring the United Nations System: Institutional Reform Efforts in the Context of North-South Relations," *International Organization,* 32(4): 993–1018.

37. "Reforming the United Nations," 20.

38. Ibid.

39. Ibid., 19.

40. Ibid., 22.

41. Ibid., 20.

42. Russett, "Ten Balances," 264–265.

43. Quote by Louise Frécette in "Reforming the United Nations," 22.

44. David D. Hale, "The IMF, Now More than Ever," *Foreign Affairs,* 77(6): 107–113.

45. One of the most common policy criticisms of the IMF is the "moral hazard" argument in which critics fear that countries will take excessive risks knowing that the IMF will later come to their rescue. See Hale, "The IMF, Now More than Ever," 10.

46. Paul Bluestein, "At the IMF, a Struggle Shrouded in Secrecy," *Washington Post*, March 30, 1998, p. A1.

47. Carol Welch, "In Focus: The IMF and Good Governance," *Foreign Policy in Focus,* 3(33); available at <www.foreignpolicy-infocus.org/briefs/vol3/v3n33imf_body.html>.

48. Joseph Stiglitz, "The Insider," *New Republic* (April 17 & 24, 2000): 56; available at <www.tnr.com/041700/stiglitz041700.html>.

49. Ibid., 57.

50. Devesh Kapur, "The IMF: A Cure or a Curse?" *Foreign Policy* (Summer 1998): 115.

51. Ibid.

52. Another thirty countries are negotiating membership. See "The WTO in Brief" on the WTO Web site at <www.wto.org/english/thewto_e/whatis_e/inbrief_e/inbr02_e.htm>.

53. Marcus Noland, "Learning to Love the WTO," *Foreign Affairs* (Sept.–Oct. 1999): 81.

54. See "Beyond the Agreements: The Tuna–Dolphin Dispute" on the WTO Web site at <www.wto.org/english/thewto_e/whatis_e/tif_e/bey5_e.htm>.

55. John Audley and Ann M. Florini, *Overhauling the WTO: Opportunity at Doha and Beyond,* Policy Brief: Carnegie Endowment for International Peace, Oct. 2001, p. 4.

56. "Who Elected the WTO? The Case for Globalisation Survey," *Economist* (Sept. 29–Oct. 5, 2001): 26.

57. As the *Economist* argued, "The WTO is no would-be tyrant. It is democratic to a fault, and has few powers of its own." Ibid.

58. Lori Wallach, "Transparency in WTO Dispute Resolution," *Law and Policy in International Business,* 31(3): 773–778.

59. Audley and Florini, *Overhauling the WTO,* 2.

60. There are still technical distinctions when referring to the European Union and the European Community, the previous name for this organization. For simplicity's sake, only the term *European Union* is used in this text.

61. Data for 2000. See "Facts and Figures" at <www.eurunion.org/profile/facts.htm>.

62. Roger Scully, "Democracy, Legitimacy, and the European Parliament," in Maria Green Cowles and Michael Smith (Eds.), *The State of the European Union: Risks, Reform, Resistance, and Revival,* Vol. 5 (Oxford, UK: Oxford University Press), 228–245.

63. See, for example, Mark Pollack, "Delegation, Agency, and Agenda-Setting in the European Community," *International Organization,* 51(1): 99–134.

64. Simon Hix, "The Study of the European Community: The Challenge to Comparative Politics," *West European Politics,* 1(1): 1–30.

65. Helen Wallace, "Politics and Policy in the EU: The Challenge of Governance," in Helen Wallace and William Wallace (Eds.), *Policy-Making in the European Union* (3rd ed.) (Oxford, UK: Oxford University Press, 1996), 3–36. See also Thomas Banchoff and Mitchell Smith (Eds.), *Legitimacy and the European Union: The Contested Polity* (New York: Routledge, 1999).

66. Maria Green Cowles, "The EU Committee of AmCham: The Powerful Voice of American Firms in Brussels," *Journal of European Public Policy,* 3(3): 339–358.

67. Ian Black, "Euro Group Calls on MEPs to Reform," *Guardian,* March 15, 2001; available online at <www.guardian.co.uk/europarl/Story/0,2763,452061,00.html>.

68. "Conflicts Cloud African Union Hopes," BBC News, July 11, 2001; available online at <http://news.bbc.co.uk/hi/english/world/africa/newsid_1433000/1433908.stm>.

69. Russett, "Ten Balances," 259–269.

70. Ann M. Florini, "The End of Secrecy," *Foreign Policy* (Summer 1998); available online at <www.ceip.org/files/Publications/annfp.asp?from=pubtopic>.

71. "The Non-Governmental Order," *Economist* (Dec. 9, 1999): 3; available online at <www.economist.com/PrinterFriendly.cfm?Story_ID=266250>. See also P. J. Simmons, "Learning to Live with NGOs," *Foreign Policy* (Fall 1998): 82–96; also available online at <www.ceip.org/files/Publications/simmfp.asp?from=pubtopic>.

CHAPTER THREE

Nongovernmental Organizations

Politics Beyond Sovereignty

Maryann Cusimano Love

> . . . proclaim liberty throughout the land to all its inhabitants; it shall be a jubilee for you.
>
> —Leviticus 25:10

The Jubilee movement is a curious coalition. The pope, Bono (lead singer of the Irish rock band U2), Harvard economist Jeffrey Sachs, and a coalition of religious organizations and nongovernmental organizations (NGOs) united behind these words from the Old Testament in an effort to get the debts of heavily indebted poor countries (HIPCs) forgiven in the millennium year. In a perverse form of foreign aid, HIPCs pay private banks and international financial institutions more in debt repayments each year than they invest in education and health care or receive in aid or foreign direct investment. Each year, $13.5 billion—$200 million per week—is drained away from Africa alone, while $7 billion to $10 billion would treat HIV and AIDS, tuberculosis, and malaria combined in Africa in one year.[1] Many of the original loans went to corrupt governments and dictators who were useful to the West during its Cold War fight against communism. For example, at least 30 percent of World Bank funds to Indonesia were pocketed by the Suharto family or its associates, according to some estimates.[2]

The idea behind the Jubilee movement is that poor people have paid enough. Most have paid the original lending amounts three or four times over—and they will never be able to pay the escalating interest owed on loans that have profited the banks of some developed countries as well as corrupt rulers, but have deprived citizens in indebted countries of resources and basic services. Initially, the Jubilee effort was declared politically dead by officials in the US Department of the Treasury, which is a strong proponent of debt repayment (US banks hold some of these debts). But through dogged persistence and savvy lobbying, the Jubilee effort prevailed on several fronts in a short time. The US government gave $434 million to international financial institutions (IFIs) for HIPC debt relief and credited the Jubilee movement for the policy switch. The IFIs forgave $34 billion in debt to 22 countries and have pledged to raise that to $70 billion over time.

Through a pincer movement of pressure commonly used by NGOs, the movement pressed democratic governments internally and externally. At rock concerts and football games, the Jubilee movement appealed directly to the public, making the abstract problem of Third World debt concrete to mobilize public opinion. Leveraging celebrity activism, Bono and others worked the halls of Congress, even winning over conservative US Senator Jesse Helms. Although the Jubilee year is over, the movement continues to push multilateral organizations to forgive more debts more quickly. For example,

> Cameroon's annual debt payments will be reduced by 40 percent over the next five years. But Cameroon will still pay, on average, $280 million per year during this period. The projected payments far exceed the amount the country spends annually on education ($239 million) and health care ($87 million). The total relief is about $2 billion, but as with most HIPCs, it will be spread thinly over the next 20 to 25 years. The amount looks especially inadequate in light of the extremely high level of poverty in Cameroon, where one-third of the children are malnourished and 60 percent of the population lack[s] access to clean water.[3]

Most HIPC debt is owed to private banks, which have done little to address debt relief. Although much remains to be done, the NGOs have pushed debt relief onto the policy agenda. The questions now to be answered are how much and how quickly debt relief should move forward—not whether it should be on the public agenda.

In a similar story of NGOs affecting foreign policy, Canadian housewife Jody Williams had enough. NGOs had warned governments about the dangers of landmines for years, but governments were not taking sufficient action. Long after wars were over, antipersonnel landmines remained in more than 90 countries, killing and maiming an estimated 26,000 people each year—or creating one new landmine victim every 20 minutes.[4] Landmines violate the rules of war because they cannot distinguish between combatants and civilians. Many victims of landmines are children, who, out of curiosity, pick up these shiny but dangerous objects. Many governments found landmines to be cheap weapons of war. They did not want to stop using them, and they did not want to pay for difficult and often deadly mine-removal programs.

So Jody Williams used the personal computer in her kitchen to organize the many NGOs that had a stake in this fight. Using e-mail and faxes, she inexpensively, quickly, and efficiently brought diverse groups on board and founded the International Campaign to Ban Landmines (ICBL). With the help of the Canadian government, the ICBL brought pressure to bear on governments to quickly ban, remove, stop producing and stockpiling antipersonnel landmines, and to increase landmine education and reduce the pain and suffering of landmine victims. The ICBL enlisted celebrity spokespeople such as Princess Diana in a direct media campaign that bypassed obstructionist governments and made emotional appeals directly to the public. Internally, governments were pressured by their own populations. Externally, they were pressed by the coalition of NGOs and states such as Canada, which led the movement to ban landmines. In record time, the ICBL succeeded in getting states to adopt an international treaty banning antipersonnel landmines in December 1997. One hundred twenty-two states have already ratified the treaty, despite opposition from the United States. In each year since the treaty's signing, landmine use, production, and stockpiling has decreased while landmine decommissioning, education, and services to landmine victims has increased. The ICBL continues in action, using a network of NGOs to monitor compliance with the treaty and pressuring states that have not joined the treaty. Jody Williams won the Nobel Peace Prize for her efforts.

These examples illustrate four main themes that will be explored in this chapter. First, not only are the power and number of NGOs increasing, but also they are more frequently joining forces in transnational advocacy networks, or mobilizations of principled actors who are committed to social change.[5] Second, NGOs are active in more sectors, taking on increased functions that were once the sole preserve of states (such as international finance) and serving as the legal monitors of arms control treaty compliance. Third, NGOs use tactics that are aimed directly at the public, multinational corporations (MNCs), or intergovernmental organizations (IGOs). They are not focused only on governments—and this is one of their greatest strengths. NGOs come with weaknesses, however, including democracy deficits, North–South divisions, and coordination complexity. Fourth and finally, these changing ideas and practices of transnational politics affect sovereignty.

NGOs: PEOPLE POWER

Although NGOs predate the current period of modern globalization, their numbers, sizes, budgets, ranges of activities, power, transnational networks, and levels of international recognition have drastically increased in recent years—to the point where commentators have suggested that "we are in the midst of a global 'associational revolution.'"[6] NGOs are an odd category, defined negatively by what they are not rather than by positive definitions of what they are. NGOs are not governments, but they may receive resources from or offer resources to governments, or they may only involve themselves in certain areas or issues with the permission of governments. NGOs are a broad and eclectic group, however, and some never accept government aid. A strong tradition of autonomy prevented the Red Cross, for example, from accepting US military airlift capabilities to transport food into Somalia during the famine in 1992.[7] After the Bush administration had publicly announced the airlift, it learned that the Red Cross could not allow its food to fly into Somalia in military-marked planes.[8] Other NGOS, such as CARE and World Vision, derive significant portions of their budgets and resources from governments as states contract out developmental assistance to NGOs.

NGOs range from small, grassroots groups run on shoestring budgets to huge international organizations with deep pockets, from single-issue outfits to umbrella organizations. NGOs are private sector organizations but

| Table 1 | | | | |
Worldwide NGO Growth				
	1909	1951	1960	1968	1976
Traditional NGOs	176	832	1,268	2,577	5,155
Special NGOs	–	–	–	741	1,067
Total	176	832	1,268	3,318	6,222
	1978	1983	1985	1987	1989
Traditional NGOs	8,347	11,523	13,768	14,943	14,333
Special NGOs	1,174	5,507	6,866	8,305	5,730
Total	9,521	17,030	20,634	23,248	20,063
	1991	1993	1995	1997	2001/2002
Traditional NGOs	16,113	12,759	14,274	15,965	18,323
Special NGOs	7,522	16,142	21,780	24,341	28,775
Total	23,635	28,901	36,054	40,306	47,098

Data from Union of International Associations (Ed.), *Yearbook of International Organizations,* Vol. 1, 2001/2002 (Brussels: K. G. Saur Verlag, 2001), Appendix 3.

are often assumed to be public interest groups, which leads to contention. Who elects NGOs and who do they speak for? Many in the United States refer to NGOs as PVOs, or private volunteer organizations. But the term *volunteer* can be misleading, because most international NGOs have permanent, full-time, paid professional staffs. NGOs are nonprofit groups. Although community development banks or Habitat for Humanity often turn a profit, the resources generated are reinvested in the community. Profit is not the organization's primary goal but a means to achieving the NGO's goals such as stabilizing communities by developing homes and businesses in poor areas where banks will not lend money.

Counts of NGOs vary, although scholars agree that their numbers are increasing. They are often referred to as part of civil society or as the third sector (government and for-profit businesses being the other two sectors). The Union of International Associations tracks NGOs and IGOs (see Table 1) and lists 18,323 traditional international NGOs in 2002, such as universal membership organizations and internationally oriented national organizations. Another 28,775 special NGOs (such as religious orders) brings a total of 47,098 international NGOs.[9]

Despite their rising numbers, NGOs raise some puzzles. NGOs have no armies. They command no states. They collect no taxes and can compel no one to follow them or to contribute to their treasuries. So what is the source of their power? NGOs trade in the currency of ideas, especially ideas of good and evil, right and wrong. The ideas compel, even when the organizations cannot. NGOs attract support more than they can enforce compliance. Many NGOs are transnational moral entrepreneurs, agents who act as reformers or crusaders to change rules out of an ethical concern to curtail a great evil.[10] Their very names are often cast as moral imperatives, proclaiming both what they value and what they do—as in Human Rights Watch and Save the Children.

Governments have legal authority, but advocacy NGOs rely on moral authority. Generally, where states have military power and MNCs have economic power, the strength of NGOs lies in their idea power. They seek to occupy the only high ground available to them, the moral high ground. If an NGO can succeed in redefining a problem as a moral issue, then it will have a greater chance of prevailing, because states and MNCs may not be able to speak credibly as bastions or brokers of morality. Religious organizations in particular often have well-developed ethics and rich institutions, resources that are useful to transnational advocacy networks and greatly needed today given the ethical and institutional gaps of globalization (discussed in Chapter 13). For example, consider the importance of church networks and leaders in abolishing slavery, as well as the importance of Archbishop Desmond Tutu in the South African anti-apartheid movement. Morally, religious organizations have legitimacy speaking on moral issues and a treasure chest of well-developed ideas available for use by transnational advocacy networks. Tactically, religious organizations can pool their power with other religious and civil society groups and use their direct pulpit access to citizens (who may be business or government decision makers) as well as their ability to attract media. Although secular NGOs may not command institutional networks (such as schools and hospitals) that are as extensive, they also develop and trade in moral ideas, such as when environmental transnational advocacy networks construct and promote environmental ethics.[11]

NGOs have information power. Especially when networked transnationally, NGOs may have access to grassroots information about how particular policies affect particular people, information that governments or

IGOs overlook or do not have. People with greater and cheaper access to information technologies can force greater transparency. Transparency and sunshine politics are important tools for NGOs. By expanding the information base of a public's or elite's discussion of previously closed matters, NGOs often impose a "Dracula" test: Will a particular policy or practice be able to survive in the daylight? Transparency alone can do much to shrink both government and corporate abuses. And discussions alone about opening the decision making process to greater transparency help to reframe issues as moral issues, again moving the issue to where NGOs have some home court advantage.

Some NGOs can use the power of their reputations as a "force multiplier" to enhance their values, ideas, and information power. Reputational power may derive from important, well-known or respected figures who are members of the group, or it may come from the NGO's own track record of strong advocacy. Or, like an MNC, an NGO may build a "brand name" around the quality and reliability of the organization's information products. Some NGOs emphasize building such reputational power through quality information products—for example, Transparency International's work on corruption worldwide.

NGOs use media and communications power as a force multiplier for their values, ideas, and information power. Although NGOs vary in their skills and access to global media, they do have certain media advantages. Global media simplify issues to attract wider audiences and compete against ever-shorter sound bites to sell their products. If NGOs often emphasize how policies or practices affect particular individuals or groups, or how global issues present clear moral choices, then they may be able to attract media attention. NGOs can use media as a megaphone for their message if they understand the care and feeding of the media and can deliver compelling stories and good pictures with clear good guys and bad guys in arenas where government, IGO, or corporate responses may be slow or lack credibility. Because MNCs may have huge marketing investments in their brand names and do not want these brands sullied or their reputations trashed, even the threat of negative media coverage can bring greater attention to an NGO's ideas. It is more difficult to wield this media power against naked, anonymous commodities and unknown, unbranded companies, however. Media and communications power are important to groups that trade in ideas. NGOs, like others who can persuade but cannot compel, must be good salespeople as well as good preachers to effectively mobilize their ideas.[12]

NGOs also have female power. Women are underrepresented in the governments of states and in leadership positions in MNCs and IGOs. But women are better represented as both leaders and members of NGOs. Women make up the majority of people on the planet, but many governments, MNCs, and IGOs throw away or underutilize the talents of more than half their populations. This can be a moral and strategic advantage for NGOs. They can provide a means for women to participate in and affect international structures that may otherwise exclude them. If women perceive NGOs as more likely to represent their interests, then this may add to popular support and reputational advantages for NGOs. Like human society in general, NGOs are certainly not free from gender conflicts; relative to other institutions, however, NGOs are more likely to be run by and for women, taking up issues—such as women's rights, human smuggling, and female genital mutilation—that other institutions ignore.[13]

NGOs also have the power of individuals. They do not accept the traditional view that states are the fundamental unit in international politics and that individuals can have little effect. Believing individuals can make a difference, they create ways to do so. Without getting bogged down in the question of which came first, the idea or the activist, activists are central to NGOs.[14] Individuals may start NGOs, splinter NGOs, and use NGOs as vehicles for both personal and community expression and activism. Even when NGOs network internationally in large campaigns, testimonials of how global problems affect real people are an enormous strength for NGOs, helping to put a face on global politics.

Although NGOs are generally legal groups that do not advocate violence, they share similarities with other nonstate actors that form transnational networks in pursuit of particular ideas: terrorists. For both groups, "victims" are strategically useful if a wider society empathizes with them either as innocent civilians, or because you can envision yourself in their shoes. A "poster child factor" also helps NGOs gain sympathy and concrete identification with their cause from either elites or masses. For terrorists, sympathy with the victims helps generate fear that is out of proportion to the acts they commit. The similarities end there, however, because terrorists target their victims with the intention of harming them, whereas NGOs target their groups with the intention of aiding them. The success of their very divergent strategies, however, depends on the esteem with which society regards them, their cause, and their targeted groups.

Another source of power for NGOs can be consumer power. If an NGO can credibly argue a connection between a corporate policy and some objectionable wider practice, then it can marshal the market power of customers, consumers, or shareholders through boycotts or pressure on advertisers and shareholders, among other forms of market pressures. This can put an economic price on objectionable practices that may make corporations or states notice and respond to NGO concerns. This is how "dolphin-free tuna" came to a grocery store near you.

NGOs have network power. They are typically organized as flatter, more flexible organizations than governments, IGOs, or MNCs. This may give NGOs greater speed to respond to pressing global issues or to quickly get their views to the media faster than some government bureaucracies. More important, networks allow NGOs to forum shop—that is, to press their issues in more favorable state or international arenas. For example, with the help of human rights NGOs, the families of four US churchwomen who had been abducted, raped, and murdered while serving the poor in El Salvador in 1980 are trying to have their day in court in Florida. Feeling that justice was blocked in the political system of El Salvador, NGOs helped to move the issue to the United States, where there are stronger legal protections on human rights and greater access to the international media.[15] What can possibly be accomplished by this? The women are dead and the civil war has ended. But NGOs trade in ideas. The trial may help shed light on the poor human rights practices of governments, as well as open a new forum for hearing other cases blocked by local governments. Margaret Keck and Kathryn Sikkink refer to this as the "boomerang pattern":

> Governments are the primary "guarantors" of rights, but also their primary violators. When a government violates or refuses to recognize rights, individuals and domestic groups often have no recourse within domestic political or judicial arenas. They may seek international connections finally to express their concerns and even to protect their lives. When channels between the state and its domestic actors are blocked, the boomerang pattern of influence characteristic of transnational networks may occur: domestic NGOs bypass their state and

directly search out international allies to try to bring pressure on their states from outside.[16]

Keck and Sikkink are correct that transnational networks often emerge as a back way around blocked local politics, but NGOs go global for other reasons as well. Even when an NGO enjoys a good relationship with the local government, as Jody Williams and the ICBL enjoyed with the Canadian government, the goal may require activating a global advocacy network. Or NGOs may perceive a better target internationally, even when local politics are not blocked.

Outlining these potential sources of power for NGOs does not mean that all organizations have all of these resources at all times. Some NGOs have denser networks that allow them to pool or access greater resources than others with fewer or sparser networks. Some issues are easier to put a face on than others. Environmentalists who are concerned with global climate change have thus far lacked a poster child, which makes it difficult for them to translate the abstractions of global warming into more concrete concern over those who are affected. If ideas are a crucial source of power for NGOs, then clearly some ideas are better than others, and some play better to particular audiences than do others. Some NGOs can craft an easily recognizable and universally sympathetic message better than others. NGOs that promulgate values and ideas with greater resonance will have advantages over NGOs with narrower and less appealing idea bases. For example, it may be easier to mobilize against child labor than to save the dwarf wedge mussel. As in all things political, context matters in assessing NGO power. It is easier to sell the idea that child labor is wrong in rich countries than in poor countries.

Different NGOs have different resources, expertise, networks, issues, and contexts. However, NGOs use their variegated supplies of people power in several common ways. NGOs raise consciousness regarding issues with elites, masses, or both. NGOs expand the idea base surrounding issues by introducing new or discrediting accepted information, or introducing alternative norms by which to evaluate information. NGOs frame or reframe issues. They put issues on the public agenda. NGOs move issues to a forum more amenable to a favorable response. NGOs change government, IGO, or MNC policy, or individual behavior. NGOs change language, beliefs, and symbols surrounding issues (which may later translate into behavioral changes). They adapt or create institutional structures or advocacy networks to further particular issues. And NGOs monitor compliance with norms or regimes once created, making actors live up to the promises they make.

Yet NGOs come with their downsides as well. Coordinating action among a wide variety of eclectic organizations with different agendas, cultures, and operating procedures is difficult. As Andrew S. Natsios, head of the US Agency for International Development (USAID) and former director of the NGO World Vision, observes, "Many of the institutional players really don't like or trust one another."[17] The abilities of NGOs to work well with states, IGOs, and MNCs in combating transsovereign problems is often inhibited by poor communication and coordination among the varying groups. IGOs, MNCs, and government foreign policy organizations too often deal with NGOs in an ad hoc, nonsystematic manner. Increased numbers of NGOs in complex combinations make coordination, communication, transparency, and accountability difficult, as is determining which groups should be included in government and IGO decision processes. NGOs may compete against one another for the supremacy of their ideas, funding, and recognition. As private sector organizations, who do NGOs speak for or answer to beyond their own governing boards or contributors? NGOs have asymmetrical resources and influence, and even within NGO advocacy networks, conflicts arise between Northern and Southern NGOs. Who guides the network? Southern NGOs are critical of donor-driven development. However, media power and reputational power can also be tools to check and balance rising NGO power. For example, public pressure against the Red Cross decision to use funds donated to the victims of September 11 for other purposes indicates these tools can yield results. Many NGOs adopt voluntary codes of conduct and publish their budgets to encourage transparency and accountability. The same questions that plague corporate codes of conduct, however, may be raised regarding NGOs: How seriously are these codes implemented, and what are the sanctions if voluntary codes are not implemented? Because NGO power frequently derives from moral and reputational capital, NGOs may have greater incentives to address democracy deficits than other organizations.

NGOs AND GLOBALIZATION: OPEN SOCIETIES

Open societies, open technologies, and open economies make it easier to establish, organize, and run NGOs. We are witnessing an explosion of NGOs worldwide precisely when liberalizing trends are spreading. The spread of democracy lowers the barriers to forming NGOs. Some of the hallmarks of democracy are freedom of expression and freedom of association. Certainly, the democratization process encourages the creation and spread of NGOs as part of the effort to build civil society. One Hungarian activist, Andras Biro, describes his efforts: "For the first time in forty years we are reclaiming responsibility for our lives."[18] Nondemocratic governments may make NGOs illegal, fearing they may form a base of opposition to the government. Organizing people in states with closed political systems—North Korea and Iraq, for example—can be a dangerous proposition to the activist, who risks imprisonment, torture, and death.

The fears of authoritarian governments are justified because NGOs have worked to bring about the fall of nondemocratic regimes. Lester Salamon notes that, "under Pope John Paul II Catholic churches in Warsaw, Gdansk, Krakow, and elsewhere in Eastern Europe provided a crucial neutral meeting ground and source of moral support for those agitating for change in the latter 1980s. The Lutheran Church played a comparable role in East Germany."[19]

NGOs also have been instrumental in pressing for open societies and advocating for human rights and democratization. During and after World War II, NGOs kept the issue of human rights on the international agenda when state representatives meeting to construct the postwar international organization (what became the UN) tried to exclude or water down such concerns. States were skeptical about including human rights in the UN Charter. They feared a loss of sovereignty over internal treatment of their citizens if the topic were broached in the UN Charter. But NGOs such as the American Jewish Committee, the American Bar Association, the National Association for the Advancement of Colored People, and the League of Women Voters reminded states that the failure to protect individual and minority rights after World War I had contributed to the conflict and genocide of World War II. Sustained lobbying by NGOs ensured that respect for human rights became one of the four purposes of the United Nations set forth in its Charter, and that the Charter called for the creation of a UN Commission on Human Rights. NGOs provided expert advice and research and helped to draft language and lobby for the adoption of the 1948 Universal Declaration of Human Rights and other subsequent human rights treaties.[20]

NGOs often are created as the locus of resistance to nondemocratic regimes. One dramatic example was the emergence of NGOs in opposition to the military dictatorships in Argentina and Chile in the 1970s and 1980s. Citizens who criticized or were seen as threats to these regimes, as well as many who happened to be in the wrong place at the wrong time, became the *desaparecidos,* or the "disappeared." They were kidnapped, imprisoned, tortured, and killed. In a final insult, the children of many of the disappeared were sold to childless military couples. "One torturer estimated that about sixty babies passed through [his clandestine detention center], and that all but two—whose heads were smashed against the wall in efforts to get their mothers to talk—were sold."[21]

> Children were tortured in front of their parents, and parents in front of their children. Some prisoners were kept in rooms no longer or wider than a single bed. And the torture continued for days, weeks, months, even years, until the victim was released or, more often, killed. The sadistic brutality did not always even end with the death of the victim. "One woman was sent the hands of her daughter in a shoe box." The body of another woman "was dumped in her parents' yard, naked but showing no outward signs of torture. Later the director of the funeral home called to inform her parents that the girl's vagina had been sewn up. Inside he had found a rat."[22]

In a heroic response to such brutality, a small group of middle-aged mothers of disappeared children organized in 1977. Calling themselves the "Mothers of the Plaza de Mayo," at first they numbered only fourteen. Frustrated in their attempts to locate their children, they began a silent vigil every Thursday afternoon in the main square of Buenos Aires in front of the president's residence and seat of government. Although the women were subject to harassment and attack (some of them even disappeared themselves), they continued their efforts to draw attention to the atrocities of the military government. They were followed by the "Grandmothers of the Plaza de Mayo," who attempted to trace and recover the trafficked children and babies. Quickly, the numbers of these groups swelled across Latin America, and they soon became the NGO known as Federación Latinoamericana de Asociaciones de Familiares de Detenidos-Desaparecidos (FEDEFAM) (Federation of Families of Disappeared Persons and Political Prisoners). Working with a wide transnational network of NGOs, they fought the military dictatorships and their brutality, always at great personal risk to themselves. When the dictatorships eventually fell, these groups helped to build democracies, strengthen the legal protections for human rights, and reunite political prisoners with their families.[23]

NGOs promote open societies in many ways. They expose the abuses of regimes by tracking facts and disseminating information, as well as by mobilizing public opinion to try to end the abuses and improve conditions. They communicate with decision makers locally and globally, dispensing information and advocating for legal changes. They are direct service providers, offering education, advocacy, and legal aid services. They teach citizens what their rights are and "how to act upon them."[24]

NGOs AND GLOBAL TECHNOLOGIES

Open technologies also greatly assist the formation and maintenance of NGOs, as seen in the landmines case. Any group with a personal computer can maintain a database and mailing list, circulate a newsletter, or e-mail information to its members. Cheap and easily available information technologies allow citizens to more easily gather and disseminate information and ideas, identify members, solicit funds, network with others, and coordinate activities. Decentralization of phone and communication companies has made it more difficult for governments to control access to or censor use of the Internet. Many governments still try to censor the Internet, although as former President Clinton put it, the attempt may be as futile as "nailing Jello to a wall."[25] NGOs also rely on independent news media to directly communicate with the public, publicize their causes, and pressure governments. For example, Greenpeace relies on satellite communications technology to launch direct media campaigns on environmental causes. When Shell Oil wanted to dump retired oil rigs at sea, Greenpeace seized one of the rigs, the Brent Spar in the North Sea, and broadcast directly from there. Media wishing to cover the controversy had to rely on

Greenpeace's satellite uplinks, putting Shell and the British government at a disadvantage in getting out their side of the story. Eventually Greenpeace was successful in mobilizing public opinion to pressure the oil companies (via boycotts) and governments to stop decommissioning oil rigs at sea, in large part because of Greenpeace's effective media strategies and use of communications technologies.[26]

NGOs also actively work to expand the reach of open technologies. Typically, international NGOs work with local counterparts, thereby spreading technology. For example, when the NGO known as Women Waging Peace began, one of the first projects it funded was equipping women's peace organizations with laptop computers and providing training in the use of the Internet and media strategies. In similar ways, environmental NGOs press for the adoption of cleaner, greener technologies, such as water- and air-filtration systems for industries that emit fewer toxic pollutants into the environment. Public health NGOs disseminate health technologies such as filtration systems for drinking water and X-ray and diagnostic equipment as parts of their disease eradication programs. Development NGOs disseminate technologies for agriculture, irrigation, water systems, and electrification.

NGOs AND OPEN ECONOMIES

The rise in NGOs is also facilitated by open economies. The information economy brings advantages for NGOs that trade in ideas and information. Economic liberalization also allows money to freely flow across borders, allowing NGOs to solicit and contribute money across sovereign jurisdictions. In addition, capitalism encourages the growth of the private sector, of which NGOs are a part. Free market economies tend to emphasize grassroots, private sector responses to societal problems rather than top-down, state-sponsored solutions. NGOs thus fit with the entrepreneurial and pluralistic norms of capitalist societies. Privatization of the economy is even encouraging the growth of NGOs in China:

> The Chinese government and party have announced a new slogan. They refer to it as "small government, big society." They want to shrink government, and they want to grow society, that is, they want to shift functions from the government sphere to the private sphere. . . .

The vehicle for doing this, in part, is to create a private nonprofit sector that can shoulder some of the social tasks that have traditionally, in recent Chinese history, been state functions.[27]

Although there are limits to the independence of Chinese NGOs, the small government, big society approach shows the spread of ideas concerning the value of the private sector.

NGOs vary in their receptiveness to open markets, however. While some trade and professional associations lobby to expand free market arrangements such as the WTO and the North American Free Trade Agreement, social advocacy NGOs in the labor, development, environment, and human rights arenas are often skeptical of economic globalization—as seen in the Battle in Seattle.

NGOs AND STATES

NGOs may work with donor states to aid people in weak or failing states, as relief and development organizations such as Catholic Relief Services are doing with the Afghan and Pakistani governments in ministering to the needs of Afghan refugees. Donor governments increasingly prefer to funnel aid through NGOs rather than give it directly to recipient foreign governments that may be neither efficient nor accountable in their use of the funds. In states undergoing transitions, new institutions may be weak and lack proven track records.

Governments believe that aid funneled through NGOs is more politically acceptable than direct government-to-government assistance. They believe that NGOs can better reach the grassroots level and are more efficient because they involve less bureaucratic red tape and overhead. They also believe that working with NGOs helps to develop the private sector. Many see contracting out to NGOs as a win–win situation. The government "has found an efficient, less costly means of carrying out its legislative mandate, while the [NGO]s have discovered a relatively dependable source of money, available in large sums."[28]

There are downsides, however. NGOs risk losing the perception of their autonomy and independence from governments if they rely too heavily on state sources for funding, which can compromise an NGO's reputational power. One NGO executive director described the question of accepting funding from the USAID as the dilemma of not wanting "to look like the tool or the fool of the United States government."[29]

NGOs are also concerned about the potential for conflict of interest between their goals and the goals of government donors. NGOs are concerned about becoming dependent on states for resources and potentially neglecting their traditional bases of support. They do not want to change their focus to fit more closely with government priorities in order to attract state funding. The "strings" that may come attached to accepting government funds (such as the "Buy American" requirement that goes along with US aid dollars) may detract from their program principles (such as, whenever possible, buy locally to help the local economy). And NGOs fear that the reporting and accounting procedures required of government contractors may make them more bureaucratic, entangle them in red tape, and drive up costs (the results donors wanted to avoid by funneling aid through NGOs in the first place).

When recipient governments are cut out of the aid loop because of corruption or weakness, animosity may develop between state institutions and NGOs, and governments such as Haiti may lack the resources to develop state capacity in crucial sectors such as education and public health.

> Critics argued that, while these approaches might provide more rapid and more accountable project implementation in the short run, they . . . failed to contribute to the institutional capacity of government to carry out long-term development projects . . . while most people would agree that the [NGO] should not be the long-term provider, this strategy may mean that no government or private institution will be ready to take over.[30]

As citizens turn to NGOs as service providers, the state is further undermined, which can perpetuate a feedback loop. NGOs may become involved to attend to problems that states are not addressing. In so doing, NGOs may further undermine the capacity and legitimacy of states, which can exacerbate transsovereign problems rather than fight them.

As an increasing number of states collapse, this is becoming a larger issue. Many NGOs do not wait for a state invitation before entering a country to provide services. This is especially true in countries such as Somalia, Rwanda, and states of the former Yugoslavia where there were no working state governments. If NGOs fulfill the functions of states where there are no functioning sovereignties, then how are sovereign states rebuilt? Some NGOs are not concerned with the question. Individuals in need, not states, are their priorities. They regard sovereignty not only as a right to nonintervention (negative or *de jure* sovereignty), but also as a responsibility to provide some benefit to citizens (positive or *de facto* sovereignty). If states are unable or unwilling to fulfill their responsibilities toward individuals in need, then NGOs must step in.

The NGO known as Doctors Without Borders (Médicins Sans Frontières) developed specifically out of the creed that physicians would provide medical assistance where needed, regardless of whether government actors existed or welcomed them.[31] Save the Children developed out of the efforts of a British woman, Eglantyne Jebb, to provide aid to the children victimized by World War I, regardless of whether they were the citizens of a winning or losing state in the conflict.[32] Similarly, Amnesty International began in 1961 with the efforts of a London lawyer, Peter Benenson, to win the release of some Portuguese political prisoners. His campaign soon developed into a worldwide watchdog and advocacy organization for human rights. Amnesty International is fundamentally concerned with protecting the human rights of individuals and groups. It is less concerned with the effect its activities may have on state capacities. Faith-based NGOs likewise are concerned with higher principles. The major world religions existed before the advent of the modern nation-state, and they likely will be around long after its demise. Although not necessarily antagonistic to states, faith-based NGOs feel they answer to a higher authority than the state.

Understandably, then, NGO–state relations are often adversarial because NGOs are often created to curb the abuses of states or to attend to issues that states ignore. In Central America in the 1970s and 1980s, NGOs were targeted by the state, particularly four types of NGOs—human rights, training, humanitarian, and organizations that represented those citizens uprooted by the violence and civil wars:

Physical attacks on NGOs started in the 1970s. . . . Governments responded violently to the growth of peasant groups in El Salvador, and to the expanding Guatemalan cooperative movement. Self-help farmers' organizations were also systematically destroyed. In the 1980s uprooted populations were methodically subjected to harassment, army abuses, disappearances, and assassinations. . . . Governments have tried to destroy human rights NGOs since their creation. They have endured because of personal courage, the mix of financial, technical, and political support received from international NGOs, and survival strategies crafted to suit local conditions. For example, the Catholic Justice and Peace Commission and El Salvador's Tutela Legal operated under the umbrella of church protection. . . . Most survived because of strong international links and small, low budget, decentralized administrative operations; some . . . perished. NGOs documenting and researching issues related to uprooted populations were also intimidated because of their infringement into policy areas considered the armed forces' preserve.[33]

One sign of the adversarial relationship between states and NGOs is the establishment of "front" NGOs by governments "to infiltrate and gather information on the NGO community. These 'government NGOs' are of particular concern in the field of human rights."[34]

NGOs AND STATE FUNCTIONS

Not only do some NGOs commandeer more resources than do many states, but also the activities of these organizations increasingly impinge on functions that previously were jealously guarded by states. NGOs carry out health, education, welfare, and development functions, especially in weak states. In abdicating educational functions to NGOs, states lose opportunities to proselytize and socialize their youth in the viewpoints of the state, as many poor Muslim states are realizing. They had welcomed Saudi charities that set up madrasas, or schools that educate students in the Wahabi form of Islam, an extreme fundamentalist version of that religion. Even in strong states, NGOs are increasingly active in issues such as economic and environmental policy making, land use, and even arms control.

Although only states make laws and sign treaties, NGOs increasingly help to write laws and treaties, lobby for their acceptance, and monitor compliance with them:

Nongovernmental organizations play an increasingly prominent role in international environmental institutions, participating in many activi-

ties—negotiation, monitoring, and implementation—traditionally reserved to states. . . . For better or worse NGOs are now a regular part of
the cooperative process. Within limits, they address delegations as a state
would. They participate actively in the corridor diplomacy which is so
central to negotiations, receive documents, present proposals, and are consulted by and lobby delegations. These changes are all relatively new. . . .[35]

Because environmental problems are indifferent to state borders, and the
information and technical expertise needed to make environmental policy
often exceeds the capacity of states, NGOs provide valuable services on
environmental issues. They can track environmental problems and effects
on resources across borders, presenting the wider perspective needed to
write treaties and create and monitor regimes. For example, in negotiations
on global warming, "NGOs set the original goal of negotiating an agreement to control greenhouse gases long before governments were ready to
do so, proposed most of its structure and content, and lobbied and mobilized public pressure to force through a pact that virtually no one else
thought possible when the talks began."[36] NGOs also provide policy
research and development, serve on government delegations, participate in
small working-group meetings at international negotiations, monitor state
commitments, report on negotiations, lobby participants, and facilitate
negotiations. NGOs even have legal standing in most of the major environmental treaties negotiated in the last decade.[37]

NGOs also develop and implement "soft law," or the voluntary codes
that often serve as stepping stones to the eventual passage of "hard law."
Finally, NGOs may change attitudes and behavior directly, changing the
ideas held by individuals and institutions. In this way, NGOs may work to
manage pressing global problems with or without the cooperation or
capacity of states.

NGOs WORKING BEYOND SOVEREIGNTY

NGOs go beyond sovereignty not only in their organization, membership,
and activities across borders, but also in their ideas and the targets of their
activities. If the public sector is shrinking or not growing as fast as the private sector, then the nonprofit part of the private sector may be needed as a
counterweight to the for-profit private sector. Citizens who believe global-

ization is out of balance or tilted in favor of corporations look to NGOs to serve as a check or counterbalance. Networks of international environmental NGOs, for example, directly pressure MNCs and the public to change environmental behavior. They do not restrict themselves to lobbying governments and IGOs for strengthened legislation or treaties. By taking their arguments directly to corporations, consumers, and public opinion worldwide, NGOs operate beyond sovereignty. McDonald's stopped using styrofoam burger packaging largely in response to NGO-fueled direct-public and consumer-pressure campaigns.[38] NGOs often prefer direct action campaigns to legislative campaigns because state actions to pass and enforce laws on particular environmental problems can be slow and are only effective within a country's territory with enforcement measures. Direct corporate and consumer campaigns, on the other hand, can achieve results across borders without government legislation or enforcement. Convincing individuals not to purchase products made from rain-forest wood can be more effective in preserving rain forests than pursuing government legislation.

Religious organizations also work beyond sovereignty, often targeting their activities directly toward individuals and communities. Religious organizations reach globally with rich, interconnected institutions in health care, education, relief and development, and refugee and resettlement services. These institutional infrastructures are so extensive, well developed, and multifaceted that some consider it misleading to consider a religious organization "just another NGO" because NGOs may be more singular in focus and rarely run global networks of schools and hospitals, for example. Too often, when religious organizations are considered at all in International Relations, they are presented as parties to ethnic and nationalist conflict and opposed to globalization, change, and modernity (or what some have termed "Jihad versus McWorld"). Samuel Huntington, among others, predicts an inevitable clash of civilizations with religious groups at war—that is, of the West versus the rest. There are alternative views, however.[39] Corporations and states are neither the only engines of globalization nor its only beneficiaries. Religious organizations have long been globalizing forces, spreading ideas, institutions, flows of people, and capital across international borders. Today, religious organizations (like other civil society groups) continue to play actives role in globalization as both global actors and mediating institutions, responding to the challenges of globalization and offering alternative ethical visions of it (beyond market or consumer dynamics).[40]

NGO ideas go beyond sovereignty. Corporations see the world as market. In this material world, people are all customers, shareholders, or investors. States see globalization as a world to be governed. People are either governed or ungovernable, citizens or those beyond government and posing problems (for example, illegal immigrants, refugees, terrorists, and criminals). Social advocacy NGOs, however, present alternative ethical visions, seeing a world in which we are all people with fundamental human dignity. Rather than mere opposition to globalization as the clash of civilizations, Jihad versus McWorld formulations suggest, NGOs present more varied and constructive reactions to globalization. Their practices of transnational networks that work to acknowledge and bridge North–South conflicts may represent one of the best ways for globalization to proceed "with a human face,"[41] thereby unleashing greater human potential than can mere materialism—and for more of the planet than currently participates in the benefits of globalization.

As NGOs (sometimes in partnership with IGOs or MNCs) fill functions instead of states and challenge the ideas of states, what effect does this have on sovereignty? Keck and Sikkink note, "If sovereignty is a shared set of understandings and expectations about state authority that is reinforced by practices, then changes in these practices and understandings should in turn transform sovereignty."[42]

The state is not going away. Rather, it is increasingly contracting out. As states downsize and decentralize in response to the pressures of globalization, and as states innovate in response to global problems, nonstate actors such as NGOs perform functions previously assumed by states and promote ideas that have unintended consequences for sovereignty.

ENDNOTES

1. Jubilee USA, "Debt and AIDS," February 2002; available at <www.jubileeusa.org/jubilee.cgi?path=/learn_more/&page=debt_AIDS.html>.
2. Rick Rowden, "A World of Debt," *American Prospect,* 12(12); available at <www.prospect.org/print/V12/12/rowden-r.html>.
3. Ibid.
4. International Campaign to Ban Landmines, "A Brief History of the ICBL" (available at <www.icbl.org>); Richard Price, "Reversing the Gun Sights: Transnational Civil Society Targets Land Mines," *International Organization,* 52(3): 613–644; Anne Peters,

"The International Campaign to Ban Landmines," case study for the Global Public Policy Network (available at <www.f2.efresh.de/public/peters%20gpp%202000.pdf>).

5. Margaret E. Keck and Kathryn Sikkink, *Activists Beyond Borders* (Ithaca, NY: Cornell University Press, 1998), 1.

6. Lester M. Salamon, "Interview on Global Civil Society," *Johns Hopkins Gazette,* Jan. 3, 2000 (available at <www.jhu.edu/~gazette/2000/jan0300/03lestxt.html>); Lester M. Salamon, *Global Civil Society: Dimensions of the Nonprofit Sector* (Baltimore: Johns Hopkins University, Institute for Policy Studies, Center for Civil Society Studies, 1999).

7. Technically speaking, the International Committee of the Red Cross (ICRC) is not an NGO. It is an international organization with a mandate assigned to it by international law in the 1864 Geneva Convention and in subsequent protocols. However, unlike most other IGOs, it is not composed of states as members, and it is not part of the UN system. Instead, it is made up of national Red Cross and Red Crescent societies, which are NGOs. Thus, the ICRC most resembles a hybrid NGO–IGO. See Andrew Natsios, "NGOs and the UN System in Complex Humanitarian Emergencies," in Thomas G. Weiss, Leon Gordenker, and Thomas Watson (Eds.) *NGOS, the UN and Global Governance* (Boulder, CO: Lynne Rienner, 1996), 73–74.

8. Maryann K. Cusimano, "Operation Restore Hope: The Bush Administration's Decision to Intervene in Somalia," in *Pew Case Studies in International Affairs* (Washington, DC: Georgetown University, Institute for the Study of Diplomacy, 1995).

9. Union of International Associations (Ed.), *Yearbook of International Organizations 2000/2001* (Brussels: K.G. Saur Verlag, 2000), 1762–1763.

10. Howard S. Becker, *Outsiders: Studies in the Sociology of Deviance* (New York: The Free Press, 1963), 148; Ethan A. Nadelmann, "Global Prohibition Regimes: The Evolution of Norms in International Society," *International Organization,* 44(4): 482.

11. Paul Wapner, *Environmental Activism and World Civil Politics* (Albany: SUNY Press, 1996); Paul Wapner, "Politics Beyond the State: Environmental Activism and World Civic Politics," in John S. Dryzek and David Schlosberg (Eds.), *Debating the Earth: The Environmental Politics Reader* (New York: Oxford University Press, 1999), 518–519.

12. Richard E. Neustadt, *Presidential Power and the Modern Presidents: The Politics of Leadership from Roosevelt to Reagan* (New York: Free Press, 1990).

13. Valerie Sperling, Myra Marx Ferree, and Barbara Risman, "Constructing Global Feminism: Transactional Advocacy Networks and Russian Women's Activities," *Signs: Journal of Women in Culture and Society,* 26(41): 1156.

14. Martha Finnemore notes that actors and interests are constituted in interaction. Martha Finnemore, *National Interests in International Society* (Ithaca, NY: Cornell University Press, 1996).

15. Specifically, the families filed a civil lawsuit under the Torture Victim Protection Act passed by the US Congress in 1991. "This federal statute permits civil lawsuits against those accused of committing torture or murder under actual or apparent authority, or color of law, of any foreign nation. As the language intended, victims or their representatives may confront not only the perpetrators of such crimes but also their superiors who bear responsibility." Information available at <www.pbs.org/wnet/justice/elsalvador.html>.

16. Margaret E. Keck and Kathryn Sikkink, *Activists Beyond Borders* (Ithaca, NY: Cornell University Press, 1998), 12.

17. Andrew S. Natsios, "The International Humanitarian Response System," *Parameters* (Spring 1995): 68–81.
18. Andras Biro as quoted in Lester M. Salamon, "The Rise of the Nonprofit Sector," *Foreign Affairs* (July–Aug. 1994): 112.
19. Salamon, "The Rise of the Nonprofit Sector," 113.
20. Felice D. Gaer, "Human Rights, Nongovernmental Organizations, and the UN," in Weiss et al., *NGOS, the UN and Global Governance,* 52–53.
21. Jack Donnelly, *International Human Rights* (2nd ed.) (Boulder, CO: Westview Press, 1998), 43; John Simpson and Jana Bennett, *The Disappeared: Voices from a Secret War* (London: Robson Books, 1985), 110.
22. Donnelly, *International Human Rights,* 39; Simpson and Bennett, *The Disappeared,* 225.
23. Donnelly, *International Human Rights,* 44–45.
24. Gaer, "Human Rights," 52–53.
25. "Nailing Jello in China," *Washington Post,* Aug. 26, 2000, p. A16.
26. Samuel Passow, *Sunk Costs: The Plan to Dump the Brent Spar, and Epilogue* (Cambridge, MA: Harvard University, 1997) (John F. Kennedy School of Government Case 1369); available at <www.ksgcase.harvard.edu/case.htm?PID=1369>.
27. Salamon, "Interview on Global Civil Society."
28. Charles Downs, "Negotiating Development Assistance: USAID and the Choice between Public and Private Implementation in Haiti," in *Pew Case Studies in International Affairs* (Washington, DC: Georgetown University, Institute for the Study of Diplomacy, 1994), 7.
29. Ibid., 8.
30. Ibid., 4–5.
31. Médicins Sans Frontières, *Life, Death, and Aid: The Médicins Sans Frontières Report on World Crisis Intervention* (New York: Routledge, 1993).
32. Angela Penrose and John Seaman, "The Save the Children Fund and Nutrition for Refugees," in Peter Willetts (Ed.), *The Conscience of the World: The Influence of Nongovernmental Organisations in the UN System* (Washington, DC: Brookings Institution, 1996), 241–248.
33. Peter Sollis, "The State, Nongovernmental Organizations, and the UN," in Willetts (Ed.), *The Conscience of the World,* 194–195.
34. Willets, *The Conscience of the World,* 6.
35. Kal Raustiala, "States, NGOs, and International Environmental Institutions," *International Studies Quarterly,* 41 (Dec. 1997): 719–724.
36. Jessica Tuchman Mathews, "Power Shift: The Age of Nonstate Actors," *Foreign Affairs* 76 (Jan.–Feb. 1997): 55.
37. Raustiala, "States, NGOs, and International Environmental Institutions," 726–731.
38. Wapner, "Politics Beyond the State," 518–519.
39. Max L. Stackhouse (Ed.), *God and Globalization,* Vols. 1 and 2 (Harrisburg, PA: Trinity Press International, 2001).
40. Maryann Cusimano Love, "Bridging the Gap: Globalization and Religion," *Journal of Social Thought,* 2003 (forthcoming).
41. United Nations Development Program Report, *Globalization with a Human Face* (New York: United Nations, 1999).
42. Margaret E. Keck and Kathryn Sikkink, *Activists Beyond Borders* (Ithaca, NY: Cornell University Press, 1998), 37.

CHAPTER FOUR

Multinational Corporations

Power and Responsibility

Richard A. Love and Maryann Cusimano Love

Globalization makes a business such as Nike possible. The founders of Nike began by selling Tiger athletic shoes, a Japanese brand, in the US market in 1964.[1] Phil Knight (later Nike's cofounder and CEO) soon realized that rather than peddle another's brand, he could use the global supply chain to produce shoes inexpensively in Asia and sell them in developed economies for a handsome profit. Over time, Nike has shifted production from Japan and South Korea to Indonesia, Taiwan, the Philippines, Vietnam, and China in search of lower costs. The labor costs are approximately $1.44 per pair of shoes. Nike buys a pair of shoes from its suppliers for approximately $20, adds transportation and marketing costs plus a profit, and sells the pair to a retailer for $40. The retailer then adds its costs and profits and sells the product to consumers for $80 and up.[2]

But why buy Nike shoes rather than another brand? The sportswear market is competitive and crowded. More than sportswear, Nike sells ideas. In Greek mythology, Nike is the winged goddess of victory, which gave rise to the company's signature winged "swoosh" symbol and the practice of making its products into wearable advertisements. Through aggressive global marketing and promotions, Nike sells an image, a lifestyle, and a creed more than a product. Close your eyes and you would be hard-pressed to tell the difference between Nike shoes and other brands. Nike is selling the dream of being a world-class athlete, the desire to belong to the club of premier athletes, and the inspiration to become the best you can be. You may never be able to play basketball as well as Michael Jordan, but you can wear his shoes. As one Nike official puts it, "We don't know the first thing about manufacturing. We are marketers and designers."[3] Nike pioneered the process of creating a market through product design, promotion, and innovative global advertising, and of associating the Nike brand swoosh with world-class athletes, male and female, of every race, from the inner cities to the more privileged classes. Nike went from $2 million in sales in 1972[4] to $9.9 billion in revenues in 2002[5]—or more than the GDP of Iceland and 100 other states.[6]

The same global media that made Nike a household name and a billion dollar company, however, also made it vulnerable to charges of labor and environmental abuses. NGOs and activists concerned with labor, environment, and human rights became concerned with the sweatshop practices of Nike factories abroad and the disconnect with Nike advertising themes of empowerment, diversity, and women's equality. Reports of sexual harassment of women workers in Nike production facilities in Asia and of seven-year-old children stitching soccer balls in Pakistan gained media and consumer attention. A young woman in China making Nike shoes would have to work nine hours a day, six days a week, for fifteen centuries to earn the yearly salary of Nike CEO Phil Knight. She would have to work more than 1,050 centuries to earn what Nike's premier athlete sponsors such as Andre Agassi or Michael Jordan earn.[7]

At first, Nike's response to the critics was denial. The factories are subcontractors to Nike, the company argued; therefore the employees who made Nike products were not company employees, and Nike was powerless to change subcontractors' behavior. When abuses at Nike's Indonesian factories came to light in the early 1990s, the Nike general manager in Indonesia responded, "It's not within our scope to investigate. I don't know that I need to know."[8] The workers were lucky to have jobs at all, and it was not the company's fault if governments in developing countries have poor labor or environmental laws or enforcement. By some estimates, more than 80 percent of the workers are young women. The company says these workers are good at sewing. Critics say they are more docile and easily intimidated. "I don't think the girls in our factories are treated badly. It's better than no job at all, than harvesting coconut meat in the tropical sun," said a company official.[9] But as the controversy grew, so did negative media coverage (undermining Nike's $280 million annual advertising budget at the time).[10] Reports continued of women being beaten by supervisors and forced to work 65 hours a week for $10 in pay without bathroom or meal breaks. Nike began to admit there were "isolated problems" that it was determined to correct, yet an internal audit done by the company and leaked to *The New York Times* revealed that workers in one factory were exposed to 177 times the legal limit of carcinogens, with 77 percent of the workers suffering from respiratory problems. Rather than being unaware, the company knew of the problem.[11]

In 1998, consumer boycotts and shareholder unrest grew while company profits fell. CEO Phil Knight announced a new course for the company. Nike would (1) increase the minimum age of its workers to 16 in apparel factories and 18 in shoe factories; (2) follow US Occupational Safety and Health Administration standards for air quality at factories abroad, especially seeking substitutes for the adhesives that were causing respiratory problems in workers; and (3) allow local NGOs and hired independent auditors to monitor and release information about the company's subcontracting factories. Nike joined corporate responsibility groups such as the Apparel Industry Partnership, the Fair Labor Association, the Global Alliance for Workers and Communities, and the United Nations' Global Compact, and increased community development loans for small business and education projects in the areas of its overseas production facilities.[12]

Nike believes it is now a leader in corporate responsibility, and some observers credit Nike with raising standards and awareness of the issues across the apparel industry. Critics charge the pronouncements are more public relations efforts than real accomplishments and that Nike's corporate codes of conduct are voluntary and unenforceable. Nike still does not pay workers adequate wages or allow international NGOs that might be more critical to participate in monitoring. College students have organized into groups such as the Workers Rights Consortium, the Clean Clothes Campaign, and United Students Against Sweatshops to pressure suppliers of college sportswear not to use sweatshop labor. Nike has withdrawn advertising sponsorships of athletics programs at many colleges and universities such as Brown University, the University of Michigan, and even for a time Phil Knight's alma mater, the University of Oregon, due to student protests of Nike and activism in these groups. While collegiate licensing is only a small part of Nike's overall business, image is everything for a company like Nike, especially image among young athletes, the company's key market. As CEO Phil Knight acknowledged, "The brand is sacred. I messed that up."[13]

The Nike example illustrates pressing debates that will be discussed in this chapter about the rising power and global reach of multinational corporations (MNCs). Do MNCs raise labor and environmental standards internationally or are they leading a global race to the bottom? Are states effectively able to regulate MNCs, or do MNCs have increasing power over states? Are MNCs exercising their power responsibly, and how do they interact with other actors (NGOs, IGOs, and states) in setting standards for responsible corporate behavior? Are corporate codes of conduct a way to go beyond sovereignty to manage pressing global problems and to make private actors better stewards of the public good? Are they nontariff trade barriers or protectionist measures that hurt development in the Global South? Or are they merely a way for corporations to deflect state regulation and public criticism? What are the effects on sovereignty?

THE GLOBAL REACH OF MNCs

Multinational corporations are enterprises that control and manage commercial ventures and operations outside their countries of origin.[14] Fueled by open economies and distributed technology, enhanced financial mechanisms and the ease of transborder trade, their power and influence is growing dramatically. Today, of the 100 largest economies in the world, a majority are multinational corporations; only 49 are countries.[15]

MNCs are not new. Foreign investment, banking, resource extraction, trade, and production were part of imperial expansion and colonial trade by the Romans, Venetians, Genoese, English (British East India Company), and Dutch (Hudson Bay Company). What is new is the global reach and influence that modern multinational firms have. In 1969, there were 7,000 MNCs.[16] Today, there are 63,312 multinational parent corporations with

821,818 foreign affiliates worldwide.[17] The sheer scope of these entities represents a rise in private, nonstate power across the globe.[18]

MNCs are a diverse and eclectic group. MNCs are organized internationally to achieve several corporate objectives: open new markets and gain access to new consumers, acquire natural resources at lower costs, and produce efficiencies through the reduction of production and labor costs or take advantage of lower environmental regulations and taxes. Some allow "host" subsidiaries greater autonomy; others insist on a high degree of "parent" company control. They range from corporations such as Royal Dutch Shell Oil and British Petroleum, which extract raw materials and natural resources; to manufacturers such as Siemens, Coca Cola, Samsung, Walt Disney Corporation, and Nikoa, which produce consumer goods; to companies such as Lloyd's of London, Barclays, and Credit Suisse, which offer banking, investment, insurance, and consulting services. Many MNCs are hybrids of these functions—such as IBM, which sells computer and business products and provides consulting services.

MNCs are not simply companies that engage in foreign trade or market their products abroad. MNCs engage in foreign direct investment (FDI) and carry out production in foreign countries. They engage in FDI because local firms have a "home court advantage." They are more knowledgeable about local business practices and consumer tastes, and it is generally less costly for local firms to do business in their home markets. Foreign firms that seek entry into a locality have an incentive to "hook up" with local firms. FDI may take many forms: buyouts of a foreign subsidiary, joint ventures, licensing agreements, or strategic alliances.

MNCs AND THE GLOBALIZATION DEBATES

The global reach of MNCs can be a positive force for profits as well as development. MNCs can assist in transferring capital and know-how to the developing world and often bring in capital goods and technology. They may create jobs and assist in developing training and education programs. MNCs also provide avenues for access to other international markets and exposure to the region that may result in additional investment. MNCs often have the incentive to develop a host state's infrastructure to maximize commerce. UN Secretary-General Kofi Annan notes that business is the best hope of alleviating global poverty, and that "economics, properly applied, and profits, wisely invested, can bring social benefits within reach not only for the few but for the many, and eventually for all."[19] For example, Nakornthon Bank works with poor villages in rural Thailand, offering training and small, low-interest loans for microdevelopment. As a result, "[i]ncome levels skyrocketed. . . . People returned to work in the village. The payoff rate for loans was 100%, and our bank now has a loyal base of customers. The project has been so successful that development agencies and the government have kept asking how it was done."[20]

But there is also a downside. MNCs can overwhelm a locality and drive traditional firms out of business. MNCs normally insist on maintaining control over technology, management, and intellectual property, which means that technology and expertise are never transferred to the host state. CEOs, boards of directors, and shareholders may all be located in developed countries so that MNC decision making and profits flow disproportionately back to developed economies. MNCs often become advocates at the local level for changing local systems in favor of gaining preferential treatment. These take the form of tax breaks, favorable laws, dispute resolution mechanisms, and ownership and property rights. In seeking lower-cost alternatives globally, MNCs exploit resources, labor, and the environment, leading critics to charge that MNCs lead a race to the bottom in worker, regulatory, safety, and environmental standards.

For example, one IGO, the International Labor Organization, reports that 250 million children under age 14 are working half- or part-time. Some of these children work for MNCs or their subcontractors such as in high-profile cases (e.g., Nike) and as forced child slave labor in Africa picking the cocoa beans for major chocolate companies like Nestles, Mars, and Hershey. Yet MNCs counter these arguments by noting that working conditions are generally no worse and are often better than those of the local employers, and prominent MNCs are likely to comply with standards that are higher than those maintained locally.[21] They also argue that age and wage standards cannot be universal but must be considered in the context of local economies.

MNCs AND OPEN ECONOMIES

It is no surprise that many MNCs are in the forefront of lobbying to increase free market economic systems and reduce barriers to FDI and trade.[22] Whether through regional trading blocs such as NAFTA or the EU, or multilateral free trade agreements such as GATT and the WTO, MNCs generally seek to decrease tariff and nontariff barriers to trade and investment, as well as decrease state control of state subsidies to key industries.[23] MNCs lobby states and multinational organizations to open up economies to market forces. In the democratizing states of the former communist bloc, Latin America, and South Africa, MNCs are pressing for protections of private property and the free movement of goods and capital in their newly liberalized economies. Once established, MNCs or their local affiliates often try to get the local host states to protect their advantages by enacting exclusionary laws and giving the established MNCs monopoly advantages. Host nations can be subject to intense pressure to acquiesce to MNC investment already in place as to appease international pressure to open its economy and markets. Each year, $365 billion is spent in protections and subsidies by developed states, which keep many of the goods from developing countries out of developed countries. This is why developing countries question how "free" the free market and free trade really are—free for whom?

Many MNCs have pushed hard for harmonizing international law, although some prefer to exploit differences in legal codes in local venues that profit foreign companies. For example, on the night of December 2–3, 1984, Union Carbide Chemical Corporation was responsible for the worst industrial accident in history. Forty-one tons of poisonous gas were released from its plant in Bhopal, India, killing 14,000 people and inflicting permanent disabilities on 150,000 more:[24]

> As people ran with their families, they saw their children falling beside them, and often had to choose which ones they would carry on their shoulders and save. This image comes up again and again in the dreams of the survivors: in the stampede, the sight of a hundred people walking over the body of their child. Iftekhar Begum went out on the morning after the gas to help bury the Muslim dead. There were so many that she could not see the ground—she had to stand on the corpses to wash them.[25]

After the accident, Union Carbide worked to see that the case was heard by a more lenient judge in India rather than face a stricter US judicial system that might have imposed hefty fines. After years of legal battles, the MNC agreed to pay survivors generally $2,857 for each death (a few received as much as $4,286). Ninety five percent of the victims compensated received only $500. These are the gross figures; subtract the legal fees, administration costs, and sometimes bribes survivors had to pay to stake their claim, and most survivors actually netted much less. These settlements are low even by Indian standards. The standard compensation offered by Indian Railways for accidental death is $5,714, and $3,429 for disability, which is disbursed quickly and with minimal additional fees.[26]

While some companies prefer to take their chances with local legal codes, most MNCs have a powerful interest in harmonizing global laws to decrease transaction costs. It is costly for them to do business internationally when each country has separate standards and rules for trade, investment, intellectual property rights, etc. MNCs push for greater harmonization to decrease their costs and risks and create a better business climate, and they stress that developing states benefit as well from such measures. They argue that international trade, global supply chains, and FDI helps developing economies and that developing states are better served by a system of established rules with transparent and regular procedures for making rules than by trying to negotiate ad hoc agreements with more powerful actors on a deal-by-deal basis. In general, developing countries have agreed and voluntarily signed up for these international agreements out of a desperate desire to attract MNCs and FDI that may bring jobs and alleviate poverty in their countries. Often, developing states fear that not to acquiesce will mean that FDI and jobs will go elsewhere and that they will be left behind. Not surprisingly, there is unequal bargaining power among the parties. Developing states riddled with poverty cannot compete with the deep pockets of MNCs that lobby state governments and the international bodies that create the rules of the road for international trade. Developing countries often lack the resources to send delegations to the international meetings that decide the rules.

MNCs AND OPEN TECHNOLOGIES

Cheap, easily available global information and transportation technologies make the growth of MNCs possible. New technology also creates new industries and presents the hope of "leapfrog" development for some developing countries. For example, Bangalore, India, is now a thriving center of the computer services industry. India is aided by an educated workforce that speaks English and a time zone differential that allows Indian computer programmers to service the information systems of companies in many developed countries while the companies' main workforces sleep. Although this model is not replicable in many developing countries, many developing countries aspire to the Bangalore model as they seek to profit from the global economy and technologies. It is not only large corporations that benefit from global technologies, but also medium, small, and even microbusinesses that can go global thanks to the Internet and shipping companies such as United Parcel Service. Australian sheepskin slippers, Turkish towels, and Mexican crafts can be marketed and sold to consumers globally without large overhead investments.

MNCs may disperse technologies in the countries where they operate as a part of their business presence, but some MNCs restrict technology transfers out of concern for retaining proprietary and competitive advantage. MNC and state interests regarding technology transfers are not always correlated either. The US government wanted limits on the sale of powerful computer encryption technologies so that law enforcement officers would have the keys to crack the codes of illicit actors using encrypted communications. Businesses did not want a lucrative new market in encryption programs regulated—and business won. States often want to restrict the sale of sensitive technologies that can have military applications, whereas MNCs may favor trade in dual use technologies. The German, British, and US governments fought the Persian Gulf War against an Iraqi army that German, British, and US firms had supplied with weapons and the ingredients to make chemical weapons. In 1987, while the United States, Japan, and Norway were officially allied to fight the Cold War against the Soviet Union, both a Japanese and a Norwegian MNC—Toshiba and Kongsberg—violated export restrictions and sold technologies to the USSR to help it build quieter and less detectable nuclear submarines.

MNCs AND OPEN SOCIETIES

The relationship between MNCs and open societies is hotly contested. In states such as China, Indonesia, and Nigeria, MNCs have pursued a capitalist economic agenda without pushing hard for democratic political reforms. In corporatist societies (such as Chile and Argentina in the 1970s), authoritarian regimes ally with and co-opt business elites, protecting business interests while repressing democratic rights and principles. Order is central for the stable, efficient, and profitable conduct of commerce. Political upheavals, even those associated with democratization, create costs and uncertainties for the investment, production, and trade of MNCs. Do MNCs favor repressive regimes as a way of ensuring a stable, orderly, and favorable business environment? In Nigeria, Shell Oil was accused of helping to arm and finance a repressive military government, as long as the government helped to keep Shell's oil flowing. Exxon–Mobile and partners, with the aid of World Bank loans, are building an oil pipeline in Chad and Cameroon, extremely poor countries with two of the most corrupt governments in the world according to ratings of government corruption by Transparency International. These governments are not democratic, and complaints are already being lodged about human rights and environmental abuses in the project. Funds have already been illegally diverted for government military purchases.

Others disagree. One study analyzed MNC cash flows to developing states from 1975 to 1986 to determine whether MNCs are more or less likely to invest in repressive states with abusive human rights records. The study concluded that "MNCs in general [avoid] locating larger amounts of [foreign investment] in those [developing states] that consistently implement fewer human rights reforms. . . . [It] does not appear that MNCs view a lack of human rights reforms and the high use of repression in [developing states] as acceptable."[27] MNCs may not favor repressive regimes for several reasons. Arbitrary exercise of police powers and military brutality affect MNC executives, workers, and citizens alike. Repressive regimes may rule by force rather than law, but respect for law (and particularly for property rights) is crucial for successful business transactions. Without the rule of law, business transactions become uncertain and potentially more costly.

The effects of MNCs on human rights can cut both ways. Sometimes just the presence of a multinational corporation can place the international media spotlight on local worker conditions, creating a "race to the top."[28] Concerned with protecting their image, companies will pressure local governments to improve workers' conditions or take the initiative to do so themselves. A multinational's instinct to protect its reputation, and thereby its bottom line, can have the beneficial side effect of exporting a concern for human rights. This may be MNC specific, however, as image conscious branded products have a greater concern for reputation than do unbranded or extractive industries. Thus, even though MNCs generally promote open economies and open technologies, their record of promoting open societies (including respect for human rights) is contested and mixed.

RISE OF PRIVATE POWER: DO CORPORATIONS RULE THE WORLD?

We are witnessing the rise of private power. Even in developed states, private standards setting bodies, contract law, and private arbitration mechanisms now fulfill regulatory functions once performed by states.[29] In emerging information technology sectors, this trend of private governance is particularly pronounced. For example, Internet commerce is often untaxed and self-regulated by companies, not by governments. A private body assigns Internet domain names and adjudicates disputes.

The critique that corporations rule the world[30] runs even stronger given the unequal bargaining power of developing states against MNCs. In developing states, grinding poverty leads states to court corporate investments because the private sector has more money than the public sector, and state-to-state aid and investment is drying up. Developing states often do not have the capacity to check corporate power, as law and order and institutions may be fragile at best in countries without resources to adequately pay, staff, equip, and train government officials. As corporations enter developing states, they often do so free of taxes (in export processing or free trade zones). The most powerful companies are also able to avoid taxes even in developed states. For example, of the top 200 corporations in the world, the majority of US corporations do not pay their full income tax rates, and seven "actually paid less than zero in federal income taxes in 1998 (because of rebates). These include: Texaco, Chevron, PepsiCo, Enron, Worldcom, McKesson and the world's biggest corporation, General Motors."[31] Export processing and free trade zones are often free of other government regulations (environmental and worker safety law enforcement).

MNCs encourage the multilateral organizations to pressure developing states to privatize their remaining state controlled industries, such as telephone systems. While done in the name of rationalizing economies and making them more efficient, privatization may also bankrupt governments because poor countries do not have the tax bases to finance basic government services—education, public health systems, clean water, roads, public safety, customs, courts, and law and order. When telephone revenues, for example, are the primary government income and the business is privatized, after the initial windfall in money from the sale of state owned industries, states may lack financing for basic government activities.

Many states have no tradition of payment of personal income taxes, and governments are too weak to be able to get citizens to pay taxes (this is a problem in Russia, Italy, and many Caribbean states). Because so many goods and incomes go untaxed, states charge exorbitant tax rates on those few goods or people that they are most able to tax—for example, automobile imports, or imports of washers and dryers. This creates greater incentives to smuggle, commit fraud, and evade taxes because taxes on the few pay the services of the many. Inability to finance basic good governance makes all government ripe for corruption because government workers are not paid a living wage and need to supplement their income with "overtime" (the euphemism for bribery in the Caribbean). Thus, governments in developing states often do not have the capacity to challenge or contain the power of corporations, and the actions of corporations (to lower their tax rates, privatize industries, and pay government bribes) may actually contribute to the weakness of state structures and governance.

Developing states sign agreements that allow corporations to operate in their territories; such arrangements are examples of bargaining among unequal parties. A developing state is signing a contract with a gun to its head—the gun being grinding poverty, unemployment, and death—and it is trying to lure corporations with its low wages and lack of unionization. A state has less ability to wrest many guarantees of good behavior, local management power, and so on from a corporation when poverty is a state's comparative advantage. The corporation has many poor states from which to choose, and it is often not building plants and capital investments from scratch but is contracting out to local subsidiary agents. The corporation can easily find another poor country that will accept its business. Literally, beggars can't be choosers.

Even strong states cannot contain corporate power alone because MNCs operate across international borders, and jurisdiction often stops at the border. Attempts to harmonize legal codes to help law enforcement work multilaterally across borders or to reign in corporate power are weak, new, and without teeth. They often are exports of Western contract law and procedures that are advantageous to corporations. They show how corporations can get laws that work for them rather than how states can effectively counterbalance the weight of corporations.

The rise of private contract law epitomizes the rise of private power in the global age. A relatively few MNCs exercise power to create law in their own interest and for their own benefit. Developed states not only condone this, but also support the trend because they hope to rationalize commercial disputes and benefit from increased tax revenue from their MNCs. The result is that local governments, especially in the developing world, experience a loss of control and influence over trade practices within their borders.

MNCs worldwide are seeking ways to fashion enforceable rights. One way they do this is by expanding private contract rights in order to avoid foreign laws. This is generally not a difficult challenge. The three most common ways of doing so are through choice of law, stabilization, and arbitration clauses. These clauses ensure the protection of property rights, right of entry into new markets, and the availability of natural resources. The effect of these clauses is not only to avoid the law of a host state, but also to develop a legal system outside traditional sovereign courts. It sets up external and private law to resolve disputes, based on the concept of the sanctity of the contract and party autonomy. Courts allow these contractual decisions, often with little or no respect for the public policy concerns of host states. Courts will often refuse to hear a controversy where clauses using alternative dispute resolution (ADR) or arbitration exist in a contract. For example, when Mexico denied Metalclad, a New Jersey metal company with toxic waste by-products, permission to build a facility because of concerns about the site's environmental impact, the NAFTA court required Mexico to pay $16.7 million to Metalclad in breach of contract compensation for earnings Metalclad could have received if it had been allowed to proceed. The case has had a chilling effect, sending the message that private contract rights take precedence over sovereign concerns.

Choiceof law clauses are perhaps the most common among the three and allow a party to avoid local law and remove issues from local courts by predetermining where controversies will be resolved and under whose law the controversy will proceed. Arbitration clauses determine who has the authority to decide controversies and usually include a reference to the specific rules that will guide arbitration. Arbitration courts have established procedures and remedies that can be adopted or amended by the terms of a contract, and the arbiters have powers similar to those of sovereign courts.[32] A stabilization clause freezes the law at the time the contract is entered into and prevents law made after a contract enters into force from having any effect on a controversy's ultimate disposition.

These clauses allow a contract to avoid the laws of sovereign states and propel controversies to a "supranational" legal arbitration body or to a court outside a local jurisdiction. Thus, they insulate foreign corporations from uncertain and unfamiliar locales. Yet this new worldwide body of private law runs counter to the sovereign concept of regulating affairs within one's state borders. These contract provisions are increasingly offensive to local legal and political institutions and affront the concept of equal dignity of sovereigns. The contract terms effectively let the parties opt out of local jurisdictions. Private contract also gives MNCs a procedural advantage because many parties in the developing world lack the expertise needed to enter into agreements with a full appreciation of the costs and consequences. Firms located outside such traditional centers of commerce as New York, London, and Geneva may also lack the resources to fully protect their rights under contract. The travel costs alone may make pursuing a dispute cost prohibitive.

While MNCs work to enlarge the private sector and earn profits, they also can facilitate the illicit economy. Money laundering, for example, is facilitated by the international banking and financial services industries. Between $500 billion and $1.5 trillion are laundered through banks every year. Money laundering involves complex financial and product transactions that mask and perpetuate the underlying criminal activity that generates the illegal gains. Money laundering finances the most egregious crimes in the global age from terrorism and drug trafficking to human trafficking, illegal arms transactions, and nuclear smuggling. It propagates corruption and corrupt regimes by providing an avenue for using illegal proceeds. Money laundering also provides a way to avoid taxes.

The underlying purpose of money laundering is to conceal the true source of the funds for free use in the open market. The mechanisms for laundering money are complex and diverse and often involve multiple transactions among several (and sometimes unsuspecting) parties, fraudulent alterations of prices for goods, and outright bribes and kickbacks. Money laundering is illegal, but some MNCs prefer the benefit of the infusion of capital. The most common form of money laundering is transfer pricing, where prices are falsified on import and export transactions in order to generate artificial values. The difference between the fair value and the artificial value is pocketed. Real estate transactions and securities trades, often between related parties and improperly priced and paid for in order to shift money across borders, offer creative avenues for generating illegal capital flight. Money laundering activities must first hide the source of the illegally received proceeds and then provide a legitimate explanation for the proceeds. Through complex layered transactions, money laundering blends criminal proceeds into the licit economy.

Most laundered money winds up in the United States and Europe through Western banks. As the beneficiaries of such an enormous inflow of capital, the banking and financial establishment traditionally favors informal money laundering controls and reporting requirements. Government efforts to curtail money laundering have failed because of the lack of "buy-in" from the private banking and business sector. The attacks of September 11 changed how many political and commercial leaders view money laundering, and they increased state and IGO pressure to regulate these industries. However, state anti–money laundering policies rely on industry self-reporting of suspicious financial activities. Even in strong, developed states, governments do not have the capacity to curtail money laundering alone without cooperation from the private sector, which shows the extent of private power.

PRIVATE POWER AND PUBLIC RESPONSIBILITY

Does the rise in private power mean MNCs can act with impunity and with no responsibilities to the common good? No. States still regulate corporations, although, as the previous section showed, MNCs may have the ability to forum shop—to have a dispute heard in a forum more amenable to their interests—and may have deeper pockets and better lawyers to evade states' regulatory capacities. However, other bodies are stepping in to fill these governance gaps. IGOs increasingly regulate global commerce, and MNCs are increasingly self-regulating, in part because of greater attention to corporate social responsibility (CSR).

There has been an explosion of CSR mechanisms for MNC voluntary self-regulation, especially in the past decade. They fall into several categories. First are internal codes of conduct and statements of company core values. Most MNCs have or are writing such in-house codes of conduct. They are frequently broad general guidelines, such as those of Levi Strauss, which state in part, "embrace diversity; be responsible, but not afraid."[33] Optimists say these are important barometers of changing corporate culture. They are attempts to educate and socialize large workforces into common values, such as that good corporate citizenship is as important as bottom line profit margins. Even broad guidelines can be helpful as a first step to more specific standards and concrete benchmarks. They are also useful because they provide a public commitment by companies to particular values. If company behavior falls short later, then the codes of conduct and value statements give reformers a basis to discuss criticisms. Skeptics argue that the codes are little more than window dressing designed to diffuse criticism and deter regulation, that they are frequently so vague and general that they cannot be implemented or measured, and that they are unenforceable because they are voluntary.

The second genre of CSR measures are sector wide agreements among companies within an industry to adopt certain standards or shared best practices. Sector wide agreements can vary from narrow technical codes on specific industrial processes to broader statements of larger CSR commitments such as the Apparel Industry Partnership to improve working conditions in the garment industry. Some sectors may develop regimes or private professional bodies to monitor and report on implementation and compliance with the standards. Many rely on the companies themselves to choose methods of monitoring and transparency to show implementation and compliance with adopted codes.

The third approach is general CSR codes that are not specific to particular organizations or industries. For example, the UN Global Compact challenges businesses to comply with nine principles drawn from UN treaties concerning human rights, labor, and the environment. The Global Compact is quite broad, as are other codes such as the Coalition for Environmentally Responsible Economies (CERES) principles on environmental responsibility, and the Caux Round Table Principles for Business. These set overarching corporate goals and rely on companies to decide their own monitoring and transparency measures. The International

Standards Organization (ISO) has its own set of standards, such as ISO 9000 and ISO 14000. The Council on Economic Priorities has SA 8000. These standards come with more specific operational guidelines and measurable benchmarks to monitor progress and implementation. As industries "buy into" ISO labeling and accreditation, they agree to regular inspections and audits by accredited auditors.

There are vigorous debates over which codes, standards, and reporting techniques are more effective in raising corporate behavior and improving labor, human rights, and environmental practices. Many are too new to be able to fully assess; MNCs are still in the adoption and implementation phases. Some critics argue that internal audits are more rigorous because only people familiar with the processes and layouts of particular factories will know where to look for problems or abuses. Others argue that internal audits lack credibility because companies have few incentives to blow the whistle on themselves. This leads to arguments in favor of external auditing procedures, but again this raises questions of competence and independence. Although professional auditors trained in particular standards sounds like an attractive way to ensure more reliability and comparability of results over time and across companies, critics argue that auditors hired and paid by industry have few incentives to issue negative reports and "bite the hand that feeds them." NGOs argue they can offer independent assessments and should be a part of the process, but this again raises the questions of which NGOs should be involved and what qualifications they have to make assessments. Some corporations do not see NGOs as un-biased and believe NGOs will never acknowledge improvements in corporate practices or issue favorable assessments. Some corporations such as Nike choose to involve local NGOs as a form of outreach to the local community where facilities are located. International NGOs question whether local NGOs are more easily manipulated to issue favorable reports because they may fear losing local jobs or may not have the resources or access to complete information to make fully informed and more critical judgments. Finally, reporting varies widely. Some reports are little more than press releases, while others are substantive and concrete assessments. The Global Reporting Initiative is a UN-sponsored effort to increase the comparability, credibility, and consistency of CSR reporting and to highlight best practices.

This explosion of CSR codes and implementation techniques shows a rising acknowledgment of the power of private governance and the power of corporations to implement social and economic change. It shows a growing attention among corporations to the "triple bottom line," a rising awareness that the environmental and social as well as economic concerns can affect business.

But why is there such growth in CSR standards and attention? Margaret Keck and Kathryn Sikkink argue that blocked politics cause activists to take their grievances to other forums,[34] including pressuring MNCs to focus on issues ignored by states. Because groups cannot lobby for environmental or human rights change in China or Vietnam, NGOs and moral entrepreneurs search for a forum where democratic politics, independent media, voters, and consumers can exert some pressure for change rather than be excluded. MNCs based out of developed democracies are open to civil society pressures, whereas authoritarian states may be less susceptible to these pressures. Blocked politics explains some of the increased attention to CSR, but not all.

Corporations often argue that they are not the correct targets for labor, environment, and human rights demands and that governments should be pressured to change. Yet even in democratic countries such as the Philippines, MNCs are targeted for CSR campaigns rather than governments, even though politics are not blocked and procedures exist for citizen advocacy. Moving away from state activism and toward CSR campaigns focused on MNCs is a way for NGOs to focus their resources and to get more bang for the buck. NGO resources are constrained, so dividing them among 189 countries may mean there will be too few resources for any one NGO to be effective, reach critical mass, and overcome threshold effects of inertia and the status quo. Just as opponents of the US civil rights movement in the 1960s tried to splinter the movement by arguing that local state governments should decide the civil rights of African Americans, NGOs find that if they successfully lobby MNCs to raise standards, the effects will be felt broadly across borders, rather than in one country only.

There are other reasons for the increased number and attention to CSR codes as well. Virginia Haufler studied private standard setting across a variety of sectors and industries and concluded that risk assessments, concern for reputation, and corporate learning were critical factors in adoption and implementing CSR standards.[35] Previous crises certainly can alert decision makers to the risks of ignoring CSR. In this way, the CERES principles were created in response to the *Exxon Valdez* oil spill.

Only publicly traded companies are vulnerable to shareholder activism, and unbranded products are less vulnerable to consumer boycotts and negative publicity. But ideas matter in pressuring corporations to address global issues. Even unbranded food products are vulnerable to claims about health and safety. And not all brands are equally vulnerable to CSR pressures. It matters what values and ideas the brand proclaims. Nike was vulnerable not just because it was an identifiable brand, but also because it advertised values of diversity, emancipating young people, and women's equality. This made it more vulnerable to brand devaluation by charges that women were being abused and children were forced to work in diverse countries. Similarly, Mattel Toys has been a leader in the Business Anti-Smuggling Coalition because, as its chief security officer puts it, "The last thing we can afford is Barbie on drugs." A shipment of Barbie toys compromised by drug traffickers would be extremely harmful to the toy's wholesome role model identity in a way that would be less damaging to a shipment of Lysol toilet bowl cleaner. It is not just the brand, but the ideas behind the brand that give traction to CSR efforts.

Several factors are important in determining whether an MNC will adopt CSR standards. The internal leadership of the company is important. The Body Shop founder, Anita Roddick, has been a force for CSR within her global franchise and throughout the wider business community.[36] Company culture, the competitive environment, and consumer demand are important. In recent years, Chiquita Brands International, the banana importer and exporter, has changed its company practices and adopted some of the industry's most enlightened age and wage policies. But if grocery stores and consumers do not factor CSR into buying decisions, then CSR policies may not be sustainable,[37] either because leadership will backslide if companies believe CSR policies are a drag to their costs that competitors avoid and consumers do not reward, or because the company goes under.

Shareholder activism also can spur attention to CSR as investments are withdrawn from companies with poor practices or ratings. For example, the Interfaith Center on Corporate Responsibility promotes socially responsible investing, and the largest private pension fund in the United States, TIAA-CREF, negotiates directly with companies regarding their CSR records.[38] Media attention to corporate shortcomings spurs MNC attention. Companies engage not only in immediate damage control within a targeted company but also in longer-range policy change across companies as MNC leaders learn lessons from the crises of others. NGOs threaten to use the sticks of negative media publicity, protests, consumer boycotts, and shareholder activism, but they can also offer the carrots of positive attention to favorable examples of CSR. Too often, however, NGOs rely more on the sticks than the carrots. Finally, IGOs and states can offer incentives for positive CSR behavior and threaten regulation or adversarial treatment to companies with negative CSR records. A combination of these factors leads companies to decide whether and which CSR policies may enhance their reputation, change their market share, or reduce their risks of adverse consumer, media, IGO, government, or shareholder reactions.

Through the CSR movement, MNCs are finding that open societies, open technologies, and open economies cut both ways. These infrastructures facilitate the operations and profits of MNCs. Yet global technologies that broadcast MNC advertising also serve as an instant and global megaphone for news of corporate abuses. Open societies allow critics to organize and apply political pressure to MNCs, and open economies allows consumer and shareholder market pressures to be brought to bear on MNCs.

MNCs, STATE FUNCTIONS, AND SOVEREIGNTY

Beyond social, environmental, and economic regulatory and arbitration functions, MNCs are also performing security functions that have been traditionally reserved for states, such as arms control negotiations, homeland security, disarmament, demining operations, and military activities. Functions traditionally reserved for the state are increasingly contracted out. For example, in 1978, when the negotiation process for the chemical weapons convention (CWC) began, few government officials had more than superficial knowledge of the chemical industry. US arms control negotiators requested assistance in the negotiation process from the chemical industry. Recognizing the importance and effect of the chemical weapons ban for their industry, the chemical manufacturers assisted the US government. An industry group, the Chemical Manufacturers Association (CMA), helped develop procedures for on-site inspections and participated in special sessions of the Conference on Disarmament. What resulted was an unprecedented industry–government partnership in forging an effective treaty. For industry, opposition to the treaty not only would have resulted in negative publicity, but also would have risked the creation of a treaty that was technically unsound and detrimental to industry interests.

The private sector has a critical role to play in protecting critical infrastructure from illicit activities, from terrorism to cybercrime. Eighty-five percent of critical infrastructure in the United States is privately owned.[39] Critical infrastructures are systems whose incapacity or destruction would have a debilitating effect on a state's defense or economic security. They include telecommunications, electrical power systems, gas and oil industries, banking and finance, transportation, water supply systems, government services, and emergency services. The events of September 11, 2001, highlighted security concerns over physical and electronic threats to critical infrastructures. Such threats are global, blur public–private distinctions, and render states, commercial interests, and individuals mutually vulnerable and interdependent.

There are limits to what governments can effectively do to provide adequate security in the absence of private cooperation. Private infrastructure owners are in the best position to understand the technology and vulnerabilities and must recognize their stake in infrastructure protection. Many challenges to effective public–private cooperation exist. Trust needs to be established between stakeholders. Public–private lines of communications and response activities need to be clarified. Technical training and expertise needs to be furthered in both sectors. Government and industry leaders must recognize the need for cooperation. Process buy-in is essential to success.

Governments of the strongest states are ceding security functions to private companies. For example, with troops stretched thin in peacekeeping operations abroad, the British government debates whether to hire and regulate private mercenary forces that would work alongside British troops. And with the US government's blessing, mercenaries trained the Bosnian army. The US government itself uses private security companies to disassemble former Soviet nuclear weapons through the Cooperative Threat Reduction program, as well as to conduct demining operations in support of US troop deployments.

Private organizations are increasingly seen not just as contributors to global problems but as crucial players in effective global solutions. We are witnessing a creative period as new private organizations arise and increased partnerships are formed with business to manage pressing global

problems. As MNCs become the target of citizen demands for social, environmental, and economic goods, ideas of authority change. As governments
cede or contract functions to the private sector (even security functions),
state power, capacity, legitimacy, and authority change relative to other
actors—and thus sovereignty is changing.

ENDNOTES

1. Phil Knight and Bill Bowerman, the head coach of the University of Oregon's track
   and field teams, each contributed $500 to start Blue Ribbon Sports Company, Nike's
   predecessor. As conflicts grew with Tiger concerning control over the company and
   exclusive rights to US distribution, Knight ordered 6,000 pairs of shoes with the now-
   familiar "swoosh" logo in 1971. The company subsequently broke with Tiger and
   became Nike.
2. Peter Schwartz and Blair Gibb, *When Good Companies Do Bad Things: Responsibility and
   Risk in an Age of Globalization* (New York: Wiley & Sons, 1999), 52.
3. Miguel Korzeniewicz, "Commodity Chains and Marketing Strategies: Nike and the
   Global Athletic Footwear Industry," in Frank J. Lechner and John Boli (Eds.), *The
   Globalization Reader* (Malden, MA: Blackwell, 2000), 158–159.
4. Ibid., 157.
5. "Nike, Inc. Reports Fourth Quarter Earnings per Share Up 28 Percent," June 27, 2002;
   at <http://www.nike.com/nikebiz/news/pressrelease.jhtml?year=2002&month=06&
   letter=d>.
6. World Bank, 2001 World Development Indicators database, July 16, 2001; available at
   <www.worldbank.org/data/>.
7. Schwartz and Gibb, *When Good Companies Do Bad Things,* 51, 53.
8. Michael Clancy, "Sweating the Swoosh: Nike, the Globalization of Sneakers, and the
   Question of Sweatshop Labor," in *Pew Case Studies in International Affairs* (Washington,
   DC: Georgetown University, Institute for the Study of Diplomacy, 2000), 5.
9. Ibid.
10. Schwartz and Gibb, *When Good Companies Do Bad Things,* 51, 53.
11. Clancy, "Sweating the Swoosh," 9.
12. Nike Web site, corporate responsibility page: <www.nikebiz.com/labor/index.shtml>.
13. Clancy, "Sweating the Swoosh," 13.
14. "Firms are considered to be more multinational if (1) they have foreign affiliates or
    subsidiaries in foreign countries; (2) they operate in a wide variety of countries around
    the globe; (3) the proportion of assets, revenues, or profits accounted for by overseas
    operations relative to total assets, revenues, or profits is high; (4) their employees, stock-
    holders, owners, and managers are from many different countries; (5) their overseas
    operations are much more ambitious than just sales offices, including a full range of
    manufacturing and research and development activities. . . . MNCs are firms that have
    sent abroad a package of capital, technology, managerial talent, and marketing skills to

carry out production in foreign countries." Joan E. Spiro and Jeffrey A. Hart, *The Politics of International Economic Relations* (New York: St. Martin's Press, 1997), 96, 98.

15. Pratap Ravindran, "The Power of MNCs over the Global Economy," *Business Line* (Sept. 11, 2001); available at <www.blonnet.com/businessline/2001/09/11/stories/041120nm.htm>.

16. *Economist* (July 30, 1994): 57; reprinted in James Lee Ray, *Global Problems* (New York: Houghton Mifflin, 1998), 465.

17. United Nations Conference on Trade and Development (UNCTAD), *World Investment Report 2001: Promoting Linkages* (New York: United Nations, 2001), 242.

18. Ibid.

19. Kofi Annan, address to the World Economic Forum, New York, Feb. 4, 2002.

20. Schwartz and Gibb, *When Good Companies Do Bad Things,* 85.

21. For example, MNCs are under growing pressure to conform to higher environmental standards from home country regulations and consumers. See UNCTAD, *World Investment Report: Foreign Direct Investment and the Challenge of Development, Overview* (New York: United Nations, 1999), 46; UNCTAD, *World Investment Report, 1999* (New York: United Nations, 1999).

22. A. Claire Cutler, Virginia Haufler, and Tony Porter, *Private Authority and International Affairs* (Albany: SUNY Press, 1999), 16.

23. In practice, this varies by MNC and country. Companies that receive subsidies favor continuing them, and industries that are hurt by foreign competition pressure governments for protection.

24. Ward Morehouse and M. Arun Subramaniam, *The Bhopal Tragedy: A Report for the Citizens Commission on Bhopal* (New York: Council on International and Public Affairs, 1986); William Board, *The Bhopal Tragedy: Language, Logic, and Politics in the Production of a Hazard* (Boulder, CO: Westview, 1989); Paul Shrivastava, *Bhopal: Anatomy of a Crisis* (Cambridge, MA: Ballinger, 1987); Rama Lakshmi, "India Seeks to Reduce Change Facing Ex-Union Carbide Boss," *Washington Post,* July 8, 2002, p. A12.

25. Suketu Mehta, "Bhopal Lives," *Village Voice* (Dec. 3, 1996): 51.

26. Ibid., 55; Lakshmi, "India Seeks to Reduce Change Facing Ex-Union Carbide Boss." Warren Anderson, CEO of Union Carbide at the time of the accident, was charged with culpable homicide in India and faced a civil suit in the United States over the accident. He has "dropped out of sight" since 2000 to avoid facing the charges against him in either country.

27. Bret L. Billet, "Safeguarding or International Morality? The Behavior of Multinational Corporations in Less Developed Countries, 1975–86," *International Interactions,* 17 (1991): 171, 184; quoted in Ray, *Global Problems,* 476.

28. Deborah L. Spar, "The Spotlight and the Bottom Line: How Multinationals Export Human Rights," *Foreign Affairs* 77 (March–April 1998): 7–12.

29. Cutler, Haufler, and Porter, *Private Authority and International Affairs.*

30. David C. Korten, *When Corporations Rule the World* (West Hartford, CT: Kumarian Press, 1995).

31. Sarah Anderson and John Cavanagh, *Top 200: The Rise of Corporate Global Power,* Institute for Policy Studies, Dec. 4, 2000.

32. These include the power to compel discovery, dispose of property and property rights, order monetary damages, and, depending on the nature of the contract and the rules of arbitration chosen, even order specific performance.

33. Schwartz and Gibb, *When Good Companies Do Bad Things*, 92.
34. Margaret E. Keck and Kathryn Sikkink, *Activists Beyond Borders* (Ithaca, NY: Cornell University Press, 1998).
35. Virginia Haufler, *A Public Role for the Private Sector: Industry Self-Regulation in a Global Economy* (Washington, DC: Carnegie Endowment for International Peace, 2001), 106.
36. Jack Quarter, *Beyond the Bottom Line* (Westport, CT: Quorum Books, 2000), 119–133.
37. Presentation to the Humanizing the Global Economy Conference of the Latin American, Canadian, and US Catholic Bishops, Washington, DC, Catholic University, Jan. 29, 2002.
38. Schwartz and Gibb, *When Good Companies Do Bad Things*, 77.
39. C. Paul Robinson, Joan B. Woodard, and Samuel G. Varnado, "Critical Infrastructure: Interlinked and Vulnerable," *Issues in Science and Technology Online* (Fall 1998); available at <www.nap.edu/issues/15.1/robins.htm>.

CHAPTER FIVE

Networked Terror

Martha Crenshaw and Maryann Cusimano Love

On the evening of December 14, 1999, US Customs agent Deana Dean decided to search the last rental car leaving the ferry from Vancouver, British Columbia, into Washington state. The driver had a Canadian driver's license that identified him as Benni Antoine Noris of Montreal, but his answers to her routine questions seemed hesitant and nervous. Customs agents removed the cover over the spare tire in his trunk and found garbage bags of white powder, as well as aspirin containers and olive jars filled with liquid resembling honey. The suspect bolted, ran across lanes of traffic, bounced off a moving vehicle, and tried to commandeer a car. Customs agents apprehended and handcuffed him and continued to search his vehicle. Thinking they had found drugs, the border guards lifted, examined, and shook the containers, while the suspect ducked behind a car. Later they learned they had by chance apprehended a 32-year-old Algerian man named Ahmed Ressam, who was wanted in France and Canada for suspected terrorist activities. Rather than narcotics, Ressam was carrying 100 pounds of volatile, high-powered explosives that could have detonated if accidentally dropped by the customs agents. His intended target had been the Los Angeles International airport. The press quickly dubbed him the "Millennium Bomber."[1]

Ressam worked with his father in a coffee shop in Algeria until intrastate hostilities intensified in Algeria in 1992. An Islamic fundamentalist party was on the verge of winning national elections, but the government prevented it from taking power and a civil war broke out. Ressam became associated with Islamic militants and then moved to France for the next two years. During that time, Algerian terrorists calling themselves the Group Islamique armé (GIA), or Armed Islamic Group, conducted a series of bombings of the Paris Metro subway system, killing 22 people and injuring more than 200 others. In an eerie preview of the September 11 attacks, in 1994 they hijacked an Air France plane, which they wanted to crash, fully loaded with fuel and passengers, into a Paris landmark, preferably the Eiffel Tower. French commandos successfully stormed the plane, freed the passengers, and shot the hijackers, thus spoiling the plan.[2]

Ressam left France, using a fake French passport, and applied for political asylum in Canada. He moved in with a group of Islamic extremists in Quebec, where he supported himself on Canadian welfare assistance and petty theft and fraud, usually by robbing tourists and using or selling their traveler's checks, cash and credit cards, passports, driver's licenses, and other identification papers. When French police upset a GIA plot to bomb a G-7 economic meeting in France, they seized an electronic organizer filled with phone numbers and addresses of others in the terrorist network. Ahmed Ressam in Montreal was included in the electronic records. Bureaucratic obstacles and delays between the French and Canadian governments and within the Canadian government kept law enforcement from apprehending Ressam. In the meantime, he forged a false Canadian birth record and obtained a Canadian driver's license and passport as Beni Noris. Posing as Noris, he traveled to Pakistan, where he met with al Qaeda members and was taken to Osama bin Laden's terrorist training camps in Afghanistan. He received training in explosives manufacturing, destruction of a country's infrastructure, use of chemical weapons, and other terrorist activities. He left with new skills, $12,000 in "seed money" from the al Qaeda network to pursue terrorist activities, and a request from one of bin Laden's chief lieutenants to steal and send them original Canadian passports so they could help establish operatives in the United States. As investigating French Judge Jean-Louis Brugiere noted, "You can't move around if you don't have false papers and passports. For these groups, passports are as important as weapons."[3] Ressam returned to Canada via South Korea, with a layover in Los Angeles International Airport. While there, he surveyed the site, calculating how long he could leave explosives-laden luggage before it would be discovered and moved, and the length of time he would have to escape the premises (apparently, he did not plan a suicide bombing).[4]

Ressam was arrested days before the millennium. Celebrations in Seattle were cancelled as a precaution until authorities could untangle the plot. Ressam's cooperation with law enforcement helped secure the arrests of some of his associates in Canada and Brooklyn, New York. International law enforcement efforts foiled other millennium plots in at least Jordan and Yemen.[5] After the September 11 attacks, Ressam was again interrogated in a high security prison in Seattle. He said he did not know any of the September 11 hijackers, but he gave authorities additional information about terrorist sleeper cells and about al Qaeda's interest in chemical and biological weapons. In return, he is seeking reduced prison time from his potential maximum sentence of 130 years.[6]

This case illustrates many trends in modern terrorism: a desire to increase casualties, global operations, use of cheap and easily available modern technologies, and networked organizational structures. The case also demonstrates how difficult it is for states to cooperate effectively to combat terrorism in a timely fashion. The purpose of this chapter is to put the transsovereign problem of modern terrorism in context:[7] in the context of the debates over defining terrorism compared to other forms of political violence, in the context of globalization,[8] in the context of what the private sector and states can do to prevent and respond to terrorism, and in the context of how terrorism ends.

DEFINING TERRORISM

The word *terrorism* was first used in describing the Reign of Terror phase of the French Revolution in 1793–94 as a newly installed regime systematically attempted to consolidate power. In nineteenth-century Russia, the People's Will proudly admitted using terrorism in its fight against the autocracy, seeing its members as "noble, terrible . . . the martyr and the hero." A successor group later proclaimed, "The terrorists are the incarnation of the honor and the conscience of the Russian revolution."[9]

Using the term *terrorism* has always been controversial. The British army in Palestine in 1947 banned use of the word *terrorist* to describe members of Menachem Begin's Irgun group, the principal Jewish rebel force, because it implied that British forces had reason to be terrified by the resistance fighters.[10]

Defining terrorism today is no less controversial, in part because the concept is "overlaid with questions of value, usually centered on the legitimacy of the use of violence. Attitudes toward terrorism are frequently based on deep moral commitments . . . the morality of political systems and governments; one has to ask what values are to be defended."[11] Because of the word's pejorative connotation, many people seek to label any use of violence they perceive as illegitimate or with which they disagree as *terrorism*. Israel tends to refer to any Palestinian violence as terrorism, whereas Palestinians call Israel a terrorist state. Pakistan regards Muslims fighting for the autonomy of Kashmir as freedom fighters, yet India regards them as terrorists. Al Qaeda contends that the United States engaged in terrorism because sanctions on Iraq kill millions of innocent women and children, and because the United States used weapons of mass destruction against civilian populations—as when it dropped atomic bombs on Hiroshima and Nagasaki in 1945.

Distinct from the word's use as an insult, however, is some core of agreement about the definition of terrorism. Why is terrorism considered to be an illegitimate use of force? One reason is that terrorism typically refers to force directed against noncombatants, which violates centuries of natural law and international law regarding the rules of war.[12]

Unlike other "isms"—communism, fascism, socialism—terrorism is a strategy or tactic, not an ideology. It is used by widely divergent groups, from Maoists in the mountains of Peru to conservative Islamic extremists in the Arabian desert. Although George W. Bush's administration has not portrayed it this way, its "war on terrorism" is similar to other efforts to delegitimize particular tactics internationally, such as the effort to ban the use of antipersonnel landmines. Similar to the campaign to ban landmines as an illegitimate tool of force against noncombatants, international coalitions, treaties, and conventions against terrorism also seek to globally undermine the use of terrorism as a tool. The war against terrorism is not a fight against a particular state, territory, group, person, or ideology. It is a battle to curtail the use of a specific method of violence.[13]

Terrorism can be defined as organized and purposive political violence that is

> perceived as unacceptable by society because of its cruelty and un-expectedness. . . . Terrorism usually occurs in situations of peace rather than war, and comes as a surprise to its victims . . . who are non-combatants, not prepared to defend themselves against attack and only in the most tenuous way responsible for the actions of the governments that terrorists oppose. . . . Terrorists intend, if not to terrorize (that is, to create the emotion of terror, a form of panic), at least to produce outrage and shock. Terrorism is a strategy of surprise. It is meant to . . . produce psychological and political effects far out of proportion to the magnitude of physical destruction. . . . [T]he physical victims of terrorism are not the targets. That they are terrorized is important only in so far as their terror is communicated to a watching audience, whose emotions the terrorists seek to manipulate.[14]

Terrorism depends on surprise to gain attention and generate fear, so terrorists must constantly be innovative in their means of attack or they lose the power to shock. If terrorist violence becomes routine, then their actions will not pressure change and their goals will no longer receive attention. Surprise is one way of compensating for what they lack in numbers. "Terrorists rarely attack well defended targets. The two factors of weakness and the desire to excite passions encourage terrorists to attack ordinary civilians."[15]

Terrorism is an inherently political act to achieving particular goals, generally to bring public pressure to bear on government decisions. For example, al Qaeda's terrorist campaign against the United States is an attempt to pressure the United States to withdraw its forces from Saudi Arabia and its support from the Saudi and Egyptian regimes, which al Qaeda regards as illegitimate. The calculus assumes that raising the costs to the United States will undermine support and encourage change of US policies in the Middle East. Thus, even though some people regard such terrorists as "mad," as a group terrorists are engaged in conscious, goal-directed, and premeditated rather than random behavior.

As opposed to mass uprisings or spontaneous violence, "Terrorism is clandestine violence organized by small groups. . . . [T]errorism is highly intentional or purposeful violence. It is not spontaneous or unplanned."[16] For example, the four simultaneous hijackings of September 11 revealed a vast, complex, and highly organized conspiracy.[17]

Because terrorism aims to arouse or intimidate civilian audiences more than reduce an opponent's military effectiveness, "Victims are representative and symbolic. Their usefulness to the terrorist lies in the regard society has for them."[18]

There are other official definitions of terrorism. The International Convention for the Suppression of the Financing of Terrorism sponsored by the United Nations defines terrorism as "an act intended to cause death or serious bodily injury to any person not actively involved in armed conflict in order to intimidate a population, or to compel a government or an international organization to do or abstain from doing any act."[19] Other UN documents stress that terrorists are nonstate actors motivated by political goals.[20]

The US Department of State defines terrorism as

premeditated, politically motivated violence perpetrated against non-combatant targets by subnational groups or clandestine agents, usually intended to influence an audience. The term "international terrorism" means terrorism involving citizens or the territory of more than one country. The term "terrorist group" means any group practicing, or that has significant subgroups that practice, international terrorism.[21]

The definitions generally share the idea that terrorism is the use of violence against noncombatants, generally by nonstate actors to generate fear in furtherance of other political goals. The "nonstate" component of the definition is important, if not universally accepted. If terrorism is only conducted by nonstate actors, then by definition US and Israeli actions against non-combatants are not terrorism, whereas similar actions by Palestinians may be so termed. International conventions, because they are signed by states, are likely to support definitions of terrorism that are more favorable to states.

It is important to note that all uses of violence by groups labeled as terrorist may not be terrorism. Although the definitions agree that terrorism is usually the resort of nonstate actors, not all violence by nonstate actors is terrorism. Terrorism is distinct from other low-level forms of political violence by nonstate actors such as guerrilla warfare, ethnic or nationalist separatist violence, and violent efforts to overthrow governments, among others. Depending on the context, nonstate groups may use a medley of tactics that includes both terrorism and other forms of political violence.[22] Sometimes, terrorist groups may engage in traditional insurgent activities of using force against military and government targets in order to gain territory or strategic advantage, not to strike at noncombatants in order to cause fear. Terrorism means not only conducting illegal actions (such as killing noncombatants), but also having certain intentions behind those actions (causing fear and psychological reactions to achieve political or other goals rather than destroy something of material value). Traditional guerrilla or insurgent actions to diminish a government's abilities to project power into a disputed region may not be terrorism. These distinctions between terrorism and other forms of low-level violence can confuse policy makers and the public, because generally once a group is labeled as terrorist, all its actions are labeled terrorism, even though groups may employ a variety of tactics, only some of which are terrorism.

Developing common definitions of terrorism is important as antiterrorism laws are increasingly enacted domestically and internationally. In the case of Ahmed Ressam, what difference does it make whether we call his actions terrorism? He committed fraud, theft, illegal immigration, and perjury and created and carried illegal explosives across state lines in a conspiracy to commit multiple homicides. Unlike many acts of cybercrime, which are not illegal in some states, terrorism is not primarily a problem of a lack of law. Most everything terrorist organizations do is already illegal: fraud, theft, murder, hijackings, bombings, conspiracy. What value is added by enacting additional domestic and international legislation that labels these activities as terrorism? The purpose of additional antiterrorism legislation is primarily political: to help free additional resources to combat terrorism, to build international political consensus and harmonize international law regarding these acts, and to further undermine the tactic's legitimacy.

GOING GLOBAL

Additional international legal conventions are also sought against terrorism because, although terrorists are increasingly global, law enforcement efforts are still stymied by state borders and jurisdictions. When terrorists attacked US military barracks in Saudi Arabia and the *USS Cole* in Yemen, Saudi and Yemeni authorities were not as cooperative as US law enforcement officials would have liked. The Saudis beheaded suspects they apprehended without giving other law enforcement officials an opportunity to question them. Because the suspects were Saudi citizens in Saudi territory, the Saudi government was well within its sovereign rights. Terrorists may go global, but state actions to pursue terrorists are constrained by sovereignty.

Although terrorism has existed for centuries, the modern period of globalization changes it. If terrorism is a form of "advertising discontent,"[23] then globalization offers terrorists the opportunity to easily and cheaply take their complaints to a global stage.[24] For example, al Qaeda's attacks on US targets can be seen as a strategic reaction to American power in the context of a globalized civil war. The United States is susceptible to international terrorism because of its global engagement and its choice of allies, most of whom face significant opposition at home.

> For many of the militants now engaged in al Qaeda, opposition to authority at home, whether peaceful or violent, was ineffective. Local regimes countered dissent with severe repression. As a result, radical frustrations apparently were transferred to the United States as a symbol of both oppression and arrogance. As a free and affluent society, America is a target-rich environment, and one where sensational attacks elicit gratifying media attention. Portraying the United States as an immoral enemy justifies terrorism to the audiences of the dispossessed, especially young men without life prospects whose only education is religious. These various strands have been knitted together in the transnational conspiracy that is al Qaeda. One cannot understand al Qaeda without understanding the domestic politics of Egypt and Saudi Arabia, or now much of the Muslim world.[25]

Globalization takes local fault lines farther afield.

Terrorists can go global by using global media as shrewdly as other political actors. Journalist Peter Bergen recalls being contacted by Osama bin Laden's media advisors, who were considering appropriate venues for bin Laden's first television interview. The advisors had a large stack of media requests, but they had narrowed it down to the BBC, CBS News's *60*

Minutes program, or CNN. Bergen, employed by CNN, recalled, "I pointed out that CNN's programs were shown in over a hundred countries, while CBS was broadcast only in the United States."[26] A month later, CNN was called on to do the interview. Bergen and his crew were blindfolded and escorted to an undisclosed location in Afghanistan and allowed to use only al Qaeda's video equipment in case their cameras were bugged or rigged with explosives.[27] After the interview, the media advisor reviewed the tape and cut out any unflattering footage of bin Laden.[28]

Besides global media, terrorists use other cheap and easily available off-the-shelf technologies. A laptop computer left behind by one of the terrorists responsible for the 1993 bombing of the World Trade Center revealed an evidence trail to other co-conspirators, as well as an al Qaeda "how-to" terrorist manual. The September 11 hijackers used the Internet to download specific airport maps, directions, flying instructions, and information about the targeted buildings. They even purchased many of their tickets online. To hide their trail, they often used general access computers in public libraries. Terrorist groups routinely set up Web sites and broadcast their political aims and encourage recruits. They create and copy homemade videotapes for use in international recruitment. From fax machines to palm pilots and cell phones, terrorist networks use the same technologies that global business networks use.

Easy access to lethal technologies facilitates another disturbing trend. Experts have noted rising casualties and increased lethality in terrorist violence in recent years. Although the Japanese group Aum Shinrikyo's release of poisonous sarin gas into the crowded Tokyo subway system in 1995 "only" killed twelve people, more than 5,500 were injured. Many more would have died if the group had been more expert in its use of chemical agents. Local terrorist groups in the past faced diminishing returns on increased bloodshed. If their activities caused too many casualties, it could decrease critical social support, recruitments, financial support, and legitimacy. The Irish Republican Army (IRA) often faced this dilemma. But today, terrorism experts fear greater casualties in coming years as terrorist groups train in and explore the use of chemical, biological, and nuclear devices. Because terrorist groups are increasingly networked globally, with training, recruitment, financing, and operations carried out in several countries, increased deaths of one country's citizens may not reduce sympathy, support, and recruitment for the group in other countries. Increased casualties may actually build support as the group gains media exposure and international recognition that it is a force to be reckoned with. Terrorists may also capitalize politically on governments' increased use of violence to combat terrorism. For example, increased violence by British troops and Protestant paramilitary units in Northern Ireland—including the British Army's firing into a crowd of unarmed Irish Catholic demonstrators in Londonderry on "Bloody Sunday" (January 30, 1972)[29]—led to the establishment of the Provisional Irish Republican Army and increased sympathy for the IRA's cause for a time, as many people asked, "Who are the real terrorists here?"[30]

Globalization also facilitates the financing of terrorist groups, because dirty money moves in the same cross-border financial flows as clean money. Terrorists can finance their operations through private charitable foundations. These NGOs may conduct social service works (such as education, health care, and care of widows, orphans, war victims, and refugees), but some of the funds raised may be diverted to illicit activities. Terrorists also engage in strategic cooperative ventures with transnational criminal groups. Terrorist groups in Latin America, for example, often derive significant financial benefit from the drug trade, just as al Qaeda profited from the Afghan heroin trade.

Terrorist organizations may also conduct legal businesses. The Aum Skinrikyo sect used its software development companies as a major source of revenue. (Computer sales at Aum-related retail shops in the cities of Tokyo, Osaka, and Nagoya alone earn the group approximately $65 million a year.) The Japanese defense ministry even used Aum-developed communications programs at twenty ground bases across Japan to gain more rapid access to the Internet. Aum programs were also used for airline-route management and mainframe computer operations. The software companies earned the business through indirect subcontracting relationships and by underbidding competitors by 30 percent to 40 percent because their employees, all Aum members, worked for virtually no pay. In an incredible irony, the Japanese government purchased software from the very group that perpetrated the sarin gas attacks in the hope of causing chaos that would lead to the overthrow of the Japanese government.[31]

Terrorist organizations may also network with other terrorist organizations. For example, the Provisional IRA historically has prized "its links with foreign terrorist movements such as the Popular Front for the

Liberation of Palestine, the Red Brigades, the Red Army Faction, and the ETA [Euskadi Ta Askatasuna, a Basque separatist group that inhabits the Spanish–French border region]. . . . Italian terrorists shared a huge consignment of Palestinian weapons between the ETA and the IRA."[32] More recently, IRA members have been arrested in Colombia, helping to train the Revolutionary Armed Forces of Colombia (Fuerzas Armadas Revolucionarias de Colombia, or FARC).

THE MISSING LINK: THE PRIVATE SECTOR AND CURTAILING TERRORISM[33]

Global infrastructures were built for speed and profit, not security. People and packages now move faster, farther, more easily, and for a lower price than ever before—but at the cost of preventive, multilateral security measures. Although attention has been placed on increasing government activities against terrorism after September 11, the private sector remains key in safeguarding infrastructure from terrorist attack.

For example, although government has increased its attention to airline security, security as a whole has not been adequately addressed in the rest of global transportation and trade infrastructure, particularly commercial shipping. Airline passengers have their tweezers and nail clippers seized at the gates, but commercial shipping cargo is loaded on these same aircraft with few security precautions. Whether by land, sea, or air, more than 21 million cargo containers enter the United States every year. Less than 2 percent of those containers are inspected in "needle in the haystack" random checks by border, customs, or Coast Guard agents. Manifests are still filed in paper, and shippers have as long as thirty days *after* a container has entered the United States to notify the government of its content or origins. This is how most illegal drugs enter the United States, and cargo containers are increasingly used in human smuggling. If terrorists were to ship and explode a chemical, biological, or nuclear device via container cargo, the US government would have no prior information to prevent its use and possibly little data to track it after it was used. The current system favors shippers and businesses, who with few reporting or inspection requirements can cheaply speed inventories for just-in-time delivery and avoid warehousing and storage costs. The shippers say they have few incentives to change the system and engage in greater public–private cooperation with government on security issues. They are not required to do so by law. Their clients, customers, and shareholders are concerned more with the bottom line than with security measures. They do not trust government competence or motives. Would information volunteered to government land in the hands of their competitors or result in higher tax bills?

Without action by shippers and businesses, however, terrorists can easily exploit the vulnerabilities of global trade and transportation infrastructure, as they did on September 11. Stephen Flynn, senior fellow at the Council on Foreign Relations and a retired US Coast Guard commander, explains the ease with which terrorists could smuggle a weapon of mass destruction into the United States using commercial shipping:

> [A] weapon of mass destruction could be loaded into a container and sent anywhere in the world. Osama bin Laden could have a front company in Karachi, Pakistan, load a biological agent into a container ultimately destined for Newark, New Jersey, with virtually no risk that it would be intercepted. He could use a Pakistani exporter with an established record of trade in the United States. The container could then be sent via Singapore or Hong Kong to mingle with the half a million containers that are handled by each of these ports every month. It could arrive in the United States via Long Beach or Los Angeles and be loaded directly onto a railcar or truck for the transcontinental trip. Current regulations do not require an importer to file a cargo manifest with U.S. Customs until the cargo reaches its "entry" port—in this case, Newark, 2,800 miles of American territory away from where it first entered the country—and the importer is permitted 30 days' transit time to make the trip to the East Coast. The container could be diverted or the weapon activated anywhere en route, long before its contents were even identified as having entered the country.[34]

Unfortunately, such a scenario is not science fiction. Businesses do little to police themselves, and pressure to facilitate trade means that established shippers receive little scrutiny from government authorities, even though they are easily compromised. In early January 2002, Federal Express unknowingly shipped a highly radioactive, 300-pound package that was emitting radiation at an estimated rate of 10 rem (radiation equivalent man) per hour. In one-half hour, a person exposed to that much radiation would exceed the annual limit for exposure and suffer the symptoms of radiation poisoning within just a few hours. Despite this case, FedEx officials do not believe the incident shows any need for greater security precautions on their part. A terrorist organization would not have been able to ship dangerous materials, the company hypothesized, "because extra precautions would have been taken in the case of an unknown shipper or recipient."[35] Would terrorists really use their own return address?

Because terrorists seek easy targets, private sector responses are crucial. The private sector is increasingly partnering with states. For example, the financial sector is working to curtail money laundering, and pharmaceutical companies are rapidly producing smallpox vaccine to prepare for potential bioterrorist attacks. Yet more private sector cooperation is needed in the war on terrorism.

Increasing the number of border control agents and the amount of equipment and increasing searches and seizures at borders are efforts that are still bound to fail because even the most up-to-date and efficient government agents cannot keep up with the volume of global trade flows. Speed and volume are crucial to maintaining the economic health of global trade and transportation systems. Just-in-time shipping and narrow profit margins that are dependent on speed and volume mean that closing down borders for old-fashioned search and seizures is an unsustainable approach and equivalent to imposing an economic embargo on ourselves.[36] Luckily we have other choices.

Flynn offers suggestions for increasing public–private sector cooperation to safeguard against terrorist attacks. Rather than focusing efforts on border control, security checks should be done at the point of origin in trade and transportation flows. Trying to manage security at borders is like "trying to catch minnows at the base of Niagara Falls."[37] Border checks should be the last defense, not the first or main check for security. Thorough security background checks should be required of all private sector employees in the shipping and transportation sectors. We should move away from paper passports and paper-based manifest and information systems globally. Modern off-the-shelf technologies such as bar coding, GPS transceivers, sensors, smart cards, and advance electronic manifests should be adopted by government and private sector agents; these would allow real-time transparency and accountability about the contents of the shipping or transportation stream at any given time. This is how United Parcel Service and FedEx track packages in transit to customers. Shippers that comply with standards and do thorough and strict self-policing will be accorded fast track processing at borders that would be the equivalent of an "EZ pass" lane. Border checks would continue but be based on intelligence and risk management baselines rather than purely on hunches. Flynn concludes:

> Governments around the world that share an interest in sustaining the free flow of people, goods, capital, and ideas must be encouraged to develop and enact common prevention and protective measures to facilitate legitimate crossborder movements while stopping illegitimate and dangerous ones. Washington has the leverage necessary to gain support for such a process, since all roads lead to and from U.S. markets. It must now put that leverage to good use. Most of the owners, operators, and users of the global transportation networks are from the private sector, however, and they must also be enlisted into any efforts to enhance security and controls. The result will be an imperfect system, but one that will do a much better job at controlling the risks and consequences of catastrophic terrorist attacks than do the arrangements prevailing now.[38]

STATE RESPONSES: HOW TERRORISM ENDS[39]

So far the discussion has focused on how to manage or curtail terrorism. More international cooperation, greater information sharing and cooperation across and within government bureaucracies, and more sustained and systematic cooperation between government and the private sector are all needed. But how does terrorism end? Context matters. As we try to formulate governmental policies aimed at ending terrorism, we must ask how such policies are likely to affect the evolution of terrorism.

The first set of questions involves the terrorist groups themselves. First, internal factors must be assessed. How does the organization make decisions? How does the organization perceive its environment? What are its internal psychological dynamics? Is the organization divided internally? The answers to all of these questions are important to know but often difficult to ascertain.

Next, external factors must be considered. How does the relative strength of the terrorist organization compare with that of the government it opposes? Are the terrorists ideologically or ethnically motivated? What kinds of ties do they have to outside groups that may support them? Is the conflict best characterized as a secessionist struggle or does the conflict involve a battle over civil society and representation?

The options that a government uses to respond to terrorism, many of which can be pursued simultaneously, must be adapted to the type of group and situation. There is no one-size-fits-all policy.

First, governments can try deterrence. They can use their coercive capacity to make terrorism too costly for those who seek to use it. They can do this by military strikes against terrorist bases, assassinations of key leaders, and collective punishment. There are several drawbacks to this approach, however. It can lead to unacceptable human rights violations, and groups may not come to government attention until their movements are so well developed that containing them through deterrent methods is insufficient.

An alternative is to use the criminal justice system to end terrorist activities and groups. Governments can treat terrorism primarily as a crime and therefore pursue the extradition, prosecution, and incarceration of suspects. One drawback to this approach is that the prosecution of terrorists in a court of law can compromise government efforts to gather intelligence on terrorist organizations. For example, al Qaeda members drastically reduced their usage of cell phones after court testimony revealed that governments could easily intercept cell phone conversations. In addition, criminal justice efforts (like deterrent efforts) are deployed mostly after terrorists have struck, meaning that significant damage and loss of life may have already occurred.

Governments can enhance prevention and defense. They can make targets harder to attack, and they can use intelligence capabilities to gain advance knowledge of when attacks may take place. As targets are hardened, however, some terrorist groups may shift their sights to softer targets. An example is the targeting of the US embassies in Kenya and Tanzania in August 1998 by truck bombs. Although the attacks were coordinated by al Qaeda, targets in Africa were chosen because of their relatively lax security compared with targets in the Middle East.

States also may try negotiations. Governments can elect to negotiate with terrorist groups and make concessions in exchange for the groups' renunciation of violence. The Good Friday Peace Accords and the associated peace process in Northern Ireland, and the Colombian government's outreach to insurgency and terrorist groups are attempts to reach negotiated settlements and end violence. Governments are often reluctant to do so when terror campaigns begin, but negotiations may be the only way to resolve long-standing disputes, especially ethnonationalist claims that have significant popular support.

The end of terrorism may result from one or more of the following situations. Success may end it. The terrorists may accomplish their objectives, such as the overthrow of a government, the end of an occupation, or a policy change. Terrorism per se cannot achieve long-term goals such as revolution or independence, but it can sometimes do so in conjunction with less violent political action.

The terrorists may also achieve partial or preliminary success. A corollary to achieving objectives is having at least achieved public recognition for an organization and the cause it espouses. It can put the issue on the public agenda. In this case, continued terrorist actions may alienate supporters, sponsors, or key third-country actors for whom continued violence is unacceptable.

Terrorists may experience organizational breakdown, as has been the case for the Tupac Amaru group in Peru. After some of its members died when a four-month siege of the Japanese embassy in Peru was put down by Peruvian forces in 1997, the group has not mounted a significant terrorist action and appears to be in organizational disarray, with dwindling numbers focused mainly on freeing their imprisoned compatriots.[40] Terrorist organizations, like any organizations, must constantly work to maintain themselves. If recruiting dries up, or if funding becomes unavailable, then the organization may be unable to sustain itself. On the other hand, the necessity of self-preservation may force organizations to continue terrorist activities even if the leadership otherwise wishes to give them up. It may be that the only way for the organization to continue to attract new recruits and financial support is to continue to gain publicity for its terrorist actions.

Terrorist groups also may face dwindling support. Organizations may lose the support of their various constituencies—the populations they seek to represent or the governments or other organizations that support them. They can do so for reasons of ideological or strategic differences, personality clashes, or simple fatigue. Terrorist actions can also provoke moral outrage and undermine support.

New alternatives to achieve political or other goals may emerge. At times, other options for political change emerge. They can include more traditional forms of warfare or revolution, mass protests, or political negotiations.

As suggested above, many of the factors and consequences already outlined may occur simultaneously. Both governments and terrorist organizations can pursue many tracks at once, and organizations may confront a wide series of challenges simultaneously.

Governmental decisions about how to confront terrorism are made more difficult by the frequently high degree of uncertainty governments have about the nature of terrorist organizations, their motivations, and the effects of government actions on those organizations. The need for understanding terrorist organizations is highlighted by the fact that such groups' calculations are based on their perceptions of costs and rewards, not those of the authorities who confront them or of objective observers.

So called get-tough measures against terrorist groups can have unintended consequences. Trying to decapitate a movement may radicalize the whole movement or some splinter faction. Assassinations and military force can provoke a desire for revenge, and raids and arrests can reinforce martial images, create mythologies of martyrdom, and feed paranoia and secretiveness (which makes the movements even harder to penetrate for reasons of either understanding motivations or foiling actions). Success in combating terrorism in one place may merely push it to another region. After the assassination of Egyptian President Anwar Sadat, Egyptian authorities cracked down on the Egyptian Islamic Jihad group. Many of its members fled Egypt and joined forces with Osama bin Laden's al Qaeda organization. Today, bin Laden's chief lieutenants all hail from Egyptian Islamic Jihad. Some observers are concerned that success in toppling the Taliban and routing al Qaeda fighters from Afghanistan may simply have pushed the organization into Yemen, Sudan, Somalia, or Pakistan.

In the event that organizations are primarily motivated by a desire for recognition, how should policy makers respond? Should the government recognize the organizations and eliminate their motivation for terrorism? Because terrorist actions most often are considered newsworthy events by media organizations, governments cannot control whether the actions garner attention. Governments can play an effective role, however, in influencing how terrorist events are portrayed to the public and thus influence (but not control) how the public interprets those events.

Public opinion is important because it can determine the amount of financial and operational support the terrorists enjoy. In some cases, support comes from abroad and is difficult for governments to control. In other cases, governments have control over populations that are sympathetic to the terrorists. In this event, they must walk a difficult line. On the one hand, repressive measures can encourage antigovernment hostility and support for the terrorists. On the other hand, fear of punishment for the terrorists' excesses can undermine a population's willingness to support terrorist activities. In this balance, the terrorists have two weapons on their side. The first is their ability to mete out punishment against those who do not support their actions, and the second is their ability to build on group solidarity to overcome reservations about their methods.

One effective tactic against many terrorist organizations may be to promote their disintegration from the inside. Governments can demonstrate to such groups that their support among the populations they supposedly represent is waning. Even where such allegations are true, however, groups may resolutely believe they enjoy support even after it has dissipated. Governments can also try to split off members from a group either by offering large rewards for information that undermines group solidarity or by making promises of leniency for imprisoned group members. Finally, governments can unilaterally enact reforms that reduce public support for the terrorists without rewarding the terrorists directly or by negotiating with them.

Another tactic may be to put pressure on states that are sympathetic to a terrorist group's goals, even if the states are not outright sponsors of the group. Expulsion from a haven often causes financial pressures or logistical difficulties and can sometimes end a group's viability. In many cases, however, affected countries lack the necessary ties to effect such pressure, or laws that govern free expression make it difficult to crack down on an organization's activities.

If the efforts to eliminate a terrorist group through compulsion fail, however, governments are left trying to reach a peaceful settlement with that group. In civil conflicts, such a settlement usually entails negotiations for amnesty of both individuals and the group. In trying negotiations, governments must confront opposition on two fronts: from the group's rank-

and-file members, who may be more disposed toward violence than the leadership; and from the inside—that is, from their own populations, who may oppose the government sitting down with killers and "rewarding violence." Groups that are opposed to a peaceful reconciliation will act to undermine the peace, often by undertaking terrorist actions of their own, as has been the case in the peace process in Northern Ireland. In this event, governments that have only a precarious grip on power will find it difficult to move decisively toward peace.

In addition, governments must time their peace overtures carefully: first, by making such gestures when their ability to reward good behavior and punish bad is strong; and second, by making them when the terrorist organization is going through some period of internal questioning. In such situations, effective intelligence can be crucial in identifying auspicious times for a peaceful gesture and in defining the context of that gesture. Yet lack of timely intelligence is often cited as the crux of the problem.

CONCLUSIONS: CONSIDER THE CONTEXT[41]

Deciding when to employ what strategy is one of the hardest problems facing government officials who deal with terrorism. There is no single solution. Governments must carefully consider the nature of their terrorism problem in context. Negotiations with those who are perpetrating violence are not the solution to every problem. By the same token, many terrorist campaigns cannot be stopped by military or law-enforcement actions alone. Many people suggest that a decisive factor that determines the effectiveness of law-enforcement activities is the support that the terrorist groups enjoy among their base. Narrowly based terrorist groups can be rooted out, but groups that rely on a broad base of support (some of them from beyond a nation's borders) have a durability that may defy such efforts. For that reason, ethnically based groups may be harder than class-based groups to eliminate through force because ethnicity has proven a stronger tie than class in most cases.

If negotiations are pursued, then two conditions should be present. First, the government should enjoy a strong popular mandate. Political opponents often portray negotiating with terrorists as "giving in" to terrorism. Such an attack can topple a weak government or, short of that, block whatever agreement has been reached through negotiations. Second, the terrorist organization should be undergoing a period of self-evaluation. In such a circumstance, the government may be able to successfully split off pragmatists from hardline terrorists, bring the population along with the pragmatists, and dry up popular support for those who continue to pursue violence.

Intelligence is important throughout. In confronting terrorism, the nature of the grievance does matter, as does the nature of the organization that puts forth the grievance. Intelligence is important not only to prevent terrorist attacks but also to understand how the organization works and how its decision making processes can be affected. Because terrorism is global, intelligence becomes an almost intractable problem. How can intelligence collection, analysis, and dissemination be conducted or shared globally? This is resisted by sovereign states.

Terrorism is an international problem and therefore requires policies that go beyond unilateral state actions. Money and weapons flow across borders, and supporters of terrorism (if not the terrorists themselves) often have established bases in other countries. Increasingly, law enforcement efforts aimed at stemming terrorism have an international component, and such a strategy will only require more international cooperation in the future. The nature of the terrorists' grievances matters. Although political violence by itself can rarely achieve its aims, it can sometimes do so in conjunction with less violent political action. By the same token, deterring terrorism and prosecuting terrorists may be insufficient to end terrorism, especially when a large population supports the terrorists' cause. In this regard, the war on terrorism may be as unsuccessful as the war on drugs if efforts to curtail terrorism focus exclusively on military, defensive, and law enforcement approaches. Without addressing underlying factors of what terrorists are fighting for, where they draw their strength from, and how to address their grievances or separate organizations from their base, it will be difficult to manage or end terrorism. The means and targets of terrorism may be global, but grievances are often still local, ensuring that governments will need to use a range of responses to manage networked terror.

Which measures are chosen will depend on the nature of the terrorist threat as well as the domestic political context. The diffusion of power in democratic governments poses a challenge for formulating and coordinating policy.[42] In addition, democracies generally promote the idea of protection of the rights of the individual, bringing pressure on governments to respond to terrorist attacks on innocent civilians. "Democracies can survive the assassinations of leaders . . . but they cannot tolerate public insecurity."[43] However, choosing a response must be tempered by the fact that no democratic regime has ever been conquered by terrorism. Terrorists often miscalculate. Their attacks may rally support for their opponent and strengthen rather than undermine the power of the state. The magnitude of terrorist destruction must also be considered in context. Terrorist destruction "is small compared not only to other forms of political violence such as civil wars or communal rioting but also to other sources of casualties in modern societies."[44] This is particularly true after September 11. The public perception of risk from terrorism generally far exceeds the reality. Citizens in developed countries are more likely to die from firearms or car accidents than from terrorism. "In 1990, 37,000 deaths in the United States were caused by firearms, while 200 deaths were caused by international terrorism."[45] Citizens in developing countries are more likely to die from tuberculosis, malaria, or AIDS than from terrorism. The spread of democracy and global media make open societies more vulnerable to terrorist attacks and place great pressure on governments to respond. Yet in choosing a response, democracies must be careful not to overreact. In fighting the war on terrorism, we must not become more like our opponents than we would like and less able to address the underlying vulnerabilities and grievances of globalization that can fuel terrorism.[46]

ENDNOTES

1. Terrence McKenna, "Trail of a Terrorist" (transcript of *Frontline* documentary, Public Broadcasting Service [PBS], Oct. 25, 2001; available at <www.pbs.org/wgbh/pages/frontline/shows/trail/etc/script.html>); Ahmed Ressam, testimony in July 2001 as a witness for the prosecution at the New York trial of co-conspirator Mokhtar Haouari, federal district court of the Southern District of New York; available at <www.pbs.org/wgbh/pages/frontline/shows/trail/inside/testimony.html>.
2. McKenna, "Trail of a Terrorist"; Ahmed Ressam testimony, July 2001.
3. McKenna, "Trail of a Terrorist."
4. Ibid.; Ahmed Ressam testimony, July 2001.
5. Vernon Loeb, "Terrorists Plotted Jan. 2000," *Washington Post,* Dec. 24, 2000, p. A01; *Frontline,* "Other Millennium Plots," PBS, Oct. 25, 2001; available at <www.pbs.org/wgbh/pages/frontline/shows/trail/inside/attacks.html>.
6. McKenna, "Trail of a Terrorist."
7. Martha Crenshaw, "Terrorism in Context," in Martha Crenshaw (Ed.), *Terrorism in Context* (University Park: Pennsylvania State University Press, 1995).

8. Maryann Cusimano Love, "Globalization, Ethics, and the War on Terrorism," *Notre Dame Journal of Law, Ethics, & Public Policy* (Violence in America issue, 2002): 65–80; Maryann Cusimano Love, "Morality Matters: Ethics, Power Politics, and the War on Terrorism," *Georgetown Journal of International Affairs* ((Summer–Fall 2002): 7–16.

9. Martha Crenshaw, "Organized Disorder: Terrorism, Politics, and Society," in Ray C. Rist (Ed.), *The Democratic Imagination* (New Brunswick, NJ: Transaction Publishers, 1994), 140.

10. Ibid., 141.

11. Ibid., 143.

12. Saint Augustine, *City of God* (trans. Thomas Merton) (New York: Modern Library Paperback Classics, 2000).

13. Cusimano Love, "Globalization, Ethics, and the War on Terrorism," 65–80; Cusimano Love, "Morality Matters."

14. Martha Crenshaw, *Terrorism and International Cooperation* (New York: Institute for East-West Security Studies; Boulder, CO: Westview Press, 1989), 6–7.

15. Crenshaw, "Organized Disorder," 150.

16. Ibid., 143–144.

17. Martha Crenshaw, "Why America? The Globalization of Civil War," *Current History* (Dec. 2001): 425.

18. Crenshaw, "Organized Disorder," 143.

19. United Nations, "International Convention for the Suppression of the Financing of Terrorism," December 9, 1999; available at <http://untreaty.un.org/English/tersumen.htm#4>.

20. Jonathan R. White, *Terrorism* (3rd ed.) (Belmont, CA: Wadsworth, 2002), 12.

21. US Department of State, *Patterns of Global Terrorism 2000* (Washington, DC: US Government Printing Office, April 30, 2001); available at <www.state.gov/s/ct/rls/pgtrpt/2000/2419.htm>.

22. Crenshaw, *Terrorism and International Cooperation,* 8.

23. Irving Louis Horowitz, "Political Terrorism and State Power," *Journal of Political and Military Sociology* (Spring 1973): 145–157.

24. Cusimano Love, "Globalization, Ethics, and the War on Terrorism," 65–80.

25. Crenshaw, "Why America?" 425.

26. Peter L. Bergen, *Holy War, Inc.: Inside the Secret World of Bin Laden* (New York: The Free Press, 2001), 6.

27. It is ironic that Afghan rebel leader Ahmad Shah Massoud, an ardent opponent of the Taliban government and the al Qaeda camps in his country, was later assassinated by opponents disguised as a camera crew.

28. Bergen, *Holy War, Inc.,* 23.

29. Prime Minister Tony Blair, "Prime Minister's Statement, Bloody Sunday Inquiry," House of Commons Official Report (Jan. 29, 1998), Parliamentary Debates (Hansard) (London); available at <www.bloody-Sunday-inquiry.org.uk/index2.asp?p=7>.

30. Paul Wilkinson, "The Orange and the Green," in Martha Crenshaw (Ed.), *Terrorism, Legitimacy and Power* (Middletown, CT: Wesleyan University Press, 1983), 117.

31. Maryann Cusimano Love, *Public Private Partnerships and Global Problems: Y2K and Cybercrime.* Paper delivered at International Studies Association, Hong Kong meeting, July 2001; Calvin Sims, "Japan Software Suppliers Linked to Sect," *The New York Times,* March 2, 2000, p. A6.

32. Wilkinson, "The Orange and the Green," 120.
33. This section derived from Cusimano Love, "Globalization, Ethics, and the War on Terrorism," 65–80.
34. Stephen E. Flynn, "Beyond Borders," *Foreign Affairs* (Nov.–Dec. 2000): 5–6.
35. Matthew L. Wald, "Fed Ex Shipped a High Radiation Package without Knowledge," *The New York Times,* Jan. 10, 2002.
36. Stephen Flynn, "America the Vulnerable," *Foreign Affairs* (Jan.–Feb. 2002): 60–75.
37. Ibid.
38. Ibid.
39. This section is drawn from Martha Crenshaw, *How Terrorism Ends* (Washington, DC: US Institute of Peace, May 25, 1999); available at <www.usip.org/oc/sr/sr990525/sr990525.html>.
40. US Department of State, *Patterns of Global Terrorism 2000.*
41. This section is drawn from Crenshaw, *How Terrorism Ends.*
42. Martha Crenshaw, "Counterterrorism Policy and the Political Process," *Studies in Conflict & Terrorism* (Oct. 2001): 329–337.
43. Crenshaw, "Organized Disorder," 149; Irving Louis Horowitz, "The Routinization of Terrorism and Its Unanticipated Consequences," in Martha Crenshaw (Ed.), *Terrorism, Legitimacy, and Power* (Middletown, CT: Wesleyan University Press, 1983).
44. Crenshaw, "Organized Disorder," 145.
45. Ibid., 145.
46. Cusimano Love, "Globalization, Ethics, and the War on Terrorism," 65–80; Cusimano Love, "Morality Matters," 7–16.

CHAPTER SIX

Global Crime Inc.

Louise Shelley, John Picarelli, and Chris Corpora

On a sweltering June day, British customs officers inspected a Dutch truck at the British border in Dover. Instead of cargo, they found the bodies of 58 smuggled Chinese men and women inside, apparently suffocated to death in the heat of their sealed container. Testimony in the criminal proceedings revealed that transnational criminal organizations known as "snakeheads," extremely well-organized traffickers of persons from China to countries in Western Europe and other developed regions, charged $20,000 per head to send the group to Great Britain. The network shipped the people with the efficiency of an international business, flying them from Beijing to Belgrade, then transporting them by auto through Hungary, Austria, France, and the Netherlands before placing the group in the sealed container aboard a trans-Channel ferry. On the same day that the courts found the driver of the lorry carrying the doomed migrants guilty, the British Immigration Service issued a report noting that 7 million people each year used smugglers to attempt entry into the European Union, creating $12.3 billion in profits for the trafficking gangs.[1]

INTRODUCTION

The "global mafia," the "next war," a "pax mafiosi," the "dark side of glob-alization," the "illicit global economy," the "retreat of the state"—all are recent terms and expressions in the literature of world politics that describe the appearance of transnational organized crime. However, such crime has a lineage that scholars have traced back to the times of pirates on the high seas and the African slave trade. So is this a new phenomenon or something that scholars of world politics have just begun to notice and explore? Furthermore, what makes the phenomenon "transnational"? Finally, what is the significance of using a term such as *transnational* or, in the context of this volume, *transsovereign?*

These are valid and often asked questions about the study of trans-national organized crime. In the span of some two decades, practitioners and scholars alike have begun to explore and analyze the different activities and processes that compose the phenomenon, developing and revising defi-nitions as they go along. Furthermore, especially in the scholarly realm, we have attempted to explain transnational criminal groups, focusing both within the traditional analytical unit of world politics—the state—as well as the state system. Finally, we have sought to identify objects and methods for responding to these criminal enterprises. This chapter will address these important issues while engaging the debates throughout the literature. It concludes by fashioning a framework for composing strategy that will respond to transnational organized crime.

TRANSNATIONAL ORGANIZED CRIME

Over the past two decades, scholarship that addresses the phenomenon of transnational organized crime has blossomed. In the 1990s, the scholarly lit-erature began a more serious focus on transnational organized crime as a phenomenon unto itself, whereas earlier literatures focused on domestic organized crime or organized criminal activities that span borders, such as the trafficking of narcotics. The scholars and practitioners who have con-tributed to this growing corpus of knowledge have sought to answer fun-damental questions: What is transnational organized crime? Why the label *transnational* versus others such as *international?* What kinds of activities com-pose this area of inquiry? In what ways does transnational organized crime interact with the state? What kinds of approaches are most appropriate for examining transnational organized crime? Each question leads us to important answers that affect the ways we view and approach world politics.

Definitional Issues

One of the first major issues that researchers and practitioners tackled was defining transnational organized crime. The United Nations established the term *transnational crime* more than twenty-five years ago, but it was a catchall term that incorporated some eighteen categories of activity, including terrorism and hijacking, alongside organized crime activities.[2] The distinction between domestic forms of organized crime and transnational organized crime developed from the increased study of narcotics trafficking and the growth in organized crime operating across international borders during the 1980s. The generation of a definition had to overcome traditional and novel hurdles ranging from the minimum number of individuals in a group to the basis for considering a group a transnational criminal entity—decisions that greatly affect the inclusiveness of the definition.

The definition of organized crime has evolved, reflecting the increasing complexity and international nature of the phenomenon. One of the first definitions of organized crime came from US law enforcement, primarily the Federal Bureau of Investigation, which states that organized crime is "continuing and self-perpetuating criminal conspiracy, having an organized structure, fed by fear and corruption, and motivated by greed."[3] With time, the FBI began to use this definition to describe what it referred to as *international* organized crime—that is, organized crime groups operating in more than one country. Note, however, that this definition retains the notion of organized crime operating internationally, and it does not seek to identify the criminal activity as a transnational phenomenon.

Thinking of crime as transnational better illustrates the ways in which these criminal organizations seek to operate outside of the state system— in essence, transcending the sovereignty that organizes the modern state system and leveraging it for their own gain. One of the first to make this distinction was Phil Williams, who in 1996 demonstrated that organized crime was recasting itself by leveraging the changes in global political economy and society being rendered by globalization and the technology revolution.[4] What resulted were criminal organizations that came to "resemble transnational corporations" that operated across the globe from a home base using networked structures to perpetuate their activities, all the while seeing borders as hindering law enforcement more than their own activities.[5]

More recently, the United Nations Convention on Transnational Organized Crime sought to provide a unified definition that is likely to serve as the benchmark for identifying transnational criminal organizations:

> "Organized criminal group" shall mean a structured group of three or more persons, existing for a period of time and acting in concert with the aim of committing one or more serious crimes or offences established in accordance with this Convention, in order to obtain, directly or indirectly, a financial or other material benefit. "Serious crime" shall mean conduct constituting an offence punishable by a maximum deprivation of liberty of at least four years or a more serious penalty. "Structured group" shall mean a group that is not randomly formed for the immediate commission of an offence and that does not need to have formally defined roles for its members, continuity of its membership or a developed structure.... [A]n offence is transnational in nature if: (a) It is committed in more than one state; (b) It is committed in one state but a substantial part of its preparation, planning, direction or control takes place in another state; (c) It is committed in one state but involves an organized criminal group that engages in criminal activities in more than one state; or (d) It is committed in one state but has substantial effects in another state.[6]

The United Nations' definition is one of the most comprehensive, addressing the issue of size, duration, and the transnational nature of criminal groups. Furthermore, it provides the flexibility to examine transnational organized crime outside of such traditional ethnic groups as the Russian Mafiya, Chinese Triads, Japanese Yakuza, and Italian Mafia families.

Transnational Criminal Activities

Transnational criminal activity involves a broad range of activities in both the legitimate and illegitimate sectors of the economy. Some groups function primarily in the illegitimate sector such as drug trafficking groups, whereas others span both sectors of the economy searching for high profits. The massive privatizations of the 1990s have given many transnational organized crime groups a large and important foothold in the economies of their home countries and in many others. Money laundering and corruption, two associated activities, are vital to the conduct of transnational organized crime.

ACTIVITIES

Experts and practitioners have identified more than a dozen criminal activities engaged in by transnational criminal organizations. The major component of most these activities is smuggling of diverse commodities and the provision of illicit goods and services. Narcotics trafficking, as Stephen Flynn details in Chapter 7, is the most common and profitable activity. Many organizations and countries cite narcotics trafficking as the most significant transnational organized crime in terms of annual profits. Furthermore, scholars such as Pino Arlacchi have demonstrated that narcotics trafficking has often served as the gateway for domestic organized crime groups to enter the transnational realm.[7] Hence, it comes as no surprise that the drug trade is often cited as the most commonly known transnational organized criminal activity.

The next most significant transnational organized crimes are trafficking in persons and in arms. An important distinction characterizes these forms of organized crime. Arms deliveries involve the transfer of inanimate goods that are used to commit other crimes or to arm regional conflicts. In contrast, trafficking in persons involves the movement of live human beings who are exploited continuously after their delivery. Likewise, human trafficking provides ongoing revenues for transnational organized crime, whereas the arms trade, if it is to be sustained, requires the perpetuation of conflict.

Trafficking in persons generally encompasses two related activities: migrant smuggling and the trafficking of persons for the purpose of exploitation. In short, both activities involve the recruitment, movement, and delivery of migrants from a host to a destination state. What separates the two activities, however, is that the traffickers enslave and exploit trafficked persons, while smuggled migrants are often freed at the end of their journey, often after a period of indentured servitude. The profits from such activities are significant and rising. The International Organization for Migration estimates that profits of $7 billion were made from trafficking in persons in 1997.[8] Crafting even inexact estimates of the number of people trafficked annually is difficult at best, and thus few solid estimates exist. Yet most every expert on trafficking in persons, practitioner and scholar alike, agrees that the problem is significant and increasing as both demand and supply are rising. The rise in demand for cheap services and labor in developed countries and the growth of population in developing countries without adequate employment will result in a rise in this phenomenon in coming decades.

Trafficking and smuggling in persons is pernicious because of both the large profits and the physical and emotional toll it takes on the victims. Numerous trafficking studies note the physical violence and mental strain that victims suffer at the hands of their captors. For example, it is not uncommon for these victims to become addicted to alcohol or narcotics, contract HIV and AIDS or other diseases, or die from strain or violence. Those that do survive often face difficult and time-consuming recoveries.

Finally, scholars note that transnational criminal organizations are increasingly engaging in the trafficking in persons. A range of transnational criminal organizations are trafficking in persons, particularly Chinese Triads, Thais, Indian, Pakistani, Russian-speaking, and Balkan organized crime groups.[9] Russian-speaking and Thai groups are particularly active in trafficking in women for the sex trade.[10] Russian-speaking groups often work with their counterparts in Asia and in the Balkans and Western Europe. None of this activity can function without the complicity of some law enforcement and the corruption of officials in source, transit, and destination countries. This telling quote from Kevin Bales also applies outside the Thai context: "To be sure, a brothel owner may have some ties to organized crime, but in Thailand organized crime includes the police and much of the government. Indeed, the work of the modern slaveholder is best seen not as aberrant criminality but as a perfect example of disinterested capitalism."[11]

Arms trafficking is another significant form of transnational organized crime. The rise of regional conflicts in the postwar era has provided transnational organized crime groups with a huge market for small arms. In some cases, transnational organized crime groups help foment regional conflict to increase demand for weapons.[12] This has been particularly true in Africa but also applies in the Balkans, Latin America, and Asia. Many of the weapons come from former Soviet states and Eastern Europe. The trafficking in arms has also led to an insidious partnership between military forces and mafia groups, especially in the post-Soviet transition states of Eastern Europe and the former Soviet Union. Graham Turbiville, Jr., for example, outlines the ways in which organized crime and the Russian military coalesced after the end of the Soviet Union, going so far as to refer to the Russian armed forces as "mafia in uniform."[13]

Transnational criminal organizations have found a niche supplying arms to areas suffering from continued conflict with small arms and even major arms systems. Organized crime has also positioned itself as the arms supplier of last resort, oftentimes delivering arms to regions under arms embargo. For example, in April 2001, Italian authorities arrested members of a Russian and Ukrainian criminal network that, for more than seven years, had supplied more than 13,500 tons of arms, including thousands of assault rifles and hundreds of missiles and antitank shells, to groups fighting in the Balkans, including the Croatian army.[14] Italian authorities then dismantled a similar Russian organized crime controlled network soon after that was supplying arms to Charles Taylor's forces in Sierra Leone.[15]

The largest profits for organized crime have been in the small weapons area, but the threat of organized crime trafficking in nuclear materials and biological and chemical weapons remains a major concern. Rensselaer Lee III and James Ford have identified organized crime as a potential facilitator for the theft and smuggling of strategic weapons and materials.[16] In the end, transnational organized crime involvement in arms smuggling is a major concern for states and international organizations concerned with maintaining international security and peace.

Smuggling and trade-related transnational criminal activities are a major profit source for transnational organized crime. For example, trade in cigarettes, once a national trade, has been internationalized by transnational criminal groups, who often work with legitimate cigarette manufacturers to obtain their commodities. These links between crime groups and legitimate corporations are now the subject of major criminal investigations within the European community.[17] Such illicit trade also thrives across the US–Canadian border.[18] Furthermore, organized crime groups are important actors internationally in the illicit trade in environmental products, ranging from banned chlorofluorocarbon-based refrigerants to toxic waste and even endangered fauna and flora.[19] Likewise, scholars have identified transnational organized crime as a player in the theft and smuggling of art and antiquities.[20] Finally, there is the smuggling of stolen automobiles, an activity that is especially prevalent in central Europe and the southwestern United States.[21] Roughly $1 billion worth of stolen vehicles is removed from the United States annually and sent to other countries.[22]

The return of a trade-related organized criminal activity that many had thought was relegated to the past—the piracy of ships in international waters—also involves the activities of transnational criminal organizations. Pirating now benefits from cheaply available global technologies. "One pirate ship captured recently in Indonesia was outfitted with bogus immigration stamps, tools to forge ship documents, and sophisticated radar, communications, and satellite-tracking equipment."[23] According to the International Chamber of Commerce, a piracy incident reporting clearinghouse, ship seizures increased 57 percent in 2000 over the previous year's numbers and were significantly more than 400 percent higher from 1991 numbers.[24] Organized crime is closely linked to these incidents, either conducting the piracy itself or supporting piracy. The benefits for the organized crime groups are significant as they can move cargo and illegal immigrants and engage in insurance fraud. The problem is most pronounced in Asia but also is common in Latin America and Africa. The crime groups are increasingly focusing on the theft of high-technology cargo.[25] Hijacking of cargo is not confined to the sea. Analysts have identified transnational organized crime involvement in the theft of land-based cargo, such as hijackings of truck and rail cargo.[26]

Many significant transnational criminal activities are now linked to the licit economy. Fraud scams originating in western Africa, primarily Nigeria, use official-looking fax and electronic mail correspondence to obtain banking information from victims that is then used to steal funds from their accounts.[27] Transnational criminal organizations have also engaged in massive credit card and identity theft rings using stolen account numbers and identities to amass millions in fraudulent charges. Recent arrests in Spain of members of a terrorist cell revealed that they supported themselves by producing fraudulent documents and airplane tickets.[28] Al Qaeda profited from heroin trafficking. Therefore, organized crime for profit not only is the domain of criminals who seek profits but also is being used by politically motivated groups.

Crime groups cash counterfeit checks, trade in bearer bonds, and manipulate the stock market in the United States, Canada, and Italy. Asian organized crime groups operating in Las Vegas were earning close to $500,000 monthly from the cashing of counterfeit checks in casinos.[29] Finally, some organized crime groups in the United States have recently infiltrated the US stock markets, purchasing or creating their own brokerage houses to engage in "pump and dump" and other types of stock manipulations for illicit gains. For example, a recent scandal occurred in Canadian markets with the manipulation of stocks by Russian organized crime in the metals trade. Italian organized crime, according to Italian investigators, is now also active in market manipulation.[30]

Violence and corruption, the traditional methods of organized crime once applied on the local level, are now being applied internationally. Protection rackets, the backbone of domestic organized crime groups, have been retained as an important activity for transnational criminal organizations, who also frequently engage in contract killings for profit or power projection. For example, the use of violence for protection rackets and other purposes is referred to as the "defining characteristic" of Asian organized crime groups operating in the United States.[31] Furthermore, Russian-speaking organized crime groups have used threats of violence to extort Russian hockey players in the National Hockey League.[32] Contract killers have been sent from Russia to carry out their hits and returned home after carrying out their missions.

A significant area of growth for transnational criminal activity is within the realm of information and high technology. Just as pirates are now focusing on high technology cargo, criminals are realizing high profits from pursuing the hardware of technology, and their Internet schemes reveal their capacity to engage in cybercrime.[33] For example, John Picarelli and Phil Williams have identified several ways criminals can use information technology as a criminal milieu, as a tool, and even as a weapon to further their activities.[34] Likewise, a recent conference that examined the ways in which organized crime, terrorist, and other groups use information technology noted that such technology can assist in the conduct of traditional criminal activities as well as serve as the gateway to new criminal endeavors. For example, panelists noted that Nigerian criminal gangs were abandoning fax machines and using e-mail in their elaborate fraud schemes, and that criminal groups were becoming increasingly involved in the piracy of intellectual property such as compact discs and computer software.[35] Finally, Richard Love notes in Chapter 8 how criminal organizations are operating online rather than in the bricks and mortar world.

Supporting Activities

Transnational criminal activity cannot survive solely in the illicit realm. Its profits must be moved into the legitimate economy to be invested. Furthermore, it requires corruption to function—to fend off arrests, obtain lucrative contracts, and obtain legitimacy in the community.

MONEY LAUNDERING

Money laundering is a universal and crucial activity for transnational criminal organizations. The previous section described the numerous methods by which transnational organized crime generates profits. These profits remain useless, however, unless the criminal groups can somehow place them into the licit global financial infrastructure without the knowledge of law enforcement or regulators. Hence, almost all transnational criminal organizations engage in some form of money laundering to dispose of their profits.

Money laundering has increased in both scope and sophistication. Although the estimates of global money laundering have continued to prove difficult to quantify, estimates of $500 billion to $1 trillion annually is a commonly held figure.[36] More anecdotal estimates provide a basis to demonstrate the significant size of money laundering. For example, in 1995 Australian officials estimated that close to $3 billion of laundered funds passed through their country.[37] Canada recently estimated that laundered funds from the narcotics industry alone accounted for roughly $5 billion to $14 billion annually from Canada.[38]

The methods that money launderers use range from placement in the licit financial sector through phony corporations, bank accounts, and the use of offshore banking centers to less traditional means such as using Internet-based banking and informal banking systems, including the *hawala*.[39] This informal remittance system is used to move funds into and from South Asia and the Middle East, and it has recently gained attention because of its uses by terrorist organizations such as al Qaeda.[40] One study showed that because increases in crime have recently been coupled with a decrease in the demand for currency, money launderers apparently are "moving away from the banking system and cash and toward parallel financial markets, sophisticated nonmonetary instruments (such as derivatives), and possibly barter (such as an exchange of boats and guns for drugs)."[41]

In the end, money laundering is the bridge that connects the illicit and licit global economies. Money laundering uses licit financial markets as a method of transfer and placement for illicit funds. Such activities, more importantly, skew economic indicators and policy in significant ways. Tanzi, for example, demonstrates that large capital inflows and outflows from money laundering affect interest rates, that the demand for dollars from money launderers supports an implicit seigniorage for US currency markets, and that money laundering generates distrust in markets, which then amplifies reactions to rumors or false statements.[42]

In recent years, international investigations have gone after the proceeds of organized crime. In the United States and Switzerland, more than $1 billion has been seized from drug traffickers and other criminal groups. Most of the proceeds of the drug trade have gone into the national treasuries of the countries where they have been seized. In Italy, unique legislation authorizes the use of seized assets for community development and drug treatment.[43]

CORRUPTION

Corruption is an important tool for organized crime, and transnational organized crime groups have exploited such relationships with politicians and government officials. Put broadly, corruption is "the misuse of office for personal gain" and "means charging an illicit price for a service or using the power of office to further illicit aims."[44] Corruption differs from clientalism in that the latter retains a vertical separation between the patron and is based on an exchange for unspecified services. Corruption blurs the line between the state and transnational criminal organizations. Some states are so thoroughly corrupt that scholars refer to them as criminal states.

Two significant and related phenomena are important for our purposes—political and economic corruption. Political corruption has received strong consideration in the literature. Only recently, however, have the links between political corruption and organized crime been analyzed—for example, the differing views on the connections between corruption[45] and political parties.[46]

Economic corruption hinges on the desire for industries to collude and establish cartels within markets, as when firms use organized crime to organize and maintain cartels among them.[47] Still, virtually no study has tackled the thorny issue of corruption within the sector of international development aid—a significant oversight given recent scandals involving skimming from aid contracts.[48]

For what ends does organized crime engage in corruption? To answer this, we refer to the triangular relationship between organized crime, the state (i.e., government), and firms.[49] Organized crime provides electoral support and intimidation powers to politicians in return for protection and legitimization of its activities. Likewise, organized crime provides protection and assistance with cartels in return for money. Finally, an important part of this equation is public contracts, which politicians can use to seek rents from both firms and criminal organizations. In turn, these contracts are a major source of mafia profits. Hence, corruption is a key factor to consider when we analyze the behavior of transnational criminal organizations.

EXPLAINING TRANSNATIONAL ORGANIZED CRIME

Transnational crime, once neglected in the study of International Relations, is now studied in different parts of the discipline because of its far-reaching effects on political systems, national sovereignty, and international political economy. The relationship between transnational crime and the state is central to this entire analysis. The following section surveys some of the approaches to studying transnational crime. Such crime can be considered from two levels of analysis: the community level and the international level with globalization.

A significant difference exists between the strategic studies literature that identifies transnational organized crime as a threat to the industrialized world and world order and the literature that focuses on the societal level at which transnational organized crime operates, shaped by the local community. Whereas organized crime has proliferated with globalization, many of the groups are still deeply entrenched in their home societies where their effects are particularly strong. It is important to consider both aspects when calculating effective responses.

Internal Analysis: Trust and Civil Society

Organized crime usually develops and operates in areas where civil society is weak or nonexistent. For example, in a landmark study, Robert Putnam describes how civil society arose in northern Italy but failed to take hold in southern regions where four organized crime groups are based.[50] In another example, Russian-speaking organized crime has emerged with potency in the states of the former Soviet Union where the communists wiped out all elements of civil society.[51]

Other related factors are trust in intrapersonal societal relations and the effects of trust on governance.[52] Weak states have poorly formed civil societies, which leads to a lack of trust in the state and a dependence on surrogate actors to address civic needs. For example, organized crime in Sicily arose when state control was absent; organized crime substituted itself for the state and provided the protection that substituted for trust in society.[53]

Trust and civil society factors help explain how transnational criminal organizations embed themselves within societal structures. A successful response must consider the societal context within which crime groups operate, particularly within the state, and at the local level where they are based. For example, Sicilian society has mobilized against the Mafia for the past century.[54] In recent decades, the movement has mobilized all levels of society simultaneously and has attempted to reeducate citizens at the local level on the need for alternatives to the Mafia. The primary objective of nearly all the anti-Mafia associations is to educate children to know and respect the law and to prevent them form acquiring a "Mafia mentality" of distrust and antagonism towards public institutions which may lead to a life of crime.[55] Such programs were introduced in the early 1980s by the first anti-Mafia groups but obtained additional impetus in the early 1990s in response to the Anti-Mafia Commission and the pressures of the mass anti-Mafia organizations of civil society. Libera, the umbrella of 800 nationwide anti-Mafia organizations, works with urban communities, schools, and the Church to implement anti-Mafia curricula.[56]

External Analysis: Globalization

Globalization is a key factor in the rise of transnational organized crime. There are several competing notions regarding how to theorize transnationality, marking a different way to configure social spaces.[57] Transnational organized crime cuts across the globalization discourse, ranging from notions of informal markets and new authoritarianism to ideas about global criminal networks.[58] The majority of the globalization literature captures transnational phenomena as dynamic, cross-sectoral, and embedded in global markets, making the concept more than a new level of analysis.

Globalization provides a theoretical boost to historical notions of national or international organized crime, emphasizing the ascendance of nonstate actors as legitimate objects of political inquiry. However, the concept of globalization is far from a settled theory and stirs great debate, ranging from downplay, through social transformation, to near chaos or turbulence.[59]

The categories of state, economics, and institutional structures are useful for capturing the majority of analysis on transnational organized crime in the globalization context. Globalization benefits the capabilities, resources, and strategies that are available to transnational organized crime.

The neoliberal understanding of globalization stresses the role that global free market capitalism and representative democracy play in making the world richer, more connected, and peaceful, as represented in the writings of Francis Fukuyama and traditional political economic interpretations.[60] In this light, transnational organized crime and other similar issues often are seen as the last vestiges of resistance to this "new world order" that eventually will be brought under control.[61]

STATES

What effects are globalization processes having on the modern state? These academic discussions directly affect our consideration of transnational organized crime. For example, Saskia Sassen posits that globalization is transforming the logic of sovereignty without eliminating the role of the state,[62] a view shared by James Mittelman and James Rosenau. Combined with weak state scenarios, such as Robert Jackson's concept of "negative sovereignty" and Susan Strange's "retreat of the state," these provide the theoretical backbone for analyzing transnational organized crime and corruption in the globalization context.[63]

Most often, scholars have posited that the weakening of state structures, either caused or enhanced through globalization processes, has created spaces that have allowed transnational organized crime to flourish.[64] Louise Shelley has examined the interplay of weakened states, civil society, and transnational organized crime, viewing criminal groups as taking advantage of new technologies and global opportunities to amplify the weakening of states.[65] Nikos Passas finds that the demise of states is a necessary part of the globalization process because it erodes the bonds of trust between state and citizenry and provides transnational organized crime with the opportunity to play surrogate for the state.[66] Peter Andreas points out how globalization processes, embodied in the form of NAFTA, directly affected the increase of transnational organized crime in Mexico by liberalizing markets without sufficient regulation and oversight.[67]

ECONOMY

The political economic approach addresses how the "illicit global economy" affects the state and the licit economy.[68] For example, the illicit Colombian economy distorts the legal economy.[69] Economic markets shape transnational organized crime, taking organizational form based on the economic context.[70] Transnational business strategies of the illicit actors increasingly mirror those in the licit economy. Specialists such as lawyers, accountants, and transportation experts now work for organized crime as they do for the legitimate economy.[71]

As the share of the international economy controlled by organized crime increases, there will necessarily be more attention to the political economy of the drug trade and other diverse forms of illicit activity. Especially since September 11, the interaction of the illicit and licit economies is receiving greater attention.

Hybrid Analysis: Security Studies

The security studies literature views organized crime as a threat. Its involvement in the weapons trade, its deleterious effects on state sovereignty, and its corruption of state structures are seen as serious threats to individual states, regional stability, and the international order. Security scholars have used several methods to explore the threat transnational organized crime poses to people, the nation-state, and global stability. Researchers of the "Copenhagen School" focus on how threats are formed and the effects they have across the social experience,[72] providing a flexible approach for looking at a broader spectrum of threats.[73] The military and state continues to be an important sector, but they are evaluated in conjunction with the economic, societal, and environmental sectors. Transnational organized crime and other negative consequences of globalization are seen as a cross-sectoral threat.

Phil Williams believes the organizational technology of networking has led to the most prolific advancement of transnational organized crime. These transnational organized crime network structures crisscross state borders and institutional boundaries, creating a nearly indecipherable web of nodes and illicit relations. These networks tie into other related networks in this clandestine space, increasing transnational organized crime's capabilities to resist interdiction and, in some cases, launch offensives against coercive state institutions.[74]

Transnational organized crime as a security threat appears most prominently in the literature of asymmetric threats, a view that has obtained more currency since September 11, 2001. Rogue states, terrorist networks, and transnational organized crime enter into alliances, creating asymmetric military threats that exploit the globalization of democracy and free market capitalism. Much of the analysis of these asymmetric alliances focuses on their capacity to acquire and deploy weapons of mass destruction.[75] Such plans or activities must be met with strong force because they are seen as threats to the survival of the West. The events of September 11 make this argument much more palatable to some, especially as evidence grows concerning the global reach and integration of the al Qaeda network.

MULTIPLE APPROACHES ARE NEEDED

Transnational crime operates on the global level but is embedded in many societies at the local level. International policies that address transnational crime at only a single level are doomed to failure. As the previous analysis has indicated, a multidisciplinary perspective is needed to understand transnational crime—one that incorporates economic, social, political, and strategic studies analyses. Yet these perspectives must also include an understanding of the historical and cultural context that led to the rise of organized crime groups in particular locales. Transnational crime has local and global, societal and state components. Effective responses to manage transnational crime must deal with each of these elements.

Globalization helps to turn once locally and regionally contained phenomena into transnational crime problems. The profits and effects of these groups are so significant in some regions that they pose threats to nation-states and undermine the national sovereignty of many countries. The global illicit trade has assumed massive proportions, and its effects are particularly great in smaller economies where the profits of this illegal trade can undermine and distort the economy. For example, tax rates escalate as the size of the illegal economy grows. Because less economic activity is conducted in the sphere where states can levy taxes, states raise rates on the remaining licit economy to recoup lost tax income and sustain government budgets. In a vicious circle, government's attempts to sustain its revenue base can push more businesses into the illicit economy (through fraud, tax evasion, and transfer pricing) to avoid the high tax rates in the licit economy. Weakened state treasuries reduce the resources that are available to states to fight organized crime.

Organized crime is necessarily, in part, a covert phenomenon. Therefore, analysis and information on the phenomenon is partial and often misinterpreted by individuals who do not understand the context in which it functions. Policy makers from one arena—law enforcement, economics, or security studies—often believe that their perspective holds the "answer" without understanding that a multidisciplinary approach is needed.

Effective strategies to control and contain transnational crime cannot address only one aspect. For example, as peacekeepers have discovered in the Balkans, Colombia, and elsewhere, transnational crime groups are now the defining actors in the political environment. Traditional military strategies cannot be used to contain their activities. As anti-Mafia activists have discovered in Sicily, the legal system can prosecute and isolate the Mafia bosses, but civil society must change community attitudes toward organized crime and must prove to the citizens of their island that there are tangible benefits for them in fighting organized crime.

CONCLUSION: A WAY AHEAD?

We propose the following framework for addressing the transnational organized crime problem through a dynamic and multidisciplinary perspective. First, any serious researcher or policy maker must ask the following questions before developing a policy. What is the process of social transformation at play? What unique and general aspects of a particular manifestation of transnational organized crime are present in the local context, and how are they embedded within it? How does the transnational crime group connect with regional, international, and multilateral actors of the legitimate and illegitimate economy? To what extent does the community understand the problems of transnational crime and have the willingness and the capacity to help address the problem? What are the costs on the local, regional, and national level of the group's continued criminality?

Because globalization reshapes both international dynamics and the local community, attempts to manage transnational organized crime must acknowledge both levels. Part of this process of social transformation is that time, space, and boundaries are collapsed or compacted. Relationships on an international scale occur more rapidly and commercial relations are more frequent. The illicit can be facilitated and more easily commingled with the licit. On the local level, culture, ideas and society are affected. Local control can be challenged in weak states (places where significant social upheaval exists), which leads to deeper divisions. Therefore, transnational groups face fewer obstacles on the local level and more ability to operate in the global economic environment.

Individual states cannot solve their problems alone. Whether one considers the rise of the European Union, the collapse of border controls of the once territorially immense Soviet state, or the rise of regional conflicts that blur national distinctions, states alone are less important. All of these changes have provided opportunities for transnational crime to work and to expand its operations. With globalization, the central state in many countries has become a less effective institution of control. It cannot sufficiently absorb the shocks, limit the dislocations, or regulate the transformation. Deepening local insecurity further strains the bonds of trust between state and citizen.

Under these circumstances, resistance to social transformation, like that found within globalization, can create the space for the proliferation of organized crime and corruption in a given locale. Local control is assumed, and services are rendered through an informal transaction between people playing the roles of criminal and citizen in exchange for certain rents and permissions. Crime groups based in the local community are not impervious to the logic of global social transformation, which changes the organization and its methods of operation. The transformation of organized criminality into a transnational phenomenon is often a logical response to the effects of globalization on the local level.

Understanding transnational crime at the different levels at which it operates requires the engagement of many different sectors of the policy and legal communities, civil society, and the media. Transnational crime groups often provide services at the local level and fulfill demands for illicit commodities and cheap services at the international level. Therefore, any strategy to address transnational crime must convince individuals that it is not in their interest to support or be complicit in its operations. To achieve this objective, media must be mobilized, independent, and supported in their efforts to report on this phenomenon. Civil society must be mobilized to address transnational crime, a mobilization that often comes only with enormous personal loss and even tragedy. Finally, legal measures must be harmonized. This includes both the criminal codes and the procedures needed to combat transnational crime. For example, much has been achieved in this area in money laundering, but the passage of needed legislation is not sufficient. Unless implementation strategies are achieved, laws remain on the books and have no practical effects.

A resource and intelligence gap divides the capacity of developed and developing and transitional countries from addressing the range of problems caused by organized crime. Affluent societies have the legal tools, personnel, and intelligence resources to pursue transnational criminals. Less affluent societies that are faced with critical health, social welfare, and other concerns often cannot allocate the financial and human resources to address transnational organized crime. Unless strategies address the enormous capacity gaps that exist between developed countries and the rest of the world, there can be little success in achieving a global effort to address this issue.

Transnational crime groups are major actors in areas with significant regional conflicts. The demand for arms and quick profits and the lack of territorial control are fertile grounds for the rise of organized crime. Unless military and peacekeepers begin to integrate the problem of transnational crime into their strategies for conflict management, the problem will undermine conflict resolution and postconflict stability.

The organized crime and corruption issues have not traditionally been part of the discourse of international relations, strategic studies, or economic development. Until these elements are integrated into these disciplines and policy planning, organized crime will continue to proliferate. Incorporating these problems into the needed framework is not a guarantee of success, but the failure to address them ensures their continued growth.

Transnational crime and corruption are not merely peripheral problems. They are central issues that need to be treated as such. September 11 was a wake up call. Although terrorism is distinct from transnational organized crime, the ability of terrorists to support themselves through transnational criminal activity provides an important lesson. Transnational crime has repercussions that far exceed the individual crime of document fraud, criminal abuse of the Internet, or trafficking in small arms. These issues merit far more attention in all spheres of education, research, and policy in the international community.

ENDNOTES

1. Reuters, "Britain's Straw Says Truck Deaths a Warning," June 19, 2000; Warren Hoge, "Trucker Found Guilty in Death of Immigrants," *The New York Times,* April 5, 2001, p. A6.
2. See Gerhard O.W. Mueller, "Transnational Crime: Definitions and Concepts," *Transnational Organized Crime* 4(3–4): 13–21.
3. National Security Council, International Crime Threat Assessment Web site (<www.terrorism.com/documents/pub45270/pub45270chap1.html>).
4. Phil Williams, "Transnational Criminal Organizations and International Security," *Survival,* 36(1): 96–113.
5. Ibid., 97.
6. UN General Assembly, "Convention against Transnational Organized Crime," Nov. 2, 2001 (New York: United Nations Publications), 25–26.
7. Pino Arlacchi, *Mafia Business: The Mafia Ethic and the Spirit of Capitalism* (London: Verso, 1986), 187–210.
8. David Kyle and Rey Koslowski, "Introduction," in David Kyle and Rey Koslowski (Eds.), *Global Human Smuggling* (Baltimore: Johns Hopkins University Press, 2001), 4.
9. Amy O'Neill, *International Trafficking in Women to the United States: A Contemporary Manifestation of Slavery* (Washington, DC: Center for the Study of Intelligence, 1999), 55–62; Donna Hughes, "The 'Natasha' Trade: The Transnational Shadow Market of Trafficking in Women" (available at <www.uri.edu/artsci/wms/hughes/natasha.htm>).
10. James O. Finckenauer, "Russian Transnational Organized Crime and Human Trafficking," in Kyle and Koslowski (Eds.), *Global Human Smuggling,* 166–186; Pasuk Phongpaichit, "Trafficking in People in Thailand," *Transnational Organized Crime,* 3(4): 74–104.
11. Kevin Bales, *Disposable People* (Berkeley: University of California Press, 1999), 50.

12. See World Bank, "Understanding Civil War, Crime and Violence through Economic Research" (at <www.worldbank.org/research/conflict>) for research papers that discuss this relationship.

13. Graham Turbiville, Jr., "Organized Crime and the Russian Armed Forces," *Transnational Organized Crime,* 1(4): 57–104 (quote on 62–63).

14. CNN, "Italy Cracks Arms Smuggling Network," 19 April 2001.

15. Jon Swain and John Follain, "Sierra Leone Arms Ring Broken," *Sunday Times* (UK), July 8, 2001, p. N24.

16. Rensselaer Lee, III, *Smuggling Armageddon* (New York: St. Martin's Griffin, 1998), 47–72. See also Phil Williams and Paul Woessner, "Nuclear Material Trafficking: An Interim Assessment," *Transnational Organized Crime,* 1(2): 206–238.

17. See *Guardian,* "BAT Exposé" (special report) (available at <www.guardian.co.uk/bat/ 0,2759,191282,00.html>); and the International Consortium for Investigative Journalists, "Tobacco Companies Linked to Criminal Organizations in Lucrative Cigarette Smuggling" (available at <www.public-i.org/story_01_030301.htm>).

18. Criminal Intelligence Service Canada, "Contraband Smuggling" (2001 annual report) (available at <www.cisc.gc.ca/AnnualReport2001/Cisc2001/contraband2001.html>).

19. Svend Søyland, "Criminal Organizations and Crimes against the Environment," report for the UN Interregional Crime & Justice Research Institute, June 2000; available at <www.unicri.it/pdf/cocae.pdf>.

20. Lauren L. Bernick, "Art and Antiquities Theft," *Transnational Organized Crime,* 4(2): 91–116.

21. Royal Canadian Mounted Police, "Organized Crime and Automobile Theft," Sept. 1, 1998 (available at <www.rcmp-grc.gc.ca/crim_int/sparkplugeng.html>); Rosalva Resendiz and David M. Neal, "International Auto Theft: The Illegal Export of American Vehicles to Mexico," in Delbert Rounds (Ed.), *International Criminal Justice: Issues in a Global Perspective* (Boston: Allyn & Bacon, 1998), 7–18; Interpol, "Vehicle Crime Profits Can Be Used to Support Terrorist Organizations, Interpol's Chief Says," Nov. 19, 2001 (available at <www.interpol.int/Public/ICPO/PressReleases/PR2001/ PR200136.asp>).

22. Anthony Lake, *Six Nightmares: Real Threats in a Dangerous World and How America Can Meet Them* (New York: Little, Brown, 2000), 46.

23. Kevin Sullivan and Mary Jordan, "High Tech Pirates Ravage Asian Seas, *Washington Post,* July 5, 1999, p. A18.

24. International Chamber of Commerce, "Piracy Attacks Rise to Alarming New Levels, ICC Report Reveals," Feb. 1, 2001; available at <www.iccwbo.org/ccs/news_archives/ 2001/piracy_report.asp>.

25. "Overview Maritime Crime," *Trends in Organized Crime,* 3(4): 68–71.

26. Julie Salzano and Stephen Hartman, "Cargo Crime," *Transnational Organized Crime,* 3(1): 39–49.

27. US Department of State, Bureau of International Narcotics and Law Enforcement, "Before You Go" (information on Nigerian advanced fee fraud), April 1997; available at <www.state.gov/www/regions/africa/naffpub.pdf>.

28. "Spain Arrests Members of Terrorist Cell," *The New York Times,* Sept. 26, 2001, p. B4.

29. Karen Zekan, "Chinese Crime Ring Ripping off Strip," *Las Vegas Sun,* Jan. 21, 1999; available at <www.lasvegassun.com/sunbin/stories/text/1999/jan/21/508304597. html>.

30. See Nichole Christian, "Officials Say Stock Scheme Raised Money for the Mob," *The New York Times,* March 9, 2001, p. B3; and Thomas V. Fuentes, "Organized Crime: Statement on the Record Before House Subcommittee on Finance and Hazardous Materials," Sept. 13, 2000 (available at <www.fbi.gov/congress/congress00/fuentes. htm>).

31. James O. Finckenauer, "Chinese Transnational Organized Crime: The Fuk Ching" (report to the UN National Institute of Justice, International Center); available at <www.ojp.usdoj.gov/nij/international/chinese.html>.

32. Robert I. Friedman, *Red Mafiya* (Boston: Little, Brown, 2000), 173–201.

33. PN Grabosky and Russell Smith, *Crime in the Digital Age: Controlling Telecommunications and Cyberspace Illegalities* (Brunswick, NJ: Transaction, 1998).

34. John Picarelli and Phil Williams, "Information Technologies and Transnational Organized Crime," in David Alberts and Dan Papp (Eds.), *Information Age Anthology: National Security Implications of the Information Age,* Vol. II (Washington, DC: NDU Press, 2000), 365–402.

35. Transnational Crime and Corruption Center, *Transnational Crime, Corruption, and Information Technology* (2000 Annual Conference Report), 4–5; available at <www. american.edu/transcrime/pdfs/TC&IT_2000_Report.PDF>.

36. Raymond Baker, "The Biggest Loophole in the Free Market System," *Washington Quarterly,* 22(4): 30.

37. Financial Action Task Force on Money Laundering, "1996–1997 Report on Money Laundering Typologies," Feb. 1997, 3; available at <www1.oecd.org/fatf/pdf/ TY1997_en.pdf>.

38. Samuel Porteous, *Organized Crime Impact Study Highlights* (Ottawa: Public Works and Government Services of Canada, 1998); available at <www.sgc.gc.ca/EPub/Pol/ e1998orgcrim/e1998orgcrim.htm>.

39. Nikos Passas, *Informal Value Transfer Systems and Criminal Organizations* (The Hague, Neth.: Netherlands Ministry of Justice Research and Documentation Center, 1999), 13–16.

40. Kathleen Day, "U.S. Islamic Cash Outlets Investigated: 'Hawalas' Suspected in Terror Funding," *Washington Post,* Nov. 7, 2001, p. A1; and Vincent Schodolski, "Terror Networks Rely on 'Hawala,'" *Chicago Tribune,* Sept. 26, 2001, p. 10.

41. Peter Quirk, "Money Laundering: Muddying the Macroeconomy," *Finance and Development,* 34(1); available at <www.worldbank.org/fandd/english/0397/articles/ 0110397.htm>.

42. Vito Tanzi, "Macroeconomic Implications to Money Laundering," in Ernesto Savona (Ed.), *Responding to Money Laundering: International Perspectives* (Netherlands: Harwood Academic, 1997), 91–106.

43. Alison Jamieson, *The Antimafia: Italy's Fight Against Organized Crime* (London: Macmillan, 2000), 128–129, 144.

44. Robert Klitgaard, R. Maclean-Abaroa, and H. L. Parris, *Corrupt Cities: A Practical Guide to Cure and Prevention* (Oakland, CA: Institute for Contemporary Studies, 2000), 2.

45. Samuel Huntington, *Political Order in Changing Societies* (New Haven, CT: Yale University Press, 1969), 59–71.

46. Donnatella Della Porta and Yves Meny, "Conclusion," in Donnatella Della Porta and Yves Meny (Eds.), *Democracy and Corruption in Europe* (London: Pinter, 1997), 166–180.

47. Diego Gambetta and Peter Reuter, "Conspiracy among the Many: The Mafia in Legitimate Business," in Gianluca Fiorentini and Sam Peltzman (Eds.), *The Economics of Organized Crime* (Cambridge, UK: Cambridge University Press, 1995), 116–135.

48. Karen DeYoung and Kevin Sullivan, "Bush Urges Nations to Use Aid as Tool against Corruption," *Washington Post*, March 23, 2002, p. A14; Neil Levine, "Fighting Corruption in Foreign Aid," speech at Second Global Forum on Fighting Corruption and Safeguarding Integrity, The Hague, Netherlands, May 29, 2001.

49. The concept is taken from Donnatella Della Porta and Alberto Vannucci, *Corrupt Exchanges: Actors, Resources, and Mechanisms of Political Corruption* (New York: Aldine de Gruyter, 1999), 236–240.

50. Robert Putnam, Robert Leonardi, and Raffaella Y. Nanetti, *Making Democracy Work* (Princeton, NJ: Princeton University Press, 1993).

51. Louise Shelley, "Post-Soviet Organized Crime," *Demokratizatsiya,* 2(3), 354–355.

52. See Valerie Braithewaite and Margaret Levi (Eds.), *Trust and Governance* (New York: Russell Sage Foundation, 1998); and Francis Fukuyama, *Trust: The Social Virtues and the Creation of Prosperity* (New York: The Free Press, 1995).

53. Louise Shelley, "Mafia and the Italian State: The Historical Roots of the Current Crisis," *Sociological Forum,* 9(4): 661–672. For more, see Raimondo Catanzaro, *Men of Respect: A Social History of the Sicilian Mafia* (New York: The Free Press, 1992), and Diego Gambetta, *The Sicilian Mafia: The Business of Private Protection* (Cambridge: Harvard University Press, 1993).

54. Umberto Santino, *Storia del movimento antimafia* (Rome: Editori Riuniti, 2000).

55. Jamieson, *The Antimafia,* 148.

56. Rita Borsellino, "In Spite of Everything: The Popular Anti-Mafia Commitment in Sicily," *Trends in Organized Crime,* 5(3): 58–63.

57. For a representation of the treatment of complexity, see Saskia Sassen, *Globalization and Its Discontents* (New York: New Press, 1998); Gwyn Prins, "Notes Toward the Definition of Global Security," *American Behavioral Scientist* (May 1995): 820–821; Robert D. Kaplan, "The Coming Anarchy: How Scarcity, Crime, Overpopulation, Tribalism, and Disease Are Destroying the Social Fabric of Our Planet," *Atlantic Monthly* (Feb. 1994): 44–76.

58. Sassen, *Globalization,* 153–158; Louise I. Shelley, "Transnational Organized Crime: The New Authoritarianism," in H. Richard Friman and Peter Andreas (Eds.), *The Illicit Global Economy and State Power* (Lanham, MD: Rowman & Littlefield, 1999), 26–33; Phil Williams, "The Nature of Drug Trafficking Networks," *Current History*, 97(618): 155.

59. The globalization debate is wide, contentious, and marked by a variety of skeptics and believers. For further treatment, see Paul Hirst and Grahame Thompson, *Globalization in Question* (Oxford, UK: Blackwell, 1996); James Mittelman, *The Globalization Syndrome: Transformation and Resistance* (Princeton, NJ: Princeton University Press, 2000); James Rosenau, *Along the Domestic-Foreign Frontier: Exploring Governance in a Turbulent World* (Cambridge, UK: Cambridge University Press, 1997); David Harvey, *The Condition of Postmodernity* (Oxford, UK: Blackwell, 1989); Richard Falk, *Predatory Globalization: A Critique* (Cambridge, UK: Polity Press, 1999); Thomas Friedman, *The Lexus and the Olive Tree* (New York: Farrar, Straus & Giraux, 1999).

60. Francis Fukuyama, *The End of History and the Last Man* (New York: Avon Books, 1992), 39–51.

61. In this regard, power is understood as an act of will that manifests itself through material and ideational expressions: coercion and knowledge. For an articulation of complex power along these lines, see Robert Cox, "Social Forces, States, and World Orders: Beyond International Relations Theory" in Robert Keohane (Ed.), *Neorealism and Its Critics* (New York: Columbia University Press, 1986), 204–254.

62. Sassen, *Globalization,* 81–81, 87–90, 92–97.

63. Robert Jackson, *Quasi-States: Sovereignty, International Relations and the Third World* (Cambridge, UK: Cambridge University Press, 1989); Susan Strange, *The Retreat of the State* (Cambridge, UK: Cambridge University Press, 1986).

64. Rosenau, *Along the Domestic-Foreign Frontier,* 114–117, 349–358.

65. Shelley, "Mafia and the Italian State," 664–669. It is important to note that Shelley's work approaches this triad from the perspective of each place, allowing for a multi-spectral analysis that can be tested in a variety of empirical contexts. Most recently, Shelley used this framework to investigate and comment on human trafficking, especially in conjunction with the global sex trade. In this same vein, Sassen (*Globalization*) examines the woman and immigrant as "undervalorized" in the globalization dynamic.

66. Nikos Passas, "Global Anomie, Dysanomie, and Economic Crime: Hidden Consequences of Neoliberalism and Globalization in Russia and Around the World," *Social Justice,* 27(2): 19–24. Passas's construction is similar to Pino Arlacchi's and Raimondo Catanzarro's, each of whom find the Sicilian Mafia a direct result of weak central authority and poor land reform. In essence, the landowners looked for protection, creating a historical link between legitimate business and organized crime, and thus creating the Mafia.

67. Peter Andreas, "The Political Economy of Narco-Corruption in Mexico," *Current History,* 97(618): 162–164.

68. Most of this scholarship owes and pays homage to the work of Susan Strange, namely, *Casino Capitalism* (Oxford, UK: Blackwell, 1986) and *The Retreat of the State*, and a handful of scholarly essays that challenged the mainstream notion of international relations that the state is the only or best legitimate object of inquiry.

69. Francisco E. Thoumi, *Political Economy and Illegal Drugs in Colombia* (Boulder, CO: Lynne Rienner, 1995).

70. Gambetta and Reuter, "Conspiracy among the Many," 118, 121–123.

71. Friman and Andreas (Eds.), *The Illicit Global Economy and State Power,* 7.

72. Bill McSweeney, "Identity and Security: Buzan and the Copenhagen School," *Review of International Studies,* 22(1): 81–93.

73. Barry Buzan, Ole Waever, and Jaap de Wilde, *Security: A New Framework for Analysis* (Boulder, CO: Lynne Rienner, 1998); Barry Buzan, *People, States, and Fear* (Boulder, CO: Lynne Rienner, 1990).

74. Following from a similar normative trajectory, the field of human security is starting to address issues that are directly related to transnational organized crime: human and arms trafficking. This literature is relatively new but rich. For a useful overview of the field, see Richard Falk, *Predatory Globalization*; Ronnie D. Lipschutz, *After Authority: War, Peace, and Global Politics in the 21st Century* (Albany: SUNY Press, 2000); and Ken Booth (Ed.), *Statecraft and Security: The Cold War and Beyond* (Cambridge, UK: Cambridge University Press, 1998).

75. Lake, *Six Nightmares,* 1–32.

CHAPTER SEVEN

The Global Drug Trade Versus the Nation-State

Why the Thugs Are Winning

Stephen E. Flynn

For US border control agents, intercepting the ripples of danger in the tidal wave of commerce is about as likely as winning a lottery. In 2000, 489 million people, 128 million passenger vehicles, 11.6 million maritime containers, 11.5 million trucks, 2.2 million railroad cars, 829,000 planes, and 211,000 vessels passed through US border inspection systems. Most of this traffic was concentrated in just a handful of ports and border crossings. One-third of all the trucks that enter the United States annually, for example, traverse just four international bridges between the province of Ontario and the states of Michigan and New York. At the binational Ambassador Bridge between Detroit and Windsor, nearly 5,000 trucks entered the United States each day in 2000. With only eight primary inspection lanes and a parking lot that can hold just 90 tractor trailers at a time for secondary or tertiary inspections, US customs officers must average no more than two minutes for each truck. If they fall behind, the parking lot fills, trucks back up onto the bridge, and the resulting traffic jam makes automotive parts suddenly unavailable in the factories, costing the US automobile industry $1 million in lost production per hour per assembly plant.

The persistent growth and dramatic spread of illicit drug markets—most notably for heroin, cocaine, and synthetic drugs—is a disturbing trend. Over the past decade, the production of opium poppies has more than tripled in the politically unstable region of Southwest Asia and nearly doubled in Latin America. Despite ten years of US-sponsored eradication programs and aggressive enforcement efforts, there were an estimated 344,630 more metric tons of Andean coca leaf produced in 2000 than in 1990.[1] Internet users can readily surf the Web for formulas to prepare controlled substances and then order the chemical ingredients from a growing menu of online suppliers. The result: synthetic drugs such as methamphetamine and LSD can be concocted by kitchen chemists around the globe.[2] The clandestine trafficking organizations that have evolved to link producers with distant consumers have also grown in number, size, and sophistication. Drug abuse and addiction, particularly near production areas and along the growing array of transit routes, has expanded into areas that had hitherto remained largely unscathed.

This growth in the drug phenomenon has taken place despite an international prohibitionary regime that is almost a century old. In the United States, even with a one-quarter trillion dollar investment in drug control programs by federal, state, and local governments since 1981,[3] the drug business continues to thrive. Indeed, for more than ten years suppliers have been compelled to lower wholesale and retail prices of cocaine and heroin and improve the street-level purity to stay competitive.[4] Around the world, drugs have become more available and affordable despite a rash of new multilateral initiatives that target not only illicit drugs but also the precursor chemicals and money connected with them.

Today, drugs represent one of the world's largest—and perhaps most lucrative—commodity trades. As an illicit enterprise, it is impossible to establish its total value with any precision. Estimates of its annual revenues range wildly from $100 billion to as much as $500 billion.[5] The latter figure would place drugs only below the global arms trade in a ranking of the world's largest industries. The lower estimate equates to a value greater than the GNP of the vast majority of the world's nations. A middle value of $300 billion would be equivalent to the world's petroleum industry.

That the marketing of drugs has become truly global is illustrated by the latest US government statistics that show Americans consume less than 40 percent of the cocaine manufactured in South America and just 1 percent to 4 percent of the world's opium supplies.[6] In 1998, the overwhelming majority of the heroin interdicted outside the production areas was in Europe, with US seizures equal to just 4 percent of the world total.[7] Virtually every country is reporting that drugs are far more available than at any time in recent history.[8]

Why is the war on drugs going so badly? The answer lies with the fact that we continue to rely on stepped-up versions of a state-centric approach to confront what is an inherently global problem that thrives in the dark corners of the international systems where traditional sovereign controls are weak or nonexistent. The end of the Cold War has dramatically expanded the realm where the writ of the state does not run. Thus, enforcement authorities who are intent on stemming the production, trafficking, and consumption of drugs often find themselves all dressed up with nowhere to go. Because most of the world's illicit drug supply is cultivated within states that are weak or failing, international source control is a house built on the sand of local enforcement bodies that are too primitive or corrupt to take the actions to stop the cultivation of drug raw materials within their borders. Interdiction efforts face the improbable task of sifting contraband from the rising tide of legitimate goods, services, and people that now wash across national borders as a result of the explosive growth of the global economy and the twin trends of liberalization and privatization. Finally, as democratization has taken root around the planet, the ability for police authorities to intrude into the lives of their citizens has been properly reined in, leaving people with greater freedom to do more of what they please—including, inevitably, socially sanctioned activities such as buying and consuming drugs—beyond the watchful eye of the state.

In short, the explosive rise of the global drug trade in the post–Cold War era highlights the fiction that the international system is the sum of its nation states. Drugs are produced and trafficked by nonstate actors who find borders essentially meaningless. In fact, the bad guys find the remaining vestiges of sovereignty to be largely an ally in their global enterprise. Because each state reserves for itself the right to draft laws, establish rules and procedures for operating its criminal justice system, and establish public policy priorities, drug control must be pursued against a backdrop of widely differing national jurisdictions. This lack of harmonization muddies the prospect for seamless multilateral cooperation among enforcement authorities. Whenever there is friction, there are "no-man's lands" that drug traffickers can occupy. The bottom line is that states must still be mindful of the sensibilities of their fellow sovereigns, but traffickers need not. As a result, the legal barriers that are supposed to prevent chemicals, drugs, and profits from circulating around the globe leak like a sieve.

Not only does the expansion of the drug trade reflect the unsteady state of states, but also, in growing measure, the trade is contributing to the turbulence. The enormous profits generated by drugs provide terrorists and insurgents with hard currency to purchase weapons. Drug moneys also make it possible for international criminal organizations to corrupt officials at every level of government, thereby undermining the legitimacy of political and judicial institutions. Because the billions of dollars associated with the global drug trade are illegitimate, they are circulated within the shadow economy, providing a substantial impetus for its growth. Finally, a rise in participation in drug-related activities, particularly when concentrated among youth and minority ethnic populations, accentuates social cleavages that are being fueled already by the pain and dislocations connected with modernization and postcommunist and postindustrial societal transitions.

Acknowledging drugs as a phenomenon that lies beyond sovereignty achieves two ends. First, it helps explain why current US and international drug control exertions are not working. Second, it points a way to a better approach. Ultimately, states must turn to the primary beneficiaries of globalization to redress its dark side. Because states have a declining presence in the economic and social spheres where the drug trade thrives, ultimately it is nongovernmental organizations, businesses, and community activists who are best positioned to create a climate that is less conducive to the rapid spread of drug supply and demand. In the end, it is not states, but nonstate actors who must be enlisted into tempering the forces that are motivating and facilitating drug-related activities.

THE RISE OF THE GLOBAL DRUG TRADE

The production and global distribution of drugs is by no means a new phenomenon. Turkish and Persian opium had been traded for centuries throughout the Middle East and in parts of Asia. By the latter part of the eighteenth century and throughout the nineteenth, large-scale production and worldwide distribution of opiates became systematically organized, often with the official sanction if not direct involvement of the governments of the major powers. On the eve of the twentieth century, legal markets in cocaine and opiates were flourishing within the United States, Europe, and the Far East, and the global drug trade could be characterized as a widely accepted sector of international commerce.

This international acceptance would change beginning with the 1909 conference in Shanghai of the International Opium Commission. Growing concern over widespread drug abuse and addiction, primarily by religious missionaries who were serving overseas and a growing number of physicians and temperance organizations at home,[9] led the US government to sponsor the Shanghai conference with the objective of convincing the principal producer countries to curtail the opium trade.[10] Although this drug control agenda was slow to take root, following World War I the League of Nations did create mandatory international controls supervised by a newly created Opium Control Board. The opium trade was to be eliminated within fifteen years and restricted to government monopolies during the interim period. This regulatory body was later reconstituted as the Permanent Central Board and charged with creating a tighter world system of controls over a wider range of drugs that would come to include cocaine and cannabis.

Resting as they did on the power and legitimacy of state authorities to enforce them, these initial steps toward developing a global prohibition regime had the unsettling effect of displacing drug trafficking, production, and consumption to places where state sovereignty was weak or non-existent.[11] Criminal suppliers stepped into the void left by long-standing government monopolies, initially basing their black market activities out of the cities of Istanbul and Shanghai. Thus began a development that would gather force over the next five decades—the tendency for the chemicals, drugs, and money that sustain the drug trade to be concentrated in areas in the international system that offered the lowest level of regulatory resistance to international trade flows. During World War II, there were few such locales, and the illicit traffic in drugs practically disappeared.[12] But after the war, as the number of these areas grew, so would the drug trade. Havana before Castro was the gateway to the Western hemisphere. Marseilles served as a base for the famous French Connection until the early 1970s. Today, transnational drug criminals have a vast menu of havens for their activities, most notably Caracas, Bogotá, Panama City, Karachi, Bangkok, Hong Kong, Lagos, Nairobi, Sofia, Moscow, St. Petersburg, and Warsaw.[13]

The tendency for trafficking activities to move toward cities where governmental authority is weakest paralleled a similar kind of shift in production of the botanical ingredients. Over time, traditional cultivation areas once controlled by colonial monopolies were largely abandoned in favor of territories effectively not under the control of any state authority. Today, nearly all coca is cultivated in rebel-controlled areas of Colombia and other remote, rural locations in Colombia, Peru, and Bolivia. Burma, Afghanistan, and Laos together account for 97 percent of opium poppy cultivation.[14] Newly emerging producers such as Kazakhstan, Kyrgyzstan, Uzbekistan, Turkmenistan, Tajikistan, Ukraine, Azerbaijan, Georgia, Nigeria, Kenya, and Vietnam all share common ingredients, seemingly validating the inverse relationship between production and viable national sovereignty. In all of these countries: (1) there is a weak central government or widespread corruption among governmental authorities, (2) there have been recently established or enhanced ties to regional or global markets, and (3) there are vast remote areas where cultivation can take place largely undetected. In addition, in several instances, production activities have been directly sponsored or protected by insurgent groups who resist, by force of arms, encroachments by the state into production regions.

While production and trafficking activities have increasingly been concentrated in the largely lawless corners of the global community, for much of the latter half of the twentieth century the end users of illicit drugs have resided largely in developed countries, with the United States serving as the primary market. Given the size and resources of the US government, it would seemingly appear that a properly committed United States could insulate itself from the wholesale and retail activities of drug traffickers. But on closer examination, it becomes clear that the government is not well positioned to do so. First, efforts to prevent retail transactions are necessarily hindered by basic civil liberty protections. Although these protections obviously apply to all criminal investigations, what makes drug crimes particularly difficult for law enforcement officials to pursue is that they rarely receive the cooperation of the victim. This is because, unlike crimes such as burglary or rape, the "victim" in a drug transaction (the consumer) does not file a police report or make evidence available because he or she is also an accomplice. Detecting a drug retail crime, therefore, generally must be accomplished unilaterally by state authorities. At the same time, these authorities must always be mindful not to interfere with the freedoms

Americans enjoy to move when and where they please, possess unfettered control over their disposable incomes, and, most important, be secure from the intrusiveness of the state in their private lives. In short, as members of an essentially free and democratic society, Americans have imposed formidable constitutional limits on the sovereign prerogatives of their government to control wholesale or retail drug-related activities within its borders.

It is not only within their societies that advanced democratic countries are confronted with serious limits to their power to pursue drug crimes. The United States and Western European states are also finding that they have a shrinking capacity to detect drug trafficking activities along their borders, partly because of conscious choices made by governments to remove restrictions on crossborder flows of a growing volume of legal goods, capital, and services. Beginning in the 1970s, for instance, the US Customs Service stopped stationing customs officers at international shipping piers and terminals where imported cargo is discharged, and it removed customs storekeepers from bonded warehouses. These traditional inspection controls were replaced with automated systems and postaudits in response to growing private sector calls for reductions in domestic barriers to international commerce. New rules, which are in place today, allow foreign goods to transit throughout the United States without prior release authorization by customs officials. The carrier needs only to assure customs authorities that it will maintain custody over these imports until the goods reach their final destination. Officials then authorize release—in virtually all instances without an on-site inspection—on receiving accounting and importers documentation. If the Customs Service receives the appropriate paperwork in advance, then it routinely authorizes release in advance. In recent years, the US Customs Service also has adopted further liberalization procedures by relaxing requirements on labeling, cords, and seals, and has virtually eliminated spot inspections of bonded goods in transit.[15]

The member states of the European Union (EU) have gone even further than the United States in adopting new rules that have substantially liberalized their national transportation sectors. Beginning in 1988, for instance, quotas and permits for transporters operating in a member country other than their own were removed. In March 1991, many Western European countries removed all restrictions on air cargo capacity and authorized a carrier based in one country to pick up goods in another and deliver them to a third. Finally, on January 1, 1993, the community granted all EU shippers who were moving cargo by road free access to any other EU country.[16] The Schengen Agreements took the ultimate liberalization step by eliminating controls on the movement of people within the European Union.[17]

These trends have not been restricted to the United States and Western Europe. Colombia, Venezuela, and Brazil have all engaged in efforts to deregulate maritime and land transport.[18] Mexico dramatically liberalized its regulations governing the trucking industry in June 1989, allowing any licensed truck to move freely within the country and to load and unload in any city, port, or railway station.[19] In May 2002, Mexican truckers received access to the highways of the United States and Canada as part of NAFTA's final arrangements.[20] Free trade zones have proliferated throughout the Caribbean and Central America as a part of a competitive effort to attract direct foreign investment and to facilitate the flow of trade. In the face of this trend, customs agents who inspect cargo that enters or leaves their jurisdictions are seen as increasingly undesirable sources of friction that should be marginalized, minimized, or eliminated wherever possible.

Global transportation and logistics trends are also complicating the lives of border control agents. Increasingly, containerized cargo moves through hub ports where cascading volumes and the imperative of rapid processing render impractical traditional efforts to examine these shipments. Kingston, Jamaica, offers a case in point. Currently, more than three-quarters of the 800,000 containers that pass through the port annually originate from outside Jamaica. Soon the port will be handling more than 1.2 million containers,[21] which undoubtedly whets the appetites of smugglers such as those who managed to insert 16,000 pounds of Jamaican ganja (cannabis) into a shipment of tires originating from Japan and destined for Savannah, Georgia, while the containers sat in a "secure" area of the port in August 2001.[22]

The challenge of filtering the bad from the good among the cross-border flows of people and goods is clearly daunting. But tracking and freezing illicit money flows represents an even more Herculean task because advanced capitalist societies have undertaken several steps to minimize the barriers to international capital movements. Governments began to surrender regulatory control over crossborder investments with the creation of the Eurodollar market and offshore banking centers in the late 1960s. The trend was given impetus by the enactment of new laws that lowered the restrictions on foreign investment by pension funds, insurance companies, unit trusts, and mutual funds, which gave rise to a proliferation of new players in international financial markets.[23] These concessions were inspired in part by the fallout from expansionary policies in the 1980s that produced large deficits in the Group of 7 countries. Confronted by the need to court foreign investors to help them finance bond issues, governments were inclined to eliminate barriers that might discourage would-be creditors. Pressures to ease reporting requirements and other controls came also from the banking and nonbanking industries. Given the volatility of exchange rates, competitive global bidding, and the explosive growth in clients who are attempting to make time-sensitive deals, financial institutions are finding that their survival depends on their ability to conclude transactions rapidly. They therefore tend to see government regulators almost exclusively as adversaries.

The deregulation of the transportation and financial sectors has been in part a reaction to the dictates of the global marketplace, which has been transformed by the extraordinary effects of the communications revolution. The power of computers, computer software, satellites, fiberoptic cables, facsimile machines, modems, and wireless technology has effectively overcome most of the practical limitations connected with geographical distances. Communications technology has made it possible for financial markets to be truly globalized with around-the-clock trading in bonds, stocks, and exchanges that are conducted over hundreds of thousands of electronic monitors linked together in trading rooms all over the world. Communications technology also provides manufacturers with the means to remotely coordinate distant operations, allowing them to disperse production activities to wherever the greatest value can be added to each stage of production. As these multinational corporations deepen these international production-based linkages, their success in turn becomes increasingly tied to their access to open capital markets and low-cost and smoothly functioning transportation and communications infrastructure. Thus, governments face nearly irresistible pressure to deregulate their financial, transportation, and communications sectors in order to compete within an increasing integrated and time-sensitive global economy.

There is little question that these liberalization trends have served to stimulate the growth in world trade and investment over the past ten years. Since the early 1980s, world merchandise exports has grown in volume at twice the rate of gross domestic product. But these widely heralded outcomes have come at a cost: International markets have been made almost as accessible to illicit commercial activities as licit. This fact has certainly not been lost on the more sophisticated drug trafficking organizations, which have increasingly shifted away from low-flying small aircraft and fast-moving cigarette boats popularized in action films to more stodgy but reliable conveyances such as the millions of commercial containers that move cargo around the planet.

Cocaine, for example, is inserted inside legitimate cargo or in the floors or walls of containers originating from international shipping centers in Central and South America, particularly in Brazil, Venezuela, Surinam, and Panama. By land, most cocaine crosses the US–Mexican border in the hidden compartments of tractor trailers and other vehicles or in commercial cargo itself. When commercial airlines are used, the drug is hidden on the plane, among perishable cargoes such as cut flowers or fruit pulp, or among passengers who conceal it by placing it in luggage with false bottoms or in hollowed-out sneakers, by taping it to their bodies, or by swallowing condoms filled with cocaine. Sometimes it is converted to liquid and smuggled in bottles of shampoo, mouthwash, baby formula, and liquor. In most instances, these shipments are accompanied by complete documentation from licensed companies with legitimate destinations.

Once the cocaine arrives in the United States, it must be distributed to the millions of drug consumers. Given the lucrative nature of this enterprise, it should come as little surprise that this is not an amateurish operation. Documents seized during a successful raid on a wholesale distribution network in New York, operated by a Cali-based organization, exposed just how sophisticated these criminals are.[24]

In its prime, the Cali cartel operated dozens of distribution cells throughout the country, with each cell made up of ten to fifteen Colombian employees who earned monthly salaries ranging from $2,000 to $7,500. They conducted as much as $25 million of business each month. Each cell was self-contained, with information tightly compartmentalized. Only a handful of managers knew all the operatives. The cell typically had a head, a bookkeeper, a money handler, a cocaine handler, a motor pool, and ten to fifteen apartments serving as stash houses.

Communications were conducted in code over fax machines, cellular phones, and pay phones. To eliminate any risk of interception, cellular phones were purchased and discarded, often weekly. When a wholesale customer wanted to make a purchase, a cell member was notified by a pager system. That cell member would proceed to a public phone and arrange a rendezvous site. He would then get a rental car from the motor pool and return it to the rental agency after the transaction. The transaction itself, including travel receipts, was logged by the bookkeeper, and the money turned over to the money handler to be shipped to the financial network set up by the cartel to hide and invest it. One favored way to ship cash within the United States was by way of the US Postal Service's express mail. There was plenty of cash to ship—as much as $200 million each year per cell.

Money laundering typically involves three independent phases. First, drug proceeds are "placed," or deposited in banks or used to purchase monetary instruments or securities that can be turned into cash elsewhere. This is often done by hiring individuals known as "smurfs" to deposit the money in small denominations in as many banks and financial institutions as possible to defeat currency-reporting requirements.[25] Second, the money is "layered," or sent through multiple electronic transfers or other transactions to make it difficult to track and to blur its illicit origin.[26] Finally, the source of the money disappears as it is "integrated," or invested into seemingly legitimate accounts and enterprises. To lower their exposure to law enforcement even more, drug trafficking organizations often contract out these last two phases, getting money handlers to provide them the money up front minus a 15 percent to 25 percent commission in return for providing these handlers the opportunity to launder and keep the full amount.[27]

Today, the notorious Medellin and Cali cartels have been largely dismantled, but the cocaine trade has not. Several smaller organizations, many with ties to Colombia's guerrilla insurgency and paramilitary groups, have been the beneficiaries of the drug kingpin strategy that was the heart of the US–Colombian enforcement efforts of the 1990s. To a large extent, these smaller trafficking organizations mirror the behaviors of successful modern global corporations. They have developed network structures that successfully support vertical and horizontal relationships with "contractors" across borders. They have invested in the most advanced information technologies to maintain secure, real-time links over long distances in order to coordinate production and distribution activities under rapidly changing conditions and in a potentially adversarial environment. Most important, they have immersed their activities within parts of the global infrastructure that are virtually unregulated—commercial containers, air cargo, overland freight, rental cars, cellular phones, overnight mail, and electronic transfers.

The Southeast Asian heroin trade mirrors the sophistication of the Latin American cocaine industry. Heroin produced in the Golden Triangle of Burma, Laos, and Thailand is typically smuggled overland to seaports in Burma, China, Thailand, Malaysia, and Vietnam, where it is packed into containers with legitimate cargo before being sent onto its intended markets in Europe, Australia, Canada, and the United States. In this transshipment process, new bills of lading are produced that mask the origin and nature of the containers' contents. After leaving the mainland ports, the containers will make an intermediary stop at a regional hub port such as Hong Kong or Singapore, which each month handles more than 1 million maritime containers. In Singapore, the average time between discharge and reloading an entire ship, which requires as many as 2,000 container moves, is less than ten hours, giving little time for Singaporean authorities to inspect or audit the cargo.[28] There are tens of thousands of importers, some of which are actually front companies that hide drug shipments within legitimate cargo.[29] There are no shortages of places to hide with 5.23 billion tons of goods plying the world's waters in 1999 and a projected two-thirds rise in the volume of seaborne trade projected over the next decade.[30]

Monitoring and inspecting commercial air traffic has become an equally formidable task for government agents. When these flights arrive in the United States, they are likely to land in a busy airport such as Miami, where more than 106 airlines moved millions of international travelers and 1.8 million tons of air cargo in 1999.[31] Frequently the goods moved by air are perishable.[32] In Houston, for example, inspectors are confronted with shipments of 2 million plants from South America each month; they must process these shipments swiftly or risk generating huge spoilage losses for importers.

Along the land borders of the United States, customs inspectors can find no relief for their overwhelming task of filtering illicit from licit traffic. A substantial proportion of the more than 489 million people who enter the United States each year do so in one of the 128 million automobiles that cross US borders.[33] The rule of thumb in the border inspection business is that it takes five inspectors three hours to conduct a thorough physical inspection of a loaded 40-foot container or an 18-wheel truck. Even with the assistance of new high-tech sensors, inspectors have nowhere near the amount of time, space, or personnel needed to inspect all of the arriving cargo.

A case in point is the Ambassador Bridge between Detroit, Michigan, and Windsor, Ontario. At this, the world's busiest commercial land-border crossing, the huge volume means that US customs officers must average no more than two minutes for each truck. If they fall behind, the backup of vehicles virtually closes the border, generating roadway chaos throughout metropolitan Windsor and Detroit. Before the terrorist attacks on September 11, 2001, US customs officials operating at busy commercial border crossings were subject to performance sanctions if they disrupted the flow of commerce by making anything more than random and token spot checks.[34] Since September 11, the business communities in Texas and Michigan have been busy documenting the disruption to the border economies associated with added delays connected with stepped-up border security measures.[35]

Given the clearly horrendous and diminishing odds of successfully discovering drugs based on random border inspections, intelligence to support law enforcement operations would appear crucial to successful interdiction of drugs along US borders and in US streets. Here, however, the traffickers' investment in state-of-the-art communications hardware and software have effectively defeated any hope of successful electronic surveillance by law enforcement officials. Communications via pagers and pay phones are, for all practical purposes, impossible to monitor. Although it is possible to listen in on a cellular phone conversation, the interception technology is scarce and expensive. Further, a court order for electronic surveillance takes time to obtain—generally longer than the brief time span a trafficker will use the phone before dumping it and getting a new one. Finally, the Internet makes it possible for traffickers to conduct completely secure communications. If the traffickers break their messages into multiple units, send each unit through anonymous remailers that move the message through a large number of routers before it arrives at its final destination, and use widely available 128-bit encryption programs such as Pretty Good Privacy (PGP), they can operate with virtually no risk from surveillance efforts by the law enforcement community.[36]

Because the prospects of interdicting drugs or investigating the trafficking organizations that move them appear to be so grim, one final temptation would be to target the money derived from this illicit business. The logic here is that retail drug sales must be made in cash and the cash is actually far bulkier than the drugs for which it is sold, so law enforcement should focus on keeping the money from finding its way back to Colombia or the other trafficking home bases. Unfortunately, given the liquidity of money and the globalization trends outlined above, this too is destined to prove illusory. There simply is no shortage of ways in which the money can be placed within the economy. Money launderers can and do use nonbank financial institutions such as exchange houses, check cashing services, and credit unions. They purchase instruments such as postal money orders, cashier's checks, certificates of deposit, and even securities (stocks and bonds). Proceeds are invested in legitimate businesses such as travel agencies, construction companies, casinos, securities dealers, real estate agencies, jewelry shops, and antique dealers—that is, businesses with high volumes of cash transactions. Money managers may soon use microchip-based electronic money or cybercurrency, giving them the ability to make instant and anonymous transfers of money around the globe.[37]

RECONSIDERING DRUG CONTROL[38]

In sum, the drug trade has grown in recent years because changes within the international system have raised the fortunes of transsovereign actors while eroding the position of states. Since the beginning of the postcolonial era, there has been an unparalleled growth in the number of state actors in the international system who lack the institutional capacity to exercise sovereignty over much of their national territories. Actors within these new states have virtually unrestricted access to the global economy as a result of the worldwide trend toward economic liberalization. Wholesale privatization and deregulation within national economies has diminished the capacity of all states—developing, postcommunist, and developed—to exercise control over production and distribution activities within and across their borders. As a result, the global economy has slid increasingly into a status of laissez faire, creating little practical distinction between engaging in legitimate and illegitimate commercial activities. Traffickers in illicit narcotics merely merge with the legitimate flows of goods, capital, and services within the global marketplace, comfortable in the realization that governments have a shrinking capacity to separate the bad from the good.

The manifold factors that influence the growth of the global drug trade render impractical traditional supply-side policies. The drug problem cannot be solved by simply working harder at both eliminating drugs at their source or seizing them before their arrival in the United States. Policies enacted with these objectives in mind are fatally flawed for two reasons. First, the centrality of enforcement makes them an inherently reactive approach to an extremely dynamic phenomenon. Law enforcement by definition cannot be preemptive—rules must be broken before the legitimate coercive authority of the state can be brought to bear to impose sanctions. Second, these policies rest on the fallacious notion that drug production and trafficking activities can be somehow readily rooted out from the context in which they exist.

By defining drugs as "bad," drug control policies rest on the normative presumption that the phenomenon is alien and that "normalcy" can be restored by isolating and exorcising the phenomenon from the body politic. But that cannot be done precisely because the phenomenon is deeply entrenched in so many of the activities that underlie modern life. Further, there is little agreement over exactly what constitutes the evil to be eradicated. Although there is nearly universal acknowledgment that the abuse of drugs such as heroin and cocaine is bad, it is difficult to formulate similar tidy judgments about the array of interwoven activities that ultimately supply addicts with their fixes. Farmers, chemists, shippers, and bankers who are directly or indirectly involved in the drug trade rarely see themselves as criminals; instead, they characterize themselves as good businesspeople striving to embrace one of capitalism's chief tenets—maximizing profits. The inventors and suppliers of new technologies who are exploited by organized criminal networks do not see themselves as accomplices to crime, but as purveyors of progress. Importers, exporters, tourists, and commercial carriers are acting in concert with the principles of economic liberalization when they strongly oppose the use of intrusive border controls that governments have traditionally relied on to detect and stop contraband. Finally, civil libertarians are embracing the core ideals of democratic society when they fight to restrict the intrusiveness of governmental authority into the individual lives of their citizenry, even if it means that some drug crimes will go undetected.

So where does this leave policy makers who are committed to stemming the burgeoning global drug trade? Obviously, it presents them with a far more complicated challenge than the one they have been willing to acknowledge—at least publicly—up to this point. It is a challenge that cannot be reduced to a state-centric crusade against evil drug producers, traffickers, and consumers. Instead it represents a vexing global problem of the first order.

By outlining the factors that are motivating and facilitating drug production, it becomes self-evident why US- and UN-funded crop eradication, crop substitution, and alternative development programs are not working. Such programs are premised on the notion that if existing growers can be either coerced or enticed to end drug cultivation, then the void will remain unfilled. But it takes the prevalence of only three rudimentary conditions to render this approach unworkable: (1) the existence of suitable alternative sites for cultivation, (2) the greater appeal of profits from drug production than from competing agricultural alternatives, and (3) the existence of jurisdictions where drug production can take place in which the host governments lack the means or the will to end it. The first condition is a function of geography; vast tracks of the global landscape are well suited to drug production. The second is a function of market demand that shows no signs of diminishing. And the third is dependent on political legitimacy and the effectiveness of regulatory and enforcement mechanisms, all of which are under significant strain in the post–Cold War era.

Similarly, it should be clear why interdiction initiatives that aim to stem the crossborder flows of processing chemicals, drugs, and drug moneys are ineffectual. As long as these activities can blend within the increasingly unregulated movements of people, goods, and services associated with an open global economy, enforcement efforts are little more than futile "needle-in-the-haystack" exercises.

Although begrudgingly acknowledging the dim prospects for real achievement, some theorists might argue that these supply-side initiatives serve an important symbolic role, providing a tangible demonstration of national and international support for antidrug norms. This rationale is found wanting, however, once the costs of undertaking this essentially normative effort are considered. For example, crop eradication programs typically end up displacing production into more remote areas that are often environmentally sensitive public lands. Because, in most of these cases, farmers neither own the land nor expect that their activities will go undetected over the long term, they clear the land with highly destructive "slash-and-burn" practices, plant and harvest a crop, and then move on. If these cultivation activities take place on mountainous terrain as is common in Southeast Asia and Latin America, then erosion can irreversibly harm the surrounding area.[39] In addition to displacement, some alternative development programs actually inadvertently facilitate the drug trade. This happens when assistance is provided to enhance the infrastructure of a drug-producing region to make the cultivation of other legitimate crops viable but farmers secretly continue to engage in illicit cultivation. The net result of these generous investments in new infrastructure is to lower the costs of moving chemicals and fertilizers into the region and to ease the transportation burden of moving drugs to their downstream markets.

Nowhere are the potential costs associated with aggressive supply-reduction efforts likely to be more painful than in Colombia. After the Colombian government rolled out Plan Colombia in 2000, the US government committed to becoming the largest donor in a multibillion-dollar plan to reign in the recent surge in coca cultivation in that long-troubled nation.[40] It is easy to predict what intensified efforts to combat drug cultivation and trafficking will do—particularly in the remote, guerilla-controlled region of Putamayo. More and more reports are documenting the spillover of kidnappings, crime, and violence, as well as the movement of refugees into Ecuador, Venezuela, Brazil, and Panama.[41] Unfortunately, none of these countries are able to cope with these effects, particularly Ecuador and Panama. Throughout this region, there are few resources and little in the way of infrastructure to promote the rule of law or advance economic development in the areas that are most susceptible to the dollars and intimidation that drug traffickers can bring to bear. None of these countries has the capacity to absorb the potential for millions of refugees from Colombia's civil war. Even if Brazilian, Venezuelan, and Ecuadorian police and soldiers are moved into the areas to harden their borders with southern Colombia, the costs are likely to be prohibitively high in economic and diplomatic terms. Militarizing the border regions will inevitably compromise the crossborder flow of trade and likely sour diplomatic relations among the neighboring countries.

Stepped-up efforts to disrupt drug trafficking activities in Colombia may also produce harmful unintended consequences. Such efforts inevitably spawn greater innovation on the part of the drug barons. The drug enforcement community often touts this result as progress because it presumably raises the cost of "doing business."[42] This may sound like a worthy objective, but it can prove counterproductive if enforcement ends up only picking the low-lying fruit. More specifically, if raising the costs only applies to entry-level competitors, then more sophisticated trafficking organizations may actually benefit from enforcement activities because they can eliminate those who might otherwise threaten their market shares.

Enforcement-generated innovation that leads traffickers to move from traditional noncommercial smuggling activities to more sophisticated schemes that involve manufacturers, commercial carriers, exporters, and financiers can also be a cure worse than the disease. This is because of the corrosive effect drug money can have across the entire commercial sector, undermining confidence in the private sector and the regulators charged with policing it. In addition, as legitimate trade becomes increasingly contaminated with illicit narcotics, it elevates the risk that all exports will be subject to delays and the added costs associated with closer inspections and destructive searches.

Perhaps the most disturbing consequence of more aggressive attacks on Colombian drug traffickers is that the most likely beneficiaries will be Mexican trafficking organizations. For some time, Mexican traffickers have benefited from the disruption of the cocaine trade in the Caribbean that led the Colombians to seek out an alternative route to the United States via its southwest border—that is, through Mexico. Mexican narcotraffickers have benefited from the aggressive enforcement efforts against the Medellin and Cali cartels. Those efforts have afforded them opportunities to move into the wholesale cocaine distribution business in the United States.[43] If the Colombian drug supplies begin to dry up, then there is little to prevent Mexican organizations from sponsoring coca production and refinement in Peru, Bolivia, and elsewhere in the Andean region, emulating the example of the Colombian drug barons of the 1970s.

It should require little explanation to show why a transfer of control over the cocaine trade to Mexican traffickers would be so disastrous. Mexico is the United States' second largest trading partner. At slightly more than 100 million, its population is two and one-half times that of Colombia. Arguably, its institutions may prove less resilient than those in Colombia to the corrosive threat of "plata o plomo" (silver or lead).[44] Its historic movement away from a one-party state has just begun. Political power in Mexico is more decentralized, with governors possessing a great deal of autonomy. Corruption within the police forces and some elements of the military is rampant. Like Colombia, Mexico has its own problems with insurgencies, particularly in the state of Chiapas. If Mexico were to become the hemisphere's new capital of drug trade, scarring its fragile political and economic institutions in ways similar to Colombia's, then the repercussions for US domestic and regional interests would be enormous.

WHAT CAN BE DONE?

We need to rethink the drug war in light of the qualities of the drug trade illuminated by considering it a transsovereign problem. By overlooking its inherently transnational character, we overlook both a threat and an opportunity. Pursuing policies that treat the drug phenomenon primarily as an enforcement problem, we see only the proverbial tip of the iceberg. The drug issue inevitably complicates the process of modernization in the developing world; the painful political, economic, and social adjustments now underway in the postcommunist world; and the difficult postindustrial transition in the developed world. Although clearly not a causal variable, the drug issue also contributes to the challenges of ethnic conflict and civil war, weapons proliferation, and environmental devastation. To tackle all these problems without acknowledging the direct or indirect relationship of the burgeoning global drug trade seems wrong-minded at best and self-defeating at worst.

Ultimately, the first step requires us to move from rhetoric to reality when addressing the concept of demand reduction. This means that the United States and other advanced societies must place their primary emphasis on providing adequate medical and social services for treating drug addicts. The strategic rationale for this is straightforward. Although an estimated 77 million Americans have experimented with drugs at least once in their lifetimes, just 5 million frequent drug users consume the majority of drugs.[45] The 50 percent decline in casual use in the United States over the past decade is a positive development, but from a drug market standpoint, the fact that there has been virtually no change in the number of drug addicts means that this drop in recreational drug use has had virtually no effect on the overall demand for cocaine and heroin.

Thanks to drug prevention programs, the cocaine industry may not be a growth business in the United States, but the demand for coca and poppies will be unchanged as long as Americans refuse to invest in long-term drug treatment.

Second, we need to recognize that the narcotics trade and the illicit dollars that go with it cannot be divorced from the informal economy that is burgeoning within the region and around the world. Trade fraud, tax evasion, sweatshops that thrive off underground labor, and the smuggling of licit products from VCRs to cigarettes all provide a growing haystack within which drugs and money laundering activities can hide. To a large extent, we should look at the drug trade as something akin to the dye that cardiologists use to detect blockages in the circulatory system. It highlights the gaping holes in the international economic system, which has facilitated the unsettling growth of what Susan Strange has called "casino capitalism."[46] If we are serious about stemming the scourge of drugs, then we must get serious about closing these holes by (1) advancing the adoption of a regional business, transportation and logistics, and investment code that brings transparency to crossborder activities, and (2) providing the means to enforce it.

Particular attention should be paid to developing meaningful and binding guidelines for trade, transshipment, and financial record keeping. Commercial records should be transmitted electronically at or as near to the point of origin as possible so enforcement and regulatory authorities can more effectively target their inspections. Also, regional organizations such as the Organization of American States could be tasked and resourced to regularly publish an "Accessories to Transnational Crime Report" that spotlights business institutions and individuals who routinely fail to abide by the established codes. The goal should be to shame the participants in the black economy and to reign in its shadows, thereby enhancing the risk of detection for criminals or terrorists who are attempting to capitalize on the legitimate flow of commerce to move contraband, weapons, or money.

Third, we need to develop and execute a comprehensive organized crime strategy that strives to deter and disrupt the ability of criminals from forming networks, corrupting governments, and prospering from their ill-gotten gains as opposed to placing primary emphasis on securing prosecutions.[47] The counterterrorism tactics that have been developed over the past two decades provide a more promising model for how to confront organized crime than does the Colombian kingpin strategy of the 1990s. There will always be a new face to fill a vacancy on the Ten Most Wanted list. Initiatives may include establishing a designated organized crime intelligence unit within each cooperating country that is responsible for coordinating crime intelligence collection and analysis within its borders and working with the intelligence units from the other countries.

Finally, we must be mindful of the human dimension associated with any effort to work internationally in attacking a global challenge such as the drug trade. An ongoing effort must be made to improve cultural understanding and linguistic abilities among agencies cooperating in multilateral efforts. Journalists and investigative reporters who write stories on crime and corruption, often at significant personal risk, deserve greater support from the international community. Efforts to intimidate media professionals or to undermine a free press should be condemned in the strongest possible terms and, when government officials are involved, subject to sanctions. A common fund should be established to train journalists and intelligence, judicial, financial, and law enforcement representatives, and to support exchange programs.

Many critics may see policy initiatives such as these as impractical within the current political and budgetary environment. But if the skeptics ultimately carry the day, what alternatives remain? Business as usual is an unacceptable option. Sticking to an approach that narrowly focuses on drug control as if it can be divorced from its wider political, economic, and social context practically ensures that drugs will continue to be widely available and that the criminal organizations that advance the trade will remain powerful and corrosive—even if they just operate out of different locales. The only remaining logical course to pursue—if we are unable to muster the political will to undertake the ambitious proposals outlined above—would be to consider dismantling the prohibitionary regime. This is because, in the final analysis, a failed prohibitionary approach to drug control does more harm than good because it ends up serving the interests of organized crime, terrorist organizations, and insurgents who benefit from the trade to a far greater extent than the national and international public welfare. If the United States and the global community are unprepared to redress the systemic weaknesses that are facilitating and motivating drug production, trafficking, and consumption, then they should begin to accommodate themselves to the fact that widespread drug use and its harmful social consequences are an unfortunate fact of life, an inevitable by-product of living in an open global capitalist system that promotes self-indulgence and instant gratification far more than community and self-sacrifice.

CONCLUSION

The persistent growth of the illicit drug trade, despite the long-standing national and international enforcement regimes designed to contain them, offers a compelling case study in the precarious status of national sovereignty. The production of illicit narcotics has gravitated to areas within the region where the writ of the state is weakest. Drug traffickers have benefited from the same revolution in communications, transportation, trade, and finance that has made it possible for so many global businesses to pursue their ends with little concern for the traditional prerogatives of nation states. Current and potential consumers of drugs are now free to use drugs with little or no risk of state intervention in a growing number of locales where there have been dramatic reductions in authoritarian social controls.

Too, the success of drug traffickers reveals widening holes within the global economy that are facilitating the free trade of an array of nefarious "commodities"—of which, drugs only rank among the more prominent. High-grade plutonium, hazardous waste, counterfeit credit cards and documents, pirated copyrighted materials, stolen vehicles, child pornography, aliens, and indentured teenage prostitutes can be found on that list. More and more, the global marketplace has come to resemble the kind of capitalism familiar to industrialized countries at the turn of the century. Then, as today, governments found themselves witnessing explosive economic growth largely from the sidelines. But the growth unleashed by the industrial revolution came at the cost of macroeconomic stability and led to widespread abuses of the environment, labor, and consumers. As the global community starts the new millennium, such negative externalities of capitalist activity cannot be absorbed as the cost of doing business without producing profound global dislocations.

There is a curious paradox in the predicament of declining sovereignty that is fueling the drug trade. To strengthen their role in the international system, states must agree to act less and less like states. That is, they must agree to embrace universal norms and empower an array of nonstate actors to advance common interests—even though these actions ultimately may limit their capacity to act independently in the pursuit of their own national interests, narrowly defined. If they delay acknowledging this Faustian bargain and sovereignty continues to erode to the benefit of nonstate actors such as organized criminal organizations, then the ailment may become terminal. The critical turning point will come when the power of criminal elements with a vested interest in an anarchical status quo co-opt some states altogether. Once that happens, the co-opted states will use their sovereign prerogatives to resist any meaningful multilateral regime that would endanger their nefarious interests.

Taking the necessary steps to prevent an irreversible erosion of the role of sovereign governments in the international system will require that the United States take a leadership role in promoting strategies of cooperative engagement that includes a broadly based alliance of international, regional, and nongovernmental organizations and the private sector. In the wake of the tragic events of September 11, 2001, the linkage between the illicit drug trade and international terrorism may provide the impetus for advancing just this kind of approach. The interconnectedness of drug profits, the illicit market in weapons, money laundering, and the operation of terrorist organizations such as al Qaeda has raised the stakes associated with persisting with a fatally flawed national drug strategy. For too long, politicians in Washington have succumbed to the temptation to pander to an American public that craves simplistic answers to complex global problems. Now more than ever, resisting that impulse is a matter of life and death.

ENDNOTES

1. More than twenty countries are now involved in the production of coca and opium. Total estimated worldwide opium gum production climbed from 3,257 metric tons in 1990 to 5,004 metric tons in 2000. Total coca leaf production grew from 306,170 metric tons to 650,800 metric tons. From US Department of State, *International Narcotics Control Strategy Report* (INCSR), March 1, 2001 (Washington, DC: US Government Printing Office, 2001): II, 26–27.
2. "The Lycaeum" at <www.lycaeum.org>, "The Vaults of Erowid" at <www.erowid. com>, and "ecstasy.org" at <http://ecstasy.org> are three such sites that provide information on optimal drug dosages and "safe" administration methods, stories on drug experiences, and technical guidance on making drugs.
3. The federal drug budget has grown from $1.5 billion in 1981 to $19.1 billion in FY2002 for a $216.8 billion total for that period (Office of National Drug Control

Policy, *Summary: FY 2002 National Drug Control Budget,* April 2001: 1). By one estimate, state and local governments spent an additional $150 billion over a 15-year period. See *Keeping Score: What We Are Getting for Our Federal Drug Control Dollars 1995* (Washington, DC: Drugs Strategies, 1995): 1.

4. In most major US cities, heroin for a single "fix" can be purchased for $10 to $20 per bag, and a bag of crack can be had in New York City for $3 (Office of National Drug Control Policy, *Pulse Check: National Trends in Drug Abuse,* November 2001 [Washington, DC: US Government Printing Office, 1995], 11, 31). In 1999, the average purity for retail heroin was 38.2 percent nationwide, up from an average of 7 percent two decades ago. In 2000, a kilogram of cocaine had purity levels of 75 percent (Drug Enforcement Administration, *Drug Trafficking in the United States,* September 2001, DEA-01020: 6, 9).

5. The $500 billion estimate was made by the former head of the Drug Enforcement Administration, Thomas A. Constantine, keynote address before the 17th Annual International Asian Organized Crime Conference, Boston, March 8, 1995.

6. The Office of National Drug Control Policy (ONDCP) estimates that approximately 714 metric tons of cocaine are potentially available for consumption each year. Domestic consumption in the United States is estimated at 275 metric tons. This leaves 440 metric tons available for consumers in source countries or in Europe. ONDCP also estimates the amount of heroin available in the United States to be about 12.9–16 metric tons, while potential global heroin production stands at 287 metric tons (*National Drug Control Strategy,* 2001: 16, 19, 97–100).

7. US seizures were 1.56 metric tons, while worldwide seizures were 33.2 metric tons (United Nations Office for Drug Control and Crime Prevention, *Global Illicit Drug Trends 2000,* 80–84).

8. For a country-by-country breakdown, see INCSR, IV 1–X 80.

9. There was a substantial American missionary presence in China where, by 1906, more than one-quarter of all adult males were estimated to be regular opium smokers (see Arnold H. Taylor, *American Diplomacy and the Narcotics Traffic, 1900–1939* [Durham, NC: Duke University Press, 1969], 6). The advent of organic chemistry in the 1800s, along with the perfection of the hypodermic needle, made it possible to isolate the active agents from drug plants and transform use patterns. By the mid-1890s, the United States was importing nearly eight pounds of opium per 1000 people to be placed in a vast array of remedies ranging from cough syrup to pain relievers; these were mass-produced by an astonishing growth in the pharmaceutical industry and marketed aggressively through advertising. For example, the Bayer Company maintained that its heroin cough syrup, developed in 1898, "will suit the palate of the most exacting adult or the most capricious child" (David F. Musto, "Opium, Cocaine and Marijuana in American History," *Scientific American* [July 1991]: 40–47).

10. Peter D. Lowes, *The Genesis of International Narcotics Control* (New York: Arno Press, 1981), 199; and David F. Musto, *The American Disease: Origins of Narcotic Control* (New York: Oxford University Press, 1987), 35–37.

11. For a discussion of the evolution of global prohibition regimes and an evaluation of their successes and failures, see Ethan A. Nadelmann, "Global Prohibition Regimes: The Evolution of Norms in International Society," *International Organization,* 44(4): 479–526.

12. A *Time* editorial remarked in 1942, "The war is probably the best thing that ever happened to U.S. drug addicts." Quoted in James A. Inciardi, *The War on Drugs II: The Continuing Epic of Heroin, Cocaine, Crack, Crime, AIDS, and Public Policy* (Mountain View, CA: Mayfield, 1992), 24.

13. National Narcotics Intelligence Consumers Committee, *The Supply of Illicit Drugs to the United States—August 1995* (Washington, DC: Drug Enforcement Administration, 1995) (Publication No. 95051), 3, 32.

14. INCSR: II–23.

15. Kevin Monroy, "Customs Automation Captures the Imagination but Not the Crooks," *American Shipper,* 35(2): 42. These details were also drawn from site visits and interviews by the author with US customs inspectors at the port of Newark, April 9, 1992.

16. Marcia MacLeod, "New Markets in the Old World," *Air Cargo World,* 82(7): 20.

17. For a detailed analysis of Schengen and other initiatives, see *Free Movement of Persons in the European Union: Specific Issues,* a working document of the Directorate General for Research, European Parliament, 05-1999.

18. World Bank, *Latin America and the Caribbean: A Decade after the Debt Crisis* (Washington, DC: World Bank Latin America and Caribbean Regional Office, 1993), 90.

19. Ibid., 89–90.

20. Joe Cantlupe, "Congressional Investigators Fault DOT on Mexican Truck Safety," Copley News Service, January 8, 2002.

21. "APM Likely to Manage Kingston Terminal," *Lloyd's List,* Oct. 26, 2001, p. 3.

22. Eric Virtue, "Big Fine for Big Ganja Find—Drugs Found on Tyre Shipment," *Jamaica Gleaner,* Sept. 30, 2001.

23. "In 1998, in a survey under the auspices of the Bank for International Settlements (BIS), global turnover of reporting dealers was estimated at about $1.49 trillion per day for the traditional products, plus an additional $97 billion for over-the-counter currency options and currency swaps, and a further $12 billion for currency instruments traded on the organized exchanges" (Sam Y. Cross, *The Foreign Exchange Market in the United States* [New York: Federal Reserve Bank of New York, 1998], 5).

24. The details on the organization and operation of the Cali distribution cells were provided in a briefing to the author at Drug Enforcement Administration headquarters on February 12, 1992, and a subsequent DEA briefing on May 18, 1994. These details were discovered after the arrest of an entire cell in New York City and the seizure of its records in December 1991. The narrative on the Cali organization draws heavily from my "Worldwide Drug Scourge: The Expanding Trade in Illicit Drugs," *Brookings Review,* 11(1): 9–10.

25. In one scheme, for instance, Cali cartel operatives recruit middle-aged Colombian couples to travel to Miami for short stays, provide them housing and a vehicle, and then send them on daily rounds to deposit money into banks in varying and uneven amounts less than $5,000. On an average day, these couples may visit ten different branch offices, making deposits in the lobby in the morning and then making deposits using the drive-through windows in the afternoon (briefing to the author by DEA's Miami field office, Jan. 11, 1994). For a description of this and other "smurfing" activities run out of New York City, see Fredric Dannen, "Colombian Gold," *New Yorker* (Aug. 15, 1994): 26–31.

26. For a description of how globalization combined with technological change has facilitated the ease at which illegal drug profits can be laundered, see Jack A. Blum, *Enterprise*

Crime: Financial Fraud in International Interspace, Working Group on Organized Crime (WGOC) monograph series (Washington, DC: National Strategy Information Center, 1997). One example of layering practices was cited by the state department in its 1994 *International Narcotics Report:* "An Asian trafficker operated more than 300 bank accounts in Hong Kong, the United States, and elsewhere in Asia. A number of these accounts were acquired when he purchased an established import/export firm, licensed in Africa, through a New York bank operating in Hong Kong. Because the shares were not publicly traded, there was no requirement to register the shares as sold, and as long as he used the same account signatories, usually nominees, none of the banks needed to be told of the change in ownership" (US Department of State, *International Narcotics Control Strategy Report–April 1994* [Washington, DC: US Government Printing Office, 1994], 473).

27. Douglas Forsh and Steve Coll, "Cocaine Dollars Flow Via New Networks," *Washington Post,* Sept. 19, 1993, p. A1.

28. In July 1995, the port of Singapore's main port operator, PSA, set the world record in the loading and unloading of containers: 229 moves per hour on the 4,000-TEU Mette-Maersk (NG Haw Cheng, *Port Facilities, Singapore, Industry Sector Analysis* [Washington, DC: US & Foreign Commercial Service and US Department of State, 1999], 2).

29. The details for this section were drawn from the US Drug Enforcement Administration, *Drug Intelligence Brief: Southeast Asian Heroin Smuggling Methods: Containerized Cargo* (Washington, DC: US Government Printing Office, September 2001).

30. United Nations Conference on Trade and Development (UNCTAD), *Review of Maritime Transport 2000* (UNCTAD/RMT [2000]/1): 3.

31. Miami International Airport, *Facts at a Glance,* Feb. 8, 2001.

32. Drug traffickers are fully aware of the enormous pressure US inspectors are under to facilitate the movement of goods, particularly seasonal, agricultural, and animal merchandise. One tactic they use is to smuggle the drugs among live animals. The US Fish and Wildlife Service upset one of these plans when an agent discovered 36 kilograms of cocaine inside the stomachs of several dozen living boa constrictors shipped through Miami International Airport ("ABC World News Tonight," Nov. 11, 1994).

33. Bureau of Transportation Statistics, *Incoming Personal Vehicle Crossings, US-Canadian Border, 2000* and *Incoming Personal Vehicle Crossings, US-Mexican Border, 2000* (Washington, DC: Department of Transportation, 2000) (based on data from US Customs Service, Mission Support Services, Office of Field Operations, Operations Management Database).

34. Stephen E. Flynn, "America the Vulnerable," *Foreign Affairs* (Jan.–Feb. 2002): 66–67.

35. Retail sales for "cross-border shoppers" have dropped by 30 percent to 55 percent in US cities along the border (Global News Service, "El Paso Businessmen Bemoan Tough Security at Border Crossings," Jan. 17, 2002).

36. PGP is based on the Rivest-Shamir-Adleman algorithm. "The basic mathematical idea behind public-key systems is that of the 'one-way function.' One-way functions are those that are much easier to perform in one direction than the other. . . . The simplest calculator can determine almost instantaneously that $987 \times 1,013 = 999,831$. But if a computer starts with the number 999,831, it will take time for the machine to determine, through trial and error, that the number can be evenly divided by 987 and 1,013.

As numbers become larger, this period of time becomes significant . . . Finding the factors of a 200-digit number on a modern top-speed computer would require not milliseconds or minutes but at least several centuries. The task is, in computer terms, 'computationally unfeasible.'" James Fallows, "Open Secrets," *Atlantic Monthly,* June 1994, p. 48.

37. INCSR, 1996: 512–527.

38. Portions of this section of the chapter are drawn from my "Asian Drugs, Crime, and Control: Rethinking the War on the Far Eastern Front," in James Shinn (Ed.), *Fires Across the Water: Transnational Problems in Asia* (New York: Council on Foreign Relations, 1997), 18–44.

39. For an overview of the pernicious environmental effects of drug cultivation, see L. Armstead, *Illicit Narcotics Cultivation and Processing: The Ignored Environmental Drama* (Vienna: UN Office for Drug Control and Crime Prevention, 1992); available at <www.undcp.org/bulletin/bulletin_1992-01-01_2_page002.html>.

40. This critique of Plan Colombia draws from my *US Support of Plan Colombia: Rethinking the Ends and Means*, which was published by the Strategic Studies Institute as a part of its monograph series on "Implementing Plan Colombia" (Carlisle, PA: US Army War College, 2001).

41. Suzanne Timmons, "The War on Coca: How Far Will the U.S. Go?" *Business Week* (Nov. 20, 2000): 60.

42. Testimony of Barry McCaffrey, director of Office of National Drug Control Policy, before the House Government Reform and Oversight Committee, Subcommittee on Criminal Justice, Drug Policy and Human Resources, "The Drug Legalization Movement in America," June 16, 1999.

43. Testimony of Donnie R. Marshall, acting administrator of Drug Enforcement Administration, before the Senate Drug Caucus on International Narcotics Control, March 21, 2000.

44. "Silver or lead"—officials are confronted by traffickers with the choice of accepting a bribe or a bullet.

45. According to the White House's Office of National Drug Control Policy, *U.S. National Drug Control Strategy: 2001,* approximately 5 million drug abusers need immediate treatment.

46. See Susan Strange, *Casino Capitalism* (Manchester, UK: Manchester University Press, 1997).

47. In this regard, the White House's *International Crime Control Strategy* (June 1998) (at <www.fas.org/irp/offdocs/iccs/iccstoc.html>) and *International Crime Threat Assessment* (Dec. 2000) (at <http://clinton4.nara.gov/WH/EOP/NSC/html/documents/pub45270/pub45270index.html >) offer useful stepping-off points.

CHAPTER EIGHT

The Cyberthreat Continuum

Richard A. Love

Coinciding with the September 11 terrorist attacks, the rate of cyberattacks in the United States—that is, computer-to-computer attacks over the Internet—increased by an estimated 79 percent in the last six months of 2001.[1] Worldwide, cyberattacks grew at an annual rate of 64 percent in the first six months of 2002, with more than 1 million suspected attempted attacks and 180,000 confirmed successful attacks.[2] Power and energy companies were heavily targeted; 70 percent suffered severe attacks,[3] a rate more than twice the mean of all companies. Technology, financial services, media, and power and energy firms showed the highest number of attacks, averaging more than 700 per company monitored for the last six months of 2001.[4]

Cyberthreats may appear in various forms. Before the September 11 attacks, it was known that terrorist organizations used communications technology to further their objectives. Sheik Ahmed Yassin, founder of

Hamas, once stated, "We will use whatever tools we can—e-mails, the Internet—to facilitate jihad against the (Israeli) occupiers and their supporters."[5] Osama bin Laden and the al Qaeda network, Hezbollah, and Hamas use computerized files, e-mail, and encryption to facilitate terrorist activities. These organizations make use of the Internet's distributive nature to organize, plan, and conduct their operations, thereby engaging in an "e-jihad," or holy war online. Captured al Qaeda computers reveal the group has been planning to destroy physical critical infrastructure such as dams and electric power grids by attacking the computer systems that control them.

Computer hackers in St. Petersburg, Russia, broke into Citibank's electronic money transfer system and attempted to steal more than $10 million by making wire transfers to accounts throughout the world.[6] All except $400,000 was recovered. The leader, Vladimir Levin, was not subject to extradition to the United States because wire and computer fraud and abuse was not a violation of Russian law. Levin, however, left the safety of Russia and was arrested at an airport outside London and extradited to the United States two years later. He pled guilty to transferring $3.7 million from Citibank customer accounts to accounts he controlled and was sentenced to a three-year prison term and ordered to make $240,015 restitution to Citibank.[7]

The ILoveYou computer virus first appeared in an e-mail attachment named Love-Letter-For-You that, when activated, produced an e-mail worm that overwrote files on hard drives and then mailed itself to every e-mail address contained in an infected Microsoft Outlook address book.[8] The virus spread its damage internationally, but when the suspected hacker was located in the Philippines he could not be prosecuted. No anti-hacking law was yet in place in the Philippines.

Computer operators at the Lawrence Livermore National Laboratory in California (operated by the University of California at Berkeley) discovered that their computer systems were being probed. Law enforcement authorities determined that because nothing of value seemed to have been stolen, no violations of law had occurred. The investigation was shelved. Cliff Stoll, a graduate student in astronomy, was not satisfied and conducted his own investigation. His research concluded that the intruders had obtained sensitive information, including weapons and munitions data from the laboratory's computers. It was later learned that the hackers sold this information to the KGB. Stoll's investigation eventually led to

Hanover, Germany. Three hackers were tried and convicted of espionage, though all were put on probation.[9]

As California suffered through a power crisis that included rolling blackouts, a hacker conducted a computer attack against a server under development at the California Independent System Operator electricity exchange. The attacker was apparently attempting to gain control of the server but was not able to access key operational systems. If the hacker had managed to gain control, then the power crisis could have been significantly worse. The California Independent System Operator discovered the hacking and reported the intrusion to authorities, but local law enforcement officials treated the incident as an isolated event. The FBI, however, recognized the potential for catastrophic and cascading damage to already strained infrastructure and began an investigation.[10]

These cases illustrate the wide cyberthreat continuum we face today. The e-jihad example demonstrates the ability of adversaries to use asymmetric capabilities provided by information technology to attack opponents who otherwise could not be confronted conventionally. The Citibank case demonstrates the difficulty in coordinating law enforcement activities globally and the vulnerability of commercial entities to planned cyberattacks. The ILoveYou virus example represents the mutual vulnerabilities that users share in the interconnected environment.[11] The Lawrence Livermore National Laboratory case shows how difficult it is to quickly and correctly characterize the nature of an attack. This attack was first considered a mere intrusion but was later revealed to be a concerted espionage conspiracy and a serious threat to national security. Finally, the California power case illustrates the potential for catastrophic and widespread damage to infrastructure, industry, and ordinary lives. Each example also reveals to some degree the difficulty commercial and government entities face in understanding and defending against cyberthreats and how those attacked—even after a close call—tend to ascribe the event to mere nuisance.

THREATS AND INTERDEPENDENCE

Computer threats are a reality in our private lives, corporate boardrooms, and government planning offices. Concern over the threat is well justified. As communications technologies converge and computer capabilities increase, the networks, systems, and computers that carry and compute data are as easily manipulated for good as for illegal purposes. This is true for several reasons.

The open architecture of the World Wide Web was developed for efficiency, not security. Although the open nature of the Web allows for easy user access, it is difficult to control or exclude wrongdoers from committing illegal acts. The anonymity of the Internet allows both honest citizens and criminals alike the opportunity to act unnoticed. Both use the same infrastructure and are protected by the same rights. Criminals can develop viruses, plan attacks, and organize complex fraud schemes in secret and in isolation and unleash their plans instantaneously or in stages if they choose, all at the touch of a few keystrokes. Criminals have the ability to act globally, irrespective of territorial and jurisdictional boundaries that constrain state-based law enforcement. The absence of effectively trained law enforcement and international coordination to combat cyberthreats is an invitation to criminals and adversaries. Cyberattackers can choose the time and place of an attack, but those on the receiving end must respond reactively; except in the infrequent case of a tip, they rarely have the ability to proactively pursue their cyberattackers. In addition, attacks are not always limited to the intended targets. They are difficult to contain and often have unintended consequences that may lead to cascading failures among other systems. Finally, states, corporations, and individuals are mutually vulnerable. In many respects, the interconnected world is only as strong as its weakest states and private computer systems. Often states and corporations assumed to have adequate protection do not. For example, the US Defense Intelligence Agency estimates that 80 percent of attacks on US computer networks and systems originate or pass through Canada, which has been described as a virtual "hacker haven."[12]

The growth of the World Wide Web also has greatly expanded the ability of individuals, states, and nonstate groups to commit crimes, challenge or undermine the national security of other states, and attack key infrastructures. Today's information technology is expanding the divide between our vulnerabilities and our ability to respond to threats. As individuals, corporations, states, and civil society are increasingly interconnected, the near future is likely to witness an increase in this divide. In 1999, business-to-business electronic commerce, or "e-business," totaled $145 billion and is expected to reach $7.29 trillion worldwide by 2004.[13] Traffic on the Internet doubles every 100 days, and 1 billion people will be connected to the Internet by 2005.[14] Maintaining security in the exponentially expanding wired environment presents a supreme challenge. How can the technology that propels the benefits of globalization (while at the same time exposing us to greater vulnerabilities) be modified or adjusted to minimize the unwanted costs?

The cyberthreat environment has prompted new thinking over how to craft solutions across the cyberthreat continuum. For example, critical infrastructures—those determined essential to the preservation of state interests—now include telecommunications networks, banking and finance operations, and access to resources in addition to traditional roads, ports, and rail lines. Private and governmental actors are working to forge partnerships to effectively combat cyberthreats, and they are organizing across borders to ease cross-jurisdictional challenges.

Since the events of September 11, 2001, security concerns over physical and cyberthreats have gained new emphasis as states struggle to develop plans and implementation regimes to enhance security. The terrorist attacks underline that many threats today are regional and global concerns that blur public–private distinctions and may not be amenable to "go it alone" solutions. In the United States, 85 percent of critical infrastructure is privately owned, rendering government solutions without private cooperation hollow and likely to fail.[15] Foreign private ownership of domestic critical infrastructures increases the level of difficulty in crafting solutions.

Much of the critical information infrastructure in place today was developed with efficiency and cost concerns at the forefront of planning and development. With the current emphasis on security, is it time to rethink basic planning assumptions that focus on guaranteeing profits and efficiency? Many people are asking not only what can be done to patch the current system, but also whether the overwhelming need for enhancing security warrants a wholesale reevaluation and replacement of more vulnerable systems. Some of the most important players in the information technology industry now acknowledge the need for added security. Bill Gates wants to make Microsoft's software less vulnerable to cyberthreats even if that means delaying the development of new applications.[16] Larry Ellison is promising that Oracle will strive to create database programs that are unbreakable.[17] John Chambers of Cisco Systems has stated that he no longer regards security enhancements on Internet routers as extras but as necessities.[18] Governments are also recognizing the need to protect against cyberthreats. In the United States, the special adviser for cyberspace security to the president is urging the information technology industry to join the government in drafting and implementing a comprehensive strategy to secure against cyberthreats.[19]

Decision makers in both industry and government face significant challenges in light of the cyberthreat continuum. The need for new laws and regulations to ensure security must be balanced with the need to provide users access and privacy, all without putting unwarranted restraint on innovation and promising technology. Industry will not partner with government if security concerns are not balanced with maintaining open markets and allowing firms to remain globally competitive. The global nature of the technology and the fact that it spans public and private boundaries not only complicates the picture for leaders, but also offers potential opportunities if effective public–private relationships can be forged. Neither government nor industry alone has the means to solve the challenges posed by cyberthreats.

The comparative technological advantages once enjoyed by developed states are eroding as essential technology is developed not by government research labs but increasingly by the private sector and is available "off the shelf." As a consequence, new, state-of-the-art technology such as sophisticated encryption is available globally, enabling everyone from money launderers, rogue states, and terrorists to enjoy an asymmetric capability without the heavy research and development budgets of the past. States are interdependent as are government and industry and must rely on each other for an effective international response to cyberthreats.

CYBERTHREATS AND NATIONAL SECURITY

In 2000, a Japanese investigation revealed that the government was using software developed by computer companies affiliated with Aum Shinrikyo, the doomsday sect responsible for the sarin gas attack on the Tokyo subway system in 1995.[20] "The government found 100 types of software programs used by at least 10 Japanese government agencies, including the Defense Ministry, and more than 80 major Japanese companies, including Nippon Telegraph and Telephone."[21] Following the discovery, the Japanese government suspended use of Aum Shinrikyo–developed programs out of concern that Aum-related companies may have compromised security by breaching firewalls, gaining access to sensitive systems or information, allowing invasion by outsiders, planting viruses that could be set off later, or planting malicious code that could cripple computer systems and key data systems.[22]

From these facts, is it clear that the suspects were likely to attempt to overthrow the Japanese government? Had they engaged in espionage, criminal violations, or possible terrorism? Was this a threat to national security? Was Aum Shinrikyo conducting a legitimate commercial enterprise? Is it possible to tell? Clearly, considering the cult's history, the Japanese government proceeded under the assumption that this was a serious state-level threat. The example highlights the key challenges posed by cyberthreats: determining intent and determining the level and nature of the threat quickly and accurately.

Cyberthreats place enormous stress on security and criminal systems that rely on proving intent to secure a criminal conviction. Computer attacks can be instantaneous, time-delayed, or staged in waves. They can be anonymous or falsely attributed to unsuspecting users. It is difficult to identify with a high degree of certainty exactly who committed an act.[23] There is also no way to know for certain an attacker's exact motives or to quickly determine whether the attacker is part of a wider conspiracy. In a broader context, while individual hacks or intrusions can be identified, it is much more difficult to quickly judge whether individual attacks are part of a wider series of attacks. Even if a state recognizes that a concerted attack is under way, an attack is not likely to have purely military objectives. The military–civilian distinction breaks down, requiring government responders to alert and work with private infrastructure and systems owners to safeguard against the attack.

Both the security apparatus that developed to pursue Cold War security objectives and sovereign law enforcement organizations are struggling to adapt to new threats ushered in by globalization. Traditional responses to new security challenges such as cybercrime and cyberterrorism are failing to keep up with the methods and tactics that are available to state and nonstate actors alike.[24]

Because of the preeminent conventional and strategic military power enjoyed by developed states and most notably by the United States, adversaries are seeking ways in which to inflict indirect or asymmetric harm on strong states and their interests abroad. Developed countries are reliant on information technology. Therefore, one area for exploitation by adversaries is attack on critical computer networks.[25]

A few examples illustrate the level to which developed states are reliant on computer networks and technology. The US Department of Defense (DOD) uses 2 million computers and operates more than 10,000 local area networks; some 200 command centers are computer-dependent. These figures do not account for the more than 2 million computer users who regularly do business with the DOD.[26] It is generally conceded that a computer network attack has the potential for causing catastrophic injury to security and could have a strategic reach that would affect cultural sensibilities, including confidence in the government's ability to protect against threats and safeguard personal and commercial interests.[27]

In the United Kingdom, there is growing concern over the threat of computer-based attack and cyberterrorism. Foreign Secretary Robin Cook warned that hacking could cripple Britain faster than a military strike because computers are managing most of the country's infrastructure.[28] Japan issued special legislation with the specific purpose of combating cyberattacks and protecting network communications systems.[29]

Adversaries are developing the tools and doctrine necessary to conduct offensive cyberwarfare programs. A major challenge will be to find ways to defend infrastructure and protect commerce while maintaining an open society. Openness and ease of connectivity promote efficiency, but these attributes also make information infrastructures vulnerable to attack. Unlike the threats of the Cold War, which required state-sponsored infrastructures and installations, cyberthreats are strategically asymmetric, require no state sponsorship, and use commercially available equipment and facilities. A computer in a basement hardly qualifies as a weapons site. These threats can affect systems anywhere in the world, disguise origins and travel routes, and do it all instantaneously.[30]

Despite the potential magnitude of the harm and the strategic nature of the threat, many states—including the United States—continue to characterize cyberthreats as a law enforcement issue with possible national security consequences rather than as a frontline national security issue. As such, a foreign or domestic adversary that develops the ability to interrupt the flow of data will have the potential to weaken any entity that is incapable of responding.

The characterization of the cyberthreat—criminal versus national security threat—is important. The law enforcement community is fundamentally concerned with trials, convictions, and punishing wrongdoers who run afoul of criminal law. Thus, it is bound by statutory authority and concerned with evidentiary trails, burdens of proof, and expert testimony. However, criminal law was not developed in democracies based on principles of efficiency. It was based on the understanding that certain principles, rights, and protections needed to be afforded to the accused. Criminal law generally requires both criminal intent and a criminal act. Proving intent, however, is difficult in many computer-related crimes. Issues that fall under national security, on the other hand, often focus solely on the act's illegality. Representing a threat to national security is sufficient for liability. An example may help illustrate this point. If a computer emergency response team detects a hacker, then the FBI may want the hacker to continue his or her activities in order to trace the hacker and develop an evidentiary trail. By following and monitoring the hacker's moves, his or her intent may become apparent. However, if such an intrusion were to occur against the military's Central Command in Tampa, Florida, during a deployment (the command is responsible for US military operations in the Middle East and South Asia), the military may wish to immediately terminate the hack and even strike back or "hack back" at the attacker.

But what if the attack is coming not from a single hacker but is being orchestrated by a state? Many countries are developing doctrines of computer attack and defense. The United States bases its information operations doctrine on its ability to attack an adversary's information and information systems while defending its own. The US approach is to blind an adversary and keep it confused over the "ground truth" of the battlefield, thus interfering with the opposing senior leadership's ability to make sound decisions.

The Russian Federation is also developing information warfare strategy and doctrine. The Russian concept of information warfare includes computer network attack and defense but is more expansive than the US concept and includes the use of information to break down the ability of the human mind and body to function effectively. China is currently developing a unique information warfare strategy based on information weapons as unconventional warfare weapons and battlefield force multipliers.[31]

What state-sponsored information warfare operations have in common is the use of information technology to achieve strategic (national-level) or tactical (battlefield-level) effects in order to achieve political or military objectives. Essentially, it is the conduct of warfare through the use of information technology. Specifically, the United States defines information operations as

> actions taken across the entire conflict spectrum to affect adversary information and information systems while protecting one's own information and information systems. Information warfare is conducted during crisis or conflict to achieve specific objectives over an adversary. Information assurance protects and defends information and information systems by ensuring their availability, integrity, authenticity, and confidentiality.[32]

If an incident appears to have the characteristics of a computer attack, then just what options are available to the government? Pursuant to the UN Charter specifically and the body of law known as the Law of Armed Conflict in general,[33] military force can only be used when responding to an armed attack on one's own territory. In addition, customary international law holds that any retaliation must be taken in self-defense and only to the extent necessary to terminate the initial attack and to prevent further intrusions.[34] Where does this leave a state after a cyberattack? The answer depends on the level and degree of damage caused by an attack. If a cyberattack causes physical damage or death to citizens by, for example, causing a dam to fail, then certainly a cyber-response would be warranted and probably a use of force would be justified. If, however, a banking system were taken down, use of force would not be permitted and a cyber-response might or might not be justified. In this case, considering the potential for unintended consequences that a response might cause, decision makers may want to find other alternatives. International practice recognizes that states may inflict great hardship on each other and their respective citizenry without such activity constituting the use of force or a violation of international law.[35] This is significant because information attacks will certainly create harm and hardship but may never constitute aggression or rise to the level of an armed attack. Law and policy have yet to evolve so that they can fully answer many of the questions posed by cyberthreats. Perhaps the events of September 11, 2001, and the recognition of mutual vulnerability will forge a new consensus on how to effectively deal with cyberthreats.

CYBERTERRORISM

Cyberterrorism presents a definitional problem. There is no recognized international definition for cyberterrorism. Each country has its own cyberterrorism rules. For example, the special legislation enacted by Japan to combat cyberterrorism defines it as the unauthorized entry into computer systems through communications networks such as the Internet and the damage caused to those systems as a result of the unauthorized access.[36] This expansive definition would constitute computer fraud and abuse in other states such as the United States, and such activities would not rise to the level of cyberterrorism.

Perhaps the best way to understand cyberterrorism is to understand it is an extension of age-old terrorist principles adapted for use in the new high-tech environment. Using violence against noncombatants to cause fear, terrorists' activities are politically motivated and seek to coerce governments or civilians in furtherance of the terrorists' political agenda. Cyberterrorists are thus politically motivated but make use of information technology and networks to further their agendas. Clearly, disrupting communications, airport, and utilities systems for the purpose of inflicting damage to achieve a political end are all cyberterrorist activities, capabilities al Qaeda is developing. In one example, a suspected terrorist group calling itself the Internet Black Tigers attacked Sri Lankan government computers with "suicide e-mail bombings" in an effort to overwhelm and disable government information systems, embarrass the Sri Lankan government, and draw attention to the cause of Tamil separatism in northern and eastern Sri Lanka.[37] Incidents such as this may become increasingly familiar as marginalized groups without political voices learn how to exploit Internet technology for their political ends.

Using the Internet to facilitate terrorist activities is also another aspect of cyberterrorism. For example, Wadih el Hage, a prime suspect in the 1998 US embassy bombings in Africa, sent encrypted e-mails under alias names to al Qaeda "associates." Ramzi Yousef, the planner of the 1993 attack on the World Trade Center, used encrypted files to hide details of a plot to destroy eleven US jetliners. Yousef's computer was discovered by Philippine officials and sent to the FBI for analysis. Two of the files took more than a year to decrypt.[38]

For terrorists, cyber-based attacks have distinct advantages over physical attacks. They can be conducted remotely, anonymously, and relatively cheaply, and they do not require significant investments in weapons, explosives, and personnel. The effects can still be widespread and profound. Consider the effects and publicity that followed when the message "Hacked by Chinese" appeared on government and corporate computers as communications networks were shut down because of the Code Red virus in July 2001.[39]

Incidents of cyberterrorism are likely to increase. They will be conducted through denial-of-service attacks that overload servers, worms and viruses, unauthorized intrusions, Web-site defacements, attacks on network infrastructures, and other methods that we are unable to envision today. One report concludes that cyberattacks in the near future will immediately accompany physical attacks and will, to an increasing degree, focus on high-value targets.[40]

So why does the vulnerability persist? Commercial off-the-shelf operating systems and applications are widely shared and their vulnerabilities are widely known. In addition, because many technology developers and producers contract out work and services, often to overseas partners, there is opportunity for mischief whenever controls and quality-assurance procedures are not in place. The Internet is also a target-rich environment in which not all systems can be protected. Finally, cultural sensitivities, such as privacy rights, preclude intrusive security measures.

CYBERCRIME

In 1995–1996, a hacker used a US-based Web site to gain unlimited access to multiple US military, university, and private computer systems. The FBI tracked the hacker to Argentina and notified a local telecommunications carrier, which in turn notified local law enforcement. An Argentinean investigating judge authorized a search of the hacker's apartment and the seizure of his computer. Julio Cesar Ardita was investigated for intrusions into an Argentinean telecommunications system, but Argentine law did not cover hacking systems in the United States, and the judge ruled that only the United States could prosecute him for these crimes. In the absence of an extradition treaty, Ardita agreed in May 1998 to come to the United States and plead guilty to felony charges of unlawfully intercepting communications and damaging Department of Defense files and NASA computers. He was fined $5,000 and sentenced to three years' probation.[41]

This example illustrates many of the challenges that law enforcement faces in overcoming cyber-related crimes. Jurisdictional, substantive, and cultural issues must be addressed. Information technologies pose a variety of challenges to criminal law and procedure. Many age-old crimes, such as fraud, theft, and money laundering have qualitatively changed because of the new cybermedium. With the aid of computers and the Web, wrongdoers can perpetrate crimes with greater ease, speed, and anonymity. Individuals can easily copy and steal information, interfere with or co-opt commercial and public assets, and gain illegal access to private information. New criminal activity, such as computer network attacks, virus disseminations, and hacking likewise pose significant challenges because of the speed at which they take place and the magnitude of damage they can create.[42]

Cybercrime and cyberterrorism are not mutually exclusive because both are intent-based. For most crimes, a state prosecutor must prove that the suspect intended to commit the crime and indeed did so.

Cybercrime is the commission of illegal acts through the use of communications and information-based technology. Cybercrime includes fraudulent activities such as e-mail schemes, identity theft, and credit card fraud, as well as theft crimes such as electronic espionage, corporate espionage, and money laundering.[43] It also includes nuisance crimes, including transmission of viruses, system shutdowns, interference with network systems, denial-of-service attacks, and Web-site defacements.

Cybercrime is also a tax because it increases the costs of doing business and passes those costs on to consumers.[44] Estimated worldwide losses to cybercrime run between $20 billion and $40 billion, although experts acknowledge that no one completely knows the full extent of the damage.[45] The FBI estimates that less than one-fifth of all cyberattacks are reported to law enforcement authorities.[46]

A FRAMEWORK FOR ADDRESSING THE PROBLEM

States, corporations, and industry are mutually vulnerable and interdependent to the threats posed by cyberthreats. States and citizens must recognize that their own self-interests lie in multinational cooperation and the development of global information-related standards and practices. The challenges posed by cyberthreats cannot be overcome by the developed world acting alone. All states are stakeholders in combating cyberthreats. However, because of the informational advantages enjoyed by developed states and the costs associated with enhancing the information infrastructures of developing states, there is some reluctance to support open and multilateral solutions. For example, even though it is vulnerable to computer network attacks, the United States enjoys superiority if not dominance in the realm of information operations and information warfare. This dominance is perpetuated by US attempts to limit the ability of other states to gain information capabilities via dual-use technology or anti-encryption limitations.

A more robust understanding of the vulnerabilities and advantages posed by cyberthreats must be developed before we can develop a cogent strategy that aligns domestic and global policy. Considering the rise in cyberincidents, a more coordinated global response is warranted.[47] In analyses of how law and public policy can be used to combat cyberthreats, solutions often suffer from a lack of practicality and applicability to real-world circumstances. Therefore, in determining the proper policy course to pursue, states and private parties must first address whether there is a need for additional public–private cooperation or regulation. In other words, is the current system working? A state must then, in coordination with industry, consider whether the nature of the threat in light of the security requirements necessitates a coordinated international approach. Finally, if international harmonization is warranted, an international framework will have to be developed.

One attempt to forge a public–private partnership was the creation of a new US government agency in 1998: the National Infrastructure Protection Center (NIPC), an interagency unit within the Department of Justice (DOJ). NIPC provides cyberthreat assessments, warnings, and vulnerability assessments and shares this information with industry and the public. For example, three days after the September 11 attacks, NIPC issued an advisory that warned of an expected increase in computer-related incidents as a result of the terrorist attacks.[48] NIPC has had some successes in fostering incident reporting and information sharing, such as the speedy notice and containment of the Melissa computer virus in 1999. NIPC was the US government's first attempt to cooperate and collaborate with industry to reduce cyberthreats, but there have been limitations to its success so far. Though NIPC does issue advisories to the public, the link to industry is modest and lacks the breadth and depth that both government officials and corporate leaders had originally anticipated.

Why the lack of success when both the government and industry acknowledged the need for cooperation? In organizing NIPC, the government did what governments do best. An interagency group was organized and key government officials were identified to lead the new center. Policies and procedures were put in place. A mission statement was drafted. Then the NIPC and its policies and procedures were "rolled out" to industry. Industry then did what it does best: It evaluated the costs of partnering with NIPC, asked why it was not consulted before, and then ignored the agency.

The reason for the failure thus lies in a lack of coordination from the beginning and in difficulties in overcoming mistrust. For public–private partnerships to work, neither side can come to the other and roll out a program with all the answers. Government and industry are organized to achieve vastly different objectives, and points of view must be aired and procedures negotiated. The government also failed to appreciate how its NIPC programs would affect industry. A one-size-fits-all approach cannot work to combat cyberthreats that cross vastly different industries. For example, NIPC provided for no Freedom of Information Act (FOIA) exemption or exclusion, meaning that any information turned over to the government could be subject to a FOIA request and wind up in the public domain. This raised concerns that information volunteered to help contain computer threats could be used against companies. Would government warnings undermine confidence in the banking industry or a specific company, for example, if the total amount of money electronically stolen from banks was made public? Furthermore, NIPC initially mandated that failure to provide the information requested could lead to fines and liability. NIPC was also physically housed in the FBI building in Washington, D.C., which led many critics to conclude that the FBI would be poring over materials looking for any wrongdoing. Would Microsoft, subject to a DOJ antitrust suit, feel comfortable turning over proprietary information to NIPC with mere assurances that the DOJ would not use it against the company later? In addition, in compiling, analyzing, and publishing threat data, what safeguards were in place if government inadvertently passed on information about a company's real computer vulnerabilities? Trust was lost early and could never be fully rebuilt.

The fact that NIPC is concerned with security and industry with protecting its competitiveness and securing profits need not be a "deal breaker" every time. Clearly, better attempts at public–private cooperation are needed. Industry, however, does not make law.

Although better public–private cooperation is needed, should additional domestic laws be enacted to combat cyberthreats? The answer changes depending on the state in question. In many developed states, comprehensive laws are on the books to punish wrongdoers; in others, no such prohibitions exist. Therefore, a case can be made for seeking international agreements on legal harmonization. International agreements should be pursued when a challenge has transboundary effects, represents an extraterritorial threat, produces a failure in effective enforcement in response to a threat, or where there are highly divergent state practices and a need to harmonize law to increase effectiveness. Cyberthreats satisfy each criterion. So what are the options?

States and private sector actors may rely on the ongoing development of international policy and law to combat cyberthreats. Although detractors term this the "do-nothing" approach, it has the advantage of a more stable and arguably more gradual and balanced development because it builds on current structures. Another approach is to clarify legal ambiguities at the margin, modifying current policy and adapting it to information technology and computer threats. This affords policy makers the chance to develop a strategy that fosters individual and specific critical information technology structures. These efforts may proceed through the United Nations or may concentrate on lower-level, bilateral, or multilateral agreements. This approach favors formalizing agreements where agreement can be found.

Finally, in a more comprehensive fashion, global leaders could seek to harmonize domestic laws and expand criminal liability in a coordinated way for agreed-upon cyberthreats. This approach relies on promoting cooperation in investigations and prosecutions. Because of the inherent importance of information infrastructures globally, certain actions could be condemned and, considering today's environment, perhaps outlawed as acts of terrorism or egregious cybercrimes.[49]

The options above should not be construed as either–or solutions but considered as appropriate responses to different challenges along the threat continuum. For example, cybercrime and anticyberterrorism laws may require a wider and more comprehensive approach, while criminal liability for fraud and hacking may better evolve at the margin.

In evaluating specific initiatives, new international agreements should be crafted to ensure that they are flexible enough to adapt to the changing technological environment, are tailored and scaled to the challenge, are reasonable and proportional to the threat they seek to overcome, and consider the unique values of the states involved (to use the US example, consider the liberal democratic principles based on underlying constitutional rights).

While assessing the current global policy on cyberthreats, its successes and failures in the past, and the economic and structural importance of information infrastructures, policy makers should consider the option to clarify legal ambiguity at the margin highly attractive and able to generate consensus on key issues. It provides flexibility to respond to technological changes and takes advantage of existing laws. This is particularly true for cyberthreats, where the relative potential harm is great and the measures that could be used to combat the threat so potentially sweeping.

A MULTILATERAL APPROACH

The effort by the Council of Europe to combat cybercrime provides an interesting case study in how to pursue cyber-related solutions. As an intergovernmental organization, the Council of Europe seeks to shape common European legislation for its member states. Among the council's stated purposes is

> to modernize and harmonize national legislation in line with the principles of democracy, human rights and the rule of law; improving justice by simple and flexible judicial procedures; seeking common solutions to the legal and ethical problems arising from scientific and technical progress by adopting regulations to cover the problems facing modern societies.[50]

In 1989, seeing the need for consistent computer-related legislation, the Council of Europe issued a recommendation on computer-related crime.[51] This was the first step in unifying European computer law. It proposed required minimum standards and activities that member countries must criminalize and another set of options that member states might wish to criminalize. Building on the success of its recommendations, the Council of Europe issued a draft Convention on Cybercrime. The draft proposes common definitions of computer-related offenses and content-related offenses.[52] Once ratified by the member states, the convention will have the full effect of a multilateral treaty with the force of law among the ratifying countries. As with any Council of Europe convention, all member European countries may sign the convention, and observer states such as the United States, Canada, and Japan that have participated in drafting the convention may also join, subject to ratification.[53] Eventually, even non-observing states may be permitted by the Council of Europe to enter into the convention.[54] Among its provisions, the draft convention makes it a crime to create, download, or post on a Web site any computer program that is "designed or adapted" primarily to gain access to a computer system without permission. It also prohibits the development of software designed to interfere with the "functioning of a computer system" by deleting or altering data, and it allows authorities to order someone to reveal his or her passwords or phrases used in an encryption key.[55] The convention also requires Web sites and Internet providers to collect information about their users, a rule that would potentially limit anonymous remailers.

The draft Convention on Cybercrime raises many issues. For example, many in the United States accustomed to protection of privacy rights are skeptical because the convention favors law enforcement capabilities over US privacy rights. Privacy advocates are concerned that the convention may interfere with the ability of online users to speak anonymously and that anonymous remailers may be outlawed. The convention also may interfere with the ability of everyone from corporations to hackers to test the security of their own information infrastructures. Internet service providers claim the draft makes unfair demands on them by asking them to track Web users' online movements.

The draft Convention on Cybercrime illustrates how good ideas can become controversial when they move from the drawing board to implementation. As early as 1989, the Council of Europe recognized that domestic regulation alone was insufficient to overcome the cybercrime threat in Europe. There was widespread industry support and both the public and private sector recognized the need for legal harmonization. The threat posed by cybercrime is clearly an extraterritorial threat, effective enforcement is lacking, and there are highly divergent state laws and practices on cybercrime. So why is there controversy? New laws, particularly regional agreements, tend to establish legal norms for the largely unregulated realm of cyberspace. Regional agreements often become customary international law that may ultimately evolve into formalized treaties. In effect, Europe is writing the first international code of conduct and criminal code that will be accepted by a multilateral body. By setting this benchmark, states and industries that did not have a voice in the process may find the European convention an attack on the unique values of other countries. Finally, and perhaps most significantly, the Council of Europe is a state-centric organization. Although industry applauded the council's efforts early on, the lack of transparency increased as the release date for the draft neared. The draft convention may be ratified by the member states, but industry is and will continue to resist. The lack of industry buy-in across the entire life cycle of the convention may leave it a blunt and ineffective tool.

CONCLUSION

Cyberthreats come in a variety of forms, including hacking, cybercrime, cyberterrorism, information warfare, and information operations. Information technology allows a wide range of actors to cause a wide range of damage and chaos across the cyberthreat continuum. To understand and overcome cyberthreats, two assumptions must be made. First, states, industry, and individuals are mutually vulnerable and interdependent. Second, neither states nor industry alone has the authority or capability to solve the problems posed by cyberthreats. Much of the key technology and infrastructure lies in the private sector, while the authority to create and enforce laws and the legitimacy to enter into international agreements resides with states. Recognizing these two key assumptions and embedding them in planning and policy will go a long way toward developing cyberthreat solutions.

ENDNOTES

1. "Riptech Releases Ground Breaking Internet Security Threat Report" (press release), Jan. 28, 2002. Available at <www.riptech.com/newsevents/release020127.html>;

"Riptech Internet Security Threat Report Volume II Quantifies Rise in Internet Attacks" (press release), July 8, 2002. Available at <http://www.riptech.com/newsevents/release020708.html>.

2. Riptech, an Alexandria, Virginia, firm that tracks computer intrusions, discovered at least 180,000 cyberattacks from January through June 2002 for its more than 400 clients across the world ("Riptech Internet Security Threat Report").

3. Ibid.

4. "Riptech Releases Ground Breaking Internet Security Threat Report."

5. Barton Gellman, "Cyber-Attacks by Al Qaeda Feared: Terrorists at Threshold of Using Internet as Tool of Bloodshed, Experts Say," *Washington Post,* June 27, 2002, p. A1; Jack Kelley, "Terrorist Instructions Hidden Online," *USA Today,* April 14, 2001. Operational details of future targets are hidden in plain view. As Kelley writes, "We recognize that cyber tools offer them new, low-cost, easily hidden means to inflict damage. Terrorists and extremists already use the Internet to communicate, to raise funds, recruit, and gather intelligence. They may even launch attacks remotely from countries where their actions are not illegal or with whom we have no extradition agreements."

6. The accounts were global indeed and included Finland, Russia, Germany, the Netherlands, the United States, Israel, and Switzerland.

7. Dorothy Denning, *Information Warfare and Security* (New York: ACM Press, 1999), 55.

8. Description of the ILoveYou virus found at <http://getvirushelp.com/iloveyou/>.

9. Denning, *Information Warfare and Security,* 206–207.

10. Charles Bickers, "Combat on the Web," *Far Eastern Economic Review,* Aug. 16, 2001.

11. Referred to as *cyberplagues* by Dorothy Denning. See *Information Warfare and Security,* 269–281.

12. Apparently, Canada is a "hacker haven" because of its large number of computers, high percentage of residents who own computers, and the heavy integration between US and Canadian computer infrastructure and systems. See David Pugliese, "Blame Canada for 80% of Cyberattacks: Country's 'Zone of Vulnerability', U.S. Military Report Warns," *Ottowa Citizen,* March 25, 2000.

13. "Gartner Group Forecasts Worldwide Business-to-Business E-Commerce to Reach $7.29 Trillion in 2004: E-Market Makers to be Key Driver of Business-to-Business Segment," Gartner Group press release, Jan. 26, 2000.

14. See Lynn Margherio, David Henry, Sandra Cooke, and Sabrina Montes, *The Emerging Digital Economy* (Washington, DC: US Department of Commerce, April 1998).

15. C. Paul Robinson, Joan B. Woodard, and Samuel G. Varnado, "Critical Infrastructure: Interlinked and Vulnerable," *Issues in Science and Technology Online* (Fall 1998); available at <www.nap.edu/issues/15.1/robins.htm>.

16. Ariana Eunjung Cha, "Cybersecurity a Top Priority: White House Adviser Presses Computer Industry to Do More," *Washington Post,* Feb. 8, 2002, p. E1.

17. Ibid.

18. Ibid.

19. Kyle Balluck, "Cybersecurity Czar Asks IT Industry for Help," *Washington Post,* Dec. 4, 2001.

20. Maryann Cusimano Love, *Public Private Partnerships and Global Problems: Y2K and Cybercrime.* Paper presented at the International Studies Association, Hong Kong, July 2001.

21. Ibid. Cusimano Love adds, "The Japanese defense ministry used Aum-developed communications programs at 20 ground bases across Japan to gain more rapid access to the internet. Aum programs were also used for airline route management and mainframe computer operations. The software companies earned the business through indirect subcontracting relationships, underbidding competitors by 30 to 40% because their employees, all Aum members, worked for virtually no pay."

22. Calvin Sims, "Japan Software Suppliers Linked to Sect," *The New York Times,* March 2, 2000, p. A6.

23. This is true even if the specific terminal from which the attack originated can be identified. It may be difficult, however, to say exactly who was at the terminal when the attack was planned and executed.

24. Virtually every benefit of the global era in some way poses a challenge to security. For example, the cheap cost of technology facilitates the rise of computer-related crime and cyberterrorism. The rapid transit of goods and people now challenges the ability of states to secure their borders. The free flow of data, people, and ideas makes it difficult to conduct intelligence gathering without running afoul of First Amendment guarantees. The growth of world markets and international investment aids in financing terrorism and engaging in money laundering.

25. But are the most technologically advanced states also the most vulnerable? According to Bangladeshi Deputy Prime Minister Datuk Seri Abdullah Ahmad Badawi, "Technologically superior states can also cripple the defenses and economies of victim states at will, again placing developing states at a disadvantage. . . . It would cost the average Bangladeshi more than eight years' income to buy a computer, whereas it would cost the average American just one month's wage. And what would this repository of information, in which more than 80 percent of the content is in English, mean to 90 percent of the people world wide who do not speak it?" See "Internet Widening Gap Between Haves, Have Nots," *New Straits Times Press,* June 5, 2000.

26. Jack Brock, *Information Security: Computer Attacks at Department of Defense Pose Increasing Risks* (Washington, DC: General Accounting Office, Accounting and Information Management Division, May 22, 1996) (publication no. GAO/T-AIMD-96-92).

27. A comprehensive list of potential computer network attacks is beyond the scope of this paper, but a few to mention are using computers to reroute trains, corrupt databases, impose information blockades in or out of computers, alter traffic control systems, interfere with law enforcement emergency response systems, and corrupt key utilities. See Roger C. Molander, Andrew S. Riddile, and Peter A. Wilson, *Strategic Information Warfare: A New Face of War* (New York: Rand Corp., 1996); and the President's Commission on Critical Infrastructure Protection, *Critical Foundations: Protecting America's Infrastructures* (Washington, DC: US Government Printing Office, Oct. 1997).

28. Nick Hopkins, "Cyber Terror Threatens UK's Biggest Companies," *Guardian,* April 3, 2001.

29. "Japan Special Legislation to Combat Cyberterrorism," *Yomiuri Shimbun,* Nov. 30, 2000.

30. John C. Gannon, "Intelligence Challenges through 2015." Remarks to Columbus Council on World Affairs, April 27, 2000; available at <www.cia.gov/cia/public_affairs/speeches/archives/2000/gannon_speech_05022000.html>. Gannon is chairman of the National Intelligence Council.

31. James Mulvenon, *China and Cyberwar.* Presentation to "Information Warfare Post Y2K: A National Security Perspective," Jane's Conference, Washington, DC, May 12, 2000.

32. This definition of information operations is provided by the Assistant Secretary of Defense for Command, Control, Communications, and Intelligence (ASD C3I) and can be found at <www.c3i.osd.mil/faq/>.

33. The Law of Armed Conflict (LOAC) is a body of international law that attempts to regulate conduct during armed hostilities in a manner that minimizes savagery but does not impede the ability of states and factions to enter into and carry out conflict. The rules and general principles of the LOAC are applicable to all conflicts, including those conducted in cyberspace.

34. Humanitarian law limits how much a state may punish an enemy. The most significant principles, to protect citizens and noncombatants, require a state to weigh the prospect of gain through military attack against harm. This principle, derived from customary law, essentially establishes that a response must be appropriate to a grievance and must be considered in light of objectives and possible casualties. See Martens Clause, 1899 Hague Peace Conference (attacks will be judged by effects rather than by methods).

35. Examples include boycotts and withholding medical aid or other needed resources.

36. "Government Drafts Plan to Combat Cyberterrorism," *Yomiuri Shimbun,* Nov. 30, 2000.

37. Jim Wolf, "Cyber Terrorism," *Scotsman,* May 13, 1998, p. 3.

38. Jack Kelley, "Terror Groups Hide Behind Web Encryption," *USA Today,* April 13, 2001.

39. "'Chinese' Virus Targets Microsoft Security Hole," CNN, July 20, 2001; available at <www.cnn.com/2001/BUSINESS/asia/07/20/hk.codered/>.

40. Institution for Security Technology Studies, *Cyber Attacks during the War on Terrorism: A Predictive Analysis* (Hanover, NH: Dartmouth College, Sept. 22, 2001), 9; available at <www.ists.dartmouth.edu/ISTS/counterterrorism/cyber_attacks.htm>.

41. David Goldstone and Betty-Ellen Shave, "International Dimensions of Crimes in Cyberspace," *Fordham International Law Journal* (June 1999): 1924, 1928.

42. In many respects, the realm of cyberspace represents the ultimate potential of economic liberalism: private self-regulation of human interaction, unfettered and instantaneous free flows of capital, and trade in a new, borderless space unconstrained by sovereign institutions.

43. Money laundering facilitates much illegal activity worldwide. However, it can also be seen as a theft crime by depriving the legitimate owners of resources the benefit of their property.

44. Anthony Lake, *Six Nightmares: Real Threats in a Dangerous World and How America Can Meet Them* (New York: Little, Brown, 2000), 46.

45. "Presidential Commission to Prepare for 'Electronic Pearl Harbors,'" *Telecom and Network Security Review,* Aug. 1996.

46. See the 2002 CSI/FBI Computer Crime and Security Survey at <www.gocsi.com>.

47. Attacks on computers are on the rise. Notable cyberattacks and viruses include the attack on the CIA on September 19, 1996; the attack on the US Department of Justice in August 1996; the attack on *The New York Times* in September 1998; the Melissa virus in 1999; the Naked Wife virus on March 7, 2001; and the Matcher virus on April 19, 2001.

48. NIPC Advisory 01-020, Sept. 14, 2001; available at <www.infragard.net/warnings/01_020.htm>.

49. Perhaps hijacking agreements could serve as a useful and instructive model.

50. Information obtained from the Council of Europe Web site; available at <www. coe.int/portalT.asp>.

51. Council of Europe, "Computer-Related Crime," Recommendation No. R (89) 9; available at <http://europa.eu.int/ISPO/eif/InternetPoliciesSite/Crime/crime1. html>.

52. For a discussion of the history of the Convention on Cybercrime, see Goldstone and Shave, "International Dimensions of Crimes in Cyberspace," 1945.

53. The US Department of Justice, which assisted the council in its discussions of the Convention on Cybercrime, is likely to urge the Senate to approve it. Other non-European countries actively involved in negotiations include Canada, Japan, and South Africa.

54. These efforts involve only developed countries; multilateral efforts in the developing world lag. It's not easy to persuade countries where Internet use is not yet pervasive to see cybercrime as an urgent problem. But an attack can be launched as easily from the Third World as from Europe or the United States, and the network will only be as strong as its weakest links.

55. Only Singapore and Malaysia have enacted such a requirement into law. This requirement may pose a substantial problem for the United States because it runs counter to the constitutional protection against self-incrimination.

CHAPTER NINE

Nuclear Smuggling

Rensselaer W. Lee and James L. Ford

The most urgent unmet national security threat to the United States today is the danger that weapons of mass destruction or weapons-usable materials in Russia could be stolen and sold to terrorists or hostile nations and used against American troops abroad or citizens at home.

—*A Report Card on the Department of Energy's Nonproliferation Programs with Russia,* Secretary of Energy's Advisory Board, Jan. 10, 2001

THE NATURE OF NUCLEAR SMUGGLING[1]

Osama bin Laden claims that the al Qaeda terrorist network has nuclear and chemical weapons "for deterrence purposes," or to ensure that weapons of mass destruction will not be used against the network. There are unmistakable indications that he has been actively seeking nuclear materials for at least six years—and is prepared to spend vast resources to achieve this ambition.[2] At the trial of those accused of the US embassy bombings in Africa, al Qaeda turncoat Jamal Ahmed al-Fadl described his role in helping to broker a deal in which bin Laden attempted to pay $1.5 million for a cylinder of South African uranium.[3] Sympathetic Pakistani nuclear scientists Sultan Bashiruddin Mahmood and Abdul Majid confessed having lengthy discussions regarding nuclear, chemical, and biological weapons with bin Laden in August 2001 in Afghanistan. During those meetings bin Laden said that he had acquired some type of radiological material from the Islamic Movement of Uzbekistan and wanted to know how to use it.

Officials cannot confirm that bin Laden has acquired either radiological material or the ability to use it.[4] Bin Laden has repeatedly called for America's destruction, saying that acquiring nuclear and other weapons of mass destruction for use in the jihad against the United States is a "religious duty" for Muslims. He entitled one such statement "The Nuclear Bomb of Islam."[5] Whether his al Qaeda terrorist group—thought by the US government to have been responsible for the September 11, 2001, airline hijackings and attacks on the Pentagon and the World Trade Center in New York City—might have a nuclear capability of some kind is a disturbing question that has been receiving serious scrutiny by international security experts. The issue highlights growing international concerns with nuclear smuggling.

Cases of illicit transactions in nuclear materials, more often referred to as nuclear smuggling, have occurred for more than twenty years virtually throughout the world, including the United States.[6] Of the 450 reported attempts of illegal trafficking recorded by the Department of Energy through 1994, most proved to be nothing more than profit-motivated scams involving bogus materials (such as "red mercury") and perpetrated by opportunists.[7] But the end of the Cold War turned what had been a minor nuisance into a major transsovereign issue. As the chairman of the President's Committee on Science and Technology noted back in 1995, "There is now a clear and present danger that the essential ingredients of nuclear bombs could fall into the hands of radical states or terrorist groups."[8]

Condoleezza Rice, President George W. Bush's National Security Advisor, aptly summed up the current situation in these words, "American security is threatened less by Russia's strength than by its weakness and incoherence. This suggests immediate attention to the safety and security of Moscow's nuclear forces and stockpile."[9] A clear shift in the nature and significance of the nuclear smuggling problem was signaled in 1994 by the unprecedented leakage of nuclear materials from the former Soviet Union (FSU). Although Western and Central European government officials, including the Russians, recognized that the reporting of such incidents was incomplete and of mixed reliability, there were unmistakable new trends: increases observed in the numbers of attempted transactions, the numbers of participants, and the types and quantities of nuclear materials offered for sale.[10] The trafficking was no longer limited to bogus or nuclear-associated materials, such as beryllium or cesium, but now included the core materials necessary for making nuclear weapons—highly enriched uranium and plutonium—being offered in militarily significant quantities.[11]

Understanding the Threat: Not Just a Bomb

Experts agree that obtaining a sufficient amount of special nuclear material is the single most difficult challenge in the construction of a nuclear weapon. The technical difficulty and expense of acquiring such material provided the principal barrier against the proliferation of nuclear weapons during the Cold War. Although still a significant challenge, that barrier has now been breached and is no longer as formidable as it once was.

The arrest of Abdullah al Muhajir, who has been accused of conspiring to build and detonate a dirty bomb on a US city, illustrates significant changes to the proliferation threat: the actors themselves, the types of materials involved, and the means of delivery.[12] The possibility of a rogue state (such as Iran, Iraq, or Libya) acquiring enough special nuclear material to construct rudimentary nuclear weapons is no longer considered the sole threat or even the most likely or worrisome possibility. Terrorist groups, subnational groups, or disgruntled individuals are attempting to use nuclear materials to construct an improvised nuclear device or a radiological dispersal device. An improvised nuclear device (or dirty bomb) is designed to produce a nuclear explosion of lower yield and greatly increases the radioactive fallout. A radiological dispersal device uses a conventional explosion to scatter radioactive materials and thus not only contaminate an area but also spread fear and insecurity among inhabitants. These scenarios both broaden the threat in terms of available materials and technologies and increase the pool of potential proliferators and the likelihood of an incident—particularly so in view of the cache of cesium, strontium, or cobalt that intelligence officials believe Osama bin Laden has acquired.[13] On this point, Harvard Professor Graham Allison disagrees with the skeptics in the intelligence community that al Qaeda does not have a nuclear capability: "I find it well within the realm of the probable that they have fissile material from Russia, which they could fashion into a device that they could put into a minivan" or could smuggle into the United States via relatively unregulated container cargo shipping.[14]

The dissolution of the former Soviet Union made large quantities of weapons-usable materials (not just radioactive medical isotopes or spent nuclear fuel) susceptible to theft or diversion while the security of at-risk facilities diminished, a paradox that is typical of transsovereign problems. Special nuclear material facilities and activities in the FSU no longer receive the same level of protection, control, and monitoring from the KGB, the Red Army, or other Soviet control organs. In addition, there is no accurate and complete inventory of FSU special nuclear materials.

Weapon delivery to a target also has been simplified, especially in terms of an improvised nuclear device or radiological dispersal device. It is not necessary to have sophisticated military aircraft or missile delivery systems. Terrorists can load one of these devices into a van and drive it to the target, as demonstrated by al Qaeda operatives' first attempt to bring down the World Trade Center in 1993, at the federal office building in Oklahoma City in 1995, in the US embassy bombings in Africa in 1998, and in the bombing of the USS Cole in Yemen in 2000. As noted by the secretary of energy's advisory board in 2001, "A nuclear engineer graduate with a grapefruit-sized lump of plutonium could fashion a nuclear device that would fit in a van like the one the terrorist [Ramzi Yousef] parked in the World Trade Center in 1993."[15]

Sen. Sam Nunn (D-GA), cosponsor of the Nunn–Lugar legislation to address problems of nuclear smuggling, described the nuclear threat emerging from the FSU as

> creat[ing] scenarios that, even if anticipated, are unfathomable in their scope. Never before in history has an empire disintegrated while in possession of some 30,000 nuclear weapons, at least 40,000 tons of chemical weapons, significant biological weaponry capability, and thousands of weapons scientists and technicians unsure of how long they will receive salaries with which to feed their families. Let loose was a vast potential supermarket for nuclear weapons, weapons-grade uranium and plutonium, and equally deadly chemical and biological weapons.[16]

Nunn's concerns were echoed in findings from investigations of the nuclear black market conducted at Harvard[17] and at the Center for Strategic and International Studies in Washington, D.C.[18]

The threat is multifaceted. It can appear in many guises and be sustained by a multitude of motivations. Although the supply of nuclear materials that are attractive to terrorist and criminal groups resides in a handful of countries, the demand is more widespread and may well include subnational groups and individuals in addition to the so-called rogue states. Large amounts of nuclear material in the FSU are now more susceptible to theft. Meanwhile, political and social turmoil throughout the world makes stealing nuclear material to amass power, exert influence, or seek retribution more attractive.

Although policy makers and analysts are not in complete agreement about the severity of the nuclear smuggling threat, there does appear to be general consensus in the national security community that early patterns of nuclear smuggling may be a prelude to more serious episodes, including major covert exports of fissile material, weapon components, and even intact nuclear weapons. The ongoing level of nuclear smuggling opens new criminal trade channels and increases opportunities for the proliferation of weapons of mass destruction.[19]

HOW SERIOUS IS THE PROBLEM?

The true dimensions of the current nuclear trafficking threat are unknown. The handful of known diversion incidents that have involved weapons-usable materials do not tell the whole story. Governments reveal little about nuclear theft and smuggling episodes, and government information channels themselves may be impaired. For example, at a recent meeting of the International Atomic Energy Agency (IAEA) on terrorist attacks on nuclear facilities, Yuri Volodin, head of the safety department for the Russian nuclear regulatory agency, reported a security violation in the past two years "of the highest possible consequence," which the Russians had not disclosed previously.[20]

Governments generally do not like to admit their security has been compromised. Previous statements of the Russian government over the years report that "not a single gram of plutonium is moving from storage" and that no diversions of nuclear warheads or weapons-grade fissile materials have taken place in Russia. Yet Western investigations indicate that plutonium smuggled to Munich in August 1994 was from a Russian facility near Moscow. There are also reports that two nuclear warheads were stolen from a weapons assembly plant in the Urals in 1993 (fortunately, the warheads were later recovered). Furthermore, according to one credible Russian observer, criminal groups have been able to commandeer the isotope separation services of Russian nuclear plants and export the products, including enriched reactor-grade and weapons-grade uranium, to various end-user countries in the Middle East and South Asia. The latter scenario is especially unsettling and points to serious possible weakness—if not an outright breakdown—in Russia's nuclear control system.[21]

Law enforcement and security officials in the newly independent states (NIS) are able to intercept only a portion of materials diverted from nuclear enterprises, some 30 percent to 40 percent in the Russia case, according to an estimate by Russia's Federal Security Bureau. Much of the rest is transported abroad or simply discarded.[22] Transnational smuggling chains have emerged to peddle stolen materials outside the NIS, principally in the Central European market. Although small compared to other illegal commodity flows (such as weapons or drugs), global illegal commerce in nuclear materials is hardly inconsequential, as different statistical indicators attest.

In late 2001, the IAEA revealed that its database contained information on more than 380 cases of nuclear smuggling reported by member states.[23] In the period from May 2000 to May 2001, the IAEA received 63 reports. Among these, 13 involved nuclear materials, including three with gram-scale quantities of plutonium. The remaining 50 cases involved other radioactive sources. In addition to the United States, the German federal intelligence service (the Bundesnachrichtendienst, or BND), also maintains a global database. During the height of the nuclear smuggling activity in Europe (from 1992 through 1996), the BND reported more than 500 cases of seizures, thefts, offers, or threats involving nuclear-related materials. Within Germany, the principal Western European entrepôt for nuclear trafficking, the German federal criminal police (the Bundeskriminalamt, or BKA), recorded 84 actual seizures and more than 576 apparently genuine offers to sell nuclear materials for the same 1992–96 period. In Poland, a key transit country for illegal nuclear commerce, between 1991 and 1996, border authorities detected an astounding 2,045 attempts to import radiation-causing substances, mostly across the country's eastern frontier. In such cases, perpetrators were turned back at the border. How many such "turnbacks" were true smuggling events and how many were innocuous (involving, for example, persons wearing radium-dial wristwatches or radioactive surgical implants) cannot be determined from the data.[24]

Qualitative factors such as the configuration of the nuclear black market and the sophistication of the actors involved in it are more difficult to measure. Such factors are subjects of much controversy in both the West and Russia. Viable evidence from seizures and other law enforcement data suggest that the nuclear smuggling business qualifies more as a minor international nuisance rather than a world-class strategic threat.[25] Few bomb-usable materials are offered for sale, bona fide buyers seldom materialize, and amateur criminals and small-time traders rather than large underworld organizations dominate the supply chain for nuclear materials.

Yet such a view probably is incomplete and misleading. On the one hand, the traffic has considerable potential as a specialty business. Smugglers can learn from their mistakes and increase the sophistication and lethality of their operations. As a report published by the National Defense University in Washington noted, "Current patterns of nuclear theft and smuggling may be a prelude to more serious episodes, including major covert exports of fissile material, weapons components and even intact nuclear weapons. The current level of nuclear smuggling opens new criminal trade channels and increases potential opportunities for proliferation of weapons of mass destruction."[26] By 2002, a more credible argument was made that the relatively innocuous visible traffic might conceal a shadow market that is organized on the initiative of the buyer or end user and oriented toward meeting the buyer's specific requirements.[27]

Some tantalizing evidence supports the argument that the nuclear-smuggling business already may be evolving in new and dangerous directions and that sophisticated mechanisms for diverting sensitive nuclear materials are firmly in place, at least in Russia. The hypothesis that two vastly different markets for nuclear materials coexist in postcommunist Eurasia is not hard to imagine. One is the disorganized, supply-driven, and amateurish traffic pattern that is visible to Western analysts and policy makers. The other is a shadow market organized by professionals and brokered by criminals or corrupt officials that poses an immediate proliferation danger and a direct challenge to Western security. The shape and extent of the shadow market are difficult to ascertain. Yet a few credible accounts of its functioning underscore the fragility of the NIS's nuclear control systems and the inherent limitations of Western counterproliferation policies and initiatives in these states.

As two US proliferation experts, Barry Kellman and David Gualtieri, noted, "The crucial truth about nuclear smuggling is that most of what is happening is covert and inferring the magnitude of the flow or the intentions of the actors from a small share of the known picture very likely is misleading."[28] Successful black market transactions are by their very nature likely to go unnoticed.[29] More recent observations support the contention that, as with drugs and other illicit commodities, what is seized may represent only a fraction of what has been shipped.[30] Supply and demand sectors might have converged in ways that are simply beyond US and allied intelligence and law enforcement capabilities to monitor and detect.

THE PRICE OF A MORE OPEN SOCIETY

The collapse of the USSR was so swift and so complete that it left a void in the governmental, economic, and social infrastructure of Russia and the other newly independent states. The transition to more open societies that is taking place in the NIS has made possible the soaring illegal trade in nuclear weapons materials. This unintended side effect constitutes a particularly alarming form of transsovereign criminality associated with the much-desired move toward greater political democratization and market-based economies.

The Impact of the Collapse of the Soviet Government

Nuclear crime was uncommon in the Soviet period. Although uranium thefts were reported at the Elektrostal Machine Building Plant in 1967 and at Krasnoyarsk 26 (a fuel-reprocessing facility) in 1971, the Russian criminal code did not incorporate laws against illegal acquisition, possession, transport, and use of radioactive materials until 1988.[31] Since the disintegration of the USSR, Russian and other NIS facilities—fuel cycle enterprises, research institutes, submarine bases, and even weapons assembly plants—have reported hundreds of thefts of such materials.

Modern-day nuclear criminality could not have existed within the framework of the Soviet totalitarian state. One Harvard study noted that one of the few benign results of that system was the unquestioned control of weapons-usable nuclear materials and nuclear weapons. But the disappearance of the Soviet order and the collapse of communism swept away this apparatus of repression and exposed glaring weaknesses in NIS systems of nuclear security. As a result, "a vast potential supermarket" of nuclear wares is becoming increasingly accessible to would-be thieves and criminal proliferators.[32]

In the Soviet period, nuclear materials security focused on preventing outsiders from spying on or penetrating the nuclear complex, not on preventing knowledgeable insiders from taking radioactive and fissile materials out of enterprises and institutes. Essential features of Soviet nuclear security included multiple and overlapping internal controls such as tightly guarded frontiers and the physical remoteness of nuclear weapons complexes from major population centers.

Physical protections—fences, gates, locks, monitoring systems, and the like—were only modest and deteriorating by the late Soviet period. Many enterprises had no specialized equipment to deter employees from walking off the site with nuclear materials. Yet in the authoritarian matrix of the Soviet Union, the nuclear complex was practically secure against break-ins. Isolation from the outside world in the closed cities of the Soviet nuclear complex and the lack of buyers or brokers of nuclear substances practically eliminated incentives for insider thefts at enterprises at least until the late Soviet period.

The collapse of the Soviet Union after August 1991 correlated with the disintegration of communist control structures and the opening of borders, as well as with significant political and economic turmoil within the NIS. The effect of these changes on civilian and defense nuclear enterprises in Russia and other NIS states was catastrophic. The system of physical protection that had depended on pervasive direct control by the central government began to unravel. The KGB was replaced by polyglot contingents of guards of uncertain reliability operating under different auspices: Ministry of Atomic Energy (MINATOM) and affiliated companies, the Ministry of Internal Affairs (MVD), the KGB's successor agencies (the Federal Counterintelligence Service and the Federal Security Service), and the individual enterprises themselves. The closed cities, which had no real *raison d'être* other than the production of nuclear weapons, became virtual economic "basket cases" (in the words of one US defense-conversion expert).[33] At the same time, the overall security environment began to deteriorate in the cities. As the city manager of one weapons development complex, Penza-19, noted, "The previous system was based on regulations and ordinances which either no longer are in place or [are] not effective and/or military discipline and a sense of responsibility which no longer exist."[34] In 1993 alone, according to the Russian MVD, employees of Russia's nuclear facilities made 700 attempts to "take out strictly protected materials and important technological documents." In the same year, the MVD recorded 900 attempts to gain unauthorized access to institutes and nuclear enterprises.[35] Internal controls and physical safeguards clearly had eroded to a dangerous extent.

The Impact of Open Society

Without the repressive controls of the Soviet period, the nuclear sectors of the NIS are painfully vulnerable both to penetration and theft. Activities that were once tightly monitored by the KGB and other control organs of the Soviet state are no longer watched over so carefully. This is the case with respect to the protection, control, and accountability of the FSU's nuclear material, especially that outside the control of the military. Some of the old institutions have disappeared, the missions of others have changed, and some have suffered deep cutbacks in personnel and resources.

Physical safeguards such as radiation monitoring devices and metal detectors, if any, are antiquated or defective. Perimeter walls and fences are frequently in disrepair. According to Russian nuclear proliferation expert Vladimir Orlov, 27 of 37 kilometers of the guarded territory of Elektrokhimpribor nuclear weapons plant (at Sverdlovsk-45) are "out of order," guaranteeing "practically free access" to the facility. Also, trucks that carry nuclear warheads out of the plant are able to "drive in without admittance documents."[36] At the Sevmorput submarine base in Murmansk, the site of a diversion of 4.5 kilograms of highly enriched uranium (HEU) nuclear fuel, fences had holes and the alarms connecting the guard post to the uranium-storage building had rusted out.[37] Gaining access to the fuel storehouse was child's play, according to investigator Mikhail Kulik of the Northern Fleet's Military Procuracy.[38]

Following the Soviet government's collapse, storage conditions at many research facilities were extremely insecure. For example, at the Kurchatov Institute's Building 116—a research reactor site housing at least 50 kilograms of 96 percent HEU and a larger quantity of less-enriched uranium— no metal detectors existed to deter theft before 1994. Employees were not searched on entering or leaving the premises, and the fence surrounding the building reportedly "had holes in it that the staff often used as a short-cut to the cafeteria."[39] Similar conditions existed in Kazakhstan and other NIS settings.[40]

Conditions in the larger society highlighted the threat posed by lax security safeguards at nuclear enterprises. In the post-Soviet (and post-KGB) era, individual security guards are open to bribes to permit nuclear materials to pass through checkpoints. "Guards will turn off any alarm system for a few moments for 1,000 rubles," commented an unnamed nuclear dealer, referring to security conditions at Elektrostal. "But if you have to bring out a kilo it will be much more expensive—and not in rubles."[41]

A further proliferation danger arises from inadequate accounting and control of nuclear materials in the NIS. Weapons-usable uranium and plutonium are stored at widely scattered sites encompassing several institutes, fuel cycle enterprises, weapons assembly plants, and naval fuel storehouses. Because each facility may comprise several storage areas, the Russian state atomic inspection agency, Gosatomnadzor (GAN), estimates that the total number of individual locations with uranium and plutonium may be close to 1,000.[42] Introducing comprehensive and up-to-date control systems at such dispersed locations is a daunting challenge for Russia's nuclear-containment policy.

Counting the material stored at different sites represents another challenge. Because there has not been a state system for materials accounting in Russia or other NIS countries, managers of facilities that house large quantities of weapons-usable uranium or plutonium often do not know how much material they have or whether any is missing. According to an American intelligence source cited in a *Newsweek* article, some Russian research laboratories "haven't opened up containers for decades to see if the nuclear material inside matches what was listed on their inventories."[43] Furthermore, according to a report by the National Research Council, some enterprises in Russia maintained stocks of material "off the books," which suggests that inventory records, where they exist, may be unreliable.[44]

A related problem concerned the Soviet practices of using standard estimates of rates of loss during fissile materials production instead of measuring actual losses. At the Luch' Scientific-Production Association in Podolsk, for example, an engineer removed 1.5 kilograms of weapons-grade uranium from the plant in 20–25 separate division episodes between May and September 1995. Laboratory procedures at Luch' allowed for a certain percentage of "irretrievable loss" in technical operations with the material. Because there were no radiation monitors at the doors of the plant, the theft went undetected until the thief was arrested at the Podolsk railway station trying to carry the uranium to Moscow to look for a buyer.[45]

Also lacking in the Soviet period were material control systems to monitor and establish custody over nuclear material. According to US nuclear experts, such a system comprises four main elements: equipping containers and vaults with seals that can indicate when tampering may have occurred, using badges and personnel identification equipment to control access to nuclear material areas, installing television cameras to maintain surveillance over nuclear inventories, and requiring two or more authorized persons to be present when materials are removed from storage.[46] Such procedures have just begun to be introduced at NIS nuclear facilities.

Most of the known nuclear smuggling cases through the end of the century involved opportunistic thieves, "insiders" within the vast Russian nuclear complex who took something of perceived value to which they had access and then tried to sell it for personal gain. Some acted individually, while others co-opted a small number of accomplices. Lacking a comprehensive analysis, it is difficult to say just what motivated these people to act—perhaps need in some cases but most assuredly greed and the hope of making big money in others. But one thing is certain: The collapse of the Soviet government affected every facet of society in Russia and the other NIS. It made possible not only the betterment of many aspects of peoples' lives, but also the desperation felt by many as they struggle through the transition.

CONFLICTING GOALS OF OPEN SOCIETY VERSUS NUCLEAR SECURITY

Transsovereign problems often manifest themselves during a time of transition, which by its very nature can be characterized by crisis or, at a minimum, competing or even conflicting goals. Within Russia and the other NIS, those forces supporting the goals of more democratization and market-based economies in open societies must compete against those who would engage in, among other things, illicit trafficking in nuclear materials.

Open Society's Crisis

Proliferation dangers abound in the NIS, where countries undergoing difficult political and economic transitions face (in varying degrees) crises of authority and legitimacy. After the fall of the USSR, the Russian central government's control over nuclear weapons-usable materials and exports of sensitive nuclear goods was clearly problematic.[47] Strains of privatization and defense conversion also took a toll on nuclear central regimes in the NIS and pushed many nuclear employees to the brink of economic ruin. Breakdown in discipline and moral standards or an increasing free market mentality also created an atmosphere conducive to nuclear materials trafficking. Powerful bureaucratic actors such as MINATOM were more interested in generating revenues than in promoting counterproliferation goals. Economically hard-pressed governments tended to "emphasize profits over non-proliferation" and turned a blind eye to violations of their own export control regimes.[48] In general, conditions in Russia and the NIS favored the growth of global black and gray markets that "could greatly accelerate the rate of proliferation by other states desiring nuclear arms."[49]

The Economy of the Nuclear Sector

Hard times befell the individual member states of the former USSR following the collapse of the Soviet order. In Russia, which contains the vast majority of nuclear sites housing weapons-grade materials, gross domestic product (GDP) dropped 55 percent from 1992 and continued in a downward spiral through 1996, when it fell 7 percent. The industrial sector of the Soviet era almost collapsed. Defense orders in Russia dropped 68 percent from 1991 to 1992.[50] The machine building industry shrank by more than 80 percent from 1992 to 1996.[51] General economic decline and the absence of new orders for nuclear weapons have forced a major downsizing of the atomic energy industry. This ongoing economic crisis had severe repercussions within the Russian nuclear complex. As Russian officials paid insufficient attention to security for nuclear materials, perimeter walls and fences disintegrated, guard forces were downsized, alarms malfunctioned, and nuclear-material accounting systems fell into disarray.[52]

The downsizing of the nuclear complex and the generally poor economic outlook also produced a catastrophic effect on employee well-being and morale. Scientists cleared for work in nuclear enterprises were once the cream of Soviet society and enjoyed a higher standard of living than their colleagues in nonsecret lines of work. But after the Soviet collapse, they ranked among the worst paid people in Russia, receiving salaries as low as

$50 per month. According to Vladimir Orlov, salaries of personnel working with nuclear weapons and weapons-grade materials at Arzamas 16 (Sarov) exceeded the minimum subsistence level by a factor of 4.5 in 1991 but averaged only one-third of the subsistence minimum throughout 1996. "And this is for people with nuclear bombs in their hands," commented Orlov.[53]

In 1996, salaries at some MINATOM facilities were only one-third to three-fifths the national average. Employees within the Ministry of Defense's direct chain of command fared somewhat better. The head of Russia's nuclear inspection agency stated that "highly qualified specialists who work in secret nuclear towns earn less than the cleaning women who work in the Moscow subway."[54] In addition, payment of wages tended to be irregular, which was true of most of the rest of the military–industrial complex in Russia. Reflecting these problems, monthly strikes and work stoppages have been reported in several of Russia's so-called secret cities. Even though the Russian economy has improved since the turn of the century, nuclear workers continue to be at the lower end of the scale, still making less than half the average Russian monthly salary of $110 to $120.[55] Not much has changed according to CIA Director George Tenet, speaking before the Senate Armed Services Committee in September 1999: "What we have noticed are reports of strikes, lax discipline, and poor morale and criminal activity at nuclear facilities."[56]

Psychological factors—a sense of loss of function and purpose among enterprise employees—also exacerbate the turn to nuclear crime. "Unneeded and unwanted, forlorn and forgotten" is how the Kurchatov Institute's security director, Nikolai Bondarev, describes nuclear workers.[57] "In just a few years, these people have gone from being valuable and respected members of society to being superfluous," declared Yevgeniy Korolev, a former nuclear scientist who heads a trading consortium in Ekaterinburg. "They are stealing not just to make a living, but also because they are angry."[58]

Further problems concern the quality and the reliability of the nuclear workforce. Nuclear enterprises have faced a hemorrhaging of talent, especially among younger people. Security clearances for new employees are perfunctory or are waived entirely (in the Soviet period, prospective employees underwent extensive KGB background checks).[59] Finally, discipline and control within the nuclear workforce have deteriorated because many employees hold down jobs outside the enterprises to make ends meet. Fully half of the Kurchatov Institute's employees moonlighted in various commercial structures, joint ventures, and laboratories, according to Kurchatov security chief Bondarev.[60]

The general malaise that affects NIS nuclear complexes has engendered criminality and corruption at higher levels of nuclear decision making, clouding the lines between criminal behavior and deliberate state policy. "Because the materials that the Atomic Energy Ministry controls certainly is the goal of serious business deals—such deals are not always legal," says Aleksandr Emelyanenkov, deputy editor of the Moscow magazine *Observer*. Emelyanenkov and other observers suspect that ostensibly private companies set up under MINATOM's aegis have been conduits for undercover export of nuclear materials, technology, and know-how.[61]

In the view of US specialists, MINATOM's insouciance about nuclear security and proliferation dangers is evident in the ministry's nuclear cooperation agreements with Iran—a country that reportedly is actively procuring technology components for atomic weapons manufacture. In a protocol with Iran's atomic energy organization, MINATOM agreed to an extensive nuclear cooperation package that included completion of a 1,000-megawatt nuclear reactor for a power plant in Bushehr. Estimates of the total value of signed contracts and planned deals with Iran range from $3 billion to $8 billion. Russia also plans to sell two light water reactors to India, a newly declared nuclear state that has refused to sign the nonproliferation treaty; the value of that deal is estimated at $3 million to $4 million. In MINATOM's view, revenue streams from these arrangements clearly outweighed the risks of advancing Iran's or India's technology and skills for nuclear weapons making.

Nuclear Smuggling's Appeal (Proximate Causes)

The many structural problems of Russian nuclear enterprises—weak physical safeguards, primitive accounting practices, and an economically desperate and increasingly undisciplined workforce—create a fertile environment for insider thefts of nuclear material. Some anecdotal evidence, though, suggests that nuclear criminality among enterprise employees and their outside associates is aggravated by media hype about the escapades of nuclear criminals and about fabulous prices allegedly paid for stolen wares and by police intervention in the market to trap unwary thieves and smugglers. For instance, Yuriy Smirnov, the engineer who made off with 1.5 kilograms of weapons-grade uranium from the Luch' Scientific Production Association, said that articles in *Komsomolskaya Pravda* (a Moscow newspaper) about people who made big money from stolen uranium gave him the idea.[62]

Arranged buys by law enforcement operatives are another proximate cause of nuclear theft and smuggling episodes. Indeed, only one of the four main Western smuggling cases in 1994—the discovery of more than six grams of nearly pure plutonium-239 in a businessman's garage in Tengen Wiechs, Germany—was not attributable to a sting operation. In that case, police were investigating the businessman, Adolf Jaekle, for intent to distribute counterfeit money.

The absence of buyers has provoked commentaries that contend that the police operations are creating an artificial demand for radioactive material and are driven by bureaucratic or political motives. Following a full-blown investigation by the German Parliamentary Control Commission into the legality of offers of money to smugglers to buy foreign plutonium, the presiding judge handed out relatively light sentences to the three smugglers, concluding that they "were provoked to commit the crime."[63]

In Russia, bureaucratic warfare between MINATOM and law enforcement agencies over appropriate methods of controlling nuclear leakage from enterprises caused problems. Then MINATOM chief Viktor Mikhailov bitterly denounced "provocateurs" within the MVD who preyed on the economic vulnerabilities of nuclear workers. He cited a visit to the Chepetsk Machine Building Plant in Glazov, Udmurtia, where MVD officials offered workers large sums of money for the depleted waste uranium ostensibly "to identify possible channels," a clear provocation according to Mikhailov.[64]

RESOLVING THE NUCLEAR SMUGGLING PROBLEM

The United Nations' International Atomic Energy Agency, based in Vienna, has collected and analyzed the available data on nuclear smuggling incidents and, in some cases, the actual nuclear material recovered from smuggling attempts.[65] Nongovernmental organizations (NGOs), both in the United States and abroad, have also been active in publicizing the proliferation threats to national and international security, as well as the hazards to the world's environment and public health from trafficking in nuclear materials.

Yet the IAEA and especially the NGOs are limited in the assistance they can bring to bear on this transsovereign problem of nuclear smuggling. Unlike other transsovereign problems (drugs, disease, the environment, refugees) discussed in this volume, nuclear smuggling is different. It involves another dimension. Nuclear materials are manufactured in strictest secrecy and controlled by only a handful of countries: the five older nuclear powers—the United States, Russia, Great Britain, France, and China—and a few newcomers (including Israel, India, and Pakistan). There is therefore an understandable reluctance on the part of Russia as the primary inheritor of the Soviet nuclear complex and arsenal, as well as the other nuclear successor states of Belarus, Ukraine, and Kazakhstan, to seek assistance from international organizations such as the IAEA. The IAEA's inspection teams could include members from non-nuclear powers. Ironically, to allow them access to highly classified processes of nuclear material protection, control, and accountability (MPC&A) could conceivably *foster* proliferation. Therefore, the United States and other Western countries have provided the bulk of assistance to counter nuclear smuggling to Russia and other NIS on a bilateral basis.

Against this backdrop, serious efforts are under way to bolster the counter-proliferation regime in Russia and other former Soviet states. Helped by the United States and other Western countries, NIS countries are improving safeguards at enterprises that house sensitive nuclear materials, strengthening export control legislation, training law enforcement officials, and upgrading customs posts along NIS borders.

The US program to use funds from the Departments of Defense, Energy, and State to address proliferation risks from the former Soviet Union originated in the US Congress in the fall of 1991, shortly after the coup attempt against Soviet President Mikhail Gorbachev.[66] Spearheaded by Senators Sam Nunn and Richard Lugar, the assistance package legislation was initially known as the Nunn–Lugar program. It was signed into law by President George H.W. Bush and had three purposes: (1) to assist the Soviet Union and its successor countries in destroying nuclear, chemical, biological, and other sophisticated weapons; (2) to assist in safely transporting, storing, disabling, and safeguarding such weapons; and (3) to establish verifiable safeguards against the proliferation of those weapons.

US–Russia cooperation to improve MPC&A began in September 1993 but got off to a slow start, initially focusing on demonstration projects as a way to build confidence between the two countries.[67] Complementing the original government-to-government program, DOE initiated a laboratory-to-laboratory program in 1994, thereby encouraging US national laboratories to cooperate directly with their Russian counterpart nuclear institutes to improve nuclear safeguards and security measures. President Clinton issued Presidential Decision Directive 41 in September 1995, giving DOE full responsibility for directing the MPC&A program. Russia's nuclear regulatory agency, Gosatomnadzor, signed a formal agreement with DOE, thus laying the groundwork for cooperation at several nuclear sites and development of a regulatory framework. In 1996, the United States and Russia agreed to expand cooperation to include several Russian navy sites. Subsequent agreements in 1997 and 1998 focused on streamlining the program and ensuring operation and sustainability of the upgraded security systems over the long term. The latter grew out of the economic crisis in Russia in 1998. At that time, DOE initiated an "emergency measures" program to provide winter clothes for the Russian sites' guard forces, heaters for vital guard force locations, and short-term operations contracts just to preserve past improvements. This was followed in 1999 by the Material Consolidation and Conversion (MCC) program, which was designed to consolidate nuclear materials into fewer buildings and fewer sites and to convert those materials into a form not usable in nuclear weapons.

Today, DOE cites a list of "significant accomplishments" in reducing the threat to US national security but notes that "much work remains to be done."[68] Included among the accomplishments at the start of Fiscal Year 2002 are the following:

❑ completed comprehensive upgrades at 38 sites;

❑ completed rapid upgrades on 37 percent of the roughly 603 metric tons of at-risk HEU and plutonium;

❑ completed comprehensive upgrades on 18 percent of the at-risk material;

❑ completed rapid upgrades on 91 percent of the estimated 4,000 at-risk Russian navy nuclear warheads;

❑ completed comprehensive upgrades on 17 percent of the at-risk Russian navy warheads;

- ❏ eliminated more than 2.9 metric tons of HEU by converting it to a less-enriched form;

- ❏ removed all weapons-usable material from 21 buildings and consolidated it into fewer locations, thus improving security and saving costs;

- ❏ conducted 45 joint US–Russian operational inspections and performance testing of installed systems; enhanced security features of 74 transport and escort trucks and 25 railcars, and provided 101 secure overpacks, thus improving security during transport;

- ❏ provided training for more than 4,000 Russian MPC&A operators and managers; created capability for 14 Russian sites to report full inventory data to the federal information system;

- ❏ completed four centers for MPC&A personnel training and education, and equipment support; and

- ❏ developed 30 federal MPC&A regulations that form the legal basis and requirement for upgraded nuclear material security.

Today, Senator Lugar urges extending these joint US–Russian programs internationally, especially to Pakistan and India. Furthermore, the issue of nuclear materials security is acquiring a more prominent place on the agenda of international concern. An International Conference on Security of Material titled "Measures to Detect, Intercept and Respond to the Illicit Uses of Nuclear Material and Radioactive Sources" was convened in Stockholm, Sweden, in May 2001. It was hosted by the Swedish Nuclear Power Inspectorate, and organized in cooperation with the World Customs Organization, Interpol, and the European Police Office.[69] The participants adopted far-reaching conclusions, including a recognition that the IAEA has a key role in supporting state efforts to improve the security of material and combat illicit trafficking by providing guidance and normative documents, promoting technical development, and, upon request, assisting states in their implementation. Earlier at a Moscow summit meeting of the heads of state of the Group of Seven plus Russia, participants agreed on a common "Program for Preventing and Combating Illicit Trafficking in Nuclear Material."[70] The program defined trafficking as a "global proliferation risk and a potential danger to public health and safety." The programs identified as fundamental tasks the safe and secure storage of sensitive nuclear materials, international law enforcement and intelligence cooperation to intercept diverted materials, and joint efforts to suppress illicit demand for nuclear substances and to deter potential traffickers. President Boris Yeltsin's proposals at the conference represented Russia's apparent commitment to the counterproliferation objective.[71]

Such signs of cooperation and progress of course are encouraging. Nevertheless, conditions in the NIS still pose a clear threat to nuclear safety and stability globally. The real proliferation danger in the transnational states derives from systemic factors: diminished economic prospects in the military–industrial complex (including the nuclear sector), a weakening political control structure, an increasingly corrupt bureaucracy, and widening penetration of the economy by organized crime. Such an environment increases the likelihood of exports of fissile materials and weaponry to countries or subnational groups with goals inimical to the United States. Infusions of Western technical assistance, the NIS's own security and export control measures, improved East–West atmospherics, and what DOE calls "the spirit of mutual understanding, partnership, and respect between US and Russian nuclear specialists"[72] can help reduce nuclear leakages. Nevertheless, existing safeguards and controls can be circumvented easily—particularly in scenarios of collaboration between senior nuclear managers, corrupt officials, and professional underworld elements. The success of counterproliferation policies hinges ultimately on progress in stabilizing NIS economies and developing effective governing institutions and criminal justice systems in the new states, a process that could take years to accomplish.

CHALLENGE AND RESPONSE: POLICY SUGGESTIONS

Overall US strategy emphasizes the containment of thefts at nuclear enterprises, but other promising lines of defense may be shortchanged as a consequence. For example, the more sophisticated collusive diversion scenarios outlined previously suggest that even well-guarded and upgraded facilities cannot prevent the eventual (and possibly even current) diversion of sensitive nuclear materials into international trafficking and marketing channels. Nonetheless, US cooperation with, and support for, Russian law enforcement has sometimes languished, beset by both insufficient funding and legal and bureaucratic wrangling. US law enforcement and intelligence officers and their counterparts in the NIS have played too small a role in bilateral dialogues on counterproliferation—accentuating the one-sidedness of US policy. Finally, US programs in the NIS suffer from an insufficient focus on the core motivations that drive the supply-side diversion of nuclear materials. Better and more comprehensive economic programs are needed to guarantee a decent livelihood for nuclear workers in post-Soviet states.

The Challenge

Containing thefts—the rationale of the MPC&A programs—is a laudable and worthy objective. The MPC&A accomplishments cited above are an impressive success story considering the legacy of hostilities in the Cold War and legendary Russian sensitivities about nuclear security and sovereignty. Whether strengthened MPC&A systems have reduced or will reduce significantly the risk of nuclear proliferation from the NIS is less clear. Certainly there are reasons to be skeptical. With few tangible achievements early after the fall of the Soviet Union, MPC&A efforts may be too little and too late, and the task is obviously far from complete. Many Russian nuclear facilities comprise many individual storage sites for nuclear materials, and additional sites continue to surface as the MPC&A program progresses. Hence, the accomplishment of MPC&A can be described as partial at best. As a sobering assessment by the National Research Council observed:

> [While] significant improvements have been made at selected facilities the task has not been completed at any facility and has only begun at many. The DOE estimates that tons of direct-use materials are contained in internationally acceptable MPC&A systems and that tens of tons are in partially acceptable systems; but adequate MPC&A systems for hundreds of tons must still be installed.[73]

Furthermore, the new MPC&A technologies are an imperfect defense against the division-by-consensus scenarios discussed earlier in this study. Russian managers contend that well-placed insiders working in concert can defeat such systems. Lack of technical discipline and irresponsible work habits also work to undermine nuclear security at enterprises. As one astute observer noted, "An MPC&A system is only as good as the scientists, technicians, and guards in charge of running it. It will take years before we can accurately assess the extent to which Russia is able fully to integrate an MPC&A system jointly designed with US engineers and scientists."[74]

Effective implementation of the new MPC&A safeguards will require monitoring and oversight from outside the MINATOM nuclear complex. The existing Russian oversight agency, GAN, lacks statutory authority to regulate facilities that manufacture nuclear weapons or explosive charges for such weapons, weapons storage sites, or naval bases that store submarine fuel rods. Furthermore, a report by the National Research Council notes, GAN "suffers from a shortage of well-trained inspectors, qualified staff, and necessary analytical and related equipment. . . ."[75] GAN is a puny instrument in terms of resources and clout compared to MINATOM, its principal object of control. GAN conducts inspections at civilian enterprises, where it found 29,000 violations of rules and norms in one year. (The typical fine is one or two dollars in such instances.) GAN also has the theoretical authority not to certify enterprises that stand in violation of safety regulations. It is not surprising that this power has never been exercised. The organization is weak overall, and it is unlikely in the near term to play a major role in countering the pro-proliferation forces in Russia.[76]

The Response

Uncertainties and concerns about the MPC&A effort argue for shifts in the emphasis of US counterproliferation policy in Russia and the NIS. The limitations of the US supply-control approach to nuclear security need to be recognized.[77] Spending more money on protection regimes—walls, fences, alarm systems, inventory controls, and the like—would not close the now largely open proliferation window in the NIS. Clever adversaries and their inside collaborators can find ways to defeat or circumvent the new systems, and the overall malaise of the nuclear economy increases the range of potential suppliers of nuclear goods. Containing the spread of nuclear intelligence, while eminently desirable, is an intrinsically difficult objective given the long history of nuclear weapons and the variety of channels through which state secrets can be disseminated. Furthermore, the United States should consider the experience of supply-side programs in other fields, most notably in the failed US international war on drugs. Similarly, nonproliferation programs that emanate from Washington are headed for defeat if NIS governments are too weak or corrupt to keep their own nuclear houses in order.

Dr. Siegfried Hecker, a senior fellow and former director of the Los Alamos National Laboratory, sees an opportunity for the current Bush administration to reevaluate these programs.[78] Although he acknowledges that much has been accomplished under the MPC&A programs, the "bad news is that the problems in the Russian nuclear complex were much greater and more pervasive than either Russians or Americans realized ten years ago." US advisors and government policies were ineffective in helping Russia deal with the root causes of the nuclear security problems—that is, in radical changes in its political, economic, and social systems. It is time for a new strategic framework for nuclear cooperation that is based more on reestablishing trust and partnership than simply increasing US funding. The US government must view nuclear cooperation with Russia as one of the principal factors shaping our future security environment and act accordingly.

ENDNOTES

1. Many of the points made in this chapter are treated in more depth in Rensselaer W. Lee III, *Smuggling Armageddon: The Nuclear Black Market in the Former Soviet Union and Europe* (New York: St. Martin Griffin, 1998).
2. Stefan Leader, "Osama bin Laden and the Terrorist Search for WMD," *Jane's Intelligence Review* (June 1999).
3. Jeffrey Kluger, "Osama's Nuclear Quest," *Time* (Nov. 12, 2001).
4. Kamran Khan and Molly Moore, "Two Nuclear Experts Briefed Bin Laden, Pakistanis Say," *Washington Post,* Dec. 12, 2001, p. A1.
5. Michael Dobbs and Peter Behr, "Analysts Debate Next Weapon in al Qaeda Arsenal: Panel Finds Terrorists More Likely to Possess Radioactive 'Dirty Bombs' Than Nuclear Weapons," *Washington Post,* Nov. 16, 2001, p. A18.
6. Eric Pianin and Bill Miller, "Nuclear Arms Plants' Security Lax, Report Says," *Washington Post,* Jan. 23, 2002, p. A15.
7. Office of Nonproliferation and National Security, *Special Report: Scams in the World of Nuclear Smuggling* (NN-62) (Washington, DC: Department of Energy, May 1997).
8. Statement of John P. Holdren, chairman of the President's Committee of Advisors on Science and Technology, Senate Foreign Relations Committee hearings, August 1995.
9. Condoleezza Rice, quoted in DOE, *MPC&A Program: Strategic Plan* (Washington, DC: US Government Printing Office, July 2001), 1.
10. James L. Ford, *Nuclear Smuggling: How Serious a Threat* (National Defense University [NDU] Strategic Forum No. 59) (Washington, DC: NDU, January 1996).

11. William C. Potter, "Before the Deluge? Assessing the Threat of Nuclear Leakage from the Post-Soviet States," *Arms Control Today* (Oct. 1995): 9–16.
12. Barton Gellman, "'Dirty Bomb' Plot Uncovered, US Says," *Washington Post,* June 11, 2002, p. A1; John Sopko, "The Changing Proliferation Threat," *Foreign Policy* (Winter 1996–97): 3.
13. Gellman, "'Dirty Bomb' Plot Uncovered," p. A1.
14. Graham Allison, quoted in Dobbs and Behr, "Analysts Debate Next Weapon in Al Qaeda Arsenal," p. A18.
15. Secretary of Energy's Advisory Board, *A Report Card on the Department of Energy's Nonproliferation Programs with Russia* (Washington, DC: US Government Printing Office, Jan. 10, 2001), 3.
16. Statement of US Sen. Sam Nunn, hearing on global proliferation and weapons of mass destruction, Permanent Subcommittee on Investigations, Senate Committee on Government Affairs, March 13, 1996.
17. Graham T. Allison, Owen R. Cote, Jr., Richard A. Falkenrath, and Steven E. Miller, *Avoiding Nuclear Anarchy: Containing the Threat of Loose Russian Nuclear Weapons and Fissile Material* (Cambridge: MIT Press, 1996).
18. Global Organized Crime Project, *The Nuclear Black Market* (Task Force Report) (Washington, DC: Center for Strategic International Studies, 1996).
19. Rensselaer W. Lee III, *Nuclear Smuggling* (unpublished manuscript) (Dec. 13, 2001).
20. Michael Dobbs, "Russian Official Reveals Attempt Made to Steal Nuclear Materials," *Washington Post,* Nov. 13, 2001, p. A22.
21. Rensselaer W. Lee III, *Nuclear Crime in Russia: Causes, Dynamics, and Implications.* Draft report for the Foreign Policy Research Institute, Washington, D.C., October 1997.
22. Kirill Belyaninov, personal communications with author (Lee), March 27, 1997.
23. International Atomic Energy Agency (IAEA), *Measures to Improve the Security of Nuclear Materials and Other Radioactive Materials.* Report issued by the Board of Governors General Conference, August 14, 2001, p. 2.
24. Tadeusz Hadys and Slawomir Sterlinski, *Polish Prevention System against Nuclear Trafficking of Radioactive Substances and Nuclear Materials* (Warsaw: Central Laboratory for Radiological Protection and Border Guards Headquarters, 1997), 5.
25. See discussion in Phil Williams and Paul N. Woessner, "The Real Threat of Nuclear Smuggling," *Scientific American,* 274(1): 40–41.
26. James L. Ford and C. Richard Schuller, *Nuclear Smuggling Pathways: A Holistic Perspective* (Washington, DC: National Defense University, 1996), 7.
27. Lee, *Nuclear Smuggling.*
28. Barry Kellman and David S. Gualtieri, "Barricading the Nuclear Window: A Legal Regime to Curtail Nuclear Smuggling," *University of Illinois Law Review,* 1966(3): 677.
29. Allison et al., *Avoiding Nuclear Anarchy.*
30. Lee, *Nuclear Smuggling.*
31. Ugolovny Kodeks Rossiiskoi Federatsii, *Severozapad* (St. Petersburg: Author, 1994), 164–165. Article 223, sections 2 through 5, deals with nuclear-related offenses. Interestingly, the code fails to specify sale of nuclear materials as a crime, apparently not envisioning that possibility.
32. Allison et al., *Avoiding Nuclear Anarchy,* 2.
33. John P. Holdren, "Reducing the Threat of Nuclear Theft in the Former Soviet Union," *Arms Control Today* (March 1996): 20.

34. Mark Hibbs, "Physical Protection Reportedly Evading at MINATOM's 10 Closed Cities in Russia," *Nuclear Fuel* (Jan. 2, 1995): 13.

35. Nikolai Bondarev, *Background Report* (Moscow: Kurchatov Institute, 1994), 8.

36. Vladimir Orlov, *Accounting, Control and Physical Protection of Fissile Materials and Nuclear Weapons in the Russian Federation: Current Situation and Main Concerns.* Paper presented at International Seminar on MPC&A in Russia and the NIS, Bonn, Germany, April 7–8, 1997, p. 9.

37. Oleg Bukharin and William Potter, "Potatoes Were Guarded Better," *Bulletin of the Atomic Scientists* (May–June 1995): 48–49.

38. Allison et al., *Avoiding Nuclear Anarchy,* 42–43; Mikhail Kulik, "Nekotorye problemy khraneniya yadernykh materialov na Severnom Flote" [Some aspects of storage of nuclear materials in the North Fleet], *Yaderny Kontrol* [*Nuclear Control*] (Feb. 1995): 12; Jessica Stern, "U.S. Assistance Programs for Improving MPC&A in the Former Soviet Union," *Non-Proliferation Review,* 3(2): 25.

39. R. W. Lee interview, Kurchatov Institute, Moscow, Oct. 25, 1996.

40. Emily Ewell, *Trip Report in Uzbekistan, Kazakhstan, Ukraine* (Monterey, CA: Monterey Center for Non-Proliferation Studies, May 1996), 8.

41. Kirill Belyaninov, "Nuclear Nonsense, Black-Market Bombs, and Missile Flim-Flams," *Bulletin of the Atomic Scientists* (March–April 1994): 48.

42. Interview with Mark Hibbs, *Frontline* (PBS), Nov. 20, 1996.

43. Tom Masland et al., "For Sale," *Newsweek* (Aug. 29, 1994): 32.

44. National Research Council, *Proliferation Control* (Washington, DC: National Academy Press, 1997), 13.

45. Interview with Yuriy Smirnov, *Frontline* (PBS), Nov. 20, 1996.

46. General Accounting Office (GAO), *Nuclear Proliferation: Station of U.S. Efforts to Improve Nuclear Materials Control in Newly Independent States* (Washington, DC: US Government Printing Office, March 1996), 13.

47. Leonard S. Spector, Mark McDonough, and Evan Medeiros, *Tracking Nuclear Proliferation. A Guide in Maps and Charts* (Washington, DC: Carnegie Endowment for International Peace, 1995), 3.

48. William Potter, "The Post-Soviet Proliferation Challenge." Testimony prepared for hearing on Russian case studies in proliferation, US Senate Governmental Affairs Subcommittee on International Security Proliferation and Federal Service, June 5, 1997, p. 4.

49. Spector et al., *Tracking Nuclear Proliferation,* 3.

50. National Research Council (NRC), *Proliferation Concerns* (Washington, DC: National Academy Press, 1997), 34.

51. Talk by Sergei Rogov, director of USA-Canada Institute Moscow, at the Foreign Policy Research Institute, Philadelphia, Jan. 22, 1997.

52. DOE, *MPC&A Program: Strategic Plan,* 1.

53. Vladimir Orlov, "Nuclear Blackmail: Threats from Enemies Within More Disturbing than Conspiracies from Without," *Nezavisimaya Voennoye Obozreniye* (Aug. 29, 1997), 1–7.

54. Olga Sitkova, "How About a Bomb," *Die Woche* (Hamburg), March 23, 1994, p. 14.

55. Valentin Tikhonov, *Russia's Nuclear and Missile Complex: The Human Factor in Proliferation* (Washington, DC: Carnegie Endowment for International Peace, 2001), 37–39.

56. Leader, "Osama bin Laden and the Terrorist Search for WMD," 34.

57. Interview with Nikolai Bondarev, *Frontline* (PBS), Nov. 20, 1996.

58. R. W. Lee interview with Yevgeniy Korolev, Yekaterinburg, Russia, Sept. 10, 1994.

59. R. W. Lee interview with Nikolai Kukharin, Kurchatov Institute, Moscow, Oct. 25, 1996.

60. Bondarev, *Background Report,* 13.

61. Interview with Aleksandr Emelyanenkov, *Frontline* (PBS), Nov. 20, 1996.

62. Interview with Yuriy Smirnov, *Frontline* (PBS), Nov. 20, 1996.

63. Mark Hibbs, "Agencies' Entrapment Justifies Mild Sentences in Munich Pu Case," *Nucleonic Week* (July 2, 1995): 2–3.

64. Viktor Mikhailov, "Intervia Mesyatsa," *Yaderny Kontrol* (Feb. 1995): 9–10.

65. IAEA, *Measures to Improve the Security of Nuclear Materials and Other Radioactive Materials.*

66. Much of the information on the MPC&A program history and accomplishments is drawn from *Nuclear Status Report: Nuclear Weapons, Fissile Materials and Export Controls in the Former Soviet Union* (Washington, DC: Carnegie Endowment for International Peace; Monterey, CA: Monterey Institute of International Studies, 2001).

67. Many of the MPC&A program details and accomplishments cited here are taken from *MPC&A Program: Strategic Plan.*

68. Ibid., 10.

69. IAEA, *Measure to Improve the Security of Nuclear Materials and Other Radioactive Materials,* 1.

70. G7/G8 Nuclear Safety and Security Summit, *Programs for Preventing and Combating Trafficking in Nuclear Material* (Moscow, April 19–20, 1996), 1.

71. "Statement by Boris Yeltsin," G7/G8 Nuclear Safety and Security Summit, *International Affairs* (Moscow, 1996), 38.

72. Nuclear Material Security Task Forces, *United States-Former Soviet Union Program of Cooperation on Nuclear Material Protection, Accounting and Control* (Washington, DC: US Department of Energy, December 1996).

73. NRC, *Proliferation Concerns,* 69.

74. Jessica Stern, *Teaching Nuclear Custodians to Fish* (unpublished manuscript) (Sept. 11, 1996), 8.

75. NRC, *Proliferation Concerns,* 13.

76. Nikolai Filonov, "O Deyatelnosti Gosatomnadzora v Oblasti Yadernoi i Radiyatsionnoi Bezopasnosti' Rossii v 1995 godu," *Yaderny Kontrol* (Aug.–Sept. 1996): 31; Gosatomnadzor (GAN) [State Committee for Supervision over the Safety of Work in Nuclear Power Engineering (Russia)], *Otchet o Deyatelnosti Federal'nogo Nadzora Rossii po Yadernoi i Radiyatsionnoi Bezopasnost* (Moscow: GAN, 1996), 149–150.

77. Lee, *Nuclear Smuggling.*

78. Siegfried S. Hecker, "Thoughts about an Integrated Strategy for Nuclear Cooperation with Russia," *Nonproliferation Review* (Monterey, CA: Center for Nonproliferation Studies, Monterey Institute of International Studies, 2001).

CHAPTER TEN

Ecological Interdependence and the Spread of Infectious Disease

Dennis Pirages and Paul Runci

The epidemic started in a remote part of Maharashtra state in India, but it soon moved to Surat, a city littered with piles of urban filth and the weekday home of more than 2 million people. Rumors of plague spread throughout the region. Within days, nearly 500,000 residents had fled to other parts of India, and business travelers stayed away. Once health officials determined that deaths were likely being caused by pneumonic plague, 80 percent of the private physicians fled the city. Word leaked out to the rest of the world. Pakistan, Sri Lanka, and many Persian Gulf states quickly banned all flights, goods, and citizens from India. The Bombay Stock Exchange crashed. Then Russia, China, Egypt, Malaysia, and Bangladesh closed all communications with the country. Flights from India were carefully inspected by health officials as far away as New York. Fortunately, the ultimate toll was "only" 6,500 infections and 56 deaths. But the economic toll for India came to more than $2 billion.

Viruses, bacteria, and various animals and plants have never respected national borders. Throughout history, microbes have hitchhiked across frontiers by wind, water, explorers, migrants, merchants, and mercenaries. Most of the time, these crossings have had little effect, but occasionally whole societies and ecosystems have been reshaped because of them. Globalization, however, increases our concern over the potential development and spread of new and resurgent diseases across increasingly porous state borders.

Over the course of history, populations of human beings have coevolved with millions of other animal and plant species as well as large numbers of potentially pathogenic microorganisms. Only during the last century did technological innovation give *Homo sapiens* a clear but perhaps temporary competitive edge in this struggle. There is now growing evidence that various kinds of destructive microorganisms are making a comeback in an increasingly interdependent and urbanized global system. In addition, various plant and animal species, having been introduced to new environments through expanded trade and more rapid transportation, are wreaking ecological havoc in many countries. The changes associated with increasingly open societies, open economies, and dependence on new technologies—growing economic integration, the gradual disappearance of national borders, more rapid movement of people and goods among regions, weakening of the authority of the state, and changing patterns of human settlements and behavior—are combining to make the resurgence of pathogenic microorganisms, as well as the worldwide spread of various kinds of other potentially destructive species, an important threat to future human security and well-being.[1]

Globalization has been quietly under way for some time. The first modern humans lived some 100,000 years ago and inhabited areas that spanned eastern Africa and the Middle East. From there, a series of expansions and migrations moved outward until most of the habitable world had been at least loosely settled 15,000 years ago.[2] Since then, there has been a slow but accelerating reintegration of these previously scattered and mostly isolated human populations into larger units as the barriers among them gradually disappeared. The Roman Empire, the Mongol empires, and European colonialism are all examples of the ways in which previously isolated human populations have been absorbed into much larger administrative units. This long-term reintegration process is expected to culminate in the emergence of an immense global village over the next few decades. But each step in this reintegration of human populations has had significant ecological, political, and socioeconomic consequences, not the least of which has been the insecurity associated with the emergence and rapid spread of disease.

INTEGRATION AND DISEASE IN HISTORY

Homo sapiens is one species among millions that share the global ecosystem. Like most other species, *Homo sapiens* lives in and identifies with basic bio-logical units called *populations.* Populations of any species are "dynamic sys-tems of interacting individuals . . . that are potentially capable of inter-breeding with each other."[3] Thus, the boundaries of human populations, which social scientists call *societies* or *ethnic groups,* could theoretically be located by mapping subtle genetic differences that result from generations of reproduction within the population. But it is easier to identify the boundaries of populations or societies through marked gaps in communi-cation efficiency. These communication gaps and inefficiencies both help to maintain and are maintained by so-called ethnic differences that are reflect-ed in different languages, behavior, values, and beliefs.[4] Throughout much of human history, the boundaries of these human populations, their politi-cal administrative units, and the local ecosystems in which they have been embedded have coincided. The early great outward dispersals of the earth's human populations resulted in a world inhabited by thousands of geo-graphically isolated human populations that were administered as clans, tribes, and kingdoms. These societies coevolved with other species and microorganisms within the constraints of shared local ecosystems. It was only with the emergence of larger administrative units, such as empires, that the large-scale mingling of previously isolated human populations and the microorganisms they carried began.

The integration of previously small and isolated populations of human beings into empires and more densely populated cities exacted a tragic death toll from disease. William McNeill has observed that the Roman Empire was repeatedly wracked by the scourge of strange diseases. There were at least eleven microbial disasters in republican times. A major epi-demic struck the densely packed city of Rome in 65 A.D., but that paled in comparison with a more widespread pandemic that began to sweep the empire in 165 A.D. Mortality as a result of this latter plague was heavy: One-quarter to one-third of those exposed to the disease died.[5]

In more recent history, the integration of growing European populations into a nascent global community has had similar disease ramifications. By the year 1350, the various kingdoms of Western Europe had become large and densely populated enough to press against the carrying capacities of relevant ecosystems and even against each other. Such pressures led to local European famines in most years between 1290 and 1350 A.D.[6] At the same time, contacts and commerce among the world's societies was increasing, manifested in the growth of lengthy trade routes between Western Europe and China. The intensification of caravan traffic across Asia and contact among those previously isolated peoples surged under the Mongol empires. At the height of Mongol power, the empires embraced nearly all of China and Russia as well as Central Asia, Iran, and Iraq.[7]

During this period of European population increase, urban growth, and expanded commerce, significant numbers of people, including messengers, merchants, and mercenaries, were moving among previously separated human populations. This increased contact resulted in the spread of new diseases to Europe from Asia, the most infamous being *Yersinia pestis*, the cause of pneumonic and bubonic plague—the infamous Black Death. The arrival of the plague in Europe in 1346 began a lengthy human pruning process by which successive waves of disease trimmed the region's population by nearly 40 percent, with the highest mortality rates being in the urban areas.[8]

Contact among previously separated peoples took another great leap forward during the age of European exploration and colonization. The ships of Christopher Columbus, which arrived in the Caribbean in 1492, were the first of a wave of European vessels that eventually brought the Europeans into contact with numerous American Indian populations. This contact not only eventually resulted in the absorption of this territory into Spanish, Portuguese, British, and French empires, but also led the microorganisms that accompanied the conquerors to wipe out a significant portion of the indigenous peoples. The military history of the period is replete with tales of miraculous conquests of huge numbers of Indians by mere handfuls of European troops. But, in reality, there were few bona fide miracles. Epidemics launched by the invaders, particularly smallpox, killed approximately two-thirds of the indigenous populations, leaving them in disarray and unable to muster a decent defense of their territories. As William McNeill has put it, "From the Amerindian point of view, stunned acquiescence to Spanish superiority was the only possible response. . . . Native authority structures crumbled; the old gods seemed to have abdicated. The situation was ripe for the mass conversions recorded so proudly by Christian missionaries."[9] The spread of smallpox was followed by measles and eventually by typhus, with such diseases from Africa as malaria and yellow fever transplanted in the American tropics. By the time these transplanted diseases had run their course, only an estimated one in twenty Amerindians in the affected areas had survived.[10] Indeed, as the European colonial networks expanded to embrace much of the world, an exchange of diseases among the conquerors and the conquered took tremendous tolls on all sides.

More recently, another spurt of disease accompanied the large-scale movement of troops during World War I. While the eyes of the world were focused on the casualties from military action, a deadly influenza epidemic spread quickly around the world with the troops. By the time the casualties began to taper off, this unexpected spin-off from the war resulted in the greatest pandemic in world history: Somewhere between 20 and 30 million people died, many more times the number of battlefield casualties.[11]

AN EVOLUTIONARY PERSPECTIVE

Since World War II, there has been a tremendous acceleration in the pace of globalization and urbanization. The historical record makes it clear that such periods of growing interactions among previously separated populations are often punctuated by serious outbreaks of disease. The last fifty years has witnessed the spread of exotic and lethal diseases in tropical areas of the world, several deadly worldwide influenza epidemics, and an AIDS pandemic that continues to spread slowly around the world. There is heightened fear that environmental change, more frequent international travel, growing bacterial resistance to antibiotics, and changing human behavior and settlement patterns are leading to outbreaks of new kinds of deadly diseases and a resurgence of others.[12] In spite of the development of a broad spectrum of antibiotics and new medical technologies, the world remains a biologically dangerous place. "At the root of the resurgence of old infectious diseases is an evolutionary paradox: The more vigorously we have assailed the world of microorganisms, the more varied the repertoire of bacterial and viral strains thrown up against us."[13]

The key to comprehending why there are so many new challenges to human microsecurity is to understand the nature and evolution of ecological interdependence. Populations of *Homo sapiens* have coevolved with other species and a variety of microorganisms within ever-changing physical environments. Ecological interdependence refers to the growth and maintenance of a delicate network of relationships among and between these organisms and the sustaining physical environments. Rapid changes in any of these relationships can rebound to the detriment of human beings, other creatures, microorganisms, and even the ecosystem itself. Thus, a mutation in a potentially pathogenic microorganism, a rapid increase in populations of voracious pests, or even a change in rainfall can destabilize an ecosystem with unfortunate results for all the creatures that share it.

For most of biological history, this coevolution has been occurring within local and isolated ecosystems. Because of mutual adaptation processes that involve the human immune system, localized bouts of nonfatal diseases have been common. But as previously isolated populations are now being forced together by the pressures of globalization, there are complex and unforeseen consequences. The world is now beginning to experience ecological interdependence on a much larger scale. The complicated network of interdependence between human populations, other species, and various microorganisms is moving to the global level.

The human immune system, which fights disease, is the product of generations of interactions between people and disease organisms. Natural-selection processes, which shape human immune systems, represent learning by bitter experience. People with weak or naive immune systems often succumb to deadly diseases and do not live to reproduce. People with stronger immune systems that have been honed by disease episodes are more likely to survive and have children with some degree of immunity to serious diseases.

Epidemics can develop when biologically naive human populations come in contact with new pathogens. Obviously, people who move into new environments are at substantial risk of contracting new illnesses. This is why traveling businesspeople or scholars attending international conferences often come down with influenza or similar illnesses on their return, or why people who move from one coast of the United States to the other are frequently ill during their first year of residence. People or animals who move into new environments can similarly bring pathogens with them. *Rattus rattus,* traveling with merchants along trade routes, brought disease-bearing fleas in their fur to Europe from Asia, introducing the Black Plague to the region in the fourteenth century. Social and cultural practices can also accelerate the spread of disease. For example, among certain African tribes, marrying and supporting a widow becomes the responsibility of a dead husband's brother. Because many African males are now dying of AIDS, this custom can accelerate the spread of the virus from widows of AIDS victims to the dead man's extended family.[14]

Problems can also arise when mutations take place in microorganisms, sometimes making them more lethal to human beings. For various reasons, including environmental changes, exposure to chemicals or radiation, or interactions with other microorganisms, destructive mutations can occur, potentially confronting the human organism with novel challenges. Similarly, prolonged exposure to antibiotics often makes bacteria antibiotic-resistant and thus more difficult to defeat.

Pathogens can also be liberated by people moving through previously unpopulated geographic locations. They also can move from animals to people. Population growth in tropical areas of the world is forcing people to clear land at the edges of rain forests, thereby liberating various kinds of microorganisms from previous isolation and their historic animal hosts. Thus, the human immunodeficiency virus (HIV, the proximate cause of AIDS) and Ebola, Marburg, and yellow fever viruses were probably first found in monkeys; Rift Valley fever in cattle, sheep, and mosquitoes; and Hantaan virus in rodents. "These pathogens probably lurked relatively undisturbed in their animal hosts in the tropics, jumping to humans only on rare occasions. They had little opportunity to adapt to humans, who usually were 'dead end' host species, because the viruses would fizzle out once they rapidly swept through a small population at the edge of the forest."[15] But these and other viruses can make successful leaps from animals to denser human populations, thus putting deadly new diseases in motion. In late 1997 and early 1998, for example, viruses made leaps from monkeys to humans in Congo (monkeypox) and from chickens to humans in Hong Kong (influenza H5N1).[16]

In a parallel process, plant and animal species can wreak havoc when they jump from their home ecosystems to naive ecosystems that have had no previous contact with them. Historically, plants and animals native to Europe had both positive and negative effects as they moved around the world with colonists.[17] In the contemporary world, it is often the unintended movement of plants and animals, largely as a result of expanded trade, that can have devastating effects. In the United States, for example, species ranging from the blue water hyacinths of South America that now clog Florida's waterways to the Africanized honeybee, an aggressive stinger that was brought to Brazil in 1959 and then escaped north, have economic and environmental effects that run from nuisance to sizably negative.[18]

In summary, major epidemics and pandemics that have transformed the nature of societies have occurred when human immune systems have encountered pathogenic microorganisms with which they have had little experience. When the Black Death arrived in Europe from Asia, nearly half the population was wiped out in many areas, thus leading to major sociopolitical transformations. Similarly, the "conquest" of the Americas was aided and abetted by new European and African microbes transplanted into naive human populations. This is one reason for the current great concern about the erosion of sovereignty, disappearance of borders, failures of states, and the rapid integration of local human populations into an emerging global village. Rapid movements of people, produce, animals and microorganisms around the world has given rise to concern about the resurgence of old diseases, the emergence of new ones, and economic and environmental damage from traveling plants and animals.

ECOLOGICAL INTERDEPENDENCE: SOME EVIDENCE

In the face of the challenges of rapidly growing ecological interdependence and associated bioinvasion, weakened and impoverished governments have been slow to react. The current political attitude toward nonhuman immigrants remains much the same as it was in the 1870s when Spencer Fullerton Baird of the US Fish Commission attempted to improve on nature by bringing a new tasty species of Eurasian carp into the United States. His venture was a great economic success and the fish became the culinary craze of the nation. But ever since then, the carp have been reproducing prolifically in US waters, destroying natural habitats and crowding out native fish. The legacy of these attempts to make nature more productive through the introduction of new species lingers on in US regulations. There is rigorous screening to catch potentially dangerous agricultural pests, but much less attention is paid to imported species that do not directly threaten to ravage crops. For example, local state governments can allow the import of exotic fish species from other countries or regions without even consulting their neighbors.[19]

Until quite recently, the potential spread of infectious diseases was similarly treated. The development and large-scale deployment of antibiotics and other pharmaceuticals has fostered complacency in the face of growing global disease challenges. In 1969, for example, the US surgeon general declared that infectious diseases had been conquered and that the time had come to focus on chronic diseases such as cancer and heart disease.[20] But things are changing, and in 1995, the World Health Organization (WHO) felt it necessary to reemphasize that infectious diseases are still the world's leading cause of death.[21] The former Clinton administration went so far as to declare HIV and AIDS a threat to US national security in April 2000. The technological optimism of an earlier era is beginning to fade in the face of the seemingly incurable HIV–AIDS complex and the resurgence of several diseases in antibiotic-resistant form. More than one-tenth of the new cases of tuberculosis (TB) worldwide are now resistant to at least one of the drugs commonly used to treat the disease. And between 1 percent and 2 percent of all new cases are resistant to multiple drugs. In addition, other serious diseases are also developing drug resistance.[22]

There is now ample evidence of the effect of growing ecological interdependence on the increasing scope of infectious diseases, but changes over time in the personal and economic effects of various diseases are difficult to quantify for several reasons. First, it is not necessary for people to die from an infectious disease for it to affect their quality of life. Various debilitating diseases can disable large numbers of people for considerable periods of time without actually making them into mortality statistics. Second, infectious-disease statistics are often deliberately manipulated downward by some countries as a matter of national pride or economics. Tourists do not often travel to countries known to be experiencing plagues. Finally, there are few reliable historical data to use as a baseline for assessing the extent to which disease has increased or decreased in many areas of the world, particularly in the most poverty-stricken countries where diseases are likely to be most prevalent.

Lower respiratory-tract infections and diarrheal diseases combine to kill approximately 5.7 million people annually, but AIDS casualties are quickly gaining on these traditional diseases.[23] Approximately 40 million people now live with HIV and AIDS worldwide, some 5 million are newly infected each year, and 3 million die from AIDS. In sub-Saharan Africa, 28.1 million people are now stricken with HIV and AIDS. In South Africa, one in nine people is living with the disease.[24] In Latin America, more than a million people have been struck with a resurgence of cholera in recent years and several thousand have died. And malaria is now active in 103 countries and is a serious threat to half the world's population. Approximately 300 million people become infected with the parasite each year, and 1 million to 2 million die.[25]

Fifty years ago, many of these diseases surely afflicted human beings. But it is unclear how much globalization and urbanization have affected the geographic scope and prevalence of these diseases; there is only anecdotal evidence for comparison. What is clear is that these diseases now move much more rapidly along with the large flow of travelers and agricultural commodities in the contemporary world. There is thus growing worry about a potential worldwide spread of killer viruses. In the 1990s, outbreaks of pneumonic plague, which can be spread through the air, killed hundreds of people in India and disrupted air travel in the region.[26] Airports as far away as Kennedy in New York City were screening dozens of flights daily for potential carriers. Also in the 1990s, an outbreak of a deadly chicken or bird flu in Hong Kong caused a major drop-off in tourism and led to the execution of 1.5 million chickens and other birds in an attempt to stop the spread of the virus.[27]

Although the many exotic species of flora and fauna that now travel around the world rarely kill people, they often do extensive damage to the recipient economies. In the United States, it is estimated that more than 4,000 exotic species of flora and fauna have become naturalized (able to survive without human help) over the past century. Just 79 of those species cost the nation an estimated $97 billion between 1906 and 1991 in damage to agriculture, ecosystems, industry, and health. Most of the species brought into the United States unintentionally have been the inadvertent by-products of commerce, tourism, or travel.[28] It is difficult to estimate the toll from invasive species on the global level, but a recent estimate of the damage to crops from nonindigenous pests put the figure at between $55 billion and $247 billion per year.[29]

Many new species make their way into the United States and other countries along with other imported commodities. Agricultural products, nursery stock, cut flowers, and timber often harbor insects, plant diseases, and snails, while bulk commodities such as gravel, sand, and wool often contain hidden seeds. Ballast water on commercial ships, taken on to provide stability at sea and often dumped when ships load at different ports, is also a major transport medium for spreading nonindigenous species around the world.

ECOLOGICAL SECURITY: CONTEMPORARY CHALLENGES

The ongoing globalization process represents a growing challenge to human health as well as ecological stability. Although ecological interdependence grew at a gradual pace for some time, it is only recently that a confluence of change drivers—rapid technological innovation and the broad, worldwide diffusion of liberal ideology—has created a historically unique climate that has accelerated these change processes.[30] As globalization proceeds in tandem with human disturbances of remote ecosystems where many pathogens reside, the likelihood of new outbreaks grows. Pathogens that have previously been restricted to isolated geographic locations have become capable of spreading rapidly and with relative ease to other areas as the world's transportation networks have expanded.[31]

Diseases are currently being spread more rapidly and widely in two obvious ways: by increased contact among people and by integration of the world's food markets. More frequent contacts are now occurring in densely populated cities and among human populations across political boundaries that once served as relatively impermeable barriers. Spatial separation in general has become a far less significant hindrance to human interaction as technological advances have accelerated and expanded the possibilities for transnational flows of information, money, goods, and people. For example, between 1950 and 1998, world exports of goods rose from a value of $311 billion to $5.4 trillion.[32]

Professional journals and mass media now carry accounts of public health incidents related to globalization with alarming regularity as pathogens old and new move worldwide along with the rising volume of trade and travel. More than 2 million people now cross an international border each day, up from only 69,000 in 1950. Since 1950, the number of passenger kilometers flown internationally has increased by nearly one hundred fold.[33] Commercial jets have been implicated in the transmission of TB among airline passengers and the reintroduction of dengue fever to the United States through cargo containing hitchhiking Asian mosquitoes.[34]

In the face of the accelerating pace of contemporary globalization, governments around the world are in many respects ill-equipped to respond to the emerging health risks associated with travel and trade, inadequate food safety, and ecosystemic changes. A major irony of globalization is that, at a time when the spectrum and level of ecological risks are growing as never before, the abilities of governments to respond appropriately may be increasingly limited.[35]

The second set of health risk factors emerges from the growth and deeper integration of the world food market. Like other economic sectors, agriculture and food production became increasingly globalized in the 1990s. Since the 1980s, food imports to the United States have more than doubled, and more than 30 percent of the fruits and vegetables the nation consumes now originate in other countries.[36] The growing crossborder traffic in food and agricultural products increases the risks to human health by creating more opportunities for pathogens to migrate from their native environments in food shipments and cause disease outbreaks among biologically naive populations in other countries. This traffic also increases the likelihood of plant and animal diseases moving from one part of the world to another. In 2001, for example, a strain of hoof-and-mouth disease that was discovered in India in 1990 made its way to England and eventually to the European continent, resulting in the slaughter of hundreds of thousands of animals to prevent further spread of the disease.

US public health officials now report a sharp increase in the number of disease outbreaks linked to imported food, particularly to produce. The lengthy list of such recent outbreaks includes raspberries from Guatemala; strawberries, scallions, and cantaloupes from Mexico; coconut milk from Thailand; and canned mushrooms from China. Imported food-borne microbes and parasites such as *Cyclospora,* hepatitis, and *Salmonella* have resulted in several thousand illnesses and deaths in the United States alone over the past ten years. The Centers for Disease Control and Prevention

(CDC) estimate that *Cyclospora,* a rare parasite linked to produce in Guatemala, accounted for more than 2,300 cases of food poisoning in the United States in 1997.[37]

But food safety concerns are not limited to products originating in less-industrialized countries. Radish sprouts grown in Oregon, for example, are thought to have caused an outbreak of food poisoning in Japan. And the South Korean agricultural ministry has claimed it found a dangerous strain of *Escherichia coli* (*E. coli*) bacteria in a shipment of frozen beef from a large US meatpacking firm.[38] The ongoing mad cow disease crisis in the United Kingdom further illustrates how unsound agricultural practices—in this case, feeding the ground carcasses of dead animals to live ones—can result in potentially serious risks to human health. Within the United States, serious health effects from high-technology food production have recently been experienced. In the Chesapeake Bay area, for example, foul agricultural runoff from poultry megafarms has been implicated in the emergence of large plumes of *Pfiesteria* bacteria in several rivers that damaged many of the region's fisheries and resulted in several cases of human illness.

Part of the emerging food-safety problem is associated with trade liberalization. Although tariff and trade barriers in the agricultural sector have been reduced and transportation technologies have more rapidly moved food products from farm to market, health and food-safety standards and practices in many exporting countries remain poor. Thus, the risk of exposure to food-borne disease is rising as more countries pursue export oriented agricultural production under various worldwide and regional free trade regimes.[39] Moreover, the tension between food safety and free trade grows more acute when it becomes a matter of international economic diplomacy. This occurs, for instance, when more stringent food safety standards in importing countries are attacked as nontariff barriers to trade. Such conflicts highlight the challenges that increased economic interdependence poses to state sovereignty. Trade disagreements are increasingly likely to be settled by the dispute resolution bodies of free trade regimes such as the WTO or NAFTA, rather than by the actions of national governments. Consequently, the limitations that trading regimes place on state sovereignty conceivably make it more difficult for countries to deal effectively with growing risks to public health. For developing countries, the policies of international financial institutions (the IMF, the World Bank, etc.) to encourage debt repayment may have unintended adverse effects on public health. Structural adjustment policies mandate that governments decrease spending in order to impose fiscal discipline and free monies to repay foreign debt. These actions, however, can lead to cuts in public health and education, two key tools in fighting infectious disease.

The increasing global traffic in food products is now straining the world's food safety monitoring systems. As one official from the Food and Drug Administration recently noted, the United States designed its system of standards, monitoring, and inspection 100 years ago for an agrarian economy that was largely domestic. That system cannot cope with the demands of a global marketplace, particularly in an era of declining government support in the face of a dramatic increase in defense against terrorism.

MIGRATION, URBANIZATION, AND DISEASE

Although there is currently much greater contact among the various neighborhoods of the nascent global village, the neighborhoods themselves are becoming more densely packed and prone to the spread of disease. People are migrating much more freely among and within countries, often carrying pathogens with them. The United Nations has estimated that by the year 2015 there will be 33 urban areas called *megacities* with 8 million inhabitants or more. Twenty-seven of these will be in less-industrialized countries. The fact that the most rapid urban growth is occurring in the cities of the poor and politically unstable less-industrialized world raises additional health concerns given the limited resources, health infrastructures, and formal institutional arrangements available to governments in these countries.[40] Because greater human population densities mean more frequent interaction, urbanization creates the conditions necessary for the potential rapid spread of infectious disease. Just as the densely populated city of ancient Rome was prone to rapidly spreading epidemics, the rise of megacities in impoverished countries, increasingly linked to each other by rapid transportation, presents growing challenges to public health.

Several forces are driving this unhealthy urbanization trend. Environmental decay in rural areas of poorer countries is a major contributor to the growing rural–urban migration. Degradation of the agricultural resource base is driven by a complex interplay of population pressures, desertification, deforestation, droughts, and salination of soils because of irrigation. These problems have contributed directly to increases in the number of migrating rural poor in many regions of Africa, Asia, and Latin America, as well as to declines in agricultural productivity, particularly in marginal areas. Compounding matters, throughout the developing world, population growth rates in rural areas are particularly high and numbers often exceed the sustaining capabilities of local ecosystems. The lure of urban areas, where industry and related economic opportunities are perceived to be growing, becomes almost irresistible to many in the countryside for whom living conditions have grown increasingly difficult. Thus, the migration of marginalized rural residents to urban centers is propelled by a complex set of ecological and economic push and pull factors.[41]

The prevalence of unemployment, poverty, pollution from municipal and industrial wastes, poor nutrition, and an inadequate public health infrastructure (particularly sanitation and sewers) in urban areas means that the urban poor of these growing megacities in less-industrialized countries frequently encounter and carry a host of First and Third World maladies. They experience the problems characteristic of poverty (for example, deaths from infectious disease and higher infant mortality rates) and those characteristic of wealth (higher rates of death form heart disease, neoplasms, and accidents). Nonetheless, many migrants in the developing world still regard themselves as better off in cities than in the countryside, where economic circumstances are often worse.[42]

This urbanization trend is now especially troubling for human health because of the rising incidence of infectious waterborne diseases (such as cholera, typhoid, and hepatitis A and E) and vector-borne diseases such as malaria that thrive around stagnant water, particularly in cities of the less-industrialized world. The ever-increasing numbers and densities of the urban poor also help to create conditions for the occurrence of epidemic outbreaks as well as for the persistence of endemic infectious disease.

Health threats associated with megacities are not limited to the less-industrialized world. Recent viral and bacterial challenges in New York illustrate the emerging threats that infectious diseases pose to urban populations, even in the industrialized world. New York witnessed a rebirth of TB in the 1990s that was facilitated by the convergence of at least three key trends: the spread of HIV and AIDS, the economic recession of the late 1980s, and budgetary reductions in public health programs. In the early 1970s, when TB appeared to be under control, programs in the United States aimed at detecting and controlling the disease were downsized and phased out. But HIV began its spread into segments of the urban population in the 1980s, creating ideal hosts through which TB could make a comeback as AIDS developed. Unchallenged by the usual defenses of a healthy human immune system, TB found hospitable breeding grounds in the systems of AIDS victims. When the economic recession of the late 1980s hit, it left poorer, TB-infected AIDS victims in New York and elsewhere unable to gain access to adequate medical care. As a result, many of the urban poor with active TB cases did not complete the necessary six-month regimen of antibiotics, thereby helping the surviving bacteria become drug-resistant.[43]

Thus, the growth of megacities in all countries affects ecological interdependence in many ways and creates conditions for the spread of infectious disease. Megacities, with their extremely dense populations, facilitate epidemic outbreaks. The ecological balance is tipped further in favor of disease-causing pathogens by virtue of the unsanitary conditions in the poorly developed health infrastructure found in poorer parts of major cities all over the world. Finally, just as in the time of the Roman Empire, the more intense intermingling of different peoples through rural–urban migration and international travel among large cities continues to make large-scale urbanization a most serious challenge to public health.

POLICY RESPONSES TO EMERGING HEALTH RISKS

These emerging health threats are symptomatic of many of the new challenges raised by increasing globalization, and they require comprehensive, sustained policy responses at both the national and international levels. But governments had been extremely lax in their approach to the menace of infectious disease until anthrax was used as a weapon in the United States in 2001. Now disease is thought of as a military matter, and there is hefty funding in the United States to fight bioterrorism but not much additional for fighting conventional disease.

Surveillance, reporting, and international response capability should be key elements to new disease prevention programs. Surveillance and reporting could rely on new telecommunications technology and a network of clinics, hospitals, and laboratories that could serve as listening posts in the United States and around the world. Each should have a staff with epidemiological expertise to recognize unusual cases and patterns of disease incidence. Ideally, each facility would be linked to a more centralized agency capable of providing information and scientific support and of mobilizing effective intervention when necessary. In this way, each associated clinic and laboratory would function as a node in a worldwide surveillance web.

A network of this sort need not be built entirely from scratch. For example, the WHO has established a global surveillance network called WHONET that links microbiology labs around the world to a central database that can be used to detect and prevent the spread of drug-resistant strains of microbes. Similarly, a group of scientists in the United States has set up a Program to Monitor Emerging Diseases (ProMED), a global e-mail network that facilitates reporting on and discussion of disease outbreaks around the world. Since ProMED was initiated in 1993, the program has rapidly grown into a worldwide unofficial disease reporting system with more than 10,000 subscribers in 120 countries.[44]

The existing surveillance network, however, has significant limitations. For example, communications and medical capabilities are inadequate in many tropical countries where new diseases are most likely to emerge. Even in the United States, for that matter, reporting to the CDC is haphazard, and, because of insufficient funding, some states' public health infrastructures have deteriorated to the extent that detection of diseases cannot be ensured.[45]

Moreover, it is of little use to report on disease outbreaks if adequate in-country or transsovereign response capabilities do not exist. In the absence of such capabilities, local doctors, scientists, and public health officials have little reason to participate in reporting networks. The CDC does deploy teams of epidemiologists to various parts of the world to assist communities where outbreaks occur, but sufficient international response demands a more centralized agency with access to state-of-the-art facilities, world-class staff, sufficient funding, and a political mandate to take the lead in responding to the threat of emerging or reemerging diseases. The WHO would appear to be the logical choice given its established role as the coordinator of international health programs. Yet, on further examination, WHO lacks all of the necessary elements—authority, mandate, funding, staff, and facilities—sufficient for the task at hand.[46]

This lack of a robust global program for the surveillance of and response to emerging disease threats highlights important political dilemmas that are characteristic of global ecopolitics. For example, the current US disposition to reduce its international commitments, minimize involvement in international organizations, and cut foreign aid flies in the face of a growing need for leadership and assistance to deal with the spin-offs of globalization, such as the need for worldwide disease monitoring and prevention. Moreover, while the largest global health risks frequently originate in poor countries and failing states, which are the least capable of managing them, countries with the resources necessary to address such problems often lack the political will to use them in the absence of an imminent crisis. From the perspective of US policy makers, for example, there is little apparent political gain and much potential damage associated with sponsoring the creation of new international programs designed to combat threats that are not perceived to be serious biosecurity concerns by the American public.

There are additional dilemmas involved in attempting to curtail the global risks of infectious disease. For instance, surveillance is intrusive, and there is a reluctance on the part of some governments to report on disease outbreaks for fear of serious international political and economic fallout. Thus, when India experienced its outbreaks of pneumonic plague in the 1990s, the government at first failed to report the incident to the international medical community, anticipating de facto quarantines and declines in trade and tourism. The Indian government's reticence is understandable in the light of the costs and benefits it must have considered. Similarly, the outbreak of bird flu in Hong Kong not only resulted in economic damage from a loss of tourism, but also damaged the political fortunes of the new government. And in South Africa, a country in which nearly one of every four adults is HIV-positive, President Thabo Mbeki has questioned whether HIV really causes AIDS and whether AIDS is the leading cause of death in his country.[47] If reporting is perceived as unlikely to muster assistance in combating disease outbreaks but highly likely to result in economic losses of various sorts, then denial rules and there is no advantage to reporting.

Finally, the status of the international policy responses to the emerging threats from infectious disease is indicative of some of the broader political dynamics incumbent in the process of globalization. In an increasingly integrated, interdependent, and technologically advanced world, the role of the sovereign state is becoming more ambiguous. The diffusion of communications and information technologies, for example, has empowered the scientific and medical communities and facilitated more effective global surveillance of infectious disease in the absence of any major government initiatives. The ProMED network demonstrates the extent to which technology can place real power in the hands of nongovernmental groups, enabling them to act swiftly to bridge gaps in existing government programs.

In effect, technology has enhanced the ability of nonstate actors to assume authority in areas where governments fail to provide leadership. The technologically augmented power of international professional networks might, on the one hand, be viewed as enhancing the authority and legitimacy of government by helping to fill vacuums in government functions. But, on the other hand, this power might as easily be viewed as further reducing governmental authority by expropriating some of the traditional responsibilities of government in the public health arena.

Thus, the nascent responses to emerging disease threats, like the threats themselves, raise questions about the future of state sovereignty in an increasingly global system. The current lack of a comprehensive response to the challenges of emerging and resurging diseases at both the national and international levels reflects two trends. First, it illustrates the continued weakening of the state and its withdrawal from some of its historic oversight and regulatory roles. This reflects the effect of the privatization of key public functions, growing budgetary constraints, and other limitations that have made private or market-based approaches appear more seductive. And, of course, it demonstrates the extent to which technology is enabling citizens or groups to act directly on matters of concern to them and circumventing government involvement and limitations.

Contemporary globalization, the intensification of trends that have been at play in the international system for several centuries, thus increases challenges to state sovereignty and capabilities. The threats from new and reemerging infectious diseases, many of which have played a major role in shaping societies throughout human history, continue to exert their influence on human populations and governance at the beginning of the third millennium in spite of humanity's best efforts to eliminate them. The complex interactions of technological advances and the growing levels of interdependence among nations are giving rise to new pathways for the transmission of disease as well as to new weapons in the war against them. In the long run, one of the casualties of these dynamics might well be globalization itself as the rapid worldwide spread of human, animal, and plant diseases leads to an antiglobalization reaction that could dramatically slow the process.

ENDNOTES

1. See Dennis Pirages, "Microsecurity: Disease Organisms and Human Well-Being," *Washington Quarterly* (Autumn 1995).

2. Luigi Cavalli-Sforza and Francesco Cavalli-Sforza, *The Great Human Diasporas* (Reading, MA: Addison-Wesley, 1995), 157–159.

3. Kenneth Watt, *Principles of Environmental Science* (New York: McGraw-Hill, 1973), 1.

4. Karl Deutsch, *Nationalism and Social Communication* (Cambridge: MIT Press, 1964), 100.

5. William McNeill, *Plagues and Peoples* (Garden City, NY: Anchor Press, 1976), 115–117.

6. Henry Hobhouse, *Forces of Change: An Unorthodox View of History* (New York: Arcade, 1990), 11.

7. See McNeill, *Plagues and Peoples,* Ch. 4.

8. Hobhouse, *Forces of Change,* 11–23.

9. McNeill, *Plagues and Peoples,* 208.

10. Ibid., 215 and references cited therein.

11. See Alfred Crosby, *America's Forgotten Pandemic: The Influenza Epidemic of 1918* (Cambridge, UK: Cambridge University Press, 1990).

12. See Laurie Garrett, *The Coming Plague: Newly Emerging Diseases in a World Out of Balance* (New York: Farrar, Straus & Giroux, 1994); Stephen S. Morse (Ed.), *Emerging Viruses* (New York: Oxford University Press, 1993).

13. Marc Lappe, *Evolutionary Medicine: Rethinking the Origins of Disease* (San Francisco: Sierra Club Books, 1994), 8.

14. See Stephen Buckley, "Wife Inheritance Spurs AIDS Rise in Kenya," *Washington Post,* Nov. 8, 1997; available at <www.washingtonpost.com/wp-srv/inatl/longterm/african-lives/kenya/kenya_aids.htm>.

15. Ann Gibbons, "Where Are 'New' Diseases Born?" *Science* (Aug. 6, 1993): 680.

16. See Keith B. Richburg, "Hong Kong Faulted on Handling of 'Bird Flu' Crisis," *Washington Post,* Jan. 4, 1998; Diane Brady and Peter Stein, "Hong Kong's Tourism Trade Gets the Chills as Airline Travelers Come to Fear Avian Flu," *Wall Street Journal,* Dec. 23, 1997; John Cohen, "Is an Old Virus Up to New Tricks?" *Science* (July 18, 1997): 312–313.

17. See Alfred W. Crosby, *Ecological Imperialism: The Biological Expansion of Europe, 900–1900* (Cambridge, UK: Cambridge University Press, 1986).

18. See Elizabeth Culotta, "Biological Immigrants under Fire," *Science* (Dec. 6, 1991): 1444–1447.

19. Ibid., 1444.

20. Cited in David P. Fidler, "Return of the Fourth Horseman: Emerging Infectious Diseases and International Law," *Minnesota Law Review* (April 1997): 773.

21. World Health Organization (WHO), *The World Health Report 1995* (Geneva: Author, 1995).

22. David Brown, "1 in 10 TB Cases Worldwide Resist Common Treatment, Survey Shows," *Washington Post,* Oct. 23, 1997; WHO, "The Big Guns of Resistance," Ch. 4 in *Overcoming Antimicrobial Resistance* (Geneva: Author, 2000) (available at <www.who.int/infectious-disease-report/2000/>).

23. National Intelligence Council, *The Global Infectious Disease Threat and Its Implications for the United States* (CIA publication NIE99-17D), Jan. 2000, pp. 8–11; available at <www.cia.gov/cia/publications/nie/report/nie99-17d.html>.

24. UNAIDS and WHO, *AIDS Epidemic Update,* Dec. 2001; available at <www.unaids. org/epidemic_update/report_dec01/>.

25. Philip J. Hilts, "Effort to Fight Malaria Seems to Have Failed," *The New York Times,* Oct. 9, 1991; Bob Drogin, "Deadly Malaria Returns with a Vengeance," *Washington Post,* Nov. 10, 1992; Eliot Marshall, "Malaria Parasite Gaining Ground against Science," *Science* (Oct. 11, 1991).

26. See Laurie Garrett, *Betrayal of Trust: The Collapse of Global Public Health* (New York: Hyperion, 2000), Ch. 1.

27. See David Brown, "World Responds Swiftly to Track 'Bird Flu' Spread," *Washington Post,* Jan. 11, 1998.

28. See US Congress, Office of Technology Assessment, *Harmful Non-Indigenous Species in the United States* (publication no. OTA-F-565) (Washington, DC: US Government Printing Office, Sept. 1993), 69, 92; available at <www.wws.princeton.edu/~ota/ disk1/1993/9325_n.html>.

29. Chris Bright, *Life Out of Bounds: Bioinvasion in a Borderless World* (New York: W.W. Norton, 1998), 176.

30. See James N. Rosenau, "The Complexities and Contradictions of Globalization," *Current History* (Nov. 1997): 360–364.

31. See Stephen S. Morse, "Regulating Viral Traffic," *Issues in Science and Technology* (Fall 1990): 81–82.

32. Hilary French, *Vanishing Borders: Protecting the Planet in an Age of Globalization* (New York: W.W. Norton, 2000), Table 1-1.

33. Ibid.

34. See, for example, Ellen Ruppel Shell, "Resurgence of a Deadly Disease," *Atlantic Monthly* (August 1997): 45–60 (available at <www.theatlantic.com/issues/97aug/ malaria.htm>); Thomas A. Kenyon, Sarah E. Valway, Walter W. Ihle, Ida M. Onorato, and Kenneth G. Castro, "Transmission of a Multidrug-Resistant Mycobacterium Tuberculosis During a Long Airplane Flight," *New England Journal of Medicine* 334 (1996): 933–938 (available at <http://wonder.cdc.gov/wonder/prevguid/p0000436/ p0000436.asp>); "E. Coli Is Found in Shipment of IBP Frozen Beef to Korea," *Wall Street Journal,* Sept. 29, 1997; Jeff Gerth and Tim Weiner, "U.S. Food Safety System Swamped by Booming Global Imports," *The New York Times,* Sept. 29, 1997; Rachel Nowak, "WHO Calls for Action against TB," *Science* (March 24, 1995).

35. For a discussion of the effects of globalization on state sovereignty, see Susan Strange, *The Retreat of the State* (Cambridge, UK: Cambridge University Press, 1996), Ch. 1; also see Ken Conca, "Rethinking the Ecology-Sovereignty Debate," *Millennium* 23 (1994): 701–711.

36. Gerth and Weiner, "U.S. Food Safety System Swamped."

37. Ibid.

38. "E. Coli Is Found in Shipment of IBP Frozen Beef to Korea," *Wall Street Journal.*

39. Gerth and Weiner, "U.S. Food Safety System Swamped."

40. United Nations Centre for Human Settlements, *An Urbanizing World: Global Report on Human Settlements 1996* (New York: Oxford University Press, 1996), 6.

41. World Commission on Environment and Development, *Our Common Future* (Oxford, UK: Oxford University Press, 1987), 95–102.

42. World Bank, *Urban Policy and Economic Development: An Agenda for the 1990s* (Washington, DC: Author, 1991), 51; Mike Parnwell, *Population Movements in the Third World* (London: Routledge, 1993), 18–24.

43. Clark Merrill and Dennis Pirages, "Ecological Security: Micro-Threats to Human Well-Being," *Futures Research Quarterly* (Spring 1997): 49–50; Richard M. Krause, "The Origin of Plagues: Old and New," *Science* (Aug. 21, 1992): 1074.

44. Stephen S. Morse, "Too Close for Our Own Good," *Washington Post,* Nov. 30, 1997.

45. See Merrill and Pirages, "Ecological Security," 59–60; and Garrett, *Betrayal of Trust,* Ch. 4.

46. See Robert Hunt Sprinkle, *Profession of Conscience: The Making and Meaning of Life-Sciences Liberalism* (Princeton, NJ: Princeton University Press, 1994), 146–155.

47. Mark Schoofs, "Doctor Group Defies South Africa AIDS Policy," *Wall Street Journal,* Jan. 30, 2002 (available at <www.thebody.com/cdc/news_updates_archive/jan30_02/south_africa.html>).

CHAPTER ELEVEN

The Nature of the Nature Problem

Environmental Interdependencies

Vicki Golich

It was 1984 and Dr. Thomas E. Lovejoy was concerned. He had been work-ing at the World Wildlife Fund (WWF) for a little more than a decade. A Yale University–trained biologist, he had been the first scientist to join the WWF's small but growing professional staff. Conservation science and preservation strategies had come a long way since the early 1960s when Rachel Carson's powerful exposé, *Silent Spring*, detailed the potential threats to human life of rapidly proliferating environmental pollution.[1] Nevertheless, nearly twenty-five years later, despite the work of thousands of scientists, naturalists, and policy makers, not to mention the burgeoning number of nongovernmental organizations (NGOs) created with a focus on environmental protection, degradation of the earth's most productive ecosystems—estuaries, coral reefs, wetlands, rainforests—was still signifi-cant. Lovejoy knew that rainforests stood as an ideal microcosm of a larger environmental global crisis.[2] Their status presaged the vitality or decline of other critical ecosystems and, ultimately, the life of the planet.

Rainforests were suffering in part because of a cycle of poverty and debt. Massive and mounting structural debt plagued most Third World countries, exacerbating the poverty of their citizens. Pressured by creditors—private banks and multinational corporations, public companies, governments, and international governmental organizations (IGOs), such as the World Bank and International Monetary Fund (IMF)—debtor states implemented aggressive policies of economic growth. But these very policies were hastening the destruction of critical resources, including the rainforests, and undermining states' abilities to repay their debts. Rainforest depletion negatively affects the vitality of geographically distant ecosystems, eventually decreasing the global capacity to produce the food, medicines, and services (e.g., the cleansing of CO_2 from the air via photosynthesis) on which all life depends. And, of course, if debtors cannot grow their economies, creditors will not be repaid.

Lovejoy's dilemma was how to protect a rapidly degrading environment threatened by seemingly unconnected short-term survival strategies unrestrained by any governance mechanisms. His dilemma was one of the oldest, best-known, and frustratingly intractable policy dilemmas: the "commons" tragedies.[3] The analogy is to the historic commons, a centrally located pasture that was open to everyone who wished to use it for grazing livestock. The "tragedy" occurred when each individual livestock owner added to his herd in order to maximize his own benefit from using the communal pasture. As a result, the livestock owners collectively overgrazed the pasture, eventually destroying the commons and their own means of survival. Although the group as a whole and as individual members would have benefited from limiting the number of grazing animals, nothing—neither incentive nor sanction—compelled any individual to limit his herd unless he could be sure that others would do the same.

Global commons abuse is a classic transsovereign problem.[4] The air we breathe, the water we drink, and the climate surrounding us flow freely across political boundaries. Each is absolutely vital to our ability to survive, yet each can be seriously degraded by activities taking place within individual sovereign countries. No one country can own or govern air, water, or the climate, but activities within any one country can pollute these critical resources. Even worse, the resulting degradation may initially wreak more havoc on surrounding countries or regions than on the polluter state itself. As a transsovereign problem, commons abuses—no matter where they may occur—share a set of interconnected characteristics that confounds any attempt to find acceptable resolution. These characteristics fall into roughly three categories: political, economic, and scientific.

Political

- ❏ No single actor owns the problems or can possibly solve them unilaterally.
- ❏ No supranational authority can impose solutions on unwilling participants.
- ❏ Domestic policy making and implementation are influenced by a wide range of disparate and potentially conflicting interests.
- ❏ The power to develop or implement policies varies among actors.

Economic

- ❏ Disagreement about whether compensation for past and present resource exploitation is reasonable or viable complicates the negotiations.
- ❏ Uncertainties persist about the actual costs of regulations for the global market in general and lesser-developed countries (LDCs) in particular and who should bear these costs.
- ❏ Disputes about economic growth strategies continue.[5]

Scientific

- ❏ The consequences of environmental degradation affect actors unevenly.
- ❏ The problems are technically complex in and of themselves.
- ❏ The search for solutions is plagued by scientific uncertainty about current levels of pollution, how long it might take for dire consequences to affect our lives as we know them, and the range of potential benefits.

Each characteristic alone challenges our capacity to find a solution to global commons abuse. The task is rendered more complicated because change in one triggers change in the others—much like a line of dominoes. Unlike dominoes, however, the changes are seldom predictable. Lovejoy knew that issue area interdependencies could enhance or inhibit the possibilities of finding a solution. Moreover, he understood the dilemma that confronted policy makers in the arena of global environmental protection: They must contend with two distinct yet inextricably connected problems—nature and economics—in a political context marked by symmetrical sovereignty but asymmetrical distribution of power. In other words, every country can legally claim the same right to implement policy within its borders (sovereignty), but each country has a different capacity to influence or determine what policy will be implemented.

This chapter explores the nature of this "nature problem." How can countries grow their economies without killing the planet on which we all depend for life as well as economics? In examining rainforest depletion and global warming, the chapter explores the connections between developed and developing states, the environment and economics (especially debt and development), the role of NGOs and IGOs in environmental problems, and global environmental problems and sovereignty.

THE NATURE PROBLEM

Nature does not respect political borders. Rainforests cover vast expanses of land, demarcated by multiple political boundaries, yet actions taken by one country *inside its own borders* could threaten the survivability of an entire rainforest. In turn, rainforest destruction could cause harmful global climate changes, triggering severe changes in the globe's biodiversity—the entire cornucopia of flora and fauna—that could eventually undermine the planet's capacity for life. A variety of economic activities damage rainforests, including ranching, farming, mining, and logging. At current logging rates, 1 percent of the primary tropical rainforests are being destroyed each year,[6] with another 1 percent degraded so much that ecosystem sustainability is threatened. In selected locations, even greater destruction is evident. In western Ecuador, approximately 95 percent of the forest has been destroyed because of "development" since 1960.[7] In Costa Rica, more than 7 percent of the rainforest was cleared each year during the early 1980s,[8] largely because of the expansion of cattle ranching.[9]

Unfortunately, the scientific community cannot predict precisely how vulnerable rainforests are to these many human activities or how dire the costs might be should tropical rainforests continue to disappear. Scientists also cannot predict the exact time line of destruction. Complicated, difficult-to-understand, and tentative information hampers negotiations by

❏ causing misunderstandings among participants who interpret the information differently,

❏ making it difficult to translate the information into policy terms, and

❏ creating uncertainty about the actual gains from implementing different policy options.

Scientific complexity and uncertainty also make it easier for stakeholders to use information to serve their own purposes.[10] Incomplete pieces of information can be used—wittingly or unwittingly—to support a policy position. The complicated nature of the global environmental protection issues is amply demonstrated by the current debate over global climate change and the Kyoto Protocol. The First World Climate Conference recognized climate change as a serious problem in 1979. Nearly twenty years later, in December 1997, the Kyoto Protocol to the United Nations Framework Convention on Climate Change was finally adopted.[11]

Even though the Kyoto Protocol has taken effect after receiving the requisite number of country signatures, the United States has refused to sign on the grounds that the science of global climate change is too indecisive. Because environmental protection in general and global climate change in particular involve a great deal of uncertainty about both the magnitude of the potential adverse effect and the significance of the potential damages, negotiations generally involve weighing vague, unproven future benefits against current known costs. Regulatory costs are relatively easy to calculate and are instantly incurred. Naturally, affected industries resist the implementation of any controls that carry expenses, and hardly any change does not, at least initially. Because environmental damage frequently occurs—or is noticed—long after the causative polluting act, it is extremely hard to prove causation. As a result, policy makers, particularly short-term elected officials, find it difficult to "bite the bullet" and decide to take action to avoid environmental damage. Instead, they walk the path of least resistance and delay decision making until improved data or information is available. This adds years to the policy making process, which further threatens the health of our global environment because many adverse environmental effects, once initiated, are not readily reversible.

The "facts" about global climate change—and its connection to rainforest depletion—have been subject to a great deal of scientific debate. As a result, a high-stakes judgment had to be made that weighed immediate economic effects against longer-term ecological benefits that may never be known precisely. On the one hand, enough scientific evidence existed to cause alarm, and even cautious scientific groups predicted severe future damage. On the other hand, sufficient scientific uncertainty remained, raising serious questions about the prudence of taking immediate action. Several crucial questions were subject to debate:

❏ What greenhouse gases are causing the greatest damage to the rainforest?

❏ Whose emissions are most responsible for which damage?

❏ How much rainforest can we afford to lose?

❏ If greenhouse gas emissions are cut back by a certain percentage, will proportional decreases in rainforest degradation occur?

Despite these exasperating uncertainties, researchers *are* learning more about the intricate symbiosis of each rainforest species to the other,[12] and about the treasure trove of benefits and values the rainforests hold for the international community.[13] Tropical rainforests play an irreplaceable role in preserving global biodiversity and stabilizing the global climate, in addition to providing all of the local benefits of an enormously productive ecosystem.

Biodiversity

Researchers estimate that tropical rainforests contain more than half the total number of species on earth, even though the forests occupy less than 10 percent of the land surface.[14] Estimates vary, but Table 1 (pages 274–275) shows the number of tropical species that are predicted to become extinct at current deforestation rates. We may destroy most of these species before we even "discover" them.[15]

Species extinction destroys a yet-to-be-developed future reservoir of food and drugs, not to mention a whole host of beneficial microorganisms.

Preserving wild species enhances our ability to develop new marketable crops, such as the recent success of the kiwi fruit; to improve existing crops by increasing their resistance to disease or pests; to expand and enhance medical pharmaceuticals; to discover naturally based, biodegradable pesticide compounds; to "clean up environmental messes" using bioremediation; and even to unravel the mysteries of the human genome.[16] The world's current food supply relies on a narrow genetic base. More than 80 percent of the world's food supplies comes from fewer than two dozen species.[17] Expanding the base opens endless possibilities. Consider the benefits flowing from the discovery of wild perennial corn in Mexico some twenty years ago:

> Previously there had been only one species of perennial corn described. . . . But unlike the species discovered in the 1970s, it did not have the same number of chromosomes as domestic corn. With the discovery of this second species of perennial corn, it became relatively easy to transfer some of the traits of perennial corn into corn agriculture, making the long-term dream of a perennial corn crop, as well as the more short-term one of disease resistance, an achievable goal. The importance of these kinds of contributions to agriculture can be underscored by noting that corn is the third most important grain supporting human societies.[18]

Similarly, many medical drugs today are derived from natural plant materials. According to pharmaceutical researcher Norman Farnsworth, "for the past 25 years, 25 percent of all prescriptions dispensed from community pharmacies in the United States contained active principles that are still extracted from higher plants."[19] Glaucoma, hypertension, malaria, heart disease, and Hodgkin's disease are only a few of the ills combated with plant products from the rainforests. Of the 3,000 plant species in the world known to contain anticancer properties, 2,100 are from the tropics.[20]

Equally important, scientific discoveries using rainforest species can unlock medical mysteries. Studies on the venom of a South American pit viper "led to the discovery of the angiotensin system that regulates blood pressure in human beings."[21] Once that system was known and understood, researchers were able to create and manufacture what is now the preferred prescription drug for hypertension.

Table 1	
Estimates of Potential Species in the Tropics	
Estimate	Source
From one species/day to one species/hour between 1970s and 2000	Norman Myers, *The Sinking Ark: A New Look at the Problem of Disappearing Species* (New York: Pergamon Press, 1979)
From 33 percent to 50 percent of all species between 1970s and 2000	Thomas E. Lovejoy, III, "A Projection of Species Extinctions," in G. O. Barney, *The Global 2000 Report to the President: Entering the Twenty-First Century,* Vol. 2 (Washington, DC: Council on Environmental Quality, 1980), 328–331
One million species or more by end of twentieth century	National Research Council, *Research Priorities in Tropical Biology* (Washington, DC: National Academy of Sciences, 1980)
Fifty percent of species by the year 2000 or by early twenty-first century	Paul R. Ehrlich and Anne H. Ehrlich, *Extinction: The Causes of the Disappearance of Species* (New York: Random House, 1981)
Several hundred thousand species in just a few decades	Norman Myers, "Forest Refuges and Conservation in Africa with Some Appraisal of Survival Prospects for Tropical Moist Forests Throughout the Home," in G. T. Prance (Ed.), *Biological Diversification in the Tropics* (New York: Columbia University Press, 1982), 658–672
From 25 percent to 30 percent of all species, or from 500,000 to several million by end of the twentieth century	Norman Myers, "Conservation of Rain Forests for Scientific Research, for Wildlife Conservation, and for Recreation and Tourism," in P. B. Golley (Ed.), *Tropical Rain Forest Ecosystems: Structure and Function* (Amsterdam: Elsevier, 1983), 325–334
From 500,000 to 600,000 species by end of the twentieth century	M. l. Oldfield, *The Value of Conserving Genetic Resources* (Washington, DC:

Table 1 (continued)	
Estimates of Potential Species in the Tropics	
Estimate	Source
	US Department of the Interior, National Park Service, 1984)
Approximately 0.75 million species by end of twentieth century	P. H. Raven, personal communication to World Resources Institute and International Institute for Environment and Development (Eds.), *World Resources 1986* (New York: Basic Books, 1986)
One-third or more of all species in twenty-first century	D. Simberloff, *Are We on the Verge of Mass Extinction in Tropical Rain Forests?* (unpublished monograph, July 1983)
From 20 percent to 25 percent of existing species by first several decades of the twenty-first century	B. J. Norton (Ed.), *The Preservation of Species* (Princeton, NJ: Princeton University Press, 1986)
Approximately 15 percent of all plant species and 2 percent of all plant families by end of the twentieth century	D. Simberloff, "Are We on the Verge of a Mass Extinction in Tropical Rain Forests?" in D. K. Elliott (Ed.), *Dynamics of Extinction* (New York: Wiley & Sons, 1986), 165–180

Source: Ariel E. Lugo, "Estimating Reductions in the Diversity of Tropical Forest Species," in E. O. Wilson and Frances M. Peter (Eds.), *Biodiversity* (Washington, DC: National Academy Press, 1988), 59.

Climate Stabilization

Standing rainforests, particularly when they cover an area as large as the Amazon basin, help to maintain stable climate patterns. Large-scale rainforest destruction may change the global climate by contributing to the greenhouse effect and consequently to global warming by increasing the concentration of atmospheric carbon dioxide.[22] When rainforest trees are burned (or cut and allowed to rot)—a common practice for clearing land for agriculture or ranching—the carbon compounds that make up the bulk of the plants are oxidized to carbon dioxide. Increases in atmospheric carbon dioxide (as well as other greenhouse gases such as methane and chloro-fluorocarbons) may cause a net warming effect. Overall, the burning of rainforests annually releases nearly 1 billion tons of carbon as carbon dioxide.[23] Approximately 25 percent of the greenhouse gases that were emitted in the 1980s came from tropical deforestation.[24]

Local or regional climate changes may presage global effects. Even if they occur in isolation, they remain a valid concern for the local community. Large-scale deforestation may trigger changes in local rainfall patterns. For example, literally half the rain in the Amazon is generated within its basin.

If the Amazon forest were to be replaced with grassland, a rough computer model predicts that about one-fourth of that rainfall would not occur, and would be accompanied by associated temperature increases. . . . These effects would spill over to other geographical areas, for example, central Brazil, which also depends on the Amazon as a source of moisture for rainfall.[25]

Ecosystem Economics

Fruits, coffee, nuts, and other economically valuable plant products such as rubber can be harvested from standing rainforests. In the past, these benefits have accrued to indigenous populations, as well as to the local rural poor. In many locations, sustainable harvesting of food and fiber from rainforests has created viable, noncash economies.[26]

Destruction of the rainforests often creates short-term profits at the expense of greater long-term benefits. The most obvious examples are projects that cut tropical rainforests to clear land for other crops or cattle. Tropical rainforests generally do not provide good long-term cropland, partly because the nutrients that sustain the forests are contained in the vegetation rather than the soil.[27] Likewise, logging and ranching are less efficient and productive on tropical than on temperate soils. "One hectare (2.5 acres) of tropical forest is worth US $6,800, if harvested yearly for non-timber products. If logged for timber, the value drops to US $3,200. If cleared for cattle ranching, that same hectare is worth only US $2,900."[28]

In the future, additional economic benefits may be derived from preserving the rainforests and developing the ecotourism industry. Ecotourists visit rainforests and wildlife preserves with carefully trained guides to see flora and fauna in their natural habitats. The economic prospects for nature-related travel are immense. The tourist industry is the world's second largest industry at $195 billion a year. Adventure travel (which includes eco-tourism) accounts for 10 percent of that market. Moreover, nature tourism, of which ecotourism is a part, has been increasing at an annual rate of between 10 percent and 30 percent a year, while overall tourism has grown at 4 percent annually.[29] Already, Kenya, an ecotravel pioneering country, earns $350 million from the industry.[30]

Finally, most rainforests support indigenous populations. In Brazil alone, more than ninety tribes have dispersed (or succumbed to disease) since the beginning of this century as a result of the destruction of their homes in the tropical rainforests.[31]

ECONOMICS AFFECTS THE ENVIRONMENT: THE DEBT CONNECTION

The international economy, and with it the entire international community, is currently struggling with a staggering structural debt. Although advanced industrial societies hold their share of debt, the overwhelming burden of this debt is borne by developing countries in the Third World. This disproportionate burden has evolved as a result of the interplay of at least four factors.[32]

First, today's lesser-developed countries face a development dilemma similar to that faced by pre–Revolutionary War colonies in North America. They actually incur debt to produce the goods and services necessary for survival (domestic consumption) and export. Developing countries typically export raw materials or light manufactures of little value. In turn, they must import products with higher value added such as the complex machinery needed for agricultural production or mining extraction. As a result, they have to pay more for the products on which they depend to produce goods and services, whether for domestic consumption or for export. This situation is exacerbated by the fact that demand for the LDCs' products tends to be elastic. When economic times get tough, First World purchases of Third World products tend to decline, and prices of LDC exports fall relative to the price of their imports. Known as *declining terms of trade,* this phenomenon forces LDCs to try to increase their exports in order to buy the same amount of imports. A negative terms-of-trade cycle is nearly impossible to break.[33]

Second, the Organization of Petroleum Exporting Countries (OPEC) accrued immense profits as a result of the oil shocks of the 1970s. Unable to absorb the profits in their own domestic economies, they invested in the banks of advanced industrialized countries (AICs). At the height of the oil boom, for example, "the Saudi monetary agency had the daunting task of investing $4 million in oil revenue every hour, nearly a $100 million a day."[34] AIC economies could not absorb all the money either, and banks sought new and often higher-risk investment sources. LDCs were often the beneficiaries of this search. The terms of the loans were not as good as those that were available from governmental or international governmental organization (IGO) sources, but LDCs were desperate for investment cash.

Unfortunately, the principal and interest payments on these loans generally must be made in US dollars or other hard currencies.[35] To earn these hard currencies, debtor countries again were forced to try to increase exports, including crops and timber, both of which involve cutting rainforests. Between 1990 and 1999, the volume of Latin American exports grew by almost 50 percent.[36] Export volume in most other developing regions increased even more dramatically. However, more exports did not bring in more profits, because of unfavorable conditions in the world market. Predictably, First World demand for Third World exports was relatively weak, and commodity prices fell. Even worse, imports increased throughout the decade; in 1990, Latin America had a positive trade balance of $22.8 billion but by 1999 it had suffered a negative trade balance of $26.4 billion.[37] So, despite increased exports, income decreased, which made debt repayment difficult.

Third, interest rates rose from the time when the developing countries took on a large share of their debt. According to World Bank analyses, throughout the 1980s real interest rates were, on average, "more than twice as high as in the 1960s and nearly six times higher than in 1974–1979."[38]

Fourth, the development policies advocated by multilateral lending agencies encouraged LDCs to build their national economies on the strength of increasing export revenues rather than on expanding domestic markets. This kept LDCs dependent on both high-priced imports and lower, fluctuating-price exports, which kept LDCs vulnerable to international commodity fluctuations. These policies also deepened the LDCs' reliance on foreign technology and capital. As a result, developing country debt service reached $388.4 billion by 1999. Between 1970 and 1988, loan payments by debtor nations calculated as a percentage of gross national product increased dramatically. In Latin America and the Caribbean, long-term debt grew from $27.8 billion in 1970 to more than $813 billion in 1999.[39] The debt burden became a major impediment to economic growth.

In 1982, Mexico announced it would be unable to pay its debts. By 1988, more than forty additional countries "made similar announcements."[40] The international community was forced to recognize that this was a structural debt problem of global proportions, not merely a Third World debt problem. After all, the banks that made the loans were key players in the economies of developed countries, too.

The effects of the debt crisis were felt by the entire international community. In debtor countries, the per-capita gross domestic product fell, and poverty increased in all countries for which data are available.[41] Concern about the size of the banks' bad-debt portfolios in turn raised questions about the effects of potential defaults on the domestic economies in First World countries and, most significantly, on the stability of the entire international monetary system. These concerns were related not only to the direct effects of the defaults on the international financial community, but also to the indirect effects—weak Third World economies would no longer provide markets for First World goods.

In short, the debt crisis was both a devastating problem from the viewpoint of the citizens of the Third World and a problem whose solution would benefit the entire international community.

INTERDEPENDENCIES:
DEVELOPMENT AND THE ENVIRONMENT

The extensive destruction of rainforests and other valuable habitat has generally occurred in the name of economic development and, in some cases, survival. Several factors converge to create this development–destruction dilemma within Third World countries, including the process of "normal" economic development. The prevalence of poverty among a large and growing portion of the population, the well-intentioned policies of multilateral agencies such as the World Bank and the International Monetary Fund, and the crushing international debt burden these states now bear encourages adoption of quick and dirty development policies.

"Normal" Economic Development

The common notion of development seeks to enhance economic growth by both exploiting a country's natural resource base and building the infrastructure that will support increased trade and economic activity. Timber harvesting, mineral extraction, and clearing land for agriculture all contribute to economic growth and provide the raw materials and cash required for domestic consumption and investment, as well as for foreign-debt payments. However, these activities directly destroy the rainforest ecosystems, while infrastructure development—housing, roads, communication systems, and public utilities—further encroaches on rainforest territories.

Promoting the exploitation of natural resources, standard theories of economic development overlook the benefits of preserving ecosystem integrity (and with it the natural resource base) for the future. Many of the economic indices by which growth is measured intrinsically undervalue *sustainable* natural resource output. For example, per-capita GNP calculations consider the benefits of rainforest clearing as "net income" without considering the costs to the economy of environmental degradation. The value of reserving natural resources for future use is heavily discounted, the external costs of exploitation are not considered,[42] and many natural resources are simply undervalued in the marketplace.[43]

Frequently the benefits derived from this "normal" development process accrue to the affluent people of the Third World countries and multinational corporations[44] rather than to the rural poor. Standard development activities characteristically have been accompanied by greater concentrations of land ownership, leaving many small farmers landless.[45] Further, many (though certainly not all) of the agricultural, ranching, and industrial production techniques are capital intensive, not labor intensive.[46] This increases the size of an already abundant labor pool, depresses wages, and further aggravates the inability of the poor to be economically productive. These societal costs, unlike the benefits, are shared by the vast majority of the domestic population and, indirectly, by the entire international community.

In sum, conservation of resources for sustainable future use has not been considered a component of economic development.[47]

Poverty

Just as commonly, environmental destruction has been inextricably linked to the poverty of the rural landless poor. The pursuit of short-term survival by local, impoverished populations often means practicing unsustainable shifting cultivation and overharvesting of animal populations—and their consequent decimation.[48] In the words of Alan Durning of the Worldwatch Institute, "poverty drives ecological deterioration when desperate people overexploit their resource base, sacrificing the future to salvage the present."[49]

Often, those who lose their lands to the economic activities associated with normal economic development, rather than move into the poverty of the cities, simply move deeper into the rainforests to clear new pasture or farmland to sustain life.[50] According to Paulo Nogueira-Neto, ecology professor at the University of São Paulo and Brazil's former secretary for the environment, "Poverty is the chief environmental problem. If people had good jobs in the cities, they would not go to Amazonia. Relief from our foreign debt would help quite a bit with the Amazon."[51]

Structural Debt

While poverty and the need for economic development in Third World countries have tended to encourage habitat destruction, the debt burden of these same countries has served to exacerbate this tendency. Debt reduction and resource abuse are not intrinsically related.[52] However, heavily indebted countries have typically chosen to raise hard currency for debt repayment through development policies that perpetuate environmental destruction, such as by promoting mining, timber harvesting, cash-crop farming, and cattle ranching. The short-term need for hard currencies has outweighed the long-term concern for fostering sustainable use of the natural-resource base.

The debt burden may also have indirect adverse effects on the local environment. Squeezed by a demanding debt load, national budgets have little room for conservation efforts or other environmental protection endeavors such as conducting research on sustainable production methods, gathering data about the consequences of development policies, or educating the population about the potential hazards of abusing the rainforests. In the view of some observers, "in times of debt-induced, economic duress, already lax pollution control and mitigation efforts receive even less financial attention."[53] A weak local economy also forces local populations to exploit natural resources for short-term survival rather than long-term sustainable use.

External Pressures

The development policies of international financial institutions (IFIs) have worsened the assault on the natural habitats and resource base of poor countries. After World War II, the IMF and the World Bank initially focused their attention on rebuilding the devastated economies of Europe and the Far East. By the 1960s, they had begun to turn their attention to the problems of the Third World. The two institutions specified conditions under which debtor states could receive IMF or International Bank for Reconstruction and Development (IBRD) loans. The IMF became an accrediting agency of sorts. Virtually all potential creditors, including private banks and central state banks, used IMF credit ratings to evaluate loans. The IBRD influenced the nature of development of Third World countries, essentially promoting transitions to industrial economies. In addition to increasing agricultural output and exploiting natural resources through expanded harvesting and mining efforts, a strong emphasis was placed on building the infrastructure that would facilitate production and trade of goods and services.

Many of the World Bank's development projects destroyed the natural ecosystem for the sake of short-term cash flow *and* decreased the sustainable output or value of the land in the longer term. The lending policies of the World Bank have come under increasing criticism from environmentalists in recent years.[54] According to a recent Environmental Defense Fund study, continued application of "orthodox stabilization and adjustment policies . . . carries the potential to further exacerbate poverty and environmental degradation in those member countries that can least afford it."[55] As a result, a gradual "greening" of World Bank rhetoric and policy appears to be under way.[56] Similarly, the IMF's structural adjustment programs have

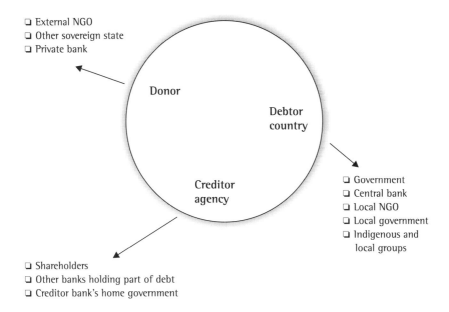

- External NGO
- Other sovereign state
- Private bank

Donor

Debtor country

Creditor agency

- Government
- Central bank
- Local NGO
- Local government
- Indigenous and local groups

- Shareholders
- Other banks holding part of debt
- Creditor bank's home government

Figure 1 Participants in Debt-for-Nature Swaps

been criticized for unnecessarily aggravating environmental problems in the name of development.[57]

LOVEJOY'S SOLUTION

As Lovejoy thought about this tangled mess of impoverished nations in debt, creditors seeking recompense to stave off more serious losses, and the degradation of the planet's environment, he had an idea. Why not swap debt for nature preservation? Nongovernmental conservation organizations could redeem part of a Third World country's debt in return for that country using funds to protect the rainforest or for other conservation work.[58] Several such arrangements have since been successfully negotiated (see Table 2, pages 284–287). The major parties to the negotiations typically represent an unusually wide range of public and private interests from both the international and domestic domains (see Figure 1). They include, at a minimum, a sovereign state (the debtor country), a donor organization headquartered in another country,[59] and a private creditor agency.

Table 2

Debt–for–Nature Swaps as of March 1991

Date	Participants*			Financial Transactions (US$)			Project Funded
	Debtor Country	Donor Organization	Creditor Agency	Cost	Face Value of Debt	Conservation Benefits Generated	
8/87	Bolivia	Conservation International	Citicorp	100,000	650,000	250,000	Beni Biosphere Reserve
12/87	Ecuador	World Wildlife Fund, Nature Conservancy, Missouri Botanical Gardens	Citibank and Bankers Trust	354,000	1,000,000	1,000,000	Fundacion Natura Galapagos Islands
2/88	Costa Rica	Fundacion de Parque Nationales, World Wildlife Fund, Nature Conservancy, Conservation International	Citibank and Swiss Bank	918,000	5,400,000	4,050,000	Convocado and Guanacaste National Parks
7/88	Costa Rica	Holland	—	5,000,000	88,000,000	9,900,000	Conservation projects
1/89	Costa Rica	Nature Conservancy	—	784,000	5,600,000	1,680,000	Guanacaste and Braúlio National Parks
1/89	Philippines	World Wildlife Fund	Bankers Trust	200,000	390,000	390,000	St. Paul Subterranean River & El Nido Nat'l Parks, training, and Philippine Dept. of Environmental Natural Resources

Table 2 (continued)
Debt–for–Nature Swaps as of March 1991

Date	Participants*			Financial Transactions (US$)			Project Funded
	Debtor Country	Donor Organization	Creditor Agency	Cost	Face Value of Debt	Conservation Benefits Generated	
4/89	Costa Rica	Sweden	Salomon Bros.	3,500,000	4,500,000	17,100,000	Guanacaste National Park
4/89	Ecuador	World Wildlife Fund, Nature Conservancy, Missouri Botanical Gardens	Bankers Trust and American Express	1,068,750	9,000,000	–	Galapagos Island National Park System Conservation Data Center
8/89	Madagascar	World Wildlife Fund	Bankers Trust and National Westminster Bank	950,000	2,111,112	2,111,112	National parks management
8/89	Zambia	World Wildlife Fund	–	454,000	2,270,000	2,270,000	Kafue Flats and Bangweulu Basin wetlands and animal habitat protection
1/90	Poland	World Wildlife Fund	–	11,500	50,000	50,000	National Foundation for Environmental Protection
3/90	Dominican Republic	Nature Conservancy, Puerto Rican Conservation Trust	MG–First Boston	116,400	582,000	582,000	Protection of several national parks
4/90	Costa Rica	Sweden, World Wildlife Fund, Nature Conservancy	–	1,953,474	10,753,631	9,602,904	National parks protection

Table 2 (continued)
Debt–for–Nature Swaps as of March 1991

	Participants*			Financial Transactions (US$)			
Date	Debtor Country	Donor Organization	Creditor Agency	Cost	Face Value of Debt	Conservation Benefits Generated	Project Funded
8/90	Philippines	World Wildlife Fund	—	438,750	900,000	900,000	Continued support for conservation projects
8/90	Madagascar	World Wildlife Fund, Conservation International	Bankers Trust, National Westminister Bank, IBM, Honeywell, Codamm (French Electric Company)**	445,891	919,363	919,363	Ecosystem management programs for four protected areas, training and education programs, sustainable-development projects, trust fund creation
2/91	Costa Rica	Rainforest Alliance, Monteverde Conservation League, Nature Conservancy	—	360,000	600,000	540,000	Continued support for conservation projects in place
2/91	Mexico	Conservation International	—	—	4,000,000	2,600,000	Data-gathering projects; conservation education programs; funding for SEDUE, Mexico's governmental environmental agency
3/91	Madagascar	World Wildlife Fund, Conservation International	Bankers Trust, Nat'l Westminister Bank, IBM, Honeywell, Codamm (French Electric Company)**	—	140,000	140,000	Continued support for conservation projects in place

Table 2 (continued)

Debt–for–Nature Swaps as of March 1991

	Participants[*]			Financial Transactions (US$)			
Date	Debtor Country	Donor Organization	Creditor Agency	Cost	Face Value of Debt	Conservation Benefits Generated	Project Funded
9/91	Ghana	Midwest Universities Consortium for International Activities, Smithsonian Institution, Conservation International, US Committee of the International Council on Monuments and Sites, Debt for Development Coalition	—	5,600,000	9,600,000	4,000,000	Create Kakum Natural Park and restore ancient buildings

[*]Debt–for–nature swaps typically involve three primary players: a creditor agency, a donor, and a debtor country. Multiple parties may influence the bargaining positions and preferences of each player. Sometimes subplayers also join in the negotiations process.

[**]This represents a variation on debt–for–nature swaps; trade credits rather than commercial bank credits are swapped for nature.

The ultimate success of the swap depends on local interests that may or may not be a party to the negotiations but are often responsible for or significantly affected by the implementation of the swap—namely, the local populace, which usually includes the landless poor and indigenous peoples.

HOW DEBT-FOR-NATURE SWAPS WORK
Bolivia: The First Example
In 1987, Conservation International (CI), an NGO headquartered in the United States, arranged to trade Bolivian debt for the expansion and long-term management of the Beni Biosphere Reserve,[60] a protected zone created in 1982 and managed by Bolivia's National Academy of Sciences. The two fundamental prerequisites to the swap—a debt problem and a nature problem—were present. Naturalists considered the increased protection of the reserve to be important because the area supports more than a dozen species of endangered plants and animals, a rich and diverse ecosystem, and the nomadic Chimane Indians.[61] Bolivian debt had grown increasingly burdensome: By 1988, principal and interest payments exceeded 5 percent of the country's gross national product.[62]

Other key ingredients also fell into place. The Bolivian government was interested in debt reduction and willing to negotiate an arrangement that involved conserving the land surrounding the Beni Reserve. The private banks that held the Bolivian debt were willing to sell it at less than face value.[63] For each bank, the decision hinged on the need to satisfy stockholders and preserve the bank's credit rating. In some cases, this meant trying to keep losses to a minimum. In other cases, it was preferable to take a larger loss in order to get the bad loans entirely off the books and eliminate any future risk of repeated default. For some banks, the desire to preserve a positive relationship with a particular debtor nation also affected the decision. Conservation International was able to raise the money to purchase the discounted debt, and the NGO was convinced that the swap was a good way to invest the money. In addition, the Bolivian National Academy of Sciences was available for the long-term oversight of the purchased conservation program.

Using funds donated by the Frank Weeden Foundation, Conservation International bought $650,000 of Bolivia's debt in the secondary financial market for the heavily discounted price of $100,000. Conservation

International then cancelled the debt in exchange for a commitment from the Bolivian government to:

- ❏ set aside 3.7 million acres of additional government lands surrounding the existing 135,000-acre Beni Biosphere Reserve as a buffer zone and allow only ecologically sensitive land use;
- ❏ provide maximum legal protection for both the reserve and the buffer zone; and
- ❏ establish a $250,000 endowment to fund the long-term management of the protected areas.[64]

It is important to note that the terms of the swap did not involve a change in land ownership. The reserve is still owned by Bolivia. Land use has, however, been limited by the swap to "carefully managed logging and farming" and other "environmentally sustainable development uses."[65] To help ensure that these restrictions are carried out, an independent commission was formed to assist the National Academy of Sciences.

Steps Involved

The precise terms of each debt-for-nature swap are unique, but all such transactions involve three basic steps: negotiate general terms, carry out the transaction, and implement the agreement.

Negotiate General Terms   Unlike many other types of negotiations, "debt-for-nature exchanges cannot be foisted upon unwilling participants."[66] Each party must consider the swap to be in its own best interest. Because a satisfactory outcome[67] depends on the swap meeting the needs of all affected parties, this first step generally requires iterative negotiations and the creative design of a package that balances a broad array of factors. The parties to the swap must determine the terms of the initial financial transaction, define the environmental benefit that the swap will buy, and decide how and by whom the agreement will be carried out in the long term.

The variables involved in the initial financial equation include:

- ❏ the price of the debt to the conservation organization (Must it be bought at or near face value or can it be purchased at a substantial discount?),

- ❏ the price debtor nations are willing to pay for the debt (Will they agree to exchange each dollar's worth of debt for the equivalent of one dollar of their own currency?), and

- ❏ the rate of exchange between the dollar—or other currency originally borrowed—and the currency of the debtor nation.

Defining the environmental benefit also involves considering a variety of options, including:

- ❏ the form of promised government programs (Will parkland be set aside immediately? Will long-term environmental management programs be implemented, such as training park personnel, managing existing parks, policing land-use restrictions, and environmental education? Will research and data collection about causes and consequences of deforestation be supported?),

- ❏ a cash distribution (Will it be distributed all at once to pay for a project or be meted out over time by setting up a local currency bond whose periodic interest payments support environmental activities?); or

- ❏ some combination of the two.

Carry Out the Transaction The next procedural steps are relatively straightforward but technically complex. First, the debt instrument must be purchased. Only debt that is available for purchase directly from a creditor bank or on the secondary market has been allowed for use in swaps in the past.[68] Moreover, the loan agreement associated with the debt must allow the swap. In many cases, foreign debt is syndicated, that is, one bank may hold the initial debt but sells portions of it to other banks. Therefore, all participants to the debt being purchased must approve its use in a swap agreement. Likewise, restructured loan agreements must allow swaps. Most rescheduling agreements have covenants that "essentially ensure that none of the major creditors dispose of the debt without approval from the others."[69] The actual purchase is generally made by the conservation organization (or its agent), whereupon title to the debt is transferred to the conservation organization.[70]

The debt instrument is then traded to the debtor nation in return for local currency, local currency bonds, or noncash consideration (such as a promise to carry out an environmentally related program). The amount of local currency received depends on whether the debt is traded at face value and on the exchange rate offered by the debtor nation's central bank. If exchanged for local currency bonds, then the debtor government must issue the bonds with the agreed-upon maturity date and interest rates. In cash transactions, the beneficiary is often a local governmental or NGO. The recipient organization must therefore set up a financial management system that meets the requirements of the other swap participants.[71]

These transactions are easier if the debtor nation has encouraged swaps and created a formal mechanism by which such swaps can be carried out. For example, in 1987 both Ecuador and Costa Rica committed to exchanging a specified amount of debt and set up a mechanism to convert the donated debt into conservation programs.

Implement the Agreement   The final step involves carrying out the actual program or purchase. Most of the swaps negotiated thus far have included at least one component that requires the long-term, continuing management of an environmental program. In some cases, the program must be initiated, while in other cases the swap provides increased financial support for an existing program.

The long-term implementation of the agreement is difficult to ensure because no strings can be attached to the agreement that will raise sovereignty concerns in the debtor nation. In response to this dilemma, most groups involved in the swaps agree it is best to include a local (debtor country) NGO in the agreement. By providing this base of domestic political support for a project, the donors feel it is less likely that the project will be scrapped (or altered enough to defeat the purpose) later.

ALTERNATIVES TO DEBT-FOR-NATURE SWAPS

Debt-for-nature swaps are one way in which NGOs, MNCs and business, IGOs and states can all play a part in environmental protection. There are other variations on this theme of public–private participation in environmental conservation or protection, however.

Conservation Exit Bonds and Green Bonds

To date, most of the intermediaries that have facilitated debt-for-nature swaps have been external nongovernmental organizations. Now other sovereign states and even multilateral institutions have begun to express interest in playing this role. This has triggered a second generation of swaps in the form of credit enhancements. *Conservation exit bonds* for existing debt are offered by multilateral development banks to commercial banks that seek to exit from a debt-restructuring process for a given country. If the commercial bank agrees to a debt swap, then it may get credit in the form of a guaranty or collateral that improves the value of the bank's other debt in proportion to the amount donated. Alternatively, *green bonds* offer credit enhancements to banks that agree to incur new debt as bonds designated for financing conservation.[72]

Debt-for-Equity Variations

A popular commercial policy involves debt-for-equity exchanges in which a portion of the developing country's debt is purchased in exchange for an equity interest in a local firm or other local asset. The debtor country is relieved of the obligation to repay the debt in hard currency, but it loses title to a valuable local asset.[73] A variation on this theme has been employed in Costa Rica with some success. Private parties were able to establish bonds in their names that were then sold on the Costa Rican bond market. The proceeds were used to finance development projects, including the management of a natural forest for sustainable production of mahogany.[74] Although, in this case, economic development was the primary criterion used for determining how to distribute the funds, it would be just as easy to add or substitute a requirement that these bonds be used to finance environmental protection projects.

Trade Debt-for-Nature Swaps

Initiated with a Conservation International–Madagascar swap arrangement, *trade debt–for-nature swaps* involve the purchase of trade debt that is turned into local currency bonds equal to the note's original value. Madagascar's trade paper was more heavily discounted than commercial debt in the secondary market, so CI was able to generate more money for conservation and preservation projects. IBM, Honeywell, and Codamm (a French electric company) were willing to sell debt to CI. The projects supported by the revenue include forest management, scientific study, conservation, and environmental education.[75]

National Conservation Trusts

An offshore hard-currency trust fund is another initiative that is gaining popularity. The Global Environmental Facility (GEF), a consortium of the World Bank and the United Nations Development and Environment Programs, has been created to funnel funds into *national conservation trusts* that can provide a permanent source of hard currency interest for conservation projects. Interest earnings from trust investments will be disbursed as needed. It is hoped that holding the trust offshore and in hard currency will be a hedge against volatile exchange-rate fluctuations and local currency devaluations. National conservation trusts should be especially appropriate for those countries that have greatly devalued currencies, not enough debt, or a macroeconomic policy that would not facilitate debt-for-nature swaps. Like debt-for-nature swaps, offshore trusts are designed to include local government and nongovernment groups.[76] Still, GEF in particular has been criticized by LDCs for underrepresenting them in the decision-making process.

Blocked Funds Donation

Foreign-exchange restrictions often restrict the ability of corporations to exchange local currency earnings for equivalent hard currency. These "unexpatriatable" assets are known as *blocked funds* and constitute an opportunity for conservation similar to that available through debt-for-nature swaps because they are sold at a discount or donated outright. A blocked funds donation is beneficial to (1) the original holder of the blocked funds because the holder can receive significant tax benefits, (2) nongovernmental environmental groups because they can purchase the funds and apply them to needed conservation projects, and (3) local governments because they keep capital in the country and the funds are applied to critical projects that would otherwise most likely be ignored.[77]

Creative Repayment Schedules

In a few, limited cases, debtors may repay a portion of their loans in national currency. This part of the payment is deposited in a special fund to be used for environmental protection projects. This approach can be employed for both private and public as well as bilateral and multilateral loans.

New Incentives Embodied in Multilateral Development Bank Conditionality

At the risk of intensifying LDC resentment toward multilateral development bank (MDB) conditionality requirements, a change in their incentive structure might prove useful.[78] Rather than encouraging short-term exploitation of natural resources with the aim of increasing export revenues, it is possible to require that natural resources be developed in an environmentally safe way. Conditionality is a concept government leaders do not like, but its debt restructuring could lead to positive economic and environmental returns.

SOVEREIGNTY AND ENVIRONMENTAL PROBLEMS

Environmental problems frequently go beyond sovereignty. The previous examples of innovative public–private tools for debt reduction and environmental conservation are examples of solutions that also go beyond sovereign states. In the first generation of environmental protection, efforts generally focused on modifying the laws and enforcement regimes of states. If states did a better job of stopping and prosecuting polluters, then environmental problems would abate. In the years following *Silent Spring*, environmental laws and enforcement agencies multiplied within states.

The second generation of environmental policy focused on intergovernmental activity. If more and stronger treaties enforced by effective multilateral regimes could be formed, then environmental problems would be better managed globally. In the past two decades, multilateral efforts at managing environmental problems have multiplied, as evidenced by the example of the Kyoto Protocol on global climate change. Both approaches to managing environmental problems focus on states, increasing the capacity of states to unilaterally or multilaterally address environmental problems. However, the approaches discussed here are a third way: manage environmental problems by engaging the private sector and civil society actors. If states are squeezed economically between the twin problems of poverty and debt, then they may not have either the resources or the incentives to address environmental problems. These methods engage the resources and incentive structures of private actors in addressing pressing public problems.

While leveraging the help of the private sector to manage environmental problems may sound attractive, some states bristle at the thought of relinquishing some control over land-use policy or development policy to private actors, especially "foreign" NGOs, IGOs, MNCs, or investors. In former colonial states, sovereignty was hard and only recently won. NGOs, however, consider debt-for-nature swaps and other innovative green investment tools to be enlightened and innovative win–win solutions. An NGO wins more bang for the buck in environmental protection. It gains a particular policy change or land-use protection while reducing the debt-repayment pressure that continues to whittle away environmental protection. The creditor—whether MNC or bank, IGO or developed state—receives repayment of some of the debt or a lessening of the loss. And the indebted country gets some relief from the pressure of debt repayment and some improvement in environmental protection.

However, what NGOs see as win–win solutions, LDCs may view as environmental imperialism. Colonialism used to be carried out by foreign, conquering armies. This form of neocolonialism, it is argued, is carried out by foreign bankers and environmentalists.

Regardless of one's assessment of debt-for-nature swaps, they do reveal important changes in sovereignty. Richard Rosecrance argues that a new form of sovereignty is emerging: the virtual state, in which territory is becoming passé. Now that the economy has changed, "land becomes less valuable than technology, knowledge, and direct investment." Debt-for-nature swaps would seem to substantiate Rosecrance's theory. When faced with a direct choice between control over potentially lucrative, undeveloped, resource-rich land, or economic growth based on attractiveness to foreign direct investment, states choose modern economies over land autonomy. The lesson of green investment tools is not that states are obsolete, but that they are integral players in reaching these agreements. However, states are not entirely free or autonomous actors in the process. They face tremendous pressure from their debts and from powerful nonstate actors (MNCs, the IMF, the World Bank, and even NGOs). They are willing to do almost anything to continue the flow of foreign direct investment and to right their swamped financial boats, even give up some of the most traditional base of sovereignty, control over territory and certain land-use policies. Especially when state-based environmental approaches are stalemated or stymied (as in the global climate change regime), efforts to manage global environmental problems will increasingly involve creative alliances among nonstate actors.

ENDNOTES

1. Rachel Carson, *Silent Spring* (Boston: Houghton Mifflin, 1962).
2. E. O. Wilson, "The Current State of Biological Diversity," in E. O. Wilson and Frances M. Peter (Eds.), *Biodiversity* (Washington, DC: National Academy Press, 1988), 3–20.
3. Garrett Hardin, "The Tragedy of the Commons," *Science* (Dec. 13, 1968): 1243–1248.
4. See Chapter 1.
5. William Easterly, *The Elusive Quest for Growth: Economists' Adventures and Misadventures in the Tropics* (Cambridge: MIT Press, 2001).
6. Estimates vary widely but are on the order of 16 million to 20 million hectares per year, or an area nearly the size of Washington state; see R. Monastersky, "The Fall of the Forest," *Science News* 138 (1990): 40–41. This roughly equates to 75–100 acres per minute.
7. Norman Myers, "Making the World Work for People," *International Wildlife* (Nov./Dec. 1989): 30.
8. Monastersky, "The Fall of the Forest," 40.
9. A. B. Durning, "Ending Poverty," in Worldwatch Institute, *State of the World* (New York: W.W. Norton, 1990), 146.
10. Barbara Gray, *Collaborating: Finding Common Ground for Multiparty Problems* (San Francisco: Jossey-Bass, 1989), 253.
11. United Nations Framework Convention on Climate Change, *Information Kit: The Kyoto Protocol;* available at <www.unfccc.int/text/resource/iuckit/index.html>.
12. William F. Laurance, Patricia Delamôica, Susan G. Laurance, Heraldo L. Vasconcelos, and Thomas E. Lovejoy, "Rainforest Fragmentation Kills Big Trees," *Nature* (April 20, 2000): 836.
13. Thomas E. Lovejoy, "Biodiversity: What Is It?" in Marjorie L. Reaka-Kudla, Don E. Wilson, and Edward O. Wilson (Eds.), *Biodiversity II: Understanding and Protecting Our Biological Resources* (Washington, DC: National Academy Press, 1996).
14. Wilson, "The Current State of Biological Diversity," 8; see also Ariel E. Lugo, "Estimating Reductions in the Diversity of Tropical Forest Species," in Wilson and Peter (Eds.), *Biodiversity,* 60.
15. Scientists have confirmed the existence of approximately 1.4 million species and estimate this represents only one-tenth or fewer of the total species on earth (e.g., Wilson, "The Current State of Biological Diversity," 8).

16. Thomas E. Lovejoy, "For Richer or Poorer: Impoverishment or Biodiversity?" Presentation to the founding workshop of the US Organization for Biodiversity, San Diego Supercomputer Center, April 12, 1996; available at <www.sdsc.edu/SDSCwire/v2.8/lovejoy-full.html>.

17. J. D. Nations, "Deep Ecology Meets the Developing World," in Wilson and Peter (Eds.), *Biodiversity,* 81.

18. Lovejoy, "Biodiversity: What Is It?" 8–9.

19. N. R. Farnsworth, "Screening Plants for New Medicines," in Wilson and Peter (Eds.), *Biodiversity,* 83–97.

20. Joel Makower, Nancy Tienvieri, and Cathryn Poff (Eds.), *The Nature Catalog* (New York: Vintage Press, 1991): 127.

21. Lovejoy, "Biodiversity: What Is It?" 9.

22. Climate patterns are partly determined by factors such as the earth's reflectivity and the amount of infrared radiation emitted by the earth. The latter is, in turn, related to the relative amounts of atmospheric gases and particles, including carbon dioxide and water. Each factor is affected when large tracts of forests are cut.

23. Lovejoy, "Biodiversity: What Is It?" 12.

24. Richard A. Houghton, "The Global Effects of Tropical Deforestation," *Environmental Science and Technology,* 24(4): 422.

25. Lovejoy, "Biodiversity: What Is It?" 10; see also Carlos A. Nobre, Piers J. Sellers, and Jagadish Shukla, "Amazonian Deforestation and Regional Climate Change," *Journal Climate,* 4(10): 957–988.

26. See, e.g., Hank Whittemore, "I Fight for Our Future," *Parade* (April 12, 1992): 4–7.

27. Slash-and-burn agriculture developed precisely for this reason. Forests are cut and the resulting slash is burned on site, which converts the nutrients and minerals in the vegetation into a natural fertilizer. Once these nutrients are gone, the soil is no longer productive, and new forest must be cut and the cycle repeated. Further, after the vegetation is removed, many tropical forest soils undergo largely irreversible chemical changes that prevent the regrowth of the native forest species.

28. Makower et al. (Eds.), *The Nature Catalog,* 128.

29. Conservation International, "Ecotourism"; available at <www.conservation.org/xp/CIWEB/programs/ecotourism/ecotourism.xml>.

30. "Ecotourism: Preserving Nature, or Helping Destroy It?" *Greenwire* (1991), no. 25.

31. Whittemore, "I Fight for Our Future."

32. Konrad von Moltke and Paul J. DeLong, "Negotiating in the Global Arena: Debt for Nature Swaps," *Resolve,* 22 (1990): 4.

33. Easterly, *The Elusive Quest for Growth.*

34. Martin Smith and Lowell Bergman, "Saudi Time Bomb," *Frontline* (PBS), Nov. 15, 2001; transcript available at <www.pbs.org/wgbh/pages/frontline/shows/saudi/etc/script.html>.

35. A hard currency is one that is accepted for purchasing goods and services in the global marketplace. US dollars, German deutsche marks, and Japanese yen are examples of currencies that are accepted by virtually all states or firms, whereas currencies such as Brazilian reals and Mexican pesos are harder to use.

36. World Bank Group, *2001 World Development Indicators* (Washington, DC: World Bank, 2001), 212 (Table 4.5); available at <www.worldbank.org/data/databytopic/databytopic.html>.

37. Ibid., 252 (Table 4.15).
38. World Bank, *Poverty: World Development Report 1990* (New York: Oxford University Press, 1990), 15.
39. Sarah Bartlett, "U.S. Efforts to Aid Debtor Nations Bring 'Profound Disappointment,'" *The New York Times,* July 24, 1989; Kristin Dawkins, "Debt-for-Nature Swaps," in Lawrence E. Susskind, Esther Siskind, and J. William Breslin (Eds.), *Nine Case Studies in International Environmental Negotiation* (The MIT–Harvard Public Disputes Program) (Cambridge, MA: PON Books, 1990), 2; World Bank Group, *2001 World Development Indicators,* 256 (Table 4.16).
40. Betsy Cody, "Debt-for-Nature Swaps in Developing Countries: An Overview of Recent Conservation Efforts," Congressional Research Service (CRS) report for Congress 88-647 ENR (Washington, DC: CRS, Sept. 26, 1988), 4; World Bank, *Annual Report 1990* (Washington, DC: Author, 1991), 132.
41. World Bank, *Poverty,* 10.
42. Also referred to as *externalities,* an external cost is generated by the producer (e.g., a mining or timber company) but borne by a different group or by society as a whole. Relevant examples include the siltation and flooding of rivers caused by logging activities upstream.
43. See, for example, Jeffrey McNeely, *Economics and Biological Diversity: Developing and Using Economic Incentives to Conserve Biological Resources* (Gland, Switzerland: International Union for Conservation of Nature and Natural Resources, 1988), 9–14.
44. See, for example, the description of rainforest logging promoted in Costa Rica for the benefit of the cattle-grazing industry in Durning, "Ending Poverty," 146.
45. Small farmers seldom have the means of shifting production to more profitable "cash" crops and are forced to sell their land.
46. For example, cattle ranching is "estimated to require not more than 6 work days per year per hectare"; see "The IMF and the Environment: A Dismal Record of Neglect; the Example of Costa Rica," mimeo from the Environmental Defense Fund (no date), 7.
47. There is evidence, however, that more value is now being placed on both sustainable resource use and human rights in the development debate; see, for example, Daniel B. Magraw, "International Pollution, Economic Development, and Human Rights," in Daniel B. Magraw (Ed.), *International Law and Pollution* (Philadelphia: University of Pennsylvania Press, 1991), 30–60.
48. E. B. Barbier, *Sustainable Agriculture and the Resource Poor: Policy Issues and Options* (London: International Institute for Environment and Development, 1988), 4–5.
49. Durning, "Ending Poverty," 44.
50. See, for example, S. G. Bunker, "The Impact of Deforestation on Peasant Communities in the Medio Amazonas of Brazil," in V. H. Stuliv, N. Altshuler, and M. D. Zamora (Eds.), *Where Have All the Flowers Gone? Deforestation in the Third World* (Williamsburg, VA: Department of Anthropology, College of William and Mary, 1981), 52; Gopal B. Thapa and Karl E. Weber, "Soil Erosion in Developing Countries: A Politicoeconomic Explanation," *Environmental Management,* 15(4): 467.
51. Quoted in George de Lama, "Brazil Resists Campaign to Save Its Rain Forests," *Chicago Tribune,* March 12, 1989, Sec. 1, p. 29.
52. See Stein Hansen, "Debt for Nature Swaps: Overview and Discussion of Key Issues," *Ecological Economics,* 1 (1989): 77–95.

53. Von Moltke and DeLong, "Negotiating in the Global Arena," 4; see also Cody, "Debt-for-Nature Swaps in Developing Countries," 6.

54. See, for example, P. Aufderheide and B. Rich, "Environmental Reform and the Multilateral Banks," *World Policy Journal* (Spring 1988): 301–321; Korinna Horta and Cathy Fogel, "No Agenda for Action" (press release from the Environmental Defense Fund and the Sierra Club, Oct. 15, 1991).

55. "The IMF and the Environment," 2.

56. See, for example, "Special Operational Emphasis: Environment," in World Bank, *Annual Report 1990*, 63–68.

57. See "The IMF and the Environment," 6.

58. The idea—first proposed in 1984 and consummated in 1987—won Lovejoy the Third World Social Invention Award in 1988. See "Social Innovation Awards up to 2000 (from 1986)" at <http://globalideasbank.org/Awards.HTML>.

59. Typically, debt-for-nature donor organizations have been nongovernmental conservation groups, but as the popularity of these agreements increases, so does the potential for other external donors to participate. For example, both the Dutch and Swedish governments have participated in debt-for-nature swaps in Costa Rica, and the United States has indicated its interest in pursuing debt-for-nature swaps through its Enterprises of the Americas initiative. See Conservation International, *The Debt-for-Nature Exchange: A Tool for International Conservation* (Washington, DC: Author, Sept. 1989), 16; "Analysis: Debt for Nature or Children? Or Both?" *Greenwire* (1991), no. 18.

60. Biosphere reserves are internationally recognized areas that receive some measure of environmental protection. The Beni Reserve has been identified by the United Nations Educational, Scientific, and Cultural Organization (UNESCO) as a part of its system of international biosphere reserves. See Alan Patterson, "Debt-for-Nature Swaps and the Need for Alternatives," *Environment,* 32(10): 5–13, 31–32.

61. Cody, "Debt-for-Nature Swaps in Developing Countries," 30.

62. World Bank, *Poverty,* 222.

63. Many banks that held large portfolios of questionable Third World loans were faced with risking default or attempting to obtain partial repayment. Default meant writing off the loans entirely and absorbing the financial loss. Partial repayment could be secured by selling the loans at a discount on the secondary market (where commercial banks buy and sell loan obligations as if they were commodities). The amount of the discount that the bank will accept varies from case to case. An increasing number of loans have been sold on the secondary market in recent years; in 1988, $55 billion to $60 billion of loans were traded, which represents an order-of-magnitude increase over the previous three years (see Conservation International, *The Debt-for-Nature Exchange,* 18). Debt payments could also be rescheduled whereby banks forgive some of the debt and create a new agreement that governs the interest payments on the remaining debt.

64. The US Agency for International Development donated $150,000 of the $250,000 endowment (see Conservation International, *The Debt-for-Nature Exchange,* 13).

65. Cody, "Debt-for-Nature Swaps in Developing Countries," 30.

66. See Conservation International, *The Debt-for-Nature Exchange,* 19.

67. *Outcome* here includes both the negotiated agreement at the end of the bargaining process and the implementation of the agreement over the long haul.

68. Thus far, debt held by the IMF and the World Bank has not been available for swaps. Hence, most swaps have involved Latin American countries because substantial por-

tions of their debt is held by commercial financial institutions. Few swaps have involved African nations because most of their debt is owed to governmental organizations, whose charter documents have been interpreted to disallow such "creative financing."

69. Von Moltke and DeLong, "Negotiating in the Global Arena," 3.
70. In some instances, the government of the creditor country has taken title to the debt instrument and then transferred it to the conservation organization. It is also possible to transfer title directly to the participating LDC's NGOs.
71. For example, a US-affiliated donor conservation group must satisfy the tax requirement that the funds be used for environmental projects.
72. Dawkins, "Debt-for-Nature Swaps," 6.
73. Cody, "Debt-for-Nature Swaps in Developing Countries," 1–2.
74. See Patterson, "Debt-for-Nature Swaps and the Need for Alternatives," 12.
75. Nancy Dunne, "Madagascar to Swap Trade Debt for Nature," *Financial Times,* Aug. 31, 1990, p. 5.
76. Steven Rubin, *Innovative Tools for Conservation Finance* (Washington, DC: Conservation International, 1992).
77. Ibid.
78. Patterson, "Debt-for-Nature Swaps and the Need for Alternatives," 31.

CHAPTER TWELVE

Leaving Home

The Flow of Refugees

Hal Kane*

The "Chunnel," the Eurotunnel under the English Channel between Britain and France, was built to foster commerce and high-speed transportation between Britain and Europe. Officials did not anticipate it would be used by refugees on foot. On one night alone, 550 refugees, most of them Afghanis, were apprehended in a cloud of tear gas by police in the Channel tunnel. The refugees were fleeing crowded Red Cross camps in France, believing liberal asylum laws in Britain would give them a chance at a better life. More than 18,500 refugees were apprehended in the Eurotunnel in the first six months of 2001 alone.[1]

Refugees and migrants move in response to the pressures of world politics, the ebbs and flows of livelihoods lost and gained, the adequacy or poverty of resources at hand, and the wars and conflicts that result. Their travels tell the story of a changing world.

For many centuries, the story they told was of a world of inequality, a world where a few people controlled many others. Migrations from 1500

*Updated by Emily Levasseur

until the early nineteenth century, for example, were mostly of slaves. Some 14 million people were transported against their will, mainly to South America, the Caribbean, and the Arabian peninsula (and a much smaller number to North America). Voluntary movements of people were smaller, possibly only 2 to 3 million people during this entire time, until voluntary migration began to rise quickly in the beginning of the last century. Thus, for centuries the causes of migration centered on domination and economic ownership.[2]

During the Middle Ages, migration was rare. That lack of movement represents a history of economic isolation and political feudalism. Peasant laborers worked near to where they were born, and feudal systems from Europe through the Middle East, Asia, and parts of Africa kept people inside their lord's domain. Even earlier, as tribes swept down into Central Asia and Europe from the north and east, migration told an altogether different story. It was one of conquest by people who carried their civilizations along with them and often battled or mixed with people they met on the way. At that time, migration was less of individuals than of whole communities.[3]

Those migrations formed history, creating an ethnic mix in Asia, Central Europe, and Africa; populating the Americas with foreigners; reducing overcrowding in Europe; and subjecting people to the tragedy of slavery. But nothing on that historical map prepares us for the sheer mass of people captured in the current picture of migration, when as many people can move in one year as previously moved in most centuries. And nothing in that history hints at the remarkable increase in the diversity of reasons why people now leave their homes and countries.

This is no aberration or temporary trend. Migration has become an ordinary activity. It occurs every day and in almost every part of the world. It has come to reflect the events of our time—the breakup of the Soviet Union, the desperation in Africa, war, and widening income disparities around the world. More people became refugees in 2000 alone than left Spain—at their leisure—to colonize the Americas in the nineteenth century, one of the times of heaviest emigration. More people fled Afghanistan following the Soviet invasion of 1979 than left Germany during the last century, yet the Germans became one of the largest ethnic groups in the United States.[4]

Today's massive movements tell of countries where organized crime is replacing aggression by militaries, where internal conflict is replacing war with neighboring countries, where young people have to look for employment abroad, and where population growth and environmental degradation are making other stresses more acute. Many of these trends are accelerating. They will add to the pressures that make people leave.

Public debate has yet to address the broad question of why so many people are leaving home. Instead, policy makers continue to focus on the refugee crisis of the moment, immigration quotas, and which individuals to allow into their countries. A fundamental resolution of the issues of refugees and migrants will require us to look deeper and understand why the politics, economics, and security situation in today's world are causing so many people to move. That is the first step toward making people more secure in their homes.

THE DISPLACED

The world's refugee population has risen to 22 million people living outside their countries of origin. In 1990, the figure was less than 15 million. And as recently as the mid-1970s, only some 2.5 million people could claim refugee status—about the same number as in the 1950s and 1960s.[5]

But these numbers reflect the strict standard established by the 1951 UN Convention on Refugees, which remains in force today. The convention defines a *refugee* solely in terms of persecution: any person who "owing to well-founded fear of being persecuted for reasons of race, religion, nationality, membership of a particular social group, or political opinion, is outside the country of his nationality and is unable to return to it." That narrow definition is a remnant of the Cold War. Its purpose was largely to weaken the former Soviet Union and other states within its domain by granting asylum to people who fled from them.[6]

The official definition hardly begins to explain why people decide to leave home today. Many fall outside it because they did not flee persecution. Those who escape famine fail to qualify, even though they had no choice but to leave or perish. Those who fear that they are losing the means to feed their children do not qualify, even though that prospect may be as terrifying as the threat of violence. Those who are pushed out by natural disasters, such as the frequent floods in Bangladesh, are also excluded. Yet all of these people can find themselves in the same conditions as official refugees.

Because these people fail to qualify as official refugees, they are not eligible for asylum in other countries. (In fact, many of them do not wish to enter other countries.) So they generally join the "internally displaced"—people who are forced from their homes but still in their home countries. Not counting people who leave their homes for economic reasons, the internally displaced number at least 25 million worldwide.[7]

Other people who fail to qualify as refugees do manage to cross a border into another country, but they do so illegally. The total number of illegal immigrants, both those who flee out of fear and those who seek better opportunities, is unknown. An estimated 8.7 million illegal immigrants live in the United States alone. As avenues for legal immigration are reduced worldwide, illegal immigration increases, facilitating human smuggling networks.[8]

Internal migration is sometimes a first step to emigration. All these movements have at their bases the failure of societies to meet the basic needs and aspirations of their citizens.

Individuals who move in an attempt to improve their standard of living—migrants, not refugees—number at least three times the number of refugees. A similar group of people—those who move from rural areas to cities within their own countries—is far larger still. In China alone they number between 80 and 100 million, and worldwide they outnumber all other kinds of migrants.[9]

All of these people are barometers of change. Their travels are symptomatic of underlying problems from poverty to human rights abuses. Travel is one solution to the problems that migrants leave behind. From abroad they can send some of their wages home to their families or communities. They have access to education and entrepreneurial opportunities they would otherwise never have had. Migration itself is neither positive nor negative. It is simply a response to the workings of modern economies, transportation systems, and communications as well as to political pressures and individual drives. Sometimes it is clearly bad. The fact that refugees flee in the night from the terror of persecution has no positive aspect. But others move to places they want to live, where they will contribute impressively to economies and cultures. Israel's innovative economy, for example, was built by Jewish immigrants and refugees whose cultures have histories of migration that go back more than three millennia.

Of course, moving is not always the most desirable solution. Most people prefer to be able to improve their lives without the stress and disruption of leaving their homes or breaking up their families. And many countries would like to avoid the so-called brain drain of mass departure.

This human drama is still being written. Few countries have 100 million people. So imagine the novelty of a "floating" country made up of more than 100 million souls and moving from countryside to city and from one town to another—as they are now in China. With that kind of motion, and with the economic change and population growth that have caused it, it is said that in southern China roads are being built so fast and in so many new directions that no maps are accurate. The same may be true of the way we think of demographics. So many people are on the move today, in so many different directions and for so many different reasons, that our old assumptions about demographic trends may be as out of date as the Chinese guidebooks that show rice fields where today there are small cities.[10]

The overwhelming majority of migrants and refugees today come from developing countries, and many of them end up in other parts of the Third World. Some of the countries least able financially to cope with new-comers have been the most accepting of them. Pakistan and Iran, for example, have been temporary homes for millions of Afghan refugees for more than a decade. Many African countries have allowed people fleeing famine and war to enter. Straining under growing numbers of their own people, these countries are hardly in a position to play host to such influxes.[11]

The United States has been a longtime passionate defender of the principle of "first asylum," which says that people may not be returned against their will to a country where they may be endangered. Surprised by the magnitude of today's still-growing flows of refugees, however, the US and other governments are now backing away from this principle. In large part, this change stems from the difference between the people who fled the persecution envisioned in the 1951 UN definition and today's refugees, who more often flee war, social breakdown, and other problems. Western governments believed they had a vested interest in fighting the persecution they saw as a part of communism in the former Soviet Union and China and of dictatorships in Southeast Asia and other places. (Some 96 percent of the refugees admitted to the United States during the Reagan administration were from communist countries.) Western policy makers feel less threatened by the social, economic, and political problems of today, no matter how severe those become.[12] This leaves refugees in a difficult position. While their numbers have increased, the interest of foreign countries in absorbing them has decreased as more and more people have sought refuge from a diverse range of problems.

Once inside some of the wealthier Western countries, newcomers have recently met with growing levels of intolerance. In the United States, immigrants face a war of intolerance waged by people who seem to forget that, in an earlier generation, their relatives were newcomers, too. Citizens' groups spend time and money lobbying to reduce quotas of newcomers, as well as to lower government spending on those already here. In Germany, xenophobia has exploded repeatedly into anti-immigrant violence. Throughout Europe, anti-immigrant sentiment has become a plank in political platforms and even fractured the 2002 French elections.[13]

But discrimination of this sort is generally based on ill-informed fears. Most studies in the United States indicate that immigrants have not taken jobs away from natives; their willingness to work for lower pay has had only a slight effect on wages overall. And immigrants rarely get credit for the positive economic effects their incomes have. According to one comprehensive study, since 1970, immigrants in the United States paid a total of $70 billion in local, state, and federal taxes, generating $25 billion to $30 billion more in public revenue than they used in public services. "That finding is sharply at odds with a number of seriously flawed studies done by groups advocating cuts in legal immigration or by governments seeking 'reimbursement' for their expenditures."[14]

It is true that the picture varies from place to place. In strong local economies, immigrants are most often found to increase economic opportunities. In weak ones, they have a small negative effect on economic opportunities for low-skilled workers. In such cases, local governments often lose revenue. Sometimes, state governments do also, but studies consistently find a net gain for the federal government and a net gain overall.[15]

THE HOUR OF DEPARTURE

When the nuclear reactor at Chernobyl exploded on April 26, 1986, some 5 percent of the core—an estimated 180 tons of radioactive material—

spread as dust over the surrounding landscape. Because of the fallout, some 116,000 residents eventually left the "Zone of Estrangement," as the Ukrainians call it. Their reason for moving was unusually straightforward. One day a power plant blew up and they had to leave. Chernobyl is a vivid symbol of the kinds of pressures that arise without warning.[16]

Natural disasters are another example of these pressures. Many Bangladeshis have left their country, one of the most densely populated on earth and a nation that suffers from frequent floods and natural disasters, in search of safety in India. Their migrations, which have touched off tensions between the two countries, are the result of people living on vulnerable floodplains and in squalid squatter settlements for lack of any place better. Acute land hunger has led people to move to places they know are risky. As the region's population grows, larger numbers of people will live on the lands that are the most susceptible to floods, hurricanes, and other disasters. That means that in the future each natural disaster will send a larger group of people looking for sustenance in other places.[17]

Other migrants are also driven by fairly simple rationales. Governments, for instance, may lure people away from their homes or even force them out. China has practiced a form of "population transfer" as part of its strategy for quashing Tibetan nationalism. Although Chinese officials have described Tibet as a barren, inhospitable land, areas that were populated entirely by Tibetans before 1950 now have majority Chinese populations. To accomplish this shift, the government has doubled the pay and many of the rations of soldiers and settlers who are willing to go there. As a result, 7.5 million Chinese now outnumber 6 million Tibetans in their own homeland.[18]

The Chinese may have read Machiavelli. "Sending immigrants is the most effective way to colonize countries because it is less offensive than to send military expeditions and much less expensive," wrote the sixteenth-century Italian philosopher. The Dalai Lama catalogs similar moves in other parts of China:

> Today, only 2 to 3 million Manchurians are left in Manchuria, where 75 million Chinese have settled. In Eastern Turkestan, which the Chinese now call Xinjiang, the Chinese population has grown from 200,000 in 1949 to 7 million, more than half of the total population of 13 million. In the wake of the Chinese colonization of Inner

Mongolia, Chinese now outnumber the Mongols by 8.5 million to 2.5 million.[19]

Eviction is another strategy that has been used against minorities. Fearing Kurdish dissent, Saddam Hussein chased 1.5 million Kurds out of Iraq and into neighboring Turkey during a three-week period in 1991. For the same reasons, he also forced Shiite Muslims from southern Iraq into Iran.[20] Ethnic cleansing was also used in the wars in the former Yugoslavia, for example, when Milosevic evicted ethnic Albanians from Kosovo. Today, some Israelis debate forced migration of Palestinians from Israeli territory.

Military invasion is a clear-cut cause for flight. In Afghanistan, for instance, the Soviet invasion coupled with internal fighting between rival Afghan forces provoked an outflow of people that peaked at 6 million. Since the US bombing campaign began in Afghanistan in late 2001, Afghan refugees have again far outnumbered those of any other nationality, "with an estimated 3.6 million or 30 percent of the global refugee population."[21]

Disease can also be a major factor in migration. In the former Czechoslovakia, pollution and industrial hazards increased disease and decreased life expectancy in certain areas, causing what the government termed frequent "inner emigrations" as people relocated from polluted to cleaner regions.[22]

Overcrowding has caused people to move as well. From time to time during history, the size of a local community would surpass the land's carrying capacity and the community would outgrow its farmland or water supply. Famous examples include the Mesopotamians and the Mayans. But today overcrowding has become widespread and plays a major role in the world's rural to urban migration. As they are divided among more and more heirs over the generations, for example, farms reach the point where they are no longer viable, and some potential inheritors must look elsewhere for livelihoods.[23]

Other people leave prejudice and head toward opportunity. One million Jews, for instance, left the former Soviet Union after the collapse of its communist government. Approximately half of them have gone to Israel, with the other half now residing in the United States and other Western countries. More people left the former Soviet Union during the early 1990s than during the entire Cold War. The loss of those emigrants, many of whom are highly educated, could trigger additional decline.[24]

In other countries, some of the efforts to remedy poverty have caused people to migrate. Public works projects, for example, have a long history of prying people from their homes. Large dams flood residential areas, roads pass over land that once held buildings, and shantytowns are cleared to make way for power stations. A World Bank study notes that public works projects uproot more than 10 million "oustees" in the developing world every year. In response, people displaced by dam construction are increasingly mobilizing against such public works projects.[25]

Environmental degradation is a common cause of flight. Millions of people have left lands where soils have become too eroded to support even subsistence agriculture. Their plights anticipate what could become the largest catalyst of migration ever: climate change. Ecologist Norman Myers has estimated that as global warming continues, rising sea levels and changes in weather patterns will probably turn 150 million people into refugees by the middle of this century, assuming a sea-level rise of thirty centimeters by 2050. Disruption of agriculture and the flooding of settled areas would be the main causes of flight. Of course, uncertainty is an element in each part of that situation, from questions about climate change to the unknowns of social and economic results.[26]

Some of these pressures will escalate in the future. Overcrowding will increase as nearly 90 million people are added to the world's population every year. Pollution will become even more widespread as economic growth and industrialization arrive in parts of Southeast Asia that have been thus far untouched. Water tables will continue to be drawn down far faster then they can replenish themselves in many countries; soils will continue to erode. And new people will react to these pressures in the future by leaving their homes.[27]

THE MOLOTOV COCKTAIL OF INSECURITY

Most displaced people are not on the move for any single or simple reason. They are forced out by a complex of pressures that are often exacerbated by underlying rapid population growth, ancient ethnic animosities, and resource scarcities. Unfortunately, accounts in the popular press have often reported singular causes for people suddenly leaving countries such as Rwanda, creating an impression that the problems are more short-term or specific in nature.

Countries with stable populations and high levels of education and public health demonstrate a resilience against war and overt persecution, so refugee flows are rare. Many countries ravaged by high infant mortality, low literacy, eroding farmland, and hunger, on the other hand, have recently seen people leaving at record rates. Often these basic deficiencies are not the immediate cause for migration. Instead, they set the stage for the despots, politically motivated bigotry, and extremist politics that eventually force people out.

The situation is analogous to the spread of a disease because the causes of infection are often complex and obscure. Malnourished people, for instance, lose the resilience of their immune systems to fight disease. They rarely die of starvation, but starvation nevertheless underlies the illnesses that kill. Lack of proper sanitation increases the likelihood of a cholera epidemic, and serious mental stress sometimes predisposes people to colds and the flu. In such cases, the disease is only the final element in a series of deeper difficulties.

A frequent ingredient in the cocktail of insecurity is war, and since the middle of the twentieth century, warfare has spread. From fewer than ten wars at any one time during the 1950s, the number of major ongoing conflicts stood at twenty-four in 2001. According to one count, the average number of annual war deaths in the second half of the twentieth century was more than double that of the nineteenth century, and seven times greater than in the hundred years before that. More than 92 percent of all conflicts since World War II have occurred in developing countries.[28]

The most spectacular examples of the complex mix of reasons why people leave their homes are in Africa. The continent has the highest crude birth rate of any region and the highest infant mortality rate. Because of its population growth, its grain production per person is lower today than it was in 1950, despite the fact that grain yields have more than doubled. At 140 kilograms per person, annual grain production is only some 60 percent as much as would be needed, without imports, to keep people healthy. In some places, hunger alone has created refugee flows. But for most of Africa's refugees, hunger and overpopulation are not the sole causes of flight—just two contributing factors.[29]

In Somalia, clan warfare had forced some half-million people out at the end of 1993, with another 700,000 internally displaced. A history of rapid population growth has hit that country hard as its soils became heavily erod-

ed and overgrazed and its forests mostly gone, the deforestation so severe
that even fuelwood is scarce in many areas. One result was migration to
cities, where tensions have flared. Demographic change and environmental
degradation in Somalia have altered the traditional community and family
structures and left people more vulnerable to the tyranny of warlords.[30]

The implosion of Rwanda brought these issues to a new level of world
attention. In the wake of the power struggle between Hutus and Tutsis, a
half million people were massacred, and huge refugee flows ensued (including a million people in one day) as people fled the violence.[31]

War orphans and AIDS orphans both played a role in the Rwandan
tragedy. Like neighboring Uganda, Rwanda was one of the countries hit
first and hardest by AIDS. Years of internal warfare had already taken many
casualties before the current tragedy. The generation of people twenty to
forty years old—today's parents—bore a disproportionate number of the
deaths from both causes. This resulted in a disruption of Rwandan family
structure. Large numbers of boys and young men lost their parents and had
dim prospects for fulfilling lives. They were more readily recruited as soldiers as a result. Tina Malone, of Catholic Relief Services, calls these children "cannon fodder—the stuff from which you can make a militia."[32]

Demographics played a part. Rwanda is the most densely populated
land in Africa. To feed itself, the country steadily expanded the amount of
land in crop production until the mid-1980s, when virtually all arable land
was in use. Today, the average farm size is less than half a hectare; and as land
is subdivided among male heirs, plot size is dwindling. The practice of fal-
lowing has virtually disappeared, manure is in short supply because many
farms are too small to provide fodder for cattle, and yields have been declining. These are threatening trends to people with too little land to feed their
children—the kind of situation that causes fear, jealousy, and hatred.[33]

These tensions were compounded by class friction between Hutus and
Tutsis, the former group having been disenfranchised. From colonial times,
Tutsis have been better educated and richer. Of course, class resentment is
sometimes a motive for slaughter. A significant part of the fighting and
killing that took place was instigated by poorer members of either group
attacking richer members within the same group—social, political, and class
struggle. Tutsi is not exactly the name of an ethnic group. Historically, it
meant "people who own cattle." And Hutu meant "people who farm."
Intermarriage between the groups has been widespread for years. When

311

fighting stemmed from hatred between Hutus and Tutsis, it was largely a result of propaganda spread by disenfranchised factions who had more to gain from war than they had to lose.[34]

Malone suggests that the warfare was motivated in part by fears that family plots were too small and by poverty and past war. "People can easily turn around and blame misfortune on the fact that there's not enough land to go around," she says. "And then someone puts the idea into their heads about Hutus and Tutsis, and it starts." Had it not been for the land scarcity and demographic disruption and pressures, Rwandan society would have been more resilient. Yet those tensions will be even more powerful in the future, with Rwanda's population expected to double in thirty years.[35]

Similar forces are at work elsewhere in the world. In the new central Asian states, political leaders are trying to create national identities within borders that were arbitrarily carved out by Stalin. The republics of Tajikistan, Turkmenistan, Kazakhstan, Kyrgyzstan, and Uzbekistan have so little national cohesion that none of them demanded independence when the Soviet Union collapsed. They became independent by default. The lack of effective political structures has created a power vacuum. Widespread poverty and an abundance of weapons have exacerbated the insecurity that many people feel. In Tajikistan, the result has been fighting between rival clan, regional, and religious groups over political power. Civil war there produced a half-million refugees in 1992 and 1993, though most subsequently returned home.[36]

With so many ethnic divisions in these countries, and with weak national identities and political structures, the involuntary movement of people in the region is likely to continue for some time.[37] The nature of war itself is changing. Warfare is taking place within states rather than between them—but it also produces refugees.[38]

In many parts of the world, people are on the move because borders are fragmenting, provinces are receiving autonomy, and states are collapsing. Yugoslavia disintegrated; Czechoslovakia broke apart peacefully. Many people have left their homes to move into newly created states that they prefer or to flee new states that they find unsafe. In the crowded countries of West Africa, state governments are said to control the borders only during the day. People flow freely across them at night.[39]

THE PUSH OF POVERTY, THE PULL OF WEALTH

The large gap in income between the rich and the poor of the world is at the root of some of the largest movements of all. Tens of millions of workers have moved from poorer countries to richer ones to take advantage of higher wages paid in stronger currencies. For example, some 900,000 Turks have relocated to Germany, Scandinavia, and other parts of Europe. Approximately 20.6 million Mexicans live in the United States. Some 400,000 South Asians and Middle Easterners were living in Kuwait before they fled war in 1991, and some 1.2 million foreign workers were in Saudi Arabia at the same time. Each migration is a response to economic disparities between countries.[40]

Globally, the remittances of migrant workers—the money they earn abroad and then send home to their families and communities—are a vital economic resource. By the end of the 1980s, remittances amounted to more than $65 billion a year according to a World Bank study, second only to crude oil in their value to the world's economy and larger than all official development assistance. Almost half these funds went to developing countries. Although that is vitally important, living abroad also poses problems. It often splits up families and communities; it can be difficult for migrant workers to adjust to their new surroundings; and it denies emigrant countries the labor and skills of those individuals. Yet without remittances, many families and communities would be in desperate circumstances.[41]

The flow of workers from poor countries to wealthier ones is likely to increase in the future. The world's labor force is projected to grow by a billion people during the next two decades. Nine out of ten of these new workers will reside in the Third World, and few of these countries will be able to create sufficient jobs for them. Even the countries that reach their goals for economic growth are unlikely to have enough jobs for their young workers. In Mexico, 1 million new jobs will have to be created every year to match the rate at which young people are entering the workforce; in Egypt, a half-million jobs a year will be needed.[42]

As young people reach working age, many will have little choice but to look for jobs abroad when too few are at home. The countries of North Africa and the Middle East are already major sources of migrant labor, and the youthfulness of their populations virtually ensures that they will be in the future as well. More than 70 percent of Arabs have been born since

1970, for example. An even more dramatic scenario exists in Africa, where almost half the population has been born since 1980. The same is true of Cambodia, Guatemala, Laos, and Nicaragua, among many other countries. These areas are likely to be major sources of migrant workers in the future unless they receive considerable investment in job-creating industries.[43]

The disparity between rich and poor also makes people move for reasons other than the search for jobs. Poverty and the scarcities that go with it make people wish for better places to live. Exhausted supplies of firewood and timber for heating and cooking and building, depleted wells, overcrowded houses and schools, and a lack of electricity all plague the regions where the poorest people live. These scarcities often band together to form a cycle of inadequacy that pushes people from their homelands. Often they move to the nearest city, where they are attracted by the glitter and the hope of new lives.

In 1970, a quarter of the developing world's population lived in cities. By 2025, 57 percent will if UN projections prove correct. In industrial countries, the urban population will have risen from 67 percent to 84 percent in that same time. One daring projection even found that in approximately fifteen years the rural population of the Third World will begin to decrease—despite rapid overall population growth—while urban populations will keep growing. Much of the urban growth will come from children born in cities, but the size of the growth is also a testament to the combined pull of urban areas and the push of poverty on rural inhabitants.[44] These cities then become international jumping-off points for migration by people trying to escape difficult living conditions. It is here that shady "travel agencies" take people's last savings in exchange for clandestine passages across state borders. For Chinese migrants, a highly specialized black market exists to move them to Europe, North America, Australia, and elsewhere.[45]

The world's already large disparities of income are rising and showing up in the growth of cities. Despite economic growth in Latin America before the Argentinean economic crisis, UN economists say that no progress is expected in reducing poverty, which is even likely to increase slightly by their calculations. And this takes place in a region whose countries already have some of the world's widest income disparities. Indeed, it is not entirely a coincidence that Latin America is by far the most urbanized region of the developing world. From 1950 to today, city dwellers have risen from 42 percent of the population there to almost three-quarters of the population.[46]

For some years, China has been an example of some of the most equal distribution of income in the world. That has been changing rapidly as incomes in the southern provinces and special economic zones soar while those in rural areas rise much more slowly. Moreover, the new income has led to inflation as the rich and foreign importers buy increasing numbers of goods, thus bidding up the prices. The poor have suffered from these price increases without benefiting from the additional income in the country. And the Chinese government counts more than 100 million "surplus farm laborers" and estimates that another 15 million are added every year. According to the Chinese Academy of Social Sciences, by 2010 half the population will live in cities, compared with 28 percent in the mid-1990s and only 10 percent in the early 1980s. So even in formerly equitable China, widening disparities of wealth play a role in moving tens of millions of people from rural lands to cities and from one region to another.[47]

Meanwhile, in some regions almost no one is getting richer. The per capita income of most sub-Saharan African nations actually fell during the 1980s. An estimated one-third of all college graduates have left the continent. That loss of talented people, due in large part to poverty and a lack of opportunities in Africa, will make it even more difficult for the continent to grow richer in the future and generate opportunities for its peoples.[48]

One attempt to lessen the push of poverty over the long term has been the structural adjustment programs of the International Monetary Fund and World Bank. However, when Poland had its first experience with this economic shock therapy in 1990, inflation hit 240 percent and 1.3 million people lost their jobs. Tens of thousands abandoned the country. Other Eastern European countries have faced similar shocks. More often, though, people are led to move by cuts in social expenditures for government subsidies on food, education, health care, and home heating fuel as well as changes in trade policies, exchange rates, and family incomes.[49]

Research by the World Resources Institute on the effects of a structural adjustment program in the Philippines found that the program worsened short-term poverty in urban areas by cutting social expenditures. That led to an urban-to-rural migration to upland regions and coastal areas as people sought livelihoods from the fields, fisheries, and forests outside Manila and other cities, where they could no longer survive.[50]

An economic liberalization program in Sri Lanka that began in the late 1970s cut social programs and increased emphasis on export industries, resulting in declining real wages, food insecurity for the lowest income group, deterioration of the social welfare system, and widening income disparities. The authors of one report argue that much of the movement of Sri Lankans to the Persian Gulf was a case of "survival migration" by those in the poorest strata of society, mostly women who went to work as domestic servants.[51]

This poses a dilemma, because the very adjustment programs that underlie unwanted emigration are needed to combat the high inflation and financial chaos that also can cause people to leave. Without adjustment, in some cases emigration will still occur, but for different reasons—because economies are completely out of control. The beginnings of a solution might come if the economists who plan adjustment programs took migration into account during their work by forecasting what movements of people could be expected. They could then at least consider the possibility of altering programs when emigration appears too severe.

DEFUSING THE PRESSURES

The problems that drive people to leave their homelands—war, persecution, famine, and environmental and social disintegration—are often treated as inevitable givens. Many people and governments feel powerless to do anything about them. But if we identify the failures and scarcities that underlie so many of these problems, then perhaps we can find ways to build more stable societies. If we see in persecution, for example, the tensions wrought by inadequate livelihoods, farmland, or water; by lack of education and health care; and by the fear that our children face a bleak future, then we can reduce the mistreatment by addressing those issues. Yet today's refugee policy consists of responding to crises as they happen rather than trying to prevent them.

Once refugees have fled their homes, no amount of money or assistance can fully restore their past lives. The fundamental solutions are those that will enable people to avoid flight in the first place. Indeed, even from a purely financial perspective, it is more efficient to head off refugee crises by spending money to make societies secure—economically, socially, and militarily—than to try to put them back together after a disruption. Preventing the emergencies that may come ten to twenty years down the road costs less, and it must begin now.

In crises, of course, the international community will have to take expensive and drastic action. But even in such cases, the money and time invested yield a huge return. The troops dispatched to Somalia, Rwanda, Bosnia, Kosovo, and Afghanistan, for instance, were able to save hundreds of thousands of lives by getting food, protection, and medical help to vulnerable people. Rarely have government programs helped so many people in so short a time. Faced with growing numbers of refugees worldwide every year, it may be time to create a permanent emergency response unit out of the world's militaries, one that would get temporary shelter, medicine, food, and safety to refugee camps. The alternatives are to assign that task to the militaries of individual countries (as happened with the French and US militaries on the border of Rwanda in 1994) or to leave the task to underfunded and understaffed voluntary organizations.

Yet governments are not jumping at the chance to turn their militaries to such tasks. "Defense Department officials cringe at the notion of becoming a kind of super, musclebound Red Cross or Salvation Army." These operations sap time and attention of senior officials, cut into combat training exercises, tie up equipment and personnel, and take increasingly scarce defense dollars away from other operations. Used for humanitarian goals, however, militaries clearly can make a huge difference. In addition to saving many lives in Somalia and Rwanda, troops have protected tens of thousands of Kurds after the Gulf War, gotten food to desperate Bosnians, and given relief to victims of natural disasters in the United States and Bangladesh. These successes clearly contribute to security and to the protection of people—the basic reasons for militaries in the first place.[52]

Of course, military action can never be a substitute for more fundamental and long-term solutions. Efforts to help people remain in their homes and countries must reach across the entire spectrum, from prevention of emergencies to protection and relief during crises and rebuilding afterward. It is only through such a complete approach that the phenomenon of refugees—no longer an aberration, but an ordinary expression of the world of globalization—can be addressed. First, prevent crises. Second, protect victims. Third, try to restore as much as possible of their past lives. The first is preferable; the second and third cost heavily in human and financial terms.

While crisis-driven expenditures are rising out of necessity, however, efforts to attack the underlying causes of flight are decreasing. Official development assistance from the world's twenty-five wealthiest countries is decreasing. Efforts to head off crises and flows of refugees or emigrants will be more fruitful if they begin today rather than waiting for chaos, as happened in Haiti, Rwanda, Somalia, and elsewhere. Perversely, often governments are willing to spend more in disaster relief than they are willing to spend to prevent disasters.[53] It is ironic that emergency assistance is siphoning away the funds needed to prevent future emergencies.[54] The goal should be to improve stability so that people who want to remain home can do so.

In this light, initiatives not normally considered relevant to refugees become central. Spending on sanitation, public health, and preventive medicine would reduce parental mortality, and intact families would give children a more secure future. Maintaining stable soils and waters for farming would defuse tensions over land and livelihoods. Investing in literacy can also have a profoundly stabilizing effect by helping people read about the actions of their governments and get more involved in solving the problems of their regions. Without such actions, the problems that people flee from will continue to return.

Many examples of attacking the underlying pressures exist. UNICEF's great successes recently at immunizing infants around the world is a significant contribution to stability. Tiny loans of a few dollars to poor villagers by the Grameen Bank in Bangladesh have brought success to people in the poorest class in one of the most densely populated countries on earth. These efforts should receive credit for their ability to enhance security.[55]

If topics such as improved literacy seem far removed from the pressures that make people refugees, then consider the fact that no democracy that has a relatively free press has ever suffered a major famine. If access by literate people to public debate seems too detached from warfare to be relevant, then consider the fact that no two democracies have ever gone to war against one another.[56]

ENDNOTES

1. "France Halts Mass Refugee Flight through Tunnel to Britain," *Washington Post,* Dec. 27, 2001.

2. Aaron Segal, *An Atlas of International Migration* (London: Hans Zell, 1993).

3. Ibid.; Colin McEvedy and Richard Jones, *Atlas of World Population History* (New York: Penguin, 1978).

4. US Committee for Refugees (USCR), *World Refugee Survey 2001* (Washington, DC: 2001); available at <www.refugees.org/world/statistics/wrs01_tableindex.htm>; Segal, *Atlas of International Migration.*

5. Based on UN High Commissioner for Refugees (UNHCR), *Refugees by Numbers: 2001 Edition* and *The State of the World's Refugees 2000: Fifty Years of Humanitarian Action* (available at <www.unhcr.org/>), later updates, and Worldwatch estimates based on press reports.

6. Gil Loescher, *Beyond Charity: International Cooperation and the Global Refugee Crisis* (Oxford, UK: Oxford University Press, 1993).

7. Global IDP Project, "Global Overview," January 2002; site available at <www.idpproject.org/global_overview.htm>.

8. Associated Press, "The Number of Illegal Immigrants in the United States More than Doubled During the 1990s, Census Bureau Estimates Show," Jan. 23, 2002; available at <www.foxnews.com/story/0%2C2933%2C43707%2C00.html>.

9. Migrant figure is from the African Commission on Human and Peoples' Rights, Conference on Migration, Globalization and Human Rights: New Challenges for Africa, Kigali, Rwanda, Oct. 28–Nov. 5, 1999. Chinese figure is from the Asian Migrant Centre, *Asian Migrant Yearbook 1998.*

10. Paul Theroux, "Going to See the Dragon," *Harpers* (Oct. 1993); William G. Rosenberg and Marilyn B. Young, *Transforming Russia and China: Revolutionary Struggle in the Twentieth Century* (New York: Oxford University Press, 1982); Myron Weiner, "Rejected Peoples and Unwanted Migrants in South Asia," *Economic and Political Weekly* (Aug. 21, 1993).

11. UNHCR, *Refugees by Numbers* and *The State of the World's Refugees 2000.*

12. Loescher, *Beyond Charity*; Morton Abramowitz, "Exodus: The World Refugee Crisis," *Foreign Policy* (Summer 1994).

13. Abramowitz, "Exodus." On refugees admitted to the United States during the Reagan years, see Loescher, *Beyond Charity.*

14. Deborah Sontag, "Illegal Aliens Put Uneven Load on States, Study Says," *The New York Times,* Sept. 15, 1994; William Drozdiak, "Rolling Up a Worn-Out Welcome Mat," *Washington Post,* July 13, 1993.

15. Jeffrey S. Passel and Michael Fix, "Myths about Immigrants," *Foreign Policy* (Summer 1994).

16. Mike Edwards, "Chernobyl: Living with the Monster," *National Geographic* (Aug. 1994).

17. *Bangladesh Flood Action Plan* (newsletter) (New York: National Audubon Society, 1993).

18. Unrepresented Nations and Peoples Organisation, "Statement on Tibet" (available at <www.unpo.org/member/tibet/0514cope.htm>).

19. Machiavelli quote from Christa Meindsma, quoted in "UN Recognizes Population Transfer as a Violation of Human Rights," Tibet Press Watch (<www.savetibet.org/>)

(Dec. 1992); Dalai Lama quoted in "Dalai Lama: U.S. Must Help Stop Chinese Population Influx into Tibet," Tibet Press Watch (May 1993).

20. Iraqi exodus cited in Raymond Bonner, "Trail of Suffering as Rwandan Exodus Continues," *The New York Times,* July 16, 1994.

21. UNHCR, *Refugees by Numbers 2001.*

22. Josef Vavrousek et al., *The Environment in Czechoslovakia* (Prague: Institute of Technical, Economic, and Ecological Information, 1990).

23. Joseph A. Tainter, *The Collapse of Complex Societies* (Cambridge, UK: Cambridge University Press, 1988); Victor Mallet, "Vietnamese Settlers in Cambodia Flee Attacks," *Financial Times,* March 31, 1993.

24. Robin Wright and Doyle McManus, *Flashpoints: Promise and Peril in a New World* (New York: Alfred A. Knopf, 1991).

25. Sanjeev Khagram, "Towards Effective Governance for Sustainable Development through the World's Commission on Dams" (Case study for the UN Vision Project on Global Public Policy Networks, 1999) (available at <www.globalpublicpolicy.net>); *Conference Proceedings: First International Meeting of People Affected by Dams* (Berkeley, CA: International Rivers Network, June 1997); World Bank Environment Department, *Resettlement and Development: The Bankwide Review of Projects Involving Involuntary Resettlement 1986–1993* (Washington, DC: 1994).

26. Bruce Rich, *Mortgaging the Earth* (Boston: Beacon Press, 1994); Norman Myers, "Environmental Refugees in a Globally Warmed World," *Bioscience* (Dec. 1993).

27. Population figures from US Bureau of the Census, published in Francis Urban and Ray Nightingale, *World Population by Country and Region, 1950–90, and Projections to 2050* (Washington, DC: US Department of Agriculture [USDA], Economic Research Service, 1993).

28. Number in 1950s from Ruth Leger Sivard, *World Military and Social Expenditures 1993* (Washington, DC: World Priorities, 1993); number of major wars from Peter Wallenstein, "Patterns of Major Armed Conflicts, 1990-2001," in Stockholm International Peace Research Institute (SIPRI), *SIPRI Yearbook 2002: Armaments, Disarmament and International Security* (New York: Oxford University Press, 2002) (available at <www.sipri.org/>).

29. UN Food and Agriculture Organization, *Food Outlook,* no. 5 (New York: United Nations, 2001); Population Reference Bureau (PRB), *World Population Data Sheet, 2002* (Washington, DC: Author, 2002); USDA, "Production, Supply, and Demand View" (electronic database) (Washington, DC: Author, Nov. 1993).

30. USCR, *World Refugee Survey 1994*; Central Intelligence Agency (CIA), "World Fact Book 2001" (available at <www.odci.gov/cia/publications/factbook/>; check under Ethiopia); USDA, "Production, Supply, and Demand View"; Bruce Byers, "Roots of Somalia's Crisis," *Christian Science Monitor,* Dec. 24, 1992.

31. Number of refugees from US Agency for International Development, *Consolidated Rwanda Report* (Update no. 10), Aug. 30–Sept. 8, 1994.

32. Tina Malone, Catholic Relief Services, Baltimore, MD, private communication, Sept. 22, 1994.

33. Population density from PRB, *1994 World Population Data Sheet*; "Rwanda: A Case of Successful Adaptation," in World Bank, *Sub-Saharan Africa: From Crisis to Sustainable Growth* (Washington, DC: Author, 1989); farm size from Centro Internacional de

Agricultura Tropical, "Rwanda Civil War Disrupts Key African Food Program," *CIAT International,* 13: 1–2.

34. Private communication with Benoit Bosquet, Africa Department, World Bank, Washington, D.C., July 19, 1994; Malone, private communication.

35. Malone, private communication; PRB, *1994 World Population Data Sheet.*

36. Gillian Tett, "Elegant Exorcism of Central Bogeymen" (review of *The Resurgence of Central Asia—Islam or Nationalism?*), *Financial Times,* July 28, 1994; Raymond Bonner, "Asian Republic Still Caught in Web of Communism," *The New York Times,* Oct. 13, 1993; number of Tajik refugees from USCR, *World Refugee Survey 1994.*

37. "Refugees on Move in Azerbaijan War," *The New York Times,* Aug. 16, 1993; Mark A. Uhlig, "The Karabakh War," *World Policy Journal* (Winter 1993); USCR, *World Refugee Survey 1994.*

38. SIPRI, *SIPRI Yearbook 2002.*

39. Robert D. Kaplan, "The Coming Anarchy," *Atlantic Monthly* (Feb. 1994) (available at <www.theatlantic.com/politics/foreign/anarchy.htm>); Jaques Attali, "An Age of Yugoslavias," *Harpers* (Jan. 1993).

40. Bureau of the Census, Census 2000 Report (available at <www.census.gov/>); Segal, *Atlas of International Migration.*

41. S. S. Russell and M. S. Teitelbaum, *Internal Migration and International Trade* (World Bank Discussion Papers no. 160) (Washington DC: World Bank, 1992).

42. UNDP, *Human Development Report 1994*; Emma Tucker, "Global Pressures Are Getting Worse," *Financial Times* (Jan. 31, 1994).

43. Kaplan, "The Coming Anarchy"; PRB, *1994 World Population Data Sheet.*

44. United Nations, *Prospects of World Urbanization 1988* (New York: Author, 1989); Jane Pryer and Nigel Crook, *Cities of Hunger: Urban Malnutrition in Developing Countries* (Oxford, UK: Oxfam, 1988).

45. See Chapter 6 of this volume; also Jorge E. Hardoy and David Satterthwaite, *Squatter Citizen* (London: Earthscan, 1989), and Segal, *Atlas of International Migration.*

46. "Latin American Speedup Leaves Poor Behind," *The New York Times,* Sept. 7, 1994; Thomas Kamm, "Epidemic of Slums Afflicts Latin America," *Wall Street Journal,* Aug. 30, 1994; United Nations, *World Urbanization Prospects* (1992 rev.) (New York: Author, 1993).

47. World Bank, China; Tony Walker, "China's Golden Era to Last Well into Next Century," *Financial Times,* Aug. 26, 1994; National Academy findings from "China's Next Revolution," *Financial Times,* Aug. 26, 1994.

48. Helene Cooper, "Sub-Saharan Africa is Seen as Big Loser in GATT's New World Trade Accord," *Wall Street Journal,* Aug. 15, 1994; brain drain from John Darnton, "Lost Decade Drains Africa's Vitality," *The New York Times,* June 19, 1994.

49. United Nations, *Expert Group Meeting on Population Distribution and Migration* (Population Bulletin nos. 34/35) (New York: Author, 1993) (summary findings of the expert group meeting held in Santa Cruz, Bolivia, Jan. 18–22, 1993); Wright and McManus, *Flashpoints.*

50. Wilfredo Cruz and Robert Repetto, *The Environmental Effects of Stabilization and Structural Adjustment Programs: The Philippines Case* (Washington, DC: World Resources Institute, 1992); R. Hakkert and F. W. Goza, "The Demographic Consequences of Austerity in Latin America," in V. L. Canak (Ed.), *Lost Promises: Debt, Austerity, and Development in Latin America* (Boulder, CO: Westview, 1989), 69–97.

51. Sharon Stanton Russell, review of *Labour Migration to the Middle East: From Sri Lanka to the Gulf* in *Population and Development Review* (Sept. 1993).

52. Bradley Graham, "Pentagon Officials Worry Aid Missions Will Sap Military Strength," *Washington Post,* July 29, 1994; Jane Perlez, "Aid Agencies Hope to Enlist Military Allies in the Future," *The New York Times,* Aug. 21, 1994.

53. Carol Lancaster, *Transforming Foreign Aid: United States Assistance in the Twenty-First Century* (Washington, DC: Institute for International Economics, 2000), 14 (available at <www.iie.com/publications/pub.cfm?pub_id=321>).

54. Wealthiest-country development assistance from Organization for Economic Cooperation and Development, *Sharp Changes in the Structure of Financial Flows to Developing Countries and Countries in Transition* (press release, Paris), June 20, 1994; UN development and peacekeeping spending from Erskine Childers with Brian Urquhart, "Renewing the United Nations System," *Development Dialogue* (Uppsala, Sweden: Dag Hammarskjöld Foundation/Ford Foundation, 1994), 1; UNHCR budget from Heather Courtney, public information officer, UNHCR, Washington, DC, private communication, Oct. 4, 1994; UNDP budget from Ad de Rad, UNDP, New York, private communication, Oct. 19, 1994.

55. Grameen Foundation USA, *Grameen Connections Newsletter Spring 2002* (available at <www.gfusa.org/>); UNICEF and World Health Organization, New York and Geneva, private communications, Feb. 17, 1994; Andreas Fuglesang and Dale Chandler, *Participation as Process: What We Can Learn from Grameen Bank, Bangladesh* (Dhaka, Bangladesh: Grameen Bank, 1988); David Bornstein, *The Price of a Dream: The Story of Grameen Bank* (Chicago: University of Chicago Press, 1997).

56. Amartya Sen, "The Economics of Life and Death," *Scientific American* (May 1993); Harald Muller, director of Frankfurt Peace Research Institute, private communication, Feb. 1991.

CHAPTER THIRTEEN

Mind the Gaps

Institutions Meet Global Problems

Maryann Cusimano Love

Every year, 8 million people die of AIDS, tuberculosis, and malaria, primarily in poor countries—approximately one Holocaust each year.[1] In one hospital in Malawi, a trickle of patients with money come in one end of the building, pay $1 a day, and receive the life-saving triple cocktail medication that manages their HIV and AIDS. The other end of the hospital corridor is where most of Malawi's AIDS patients go. Too poor to afford the $1 treatment, they are brought to the hospital not for medicine or care but to die. They are warehoused four to a bed, two head to foot on the mattress, and two on the floor below. Families gather to say goodbye, and the hospital waits for the disease to run its deadly course as others are treated just steps away.

This scenario is repeated every day throughout sub-Saharan Africa and developing countries in a life-and-death example of institutional gaps. The public health and government institutions of these regions do not have the capacity to save their citizens. Other countries have public health institutions with greater capacity, but Malawi's problems are beyond their jurisdiction. Because of sovereign jurisdictions, other governments do not regard it as their responsibility to help the dying. Each US citizen (through US government contributions) spends a mere 75 cents per year toward the global fund to treat AIDS, tuberculosis, and malaria. Until the Doha meeting, World Trade Organization (WTO) rules protected the profits of pharmaceutical companies more forcefully than they protected the lives of the sick and poor—and denied affordable generic drugs because of WTO rules that protected pharmaceutical patents.[2] Now more lenient WTO rules allow governments to license generic production of essential medicines to fight public health emergencies. But this does little to aid the sick in Malawi, where life expectancy is thirty-seven years and more than half the population lives below the poverty line.[3] Malawi is too poor to produce generic drugs locally, and WTO rules are still being resolved regarding the export of cheaper generics. Although a few multinational corporations (MNCs) have pledged to sell their medications at reduced prices, these prices are still beyond the purchasing power of the poor in Malawi.

As a heavily indebted poor country, Malawi has implemented structural adjustment programs required by the international financial institutions (IFIs) since the 1980s, cutting public spending internally (including on health care and education needed for HIV and AIDS treatment) in order to increase external debt repayment.[4] Such actions have led to legitimacy gaps as the poor of the world question whether the WTO and other IFIs rightly represent their interests. It also is evidence of an ethical or values gap, as the market values pursued by pharmaceutical companies, governments, and IFIs are at odds with important societal values of saving human life. UN Secretary-General Kofi Annan notes, "It is a shocking fact that, out of the 1,233 drugs licensed in the world between 1975 and 1997, only 13 were for tropical diseases, and only four were commercially developed specifically for tropical diseases suffered by human beings."[5] At the same time, many more drugs were created for developed markets for non–life threatening afflictions such as acne. The disparity results from market assessments of who can pay rather than from medical assessments of pressing human needs. Efficiently functioning markets can still allow millions to die. Markets create profits. They do not solve all human problems.

INSTITUTIONAL GAPS

Global economic and technological change is fast, while government, legal, and intergovernmental responses are slow. This creates institutional gaps between the problems of globalization and attempts to manage them.[6] These institutional gaps are growing, tall enough to swallow the twin towers of the World Trade Center and wide enough to make the Pentagon a quadrangle for a time. As on September 11, governments are often surprised by these gaps. For example, when the governments of the Philippines, Britain, and Japan wanted to combat problems of cyberthreats, they found they had neither the organizational nor the legal tools to do so.[7] They had to create new institutions.

Institutions range from "formal organizations, which have explicit rules and forms of administration and enforcement, to any stabilized pattern of human relationships and actions."[8] Generally agreed-upon societal norms and specific treaties or organizations with a routine way of doing business may be referred to as institutions. The institutions considered here, however, are a much narrower group: the organizations (whether unilateral or multilateral) that carry out foreign policy. By taking a narrower focus, we can examine theories of bureaucratic organizations as well as institutions writ large. Unlike the broader definition of institution (which can incorporate ideas, behavioral patterns, roles, and even ceremonies such as marriage), the institutions addressed in this chapter are specific in time and space. They have addresses. They are organizations that are generally arranged bureaucratically and hierarchically.

Existing states and international regimes are having difficulties coping with the challenges globalization brings because globalization creates and exacerbates institutional gaps. These institutional gaps fall into several categories of gaps: capacity, jurisdictional, participation, legitimacy, and ethical value. Capacity gaps are shortfalls in organizations or organizational strength, resources, personnel, competence, or standard operating procedures that hinder a state's ability to effectively respond to problems of globalization. Jurisdiction gaps are found when the writ of the problem extends farther than the authority of the institutions charged with responding to the problem. Participation gaps exist when people affected by globalization are excluded from partaking in the decision processes of managing or guiding globalization, earlier described as "democracy deficits." Legitimacy gaps are found when the institutions that manage or regulate globalization are not perceived by society as rightfully representing them. Ethical or values gaps arise when globalization is perceived either to have no ethical base or to promulgate values that are at odds with societal values or the common good.

All of the preceding chapters discussed capacity gaps, ways in which global problems challenge institutions' abilities to effectively respond. From containing terrorism to containing disease, capacity gaps vex state, multilateral, and private sector institutions. Besides the problem of speed (institutions moving slower than global problems), there are other reasons why governments alone cannot effectively respond to globalization's problems. Many regimes have only shaky control over their respective territories. The last decade has seen an increase in the number of failed states and states destabilized by democratic and market transitions and internal conflict. Lack of institutional capacity and resources hamstrings many governments' abilities to respond to global problems.

Comparatively speaking, developed democracies are better equipped to adapt to the challenges of globalization because they have adaptive and well-resourced political and economic institutions that are capable of responding to the dislocations, disruptions, and unintended consequences that globalization brings. States with adequate educational and public health systems and access to technology, coupled with stable governance, allow people access, an on-ramp to the globalization highway. But for many developing and newly democratizing states, rule of law and political and economic institutions are weak; they lack the capacity and resources to respond to globalization's challenges. Even strong states may lack capacity, as growth in the private sector (legal and illegal) has outpaced growth in the public sector by design. Weak and strong states both have capacity gaps, as evidenced by the September 11 attacks. They are more severe for developing states, collapsing states, and states undergoing transitions.

Yet even strong states cannot manage global problems alone because the issues cross jurisdictional and territorial boundaries. Jurisdiction gaps are described throughout this book in which problems cross borders but governments are still constrained by borders in their abilities to respond. Cybercriminals and international terrorists attack from a distance. Bringing them to justice is complicated by these jurisdictional gaps. In addition, the private sector often has better information and technology for containing global problems, while public sector capabilities lag behind. For example, the transportation and financial infrastructures exploited by the September 11 terrorists were all privately owned and operated, further complicating government's jurisdictional reach. Terrorism crosses international and public–private jurisdictions, making governmental responses to these problems necessary but insufficient to successfully manage these problems. As democratization and the Washington consensus spread liberal political and economic systems globally, more states find themselves constitutionally limited in what interventions they may undertake in the private sphere. IGOs are also increasing in number, resources, functions, and power, but IGOs and states alone cannot solve globalization problems because many of the factors that constrain individual states also constrain collections of states. This again creates gaps between what institutions can do and what they are needed to do.

Institutional gaps also exist between rich and poor. Generally, the wealthy have institutions with more capabilities to act on their behalf; the poor often do not. The rural poor have less opportunity to access globalization's benefits. Poor countries and peoples face institutional gaps that fuel the increasing backlash against globalization. Lacking resources, the institutions of poor countries are disadvantaged when bargaining with more powerful countries' institutions over the rules and regimes that govern globalization. For example, although most of the planet's populations are poor people living in developing countries, multilateral institutions such as the WTO and WIPO often favor the intellectual property rights and profits of MNCs at the expense of the poor (through TRIPS and TRIMS).[9] In what developing countries refer to as "biopiracy," local farmers are being told they cannot continue practices of creating seed banks or certain traditional medicines without paying fees to MNCs who now own the intellectual property, patents, and copyrights for these. Although multinational pharmaceutical companies use the populations of developing countries for human testing of potential medicines in the research and development phases, these poor people and countries often do not share in the benefits of these medicines once they are approved because the poor cannot afford the cure.

Poor peoples and countries do not have adequate participation in the decision making processes that channel globalization from corporate boardrooms to annual World Economic Forum summits to the Group of

Eight meetings. The thirty poorest member states of the WTO cannot afford to send delegations to represent and negotiate on their own behalf in Geneva. The participation gaps, capacity gaps, and asymmetric distribution of costs and benefits intensify dissatisfaction and backlash against globalization. Institutions that do not adequately protect developing countries or exclude them from decision making processes are increasingly seen as illegitimate by those who are excluded. These various institutional gaps are reinforcing. Institutions must be perceived as legitimate to be effective; participation gaps exacerbate legitimacy gaps, which intensify capacity gaps.

The participation and legitimacy gaps also further the ethical and values gap. Many observers believe that corporations rule the world,[10] and that globalization puts profits ahead of people. Although powerful multinational corporations seek profits, states seek wealth and development in globalization. Many decry the degree to which rich states, particularly the United States, drive globalization, putting market values ahead of other values. Most of the world's poor are not citizens of the developed states, leaving rich states with no jurisdictional or perceived ethical obligations to the world's dispossessed. Thus, whether driven by powerful companies or powerful states, many observers decry the ethical basis of globalization, believing globalization is driven by an ethic of crass materialism and consumption or Western (especially US) cultural imperialism.[11] To the extent that this ethos pervades globalization, many people suggest that the violence and backlash against globalization will increase, producing a world in which the benefits of globalization reach too few people and countries, making the dynamics of globalization politically unsustainable.[12]

The ethical gaps are large and growing. Today, more than half of the world's citizens are not receiving the benefits of globalization, either because they are not plugged into the global economy or because they do not have institutions that can advance or protect their interests as participants in the global economy. Human life is lost, human development unfulfilled, and creation destroyed. This disparity between those who benefit from globalization and those who are left behind or vulnerable to its challenges is increasing. The world's poorest populations are growing, while the populations of developed countries are stable or slightly declining with the graying of the baby boomers. For example, world population is expected to grow from its current 6 billion to 7.2 billion in the next fifteen years. Ninety-five percent of that population growth will occur in developing countries and in already stressed urban areas—megacities such as Lagos and Mexico City.[13] Therefore, globalization's moral and ethical problems will only intensify. The values gap is exacerbated by the legitimacy, jurisdictional, and participation gaps. As Archbishop Diarmuid Martin, Vatican Representative to the United Nations and Specialized Agencies in Geneva, put it, "The human family is a dysfunctional family. What is needed is a network of structures, institutions, principles and elements of law to help manage in the best possible way the world's common good, which cannot be protected only by individual governments."[14]

POLITICAL SCIENCE AND OBSTACLES TO ORGANIZATIONAL CHANGE

How can we build institutions that better address global problems and better protect and promote peace and prosperity for more people on the planet? How can we change institutions to address the institutional gaps exacerbated by globalization? Political scientists have many theories about institutional change, but most of them tend to be pessimistic, emphasizing the obstacles to changing institutions. This chapter will consider five approaches in the political science literature on institutional change, those of rationalists, reflectivists, institutionalists, bureaucratic and organizational theorists, and political psychologists.[15]

Rationalists

Rationalists stress that institutions are rational reactions to the environments that states face. States create institutions because it is in their interest to do so. They expect that benefits will flow to them from the institutional arrangements that will be worth the cost.[16] Institutions reflect the power, resources, and interests of states at the time of their creation (which is why Germany and Japan, defeated powers when the UN Security Council was created, do not have veto power or status as permanent members of the Security Council). States create institutions and thus states can change institutions whenever they want, which usually occurs when the distribution of power or resources has changed.

Sunk costs are an obstacle to institutional change, however. States are attentive to how much time, attention, and resources they have already poured into an institution, and thus they are not likely to change institutions quickly or lightly. The other permanent members of the Security Council have few incentives to change the institution to now include Germany and Japan.

Reflectivists

Reflectivists emphasize that institutions are constructed based on ideas, norms, values, culture, and history.[17] For example, although the structure of the United Nations represented the interests of the World War II victors, it also reflected the lessons learned from the failure of the League of Nations. The structure of NATO represented not only the interest of containing the USSR's power, but also ideas about promoting democracy in Western Europe and cooperation among democratic states. States are not billiard balls moved only by power dynamics, and institutions are not mere puppets of states. An institution can assume a life of its own. Actors often do not know exactly what outcomes they want in advance, and value-based institutions help shape and create their interests. Ideas and norms change, and so institutions can change. But existing institutions will affect and constrain change.[18]

Institutionalists

Institutionalists stress the importance of history, path dependency, and chance. Actors never have the entire universe of possible organizational varieties from which to choose. They must choose from the options that are available to them; earlier selections narrow the options.[19] Even if another choice later appears more efficient, changeover costs may wipe out any gains. Gatekeeping and self-censorship are also obstacles to change. Dominant forms may actively work to keep out alternative forms, or alternatives may try to make themselves resemble the dominant form so they will be accepted into the system. People conceive of the world and themselves within current institutional frameworks (vertical linkages), and existing organizations have many standardized ways of doing business with other organizations (horizontal linkages). Vertical and horizontal linkages (concepts and relations with others) allow institutional structures to persist even after the circumstances they were created to deal with have changed and institutions have become inefficient or outmoded. These links create formidable obstacles to institutional change.[20]

Change happens in fits and starts (punctuated equilibrium) and is constrained by the weight of existing organizational structures. Rapid change can occur unexpectedly if "a stable structure is stressed beyond its buffering capacity to resist and absorb [change],"[21] but such examples are rare because institutions actively influence the environment to promote their own survival. More often, old institutions are retrofitted to do new tasks. Even though these structures may not be the most efficient or logical way to tackle a new problem, the existing structure has the advantage of being available. "Credit cards can be used to open doors."[22] UN peacekeeping troops may be used to fight famine in Somalia; commercial airlines may be used as weapons. Having the tool often leads to its use.

Bureaucratic and Organizational Theorists

The bureaucratic and organizational approach stresses the role and effect of domestic and internal politics on institutional structures. Many theorists of this approach are "in-and-outers" in government service, so they focus on characteristics that policy makers and practitioners believe are important.[23] They describe bureaucratic organizations as semifeudal agencies, each fighting to protect its turf and to guard its missions, budgets, functions, personnel, resources, and autonomy. Internal conflicts may exist in organizations between bureaucratic chiefs and followers, but in general personnel are socialized (through training, standard operating procedures, and advancement incentives) into certain shared organizational viewpoints (vertical linkages).[24] Bureaucratic organizations may engage in strategic bargains with others. Agencies may give up subsidiary functions in order to protect primary ones. They may bow out of fights with more powerful agencies if they believe they cannot win and want to survive and preserve resources. But regardless of the specific strategy, organizations will seek to promote their own survival—and change will come slowly, in an incremental fashion, and when viewed as necessary to organizational survival. Change that is seen as threatening to the organization's missions, functions, budgets, autonomy, or personnel will be resisted.

Much of what is perceived as bureaucratic waste and inefficiency is actually the result of conflicting purposes given to public sector organizations. Different expectations exist for public and private organizations. As Milton Friedman put it, "the moral responsibility of business is to make a profit."[25] Government organizations raise different expectations. We care about what they produce as well as how they produce it. In some cases, what is produced is so nebulous (national security, for example) and hard to measure that greater emphasis and constraints are placed on the process (which can be seen and measured). We may not be entirely sure what we want the military to do or how it may best produce national security, but we know a lot about how we expect the military to operate. For example, the US military was under strict orders to integrate the armed services decades before the rest of American society integrated. We expect the marketplace to offer better treatment to those who can pay more. We expect the government to treat all citizens equally.

Because government bureaucracies face greater operational constraints than private bureaucracies, it is unrealistic to expect them to operate as efficiently as their private counterparts, but many organizational reform proposals are based entirely on this flawed premise. Proposals for UN and IMF reform focus on downsizing, defunding, and privatizing the existing machine for budgetary purposes (less is more, according to this view). Although cost savings, organizational efficiency, and simplified chains of command are all laudable goals, these reforms are not aimed at making the organization better able to manage global issues. Focusing exclusively on cutting budgets and bodies may actually hamper the United Nations' capacities to respond to global problems. Scholar James Q. Wilson is skeptical of trying to change organizations through additional regulations or external reorganization plans without parallel changes in internal incentives. If executives favor change, if they change the incentive structure (through training and promotion opportunities) to reward innovation and encourage the rank and file to innovate, then organizations may change—but such change will not be quick or easy.

Institutions are inherently political animals. Every organizational structure was created as a result of political negotiation enacted into law. Thus, every organization is based on the political coalitions that won out or the compromise that was reached in order to create an institutional structure. Powerful actors rarely get what they want because institutional structures represent compromise and bargaining among groups. In addition, institutions are not particularly adaptive or efficient in response to changes in the external environment:

> The choices about structure that are made in the first period, when the agency is designed and empowered with a mandate, are normally far more enduring and consequential than those that will be made later. . . . Most of the pushing and hauling in subsequent years is likely to produce only incremental change. This, obviously, is very much on everyone's minds in the first period.[26]

Structures may be quite ill-suited to organizational goals by design. In democracies, organizational structures were created by groups who wanted to address particular needs, curry favor with political constituents, or wrest power or functions from existing organizations. Controlling mechanisms were foisted on organizations by opponents who either did not want particular issue areas addressed or did not want the new organization to succeed or become too powerful, or sometimes by proponents of the original organization who, fearful that political opponents would control the organization at some future point, wanted to limit the damage the opponents could do. Changing institutions is therefore not about making more efficient structures, but about changing political balances. There are no easy answers—or they would have been implemented long ago:

> It would be nice to say that there is an easy way out of all this, that the nation can have an effective public bureaucracy if only it wants one. But this is probably not so. A bureaucracy that is structurally unsuited for effective action is precisely the kind of bureaucracy that interest groups and politicians routinely and deliberately create . . . [B]ecause they are forced to design bureaucracy through a democratic process, their structural choices turn out to be very different indeed from those intended to promote effective organization.[27]

Moe expects bureaucratic structures to be "grotesque" and "bizarre," not efficient or easily adapted. Ironically, this point is lost on many think tanks that produce many ideas of how to reform specific foreign policy organizations for greater efficiency and effectiveness without attention to changing the underlying political coalitions. Without the political support to bring them to fruition, these ideas often die on the vine.

Political Psychologists

Another helpful academic approach to understanding institutional change has been undertaken by political psychologists. These authors also stress the difficulty of changing conceptual or belief systems, and the ways in which outmoded beliefs can persist despite changes in external circumstances. Individual decision makers and small decision making groups are important in international politics. People make policy and people create and lead institutions, so people can bring about change. Conceptual change is necessary for institutions to change, but it does not come easily or precipitously, because change in beliefs is "gradual and ragged."[28]

For example, Deborah Larson studied the origins of Cold War ideas and institutions. For an extended period, policy makers themselves did not know what course of action to pursue and what to think about Soviet behavior and the nature of the new postwar world. They did not develop new beliefs in the abstract, but they were forced by circumstances to deal with the changed environment. They improvised and developed ad hoc policy responses, tinkering with a variety of sometimes contradictory approaches. Policy makers often knew their old ideas were inadequate, but they did not discard them quickly because they had no replacement theory. Decision makers were forced to act, and out of those actions they gradually developed new ideas, which they then used to justify their past and subsequent actions and to create new organizations. "Forged in the fires" of action and crisis, "ideology leads to the development of policy doctrines that become institutionalized through the creation of bureaucracies. In particular, the Cold War ideology underlay a vast expansion of the power and resources of the executive branch of the U.S. government."[29] Changing ideas made organizational change possible. Larson's account parallels our current period of institutional tinkering.

The literature agrees that change is difficult. It will be resisted by bureaucracies that see change as threatening to their missions, functions, budgets, personnel, autonomy, or standard operating procedures. Peripheral tasks will be easier to change than core tasks. In democratic systems, change can be initiated by legislators, prime ministers or presidents, interest groups, and voters, but even externally imposed changes need some degree of internal support if the proposed changes are to be carried out in accordance with the spirit of the law and not just its letter. Ideas may need to change before organizations can change, and they may change only through hands-on experience in grappling with a changed environment. Leadership, concepts, and coalitions are needed for change.

MACHIAVELLI WAS RIGHT: CHANGE IS THE ONLY CONSTANT

What is often overlooked in the literature's emphasis on the obstacles to organizational change are the facts that (1) change does occur, and (2) sometimes the same characteristics of bureaucratic and organizational behavior that are cited as obstacles to change can be marshaled to promote institutional change. It seems, after all these years, that Machiavelli is still right. Change is the only constant in politics. Perhaps the only thing organizations fear and resist more than change is their own obsolescence or threats to their survival. If organizations are seen as ineffective, outdated anachronisms, then they may have powerful incentives for reinventing themselves to survive with the changing times. It is not merely a matter of cosmetics. Organizations do not want to put their personnel or resources at risk. If older standard operating procedures are seen as no longer being able to protect personnel or resources, then organizations will have powerful incentives to change the way they do business. After September 11, there was little argument that institutions must change to better contain the threats of terrorism. The only debates have been over how best to do so.

Organizations do not want to appear outdated—and not just because they want to convince political decision makers of their validity, necessity, and fiscal worth. Although some bureaucrats may be concerned only with maintaining their paychecks, many others want to use their organizations to effectively perform tasks. Most bureaucrats consider themselves members of some profession, and their professional ethics prompt them to want to pursue effective action in their field. Thus, there will always be advocates for change within any institution, people who see better ways to do their jobs or who want to improve their institutions' abilities in a changed world. Once these agents for change begin interacting with the environment, the results may be unpredictable. Gorbachev did not set out to dismantle the

USSR. He tried to improve worker productivity and cut down on alcohol abuse on the job in an attempt to improve the performance of Soviet institutions. But the changes he unleashed had the unintended but eventual consequence of ending the Soviet empire.

As people engage in the process of changing institutions, the process may change the people as well. Perhaps you can't always get what you want in institutional structure. But if Larson is correct about how people revise their belief systems, then we may not know what we want until we engage in the process and begin to learn from experience. Thus, although action for change may come from individuals or political coalitions in alliance with reformers within institutions, the process may change as the institutions interact with the agents for change and vice versa.

Institutional change is occurring in fits and starts. As we experience the institutional gaps posed by globalization, new concepts for change, leaders, and coalitions are emerging to address globalization's gaps with the aid of reformers within organizations. Governments, multilateral institutions, and private institutions are hard at work, especially in addressing capacity gaps. Developed country governments address capacity gaps by creating new bureaucratic organizations or changing old ones, changing laws and policies that direct these institutions, and adding resources. Poor countries have fewer resources to address their governments' capacity gaps, so IGOs and NGOs also work to bridge them. Multilateral organizations and NGOs address capacity gaps of state institutions in developing countries by offering technological assistance or training, for example, to bridge the digital divide. Although some businesses exploit low capacity in developing governments, most MNCs desire greater capacity in developing countries' institutions in order to have a stable and predictable business environment governed by rule of law. But poorer countries will always have fewer resources to fund their institutions, and in the effort to attract foreign direct investment may even forgo further tax revenues, further exacerbating capacity gaps.

State and multilateral institutions are increasingly trying to borrow or buy capacity from the private sector. Whether in deterring cyberthreats or terrorism, protection of critical infrastructure (largely privately owned and operated) requires the cooperation of the private sector. Governments and IGOs increasingly contract out to the private sector to provide key capacities. The Australian government, for example, hires a private company to run refugee camps. Private companies are demining Afghanistan and de-nuclearizing the arsenals of the former Soviet Union on behalf of the US government. Through the voluntary Global Compact, Kofi Annan and the United Nations work to harness the capacity of businesses to fight environmental, human rights, and labor abuses. Working with the private sector has meant forming new collaborative networks to help monitor, report, and share information on problems; contribute to policy solutions; and implement policy to manage global problems. Across a variety of issue areas, diverse foreign policy institutions are widening their contacts and partnerships with the private sector.

Rather than creating entirely new state agencies to deal with global problems, existing institutions are developing new integrating and coordinating mechanisms that cross agency and public–private sector boundaries. For example, to avert Y2K-related problems globally, unprecedented public–private partnerships shared information about problems and best practices for solutions. Governments had neither the resources nor the know-how to tackle the problem, and most of the infrastructure to be protected was in the private sector. The private sector had selected sets of information but no forum by which to share that information across organizations and internationally. The costs of Y2K-related repairs was estimated at between $300 billion and $500 billion internationally. Problems still occurred. Some Italian prisoners had a century added to or subtracted from their jail sentences. France lost satellite communications with its troops in Bosnia. Four thousand US small businesses failed to download Y2K-compliant credit-card billing software and lost business while banks reversed erroneous double and triple credit-card charges to more than 40,000 customers who made purchases in the first days after the date change to 2000. But Russian nuclear missiles were not accidentally fired, air traffic control systems generally worked, and many other Y2K-related concerns were averted.[30]

Borrowing ideas from the private sector and from computer technology about connectivity, institutions are generally not trying to create large, new federal bureaucracies that attempt to control activities and impose policy solutions from the top down (as was done after World War II). Instead, state institutions are trying to serve as better facilitators, coordinators, and integrators of information and action across a wide variety of actors and issues. Networking may be difficult for government organizations because they are organized as hierarchical bureaucracies, whereas NGOs and other nonstate actors may not be. State institutions' roles, missions, functions, procedures, authority, accountability, and chains of command are often more clearly demarcated than those of nonstate actors. NGOs often have flatter and looser organizations, and bureaucratic government organizations may find it difficult to determine who's in charge. When a bureaucratically organized institution attempts to coordinate and integrate information and action with a less hierarchically organized institution, they may "talk past each other." The bureaucratic organization wonders how anyone can function in such fluid chaos without standardized ways of doing business. The nonbureaucratic organization wonders why the bureaucracy cannot be more flexible to the nuances of the emerging situation. Differences in communication, culture, and organization make networking difficult but not impossible, as when international bankers in the IFIs try to reach out more systematically to the NGO community.

To create new or adapt existing institutions to better leverage the resources of the private sector, institutions must increasingly go not just beyond sovereignty but also beyond bureaucracy. Called *postbureaucratic organizations,* these organizational forms stress integrative and interactive networks that are based on ideas drawn from successful entrepreneurs and technologies.[31] Often when government reformers talk of moving beyond bureaucracy and "reinventing government," what they really mean is cleaning up bureaucracy and making government more like a business.[32] Despite the grandiose language of a "paradigm shift,"[33] these reforms really do not demolish bureaucracy but streamline and downsize overgrown and inefficient bureaucracy. Although it has some advantages, this approach is limited in how far it can go given the differences discussed earlier between businesses and governments. But some of the current reforms break down or circumvent bureaucracy's formal, rule-bound structures based on clear demarcations of hierarchy and office.

These postbureaucratic organizational forms are flatter and more adaptive, based not on hierarchical chains of command but on interdependent webs of actors.[34] The benefits to this type of structure are increased flexibility, increased information sharing regardless of rank or organizational affiliation, a greater emphasis on the job to be done than on bureaucratic rules or routines, and more fluid boundaries. These trends are facilitated by both career patterns that no longer assume people will spend entire careers in one organization and information technologies that allow the building of temporary networks of people who work together virtually on specific problems and may never meet face-to-face.[35] The problems are challenges in coordination, greater complexity, and questions of transparency and accountability.

These changes in organizational forms may help combat global problems. When the models of organization from business were large, cookie-cutter bureaucracies such as IBM, and when the external threat was a stable, monolithic, universal, hegemonic Cold War adversary, foreign policy organizations responded with large, bureaucratic, and hierarchical structures that heavily emphasized stable routines, rules, and standard operating procedures. Change makes sense now that external threats come from diffuse and decentralized networks such as terrorism and international crime. Institutions need to be organized as networks to better fight networks. Yet sustained leadership, fresh concepts, and new political coalitions are necessary to make these changes.

MIND THE GAPS: BRIDGING INSTITUTIONAL GAPS

Globalization is intensifying institutional gaps, and there are many obstacles to institutional change. Yet change *is* occurring. To address capacity gaps, states and nonstate actors are partnering in new ways and using new, more networked institutional forms. To address jurisdiction gaps, governments harmonize laws and develop new or strengthen existing international regimes to better manage problems that go beyond state borders and jurisdictions. To address participation gaps, IGOs try to include NGOs in some manner in their activities. To address ethical gaps, some IGOs, NGOs, and MNCs adopt voluntary codes of conduct. To address legitimacy gaps, IGOs are increasing transparency, primarily by posting information about their activities on Web sites. But Web sites and ad hoc codes of conduct and NGO forums are not enough to bridge these gaps. Powerful political coalitions remain that form obstacles to better address participation, legitimacy, and ethical gaps. NGOs often work to build new political coalitions to bridge these gaps through organizing grassroots support and direct-media campaigns that pressure democratic governments internally and externally, as well as applying direct pressure on MNCs to better address pressing global issues. Governments and IGOs are more concerned with capacity and jurisdiction gaps than legitimacy, participation, and ethical gaps, but IGOs cannot be effective or sustainable if these other gaps are not addressed. Powerful governments and IGOs will be increasingly targeted for sometimes violent protests as long as these gaps worsen or go unaddressed.

In Lewis Carroll's classic story *Alice in Wonderland,* the white queen chastises Alice for an insufficient imagination and tells her that expanding her imagination requires daily practice. "My dear, sometimes I think six impossible thoughts before breakfast."

Perhaps during the stability of the nearly fifty-year Cold War period, our imaginations atrophied. We did not give our imaginations much practice, as indicated by an exchange in 1986 between then-director of the CIA Richard Gates and Senator Daniel Patrick Moynihan. The senator, a former academic, had noticed that all economic indicators from the Soviet Union seemed to be pointing to an end to the Soviet empire. No one in Washington agreed with Moynihan's analysis because the Reagan administration and Congress were involved in unprecedented peacetime defense spending levels in order to combat the evil empire of the Soviet threat. Moynihan asked Gates in a Senate Intelligence Committee hearing what plans the agency was making for how to deal with a post-Soviet world.[36] Gates responded, "[M]y resources do not permit me the luxury of sort of just idly speculating on what a different kind of Soviet Union might look like."[37] He did not see the point of making plans for the impossible.

Today we find that the impossible has occurred. The Soviet empire collapsed, and a small band of nonstate actors brought thousands of deaths and billions in damages to the world's most powerful state. Our thoughts have not caught up with the impossible. Like Alice, we have not figured out how to think about the strange new world into which we have unexpectedly fallen.

Markets and global problems are moving faster than institutional and conceptual responses to the challenges of globalization. Of all the obstacles to organizational change, the biggest one appears to be ourselves and our limited ways of thinking about our changed world. Too often the debates over globalization are portrayed as a choice between a globalization that puts profits over people versus no globalization at all. In reality, there are more choices than that. We do not have to choose between the current form of globalization, with its mix of benefits along with its excesses and problems, or a return to a more closed, isolated, and less interdependent world. Instead of debating over false choices, we can build institutions that better represent important values; better distribute the benefits of globalization; better mitigate the problems of open economies, open societies, and open technologies; and better protect and promote the common good, building a global infrastructure that advances more authentic human development.

Change is not easy, direct, or logical, and institutions created by democracies will not be efficient in the narrow economic sense. But these observations about the obstacles to change should not obscure the fact that change is occurring, even if it is hard-fought, long in coming, constrained by political parameters, and occurring unevenly in fits and starts. Institutions are minding globalization's capacity and jurisdictional gaps, though much work remains, especially with gaps in legitimacy, participation, ethics and values. If we learn by doing and we change our ideas about the world as a result of our actions in the world (not before our actions), then we will see greater change as a result of our experiences in the changed international environment. A silver lining from September 11 could be increased leadership, attention, urgency, and changed concepts and coalitions toward the problem of institutional gaps, bringing more communication, cooperation, and coordination among a wide variety of public and private actors.

ENDNOTES

1. Jeffrey Sachs, speech to the "Humanizing the Global Economy" conference of the Catholic bishops of Latin America, Canada, and the United States, Catholic University, Washington, DC, Jan. 31, 2002.

2. World Trade Organization (WTO), *Declaration on the Trips Agreement and Public Health*, Nov. 14, 2001 (Doha); available at <http://docsonline.wto.org/> (search for "Declaration on the Trips Agreement and Public Health").

3. Central Intelligence Agency, "The World Factbook 2001"; available at <www.odci. gov/cia/publications/factbook> (check under Malawi).

4. WTO, "Trade Policy Reviews: Summaries and Conclusions," at <www.wto.org/ english/tratop_e/tpr_e/tp_rep_e.htm#malawi2002>.

5. UN Secretary-General Kofi Annan, address to the World Economic Forum, Feb. 4, 2002.

6. Maryann Cusimano Love, "Globalization and Religion," International Studies Association annual meeting, Chicago, Feb. 24, 2001; Maryann Cusimano Love, "Bridging the Gap: Globalization and Religion, and the Institutions of the U.S.

Catholic Church," American Academy of Religions annual conference, Denver, CO, Nov. 20, 2001; Maryann Cusimano Love, "Globalization and Religion," *Journal of Social Thought* (forthcoming); Maryann Cusimano Love, *Unplugging the Cold War Machine: U.S. Foreign Policy and Globalization* (Thousand Oaks, CA: Sage, forthcoming).

7. Maryann Cusimano Love, *Public–Private Partnerships and Global Problems: Y2K and Cybercrime.* Paper delivered to International Studies Association, Hong Kong meeting, July 2001.

8. Jack Knight, *Institutions and Social Conflict* (Cambridge, UK: Cambridge University Press, 1996), 2.

9. WIPO is the World Intellectual Property Organization. TRIPS are Trade-Related Intellectual Property Rights, and TRIMS are Trade-Related Investment Measures.

10. David C. Korten, *When Corporations Rule the World* (West Hartford, CT: Kumarian Press, 1995); Richard Falk, *Predatory Globalization: A Critique* (Malden, MA: Blackwell, 1999); John Gray, *False Dawn: The Delusions of Global Capitalism* (New York: New Press, 1998).

11. Ignacio Ramonet, "Dueling Globalizations: Let Them Eat Big Macs," *Foreign Policy* (Fall 1999): 116–121, 125–127; Thierry Linard de Gueterchin, S. J., "A Christmas Present for the Ford Workers in the ABC of Sao Paulo," Centro Cultural de Brasilia: Global Economies and Culture Project, in conjunction with the Woodstock Theological Center, Georgetown University, Washington, DC, April 6, 1999; Dani Rodrik, *Has Globalization Gone Too Far?* (Washington, DC: Institute for International Economics, 1997).

12. James Mittelman, *The Globalization Syndrome: Transformation and Resistance* (Princeton, NJ: Princeton University Press, 2000); Mark Juergensmeyer, "The Worldwide Rise of Religious Nationalism," *Journal of International Affairs,* 50(1); Benjamin R. Barber, *Jihad vs. McWorld: How Globalism and Tribalism Are Reshaping the World* (New York: Ballantine, 1995); Samuel Huntington, "Clash of Civilizations," *Foreign Affairs,* 72(3), 22–28.

13. National Intelligence Council, *Global Trends 2015: A Dialogue About the Future with Nongovernment Experts* (Washington, DC: US Government Printing Office, December 2000); available at <www.cia.gov/cia/publications/globaltrends2015/>.

14. Archbishop Diarmuid Martin, speech to the "Humanizing the Global Economy" conference of the Catholic bishops of Latin America, Canada, and the United States, Catholic University, Washington, DC, Jan. 28, 2002.

15. Robert Keohane, "International Institutions: Two Approaches," *International Studies Quarterly* (1988): 379–396; Steven Weber, "Institutions and Change," in Michael W. Doyle and G. John Ikenberry (Eds.), *New Thinking in International Relations Theory* (Boulder, CO: Westview Press, 1997), 229–265; Stephen Krasner, "Sovereignty: An Institutional Perspective," *Comparative Political Studies* (April 1988): 66–94; Graham Allison and Philip Zelikow, *The Essence of Decision: Explaining the Cuban Missile Crisis* (2nd ed.) (Reading, MA: Longman, 1999); I. M. Destler, *Presidents, Bureaucrats, and Foreign Policy* (Princeton, NJ: Princeton University Press, 1972); Francis Rourke, *Bureaucracy and Foreign Policy* (Baltimore: Johns Hopkins University Press, 1974); Morton Halperin, *Bureaucratic Politics and Foreign Policy* (Washington, DC: Brookings Institution, 1974); Terry Moe, "The Politics of Bureaucratic Structure," in John E. Chubb and Paul E. Peterson (Eds.), *Can the Government Govern?* (Washington, DC: Brookings Institution, 1989); Deborah Larson, *The Origins of Containment: A Psychological Explanation* (Princeton, NJ: Princeton University Press, 1985).

16. Keohane, "International Institutions: Two Approaches," 386–387.

17. Weber, "Institutions and Change," 235; Martha Finnemore, *National Interests in International Society* (Ithaca, NY: Cornell University Press, 1996).

18. Finnemore, *National Interests in International Society*.

19. Krasner, "Sovereignty: An Institutional Perspective," 83.

20. Ibid., 66.

21. Ibid., 79.

22. Ibid., 80.

23. Allison and Zelikow, *The Essence of Decision*; I. M. Destler, *Presidents, Bureaucrats, and Foreign Policy* (Princeton, NJ: Princeton University Press, 1972); Rourke, *Bureaucracy and Foreign Policy*; Halperin, *Bureaucratic Politics and Foreign Policy*; Terry Moe, "The Politics of Bureaucratic Structure," in Chubb and Peterson, *Can the Government Govern?*

24. This is the most critiqued part of bureaucratic theory, the idea that, "where you stand (on an issue) depends on where you sit (in which organization)." A cottage industry has developed to critique this aspect of bureaucratic theory. As convincing as these studies are that issue positions are not determined by organizational membership alone, it is important to note that Allison never said this was the only determinant of an actor's position; it is one factor among many. Also, many of these studies mistakenly conclude that bureaucratic and organizational dynamics were not involved when no conflict is seen among bureaucratic actors. If agencies often pursue strategic alliances, and especially if actors seek to reduce uncertainty and be sure in advance of a meeting that they will not be blindsided, then a lack of conflict along agency lines at key meetings might not be evidence that bureaucratic politics theory has been disproved, but the phenomenon might actually be explicable according to the theory. Thus, the problem for Allison's theory is not that it has been proved wrong by numerous critical studies, but that it is too poorly specified to be proved wrong or right. Both evidence of conflict and evidence of its absence among agencies can be interpreted in light of the theory.

25. Charles Heckscher, "Defining the Post-Bureaucratic Type," in Charles Heckscher and Anne Donnellon (Eds.), *The Post-Bureaucratic Organization: New Perspectives on Organizational Change* (Thousand Oaks, CA: Sage, 1994), 27.

26. Moe, "The Politics of Bureaucratic Structure," in Chubb and Peterson, *Can the Government Govern?* 285.

27. Ibid., 329.

28. Larson, *The Origins of Containment,* 341.

29. Ibid., 349.

30. Cusimano Love, *Public–Private Partnerships and Global Problems*.

31. Heckscher and Donnellon, *The Post Bureaucratic Organization.* Also, a growing literature is developing in sociology on diffuse networks; see Mary Durfee and Paul Lopes (Eds.), "Networks of Novelty: The Diffusion of Ideas and Things," *The Annals of the American Academy of Political and Social Sciences* (Philadelphia: AAPSS, November 1999).

32. Al Gore, *Common Sense Government: Works Better and Costs Less* (New York: Random House, 1995); Al Gore, "Report on the National Performance Review," White House press releases on July 14, Sept. 14, Oct. 13, and Dec. 5, 1994, and Jan. 26, 1995; also see White House Documents, Office of the Press Secretary, "Gore Announces Initial Restructuring of Foreign Affairs Agencies," Jan. 27, 1995; Donald F. Kettl, *Reinventing Government? Appraising the National Performance Review* (Washington, DC: Brookings Institution, 1994); Donald F. Kettl and John J. DiIulio, Jr., *Cutting Government*

(Washington, DC: Brookings Institution, 1995); Ronald C. Moe, "The 'Reinventing Government' Exercise: Misinterpreting the Problem, Misjudging the Consequences," *Public Administration Review* (March–April 1994): 111–122; Gerald E. Caiden, "Administrative Reform American Style," *Public Administration Review* (March–April 1994): 123–128.

33. James P. Pinkerton, *What Comes Next: The End of Big Government and the New Paradigm Ahead* (New York: Hyperion, 1995).

34. Heckscher, "Defining the Post-Bureaucratic Type," 25.

35. Ibid., 27.

36. Daniel Patrick Moynihan, "Our Stupid but Permanent CIA: What Are We Going to Do about Reforming the Agency? Nothing," *Washington Post,* July 24, 1994, p. C3.

37. Richard Gates, as quoted in David M. Kennedy, *Sunshine and Shadow: The CIA and the Soviet Economy* (Cambridge, MA: Harvard University, 1991), 18.

CHAPTER FOURTEEN

Sovereignty's Future

Changes Among Us

Maryann Cusimano Love

Much of this book has been about unintended consequences. States, IGOs, and MNCs worked to build international markets and to create the political, economic, and technological infrastructure that made the global marketplace possible. States courted foreign direct investment and technological advancement. Through a variety of economic and political liberalization policies, states deliberately worked to increase the size of the private sector while curtailing public sector expenditures so the private sector would not be "crowded out." They pursued these policies to increase economic development and prosperity, believing that wealthy states are strong states.

Western states sought to promote open societies, believing that democratic states are more stable trade partners and are less likely to go to war with other democracies. States did not intend, however, to create the infrastructure for transsovereign problems to thrive. State governments did not realize that the new actors and dynamics created by globalization would also drain autonomy, choice, and freedom of action away from states. Sovereignty is based on territory, yet the new economy and new actors' prosperity does not derive from territory, making them less beholden to states. How can these new dynamics and actors be managed within a system of sovereign states? How can states maintain law and order, justice and peace against licit and illicit private sector actors who are increasingly powerful?

THE POLICY PRESCRIPTIONS

Policy prescriptions for managing globalization and the global problems created by open societies, economies, and technologies fall into three main categories: state-centric (public sector) approaches, nonstate-centric (private sector) responses, and mixed (public–private) responses.

The State-Centric Approach

The state-centric approach to global problems suggests that states strengthen their capacity to fight global problems, enhancing law and order institutions, control over borders, markets, multilateral cooperation among states, and interagency cooperation within states to increase states' efficacy of response. In essence, this approach argues that the same forces that facilitate global problems and undermine sovereignty (open technologies, economies, and societies) can be harnessed or managed to fight global problems. States need to better use the same new technologies and market forces that are being used against them in global problems. If we could just make states smarter and work together better, then states would be able to meet these challenges more effectively. If states were equipped with better technologies, with enhanced state capacity, then cooperating and sharing information and implementation would be possible and more effective across and within governments. After all, terrorists and drug traffickers are using the most advanced emerging technologies and are developing strategic relations with other criminal cartels. Why can't states do the same in their efforts to stop these illicit activities? State-centric responses can be unilateral, focusing on building the capacity of states internally. They can also be multilateral, focusing either on increasing IGO capacity or on federal, functional cooperation among government agencies (as when police or judges share information and cooperate across borders).

State-centric responses are seen most often in the efforts to fight the global problems of drug smuggling, terrorism, cyberthreats, transnational crime, and nuclear proliferation. This is not surprising: These issues touch most closely to the security sectors where state identity and activities are strongest and where states have always been active. Interdiction, improved intelligence and law enforcement capabilities, interagency and IGO efforts to improve information sharing, cooperation, and enforcement are all examples of state-centric responses to global problems. Even progressive and creative programs that are fully in the cooperative security rubric—such as the Cooperative Threat Reduction program between the United States and the states of the former Soviet Union (FSU) to stem nuclear proliferation from the FSU—fit into this category. Attempts to increase nuclear material protection, control, and accountability (MPC&A) by increasing security at FSU nuclear labs and facilities by installing security cameras, detection devices, modern accounting and storage procedures, and so on are oriented at strengthening the capacity of states.

The Nonstate-Centric Approach

The nonstate-centric policy approach emphasizes the importance of the private sector in responding to global problems. It also emphasizes the limitations of trying to work through the state for help in curtailing activities that largely fall in the social and economic sectors where the reach of liberal, capitalist states is the shortest. If state capacity is (or should be) weakening, then why ask the state to solve global problems? Why not go directly to the private sector, where the resources exist to attack the problem?

This approach emphasizes developing new responses and infrastructure that utilize nonstate actors such as NGOs and MNCs. Corporate codes of conduct to improve international environmental and labor standards, efforts to get pharmaceutical companies to voluntarily reduce the prices and increase access to essential medicines for poor countries and people, market solutions to overcoming poverty problems through FDI, increased trade, and microbusiness (for example, Nakornthon Bank) are nonstate-centric policy prescriptions. Direct action campaigns by NGOs to change corporate or consumer behavior (for example, convincing the tuna industry to adopt dolphin-safe fishing techniques) are also instances of action directly affecting change regardless of governmental participation. Efforts to fight global problems of refugee flows, disease, and environmental degradation tend to focus more readily on nonstate-centric approaches. NGO activities have traditionally been strongest in these areas. The efforts of the Gates Foundation to immunize children in Africa, and the efforts of ProMED (the Program to Monitor Emerging Diseases), a global electronic mail network that facilitates reporting on and discussion of disease outbreaks around the world, are also nonstate-centric responses.

Mixed or Public–Private Approaches

Finally, there is a third way. If public and private sector responses alone cannot effectively manage global issues, then why not combine the two? Public–private partnerships can reap the benefits of each separate approach while minimizing some of the problems of one approach alone. By combining the benefits of state legitimacy and enforceability with the flexibility and resources of the private sector, more traction can be brought to bear on difficult global issues.

The state still has important levers that can be used to fight global problems. David Victor of the Council of Foreign Relations invokes a *Star Wars* analogy. The dark side of enthusiasm about using private sector responses is that you still need the force of the state. A state can provide threats or force, serve as negotiator or facilitator of private sector interactions, and backstop private sector initiatives with a safety net baseline of law that provides more universally implementable and enforceable norms. States provide not only the sticks but also the carrots of incentives, and they can focus direction. The state has the added advantage of being familiar and available. But neither the state nor the private sector can do it alone. The choices are not between multilateralism and unilateralism, integration and fragmentation, federal government and local government, and public sector and private sector. To manage global problems, we must use all of the networks at our disposal. Choice of the institutional instrument will be based on who has the established network assets in a sector. She who has the network becomes the partner with the foreign policy organizations.

For example, Stephen Flynn argues that greater cooperation between the government and private sector shipping firms through information sharing and increased security measures at the point of origin would greatly reduce trafficking in refugees, persons, drugs, and weapons, as well as terrorism. The private sector wins with faster, more assured shipping, less money lost to stolen shipments, less time lost to backups at the border, and fewer invasive border inspections. The government wins allies in trying to manage global problems and gains information with which to better target government border control resources.[1] Debt-for-nature swaps; the financial action task forces that develop anti–money laundering standards for member states as well as private banks; and the US treasury department's Financial Crimes Enforcement Network (FinCEN), which works with banks to identify and track suspicious financial transactions—all of these are public–private partnerships.

If states alone cannot adequately respond to global problems, then why is it important that they be part of the multipronged approach? The most important advantage states have is that they exist. They do not have to be built from scratch. They are familiar, with addresses and known processes that are understood and available for interaction, allowing the opportunity for transparency and accountability. States may not have the ability to command or compel resolution of a global problem, but they are uniquely positioned to coordinate, communicate, facilitate, and cajole action from a variety of other actors who look to the state to fill that conduit function. States are a focal point for citizen imagination and demands. Whether or not states can solve global problems alone, the question is still raised by the public and the media, "What is the state doing about it?"

In addition, governments are often perceived to have the political legitimacy to act on behalf of the populace in foreign affairs. Although foreign policy bureaucracies in democracies are generally not staffed by elected officials, they are created and funded by elected officials, and they can be held responsible to elected officials. Thus, state institutions must have some degree of political support to exist at all; on the other hand, it is not clear whom MNCs and NGOs represent, to whom they are accountable or how they can be held accountable, or how much political legitimacy and support they command. Why not use the institutional advantages states have of being available as a forum?

Underlying these differences over how to best respond to global problems are different assumptions about the future of the sovereign state. Is the sovereign state retreating, its power becoming more diffuse in a globalized economy? Susan Strange argues that power is moving from states to markets as states either abdicate more functions to nonstate actors or vacate certain functions altogether.[2] There is some evidence from the preceding chapters in favor of this view. Nonstate actors are increasingly taking on functions that were traditionally performed by states, even in the security sector. The example of debt-for-nature swaps supports Rosecrance's idea of the declining importance of territory relative to the rising importance of market forces.[3] If states are losing power to nonstate actors and market dynamics, then responses to global problems should be aimed at nonstate actors and market forces.

Others argue that the sovereign state is still the fundamental unit in the international system. Sovereignty took centuries to develop and will not disappear in a few decades, and there are no well-developed alternative organizing units ready to replace sovereign states.[4] The preceding chapters offer some evidence to support this view. Terrorism highlights that the state is still important enough to be worth fighting for. Likewise, Ford and Lee believe that states created nuclear weapons, and only state actions can effectively contain nuclear smuggling. If this is the case and state actors still reign supreme, then efforts to fight global problems should still be aimed at states and strengthening state institutions or perhaps at developing more cooperative ventures among states.

There is a third way. If sovereignty is denigrated but not dead, then fighting global problems may require a combined approach in which a wide spectrum of policy responses are undertaken and coordinated, aimed at both state and nonstate sectors. If we are in a period of transition or turbulence[5]—in which a changed economic system has created new actors and dissipated the power of states in crucial economic and social sectors, but in which state actors are still important in the law enforcement and security sectors—then a combined approach is necessary. Just as new interstate highways are often built alongside existing two-lane highways, new networks using new actors must be built at the same time while the old state actors are still functioning.

For all of the advantages of pursuing public–private partnerships, there are also obstacles. Many were discussed in the last chapter, but there are also the problems of working with many different actors and integrating a wide variety of responses. More actors require greater coordination, communication, cooperation, prioritization, transparency, and accountability, which increases the level of difficulty. Pursuing a combined approach also necessitates vigilance for threshold effects and unintended consequences. For example, policy responses may need a certain level of funding for a protracted period of time before a program may yield results. But if policy responses are split over a variety of state and nonstate venues, then resources may be diluted or a plan of attack may be pursued for too short a period, never reaching the threshold necessary for effective action. Unintended consequences apply to every approach. Because action must be coordinated among a wider variety of players, it may be more difficult to anticipate the full ramifications of a wider array of actions in public–private partnerships. For example, funneling attention and funding to nonstate actors and sectors could further undermine state sectors and actors. As new highways are built, sometimes the old roadways fall into disuse.

Continued monitoring and attention to coordination, prioritization, and accountability are necessary. Yet none of these critiques is unique to public–private approaches, though they may be more intense with them. State-centric and nonstate-centric prescriptions also share these obstacles. Combating terrorism, organized crime, or drug trafficking in one sector or region may merely drive it into another area. All approaches require building political support, coordination, communication, prioritization, transparency, and accountability—and all may encounter resistance to change by existing organizations, threshold effects, and unintended consequences.

DOES SOVEREIGNTY STILL REIGN?

If state-centric responses are still necessary along with other approaches in dealing with global problems, then does this mean that Krasner and Spruyt are right? Is there no competitor to the sovereign state out there right now, so sovereignty still reigns by default? Not exactly, because sovereignty is changing in significant ways. Vertical and horizontal linkages may still anchor sovereignty in place, but they are breaking down. The anchor is becoming dislodged.

It is instructive to remember Hendrik Spruyt's story of how fundamental change came about the last time and ushered in the sovereign state: the economy changed. New elites were created who benefited from the new economic system and needed a new form of political organization to better accommodate them and their economic practices. Ideas changed, new organizational forms emerged and competed, and, after centuries of flux, the sovereign state eventually won out.[6]

There are many parallels today. The economy has changed. The new economic system is increasingly based on information, technology, and services, which are less dependent on the control of territory. The means of production, capital, and labor are mobile, not fixed. Players who make use of modern information, communication, transportation, and financial technologies reap the benefits of increasingly open borders and economies. Political systems that make room for the new economic system reap profits in foreign direct investment, and so regime types as distinct as the Chinese communist system, the Mexican emerging democracy, and the Iranian theocracy are all simultaneously undertaking reforms to make themselves more attractive to investors' capital and technology flows.

New elites are emerging who profit from the new economic system. Typified by George Soros, Bill Gates, and Ted Turner, these "new imperialists"[7] increasingly follow no flag. They are passionate about expanding technologies and markets, and they are frustrated by what they see as anachronistic state barriers to investment and trade flows. The international business classes attend the same schools, fly the same airlines, vacation at the same resorts, eat at the same restaurants, and watch the same movies and television shows. Independent of national identities, these elites mobilize to try to make states facilitate market dynamics. Some call it the "Davos culture" after the Swiss luxury resort where the annual World Economic Summit meets.[8] Sociologist Peter Berger calls it the "yuppie internationale," a culture typified by the scene in a Buddhist temple in Hong Kong of "a middle aged man wearing a dark business suit over stocking feet. He was burning incense and at the same time talking on his cellular phone." Berger believes these cultural ties have made peace talks in South Africa and Northern Ireland go more smoothly: "It may be that commonalities in taste make it easier to find common ground politically."[9] Can it be that leaders who all shop at the Gap and Benetton and eat at McDonald's find political antagonisms quaint and unnecessary? In what he deems the "Golden Arches Theory of Conflict Prevention," Thomas Friedman argues that no two countries with McDonald's restaurants have ever gone to war with one another.[10] Even though clearly there are many economically underprivileged people around the world who do not partake of this lifestyle, the values of this new elite percolate into the rest of society as people mimic the behavior of the elites and strive to better their economic situations to one day rise into the wealthier classes.

Ideas are changing (including ideas of authority, identity, and organization), facilitated by the new information technologies and changes in the economy. Never before in human history have we been able to spread ideas so quickly and widely. Modern communication technologies allow an ever-wider swath of the planet to be tuned in to the same advertisements, the same television shows, and, thereby, to some of the same ideas about consumerism and personal freedoms. Identity is becoming less tied to territory. If identity and authority do not stem from geography, then what is our new church, our new religion? In the European Middle Ages, identity came from Christendom, the Church, while authority stemmed from spiritual connections. In the modern era, identity was tied up with the nation state; authority corresponded with geography. Now authority and identity are increasingly contested. Strange believes we now have Pinocchio's problem: The strings of state control, authority, and identity have been cut, but no new strings have been fastened.[11] States no longer are the supreme recipient of individual loyalties, especially because they no longer fulfill basic services and functions and other actors have stepped into the gap. Firms, professions, families, religions, and social movements have all significantly challenged the state's territorial and security-based claim to individual loyalty. We are left to choose among competing sources of allegiance, authority, and identity, with no strings to bind us like puppets to one source of authority, and with more freedom to let our conscience be our guide.

Certainly the new economy would like identity to be formed around consumer products—you are what you wear, what you consume. Advertisers spend billions to imprint brand loyalty at an early age, and all the advertising of Planet Reebok, I'd-like-to-buy-the-world-a-Coke, and Microsoft's One World Internet Explorer icon share a common theme: that identity stems not from national borders but from consumer products. Identity is therefore just as mobile as the economy. You are not born with it. You can buy it. Alternatively, some see identity as increasingly flowing from professions and firms: You are what you do, and your commitment is to your profession rather than to a specific state. As Rosecrance describes it, "Today and for the foreseeable future, the only international civilization worthy of the name is the governing economic culture of the world market."[12] Benjamin Barber refers to this popular, consumer market culture as "McWorld."[13] As market values permeate various cultures, certain ideas emerge as prized: the value of change, mobility, flexibility, adaptability, speed, and information. As capitalism becomes our creed, with technology as our guide, distinct national and religious cultures are becoming permeated with common market values.

There are alternatives to market values, however. Religious organizations and NGOs promulgate alternative ethics to materialism, a globalization in which we are not merely consumers or a governance problem but human beings, each with irreducible sacred dignity. This vision of globalization prescribes putting people before profits, ethical values before market values. These organizations use the tools of globalization to promote their views of humanizing globalization. For example, the Internet is a popular tool for organizing and proselytizing by many faith groups, including traditional Islam.[14]

Ideas of organization are also changing and are based on models from the marketplace and technology: Computers, the Internet, and the market are diffuse, decentralized, loosely connected networks with a few central organizing parameters but strong ties to the activities of individual entrepreneurs. Foreign policy organizations are, in some instances, going beyond bureaucracy, creating flexible, innovative, coordinating networks.

Creative public–private partnerships are the wave of the future in solving global problems. Rather than trying to become draconian, big brother states (which would conflict with the goals of open societies, open economies, and open technologies), it makes sense for governments to look toward civil society for help in managing global problems. But states must be aware of the costs of contracting out. In privatizing, not only do governments lose some control over policy, but also private entities may present obstacles to the government's agenda as profit or other motives conflict with important public policy goals.[15] Although *privatization* and "moving beyond bureaucracy" are popular buzzwords and phrases in today's budget-conscious political climate, changes in state architecture have consequences for how we think about political authority, identity, and organization.

Ideas drawn from experience of the new economic system are helping to shape new ideas of political organization. A resurgence of IGOs simultaneous with increased attention to local governance may not seem at all strange to a civilization used to surfing the Internet and using a system that is simultaneously globally connected and only as good as the local link.

Rosenau believes that as individuals become more analytically skillful, the nature of authority shifts. People no longer uncritically accept traditional criteria of state authority based on historical, legal, or customary claims of legitimacy. Instead, authority and legitimacy are increasingly based on how well government authorities perform.[16] Kane's description of the huge increase in refugees and migrants voting with their feet seems to support this claim. Thus, while scholars disagree about the sources of identity and authority in the emerging era, they agree that these ideas are changing.

Finally, new forms of political organization are beginning to emerge, as evidenced by the European Union and the increasing roles and profile of IGOs. Thus, even if, as Spruyt maintains, the sovereign state is still supreme, three out of four of his indicators of fundamental change are already here: Change in economy, elites, and ideas are in evidence, and even though no new form of political organization has unseated the sovereign state, new forms are beginning to emerge around the sovereign state that are chipping away at functions previously performed by it and changing its role.

GOING GLOBAL VERSUS GOING LOCAL: THE STATE CONTRACTS OUT

Are new forms of political organization emerging to accompany these changes? Many commentators have noted the irony that globalizing forces are spreading and deepening at the same time that virulent forms of nationalism are evident in internal wars. There are several reasons why this is not surprising. First of all, scholars on nationalism note that ties to ethnic or national groups increase under threat.[17] Therefore, it makes sense that at precisely the time when globalizing forces threaten local identities, there is resurgent attention to local ways of life.

Threat is only one piece of the puzzle, however. Transitions to liberal economic and political forms are destabilizing. Virulent nationalisms can be resuscitated as a means of finding a scapegoat for tough times. The fact that there once was a violent form of nationalism does not mean, however, that future conflicts will break out along national or ethnic lines. Many of the most highly developed states today once endured bloody civil wars—the United Kingdom, the United States, and France.

Previous conflict by itself is neither an indicator nor an explanation for later conflict. This is where the case of Bosnia becomes critical. Most journalists and pundits peg the cause of conflict in the Balkans as "ancient ethnic hatreds."[18] But this no more explains the conflict than does noting that the sun rose before the fighting took place, and because A came before B, A therefore caused B. Poland and Czechoslovakia also experienced "ancient ethnic hostilities," yet violent nationalism did not plunge these societies into internal war as occurred in the former Yugoslavia. Economics was a pivotal trigger in bringing violent nationalism to Yugoslavia, while Poland and Czechoslovakia had gentler transitions from communism. As the economic situation deteriorated in Yugoslavia, politicians sought to protect their own national groups. Leaders exploited nationalist tensions to explain away economic woes and distance themselves from their communist pasts, often using the media as their megaphones of hate.[19] Michael Brown notes that bad leaders, bad neighbors, bad internal problems, and bad neighborhoods can also fire nationalism into internal conflict.[20] There is no straight causal line between violent nationalism in the past and violent nationalism in the future. However, states undergoing difficult transitions can be more vulnerable to such violent forms.

Going global and going local are connected in another way as well. A study of twelve states over the past twenty years showed a correlation between indicators of open societies, open economies, and open technologies and government decentralization. States that increased in openness over the time period also increased in government decentralization (the amount of money and decision-making power that went to the local government level as opposed to the central government). States that stayed closed in the same time period did not experience government decentralization. Correlation is not causation, and so the forces of open economy, open technology, and open society and government decentralization might be caused by some third factor (the IMF, for example, as international investors pressure states both to decentralize governments and to privatize markets). But initial evidence does show that there are "simultaneous trends in globalization and decentralization."[21] Decentralization and open society, open market, and open technology forces go together.

By this view it is not an accident that the highly centralized states of the communist Soviet Union and Eastern Europe, the apartheid state of South Africa, the military regimes in Argentina, and the social-welfare states of the United Kingdom and the United States are undergoing decentralization simultaneously. Big government is being downsized all over the planet,[22] and power is increasingly moving to local governments in federated systems and to nonstate actors. Sometimes, the central state government retains authority over certain functions but no longer performs the functions itself, as when Australia contracts refugee camps out to private companies or Britain debates hiring mercenary soldiers:

> When a country's political, economic, and development activities become globalized, the national government may no longer be the dominant entity; transnational cooperations emerge at all levels of government (national and subnational) and among all types of organizations (public organizations, multinational organizations, and NGOs). . . . Global changes occurring today are creating new, complex, and decentralized systems of networks that are radically different from the old centralized systems of governance which controlled the process of international activities and decision making.[23]

How can it be that local government is making a comeback all over the globe at the same time that IGOs are becoming more important? The state is contracting out functions to several actors simultaneously: IGOs, NGOs, MNCs, and local governments. The strong central governments of the twentieth century—the fascist states, the communist states, and the Rooseveltian social security state—are receding. At the dawn of the twenty-first century, the sovereign state remains. But this is not the state that we drove into the last century. This is not your father's Oldsmobile.

THE SPEED OF CHANGE

If the sovereign state is changing and new forms of political organization are emerging, then will change take centuries this time around? When sovereignty emerged, competing political forms coexisted for centuries before feudalism receded and the sovereign state emerged as the standard. Skeptics believe that it will take a similarly long time before current changes in economic or social structures mount a fundamental challenge to the sovereign state system, in part because those who benefit from the existing state system will fight to keep it. But the end of feudalism and the rise of sovereignty took place in an era when the modes of transportation and communication were horseback and slow-moving ships. Might change occur more quickly now in an era of jet planes, the Internet, faxes, e-mail, personal computers, and cell phones?

The rate of change is different than it used to be. As Susan Strange notes

> What is new and unusual is that all (or nearly all) states should undergo substantial change of roughly the same kind within the same short period of twenty or thirty years. The last time that anything like this happened was in Europe when states based on a feudal system of agricultural production geared to local subsistence, gave way to states based on a capitalist system of industrial production for the market. The process of change was spread over two or three centuries at the very least and in parts of eastern and southern Europe is only now taking shape. In the latter part of the twentieth century, the shift has not been confined to Europe and has taken place with bewildering rapidity.[24]

Ideas are spread instantaneously in an era of satellite television, as fast as an Internet connection. The "one world" advertising themes of Nike, IBM, and UPS may contain a grain of truth in highlighting the ramifications of a wired planet to which many of us are plugged in.

The idea of punctuated equilibrium draws the analogy that institutional change may occur rapidly over a limited period of time in unexpected ways. Rather than the Darwinian idea of change as slow, steady, continuous, and gradual, punctuated equilibrium stresses that change is "usually accomplished rapidly when a stable structure is stressed beyond its buffering capacity to resist and absorb. . . . These evolutionary shifts can be quirky and unpredictable as the potentials for complexity are vast."[25]

Is the fast rate of change that open economy, society, and technology forces have unleashed comparable to the rate of change of sovereign states to keep up with new environmental circumstances? This is particularly important as more states become democratic, because democratic state institutions are often slow to act, with opportunities for gridlock and delay built into the state structure. Democracy was never organized to be effective or efficient. Shared powers and separate institutions with checks and balances among them is a hedge against tyranny, not a recipe for efficiency. By putting different parts of government at each other's throats, it was hoped that government might stay off the people's backs and that deliberation and perspective might result from democratic procedures. Tyranny has many faults, but it can act quickly. The government does what the ruler says, whether it is right, just, legal, or in the public interest. The Nazi government, for example, was chillingly systematic and efficient in its use of industrial technology to conduct the Holocaust. Government becomes much more slow and bothersome when those in charge have to consult others about what to do, and when they have to factor in civil rights, civil liberties, and accountability to the law. In an era of e-mail, cell phones, and laptop computers, where the economy and technology place great value on speed and efficiency, we forget that democratic institutions were not built for speed. As Alexis de Toqueville noted, the miracle of the system is that it works at all.

If the rate of external change vastly supercedes the institution's ability to respond, then will sovereign institutions be stressed beyond their ability to evolve and adapt? Buffeted by external blows, sovereignty continues to limp along, pocked by capacity, jurisdiction, and other institutional gaps. But as the speed of technological change outpaces the sovereign state's ability to hobble and hotwire responses, the limp may become more pronounced and perhaps (though no time soon) eventually be fatal to the sovereign state.

CONCLUSION: THE SHIP OF STATE

At what point do we have a new ship of state? Scholars agree that change is occurring. The sovereign state is not obsolete, and will continue to play a role along with other actors on the international scene. But there is disagreement over sovereignty's future. We are in a period of transition. We do not know yet whether the state can be retrofitted to weather the storms of changes in economy, elites, and ideas, or whether these changes will someday bring about new forms of political organization.

The situation is analogous to a famous puzzle in the study of philosophy: the ship of Theseus. There are three different ways the ship of Theseus problem is discussed. The first stems from its origins in Greek mythology. Theseus was the son of Aegeus, the king of Athens. Theseus sailed away to fight a heroic battle, but after slaying the Minotaur he forgot to change the sails to indicate the victory to his father. Sailing in the same old sails unwittingly brought about tragedy, as his father did not realize the battle had been won because the changed situation was not immediately apparent by viewing his son's ship. In a fit of despair, Theseus's father committed suicide, throwing himself from a cliff into the sea.[26] The analogy here is to the discussion in Chapter 13 about institutions. Many of our foreign policy institutions were built to fight strong states, not weak states and global problems. We have not changed our institutional sails consistent with the new situation, and we flirt with disaster by traveling with our old sails.

The more pressing analogy, however, concerns the other two ways in which the problem of the ship of Theseus is discussed, questioning the nature of change and identity. If the planks of a ship are removed one by one over intervals of time, and each time an old plank is removed it is replaced by a new plank, then is it a new vessel? At what point did it reach critical mass to call it something new?[27]

This is the question we now face in considering the sovereign state. In Chapter 1, we considered ten functions of states that Susan Strange believed are either no longer being performed or are at least being shared with other, nonstate actors. Scholar William Zartman posts his own list. In discussing failed or weak states that are collapsing, he lists five basic roles states perform: as the decision-making center of government, as a symbol of identity, as controller of territory and guarantor of security, as an authoritative and legitimate political institution, and as a system of socioeconomic organization, the target of citizen demands for providing supplies or services.[28] Although Zartman offers this list as a litmus test for when weak states are failing because basic state functions are no longer being performed, many of these functions correspond with Strange's and other authors' observations of roles that all states (weak and strong) used to undertake but no longer fulfill.

The chapters of this book show that states are no longer the sole decision making centers. MNCs, IGOs, and NGOs increasingly make decisions about matters that were traditionally handled by states. Economic decisions increasingly take place in corporate boardrooms, on the floors of international stock exchanges, and in the conference rooms of the IMF, and states increasingly react to rather than generate these key decisions. States are being challenged as symbols of identity and as authoritative, legitimate political institutions, as citizens increasingly place their loyalties elsewhere. Even strong states no longer can unilaterally control territory or borders or secure territory from external threats.

Alternative institutions—from MNCs to NGOs and IGOs—are increasingly the targets of citizen demands for services that citizens do not believe the state can supply. If the sovereign state is no longer performing the basic functions associated with sovereign states, then at what point does sovereignty cease? If the primary innovation of the sovereign state was its connection of authority to territory, then what does it mean for sovereignty if the state's connection to territory is being severed and states derive less authority or power from territory?[29] Rosenau argues that authority is no longer automatically conferred to the traditional sources on the basis of customary legitimacy claims, be they legal or geographic, but that people are instead judging legitimacy and authority on the basis of performance. If sovereignty is no longer about territory, then what is it about? If territory is at the heart of sovereignty and territory is removed, then is what's left still sovereignty? How many planks must be pulled for us to recognize it as something different?

The difference between the case of sovereignty and the changes that occurred to the ship of Theseus are these: The ship's planks were replaced exactly in the same manner and to fulfill the same functions. The planks were not altered to turn the ship into a rocket. In the case of sovereignty, however, materials are changing to slowly give the vessel a facelift. Such changes might be correlated to the changes in regime and administrative type between the authoritarian regimes and regimes with the strong central government functions typical of the twentieth century rather than the decentralized, capitalist, and democratic regimes of the twenty-first century.

However, the changes this volume discusses are not just changes in sovereignty's face or outward appearance; they are changes in its nature. Unlike the ship of Theseus, the ship of state is changing the very functions it performs and how it performs them. If sovereignty is as sovereignty does, and what sovereignty does is changing, is what sovereignty is changing?

The final analogy with the ship concerns the nature of change. Some philosophers argue for foundationalism—that sound principles need to be laid out first before new concepts can be built on them. But Otto Neurath argues that we seldom have the luxury of changing our ideas in a pristine vacuum and starting from scratch. Instead he argues that "we are like sailors who must rebuild their ship on the open sea, never able to dismantle it in dry dock and to reconstruct it there out of the best materials."[30]

Certainly this is analogous to the descriptions of change offered by political psychologists, as forged in experience. Humans learn by doing, and as we experiment with states contracting out and public–private partnerships, we learn new ways of thinking about human organizations. These experiences are changing how we exercise and think about sovereignty. The ship's wheel is being replaced while the ship is still in operation. New planks are added and old functions are jettisoned while we are under way. Nonstate actors are cropping up and assuming functions that states used to perform. New policies toward global problems are evolving, utilizing nonstate sectors at the same time that state responses are being fine-tuned. We are not dry-docked and awaiting the emergence of a new ship of political organization, but we must go forward while we are in the midst of major construction.

The problem with our ability to track changes in the sovereign state is that we are used to the system; we are not good even at contemplating what the alternatives to sovereignty might look like. We are truly conceptual prisoners. Ideas matter, and outdated ideas can kill. Changes can occur in unintended ways, and they can occur rapidly when threshold effects are reached. Even though Krasner concludes that the sovereign state "will not be dislodged easily, regardless of changed circumstances in the material environment" and that sovereignty is so entrenched that "[i]t is now difficult to even conceive of alternatives," he acknowledges that surprises are possible.[31]

The *Titanic* was a supposedly unsinkable ship that hit an iceberg in the dark and sank within hours, killing more than 1,500 passengers and crew members. Similarly, the sovereign state is hitting many unforeseen obstacles in the dark side of globalization. Gaps in our institutions are already painfully apparent. Because the seas of change are turbulent, we have a moral obligation to think about the unthinkable, build better institutions, and consider alternatives if the impossible were to occur and the ship of sovereignty turned out not to be unsinkable after all. Urgently needed are new thoughts on how we might better organize humans, as well as more specific ideas about the organizational shapes into which sovereignty might morph or that might rival or replace sovereignty at some time in the unknown future. These ideas are developing out of our experiences of economic and technological change as our ideas about organization are informed by the new organizational structures we use in the marketplace and on the Internet.

Sovereignty is not going away, but it is evolving, decentralizing, and contracting out. States increasingly coordinate policy among a wider variety of public and private actors. Richard Neustadt describes a US political system in which the president is more powerful than other political actors but rarely has the ability to command or compel. Instead, the president must persuade others to pursue his preferred outcomes.[32]

The state is entering a similar position. It may be more powerful than NGOs, IGOs, and MNCs, depending on the case and the situation, but it rarely has the power to command or compel outcomes on global problems. Instead, states have to assume new roles as coordinators, facilitators, initiators, and salesmen in order to persuade action on global problems. This places burdens on state institutions, requiring organizational changes and adding more functions for states to undertake though not necessarily control. Neustadt notes that an increase in duties does not equate to an increase in power or in the capacity to fulfill new duties, and that more duties without means is equivalent to being a glorified clerk, not a powerful entity. For the immediate future, sovereignty will be first among competing forms, but there will be a "return to history" in the sense of a return to cross-cutting, nonhierarchical, ad hoc, and relative forms of order and organization.

Yet integrating action among a wider variety of players also opens new opportunities for policy and offers greater possibilities for effectively managing global issues than old-style unilateral responses. NGOs and MNCs frequently "forum shop"—that is, move an issue across borders to a more hospitable institutional venue for a chance at better resolution. We are no longer stuck with sovereignty only; we can often choose from and move among a variety of institutions. We are engaged in an exciting period of organizational pluralism and experimentation. International political problems have gone beyond sovereignty. We must also go beyond sovereignty in theory and in practice, changing our ideas and our institutions to better respond to the life-and-death challenges of globalization's gaps.

ENDNOTES

1. Stephen Flynn, "America the Vulnerable," *Foreign Affairs* (Jan.–Feb. 2002).
2. Susan Strange, *The Retreat of the State: The Diffusion of Power in the World Economy* (Cambridge, UK: Cambridge University Press, 1996), 189.
3. Richard Rosecrance, "The Rise of the Virtual State," *Foreign Affairs* (July–Aug. 1996): 59–60.

4. Stephen D. Krasner, *Problematic Sovereignty: Contested Rules and Political Possibilities* (New York: Columbia University Press, 2001); Stephen D. Krasner, *Sovereignty: Organized Hypocrisy* (Princeton, NJ: Princeton University Press, 1999); Stephen D. Krasner, "Sovereignty: An Institutional Perspective," *Comparative Political Studies* 21 (April 1988): 74; Kenneth Waltz, "Globalization and Governance," *PS: Political Science & Politics* (Dec. 1999): 693–700; William H. McNeill, "Territorial States Buried Too Soon," *Mershon International Studies Review* 41 (1997): 269.

5. James N. Rosenau, *Turbulence in World Politics* (Princeton, NJ: Princeton University Press, 1990).

6. Hendrik Spruyt, *The Sovereign State and Its Competitors* (Princeton, NJ: Princeton University Press, 1994), 62, 75.

7. Mark Leibovich, *The New Imperialists* (New York: Prentice Hall, 2002).

8. Samuel Huntington, *The Clash of Civilizations and the Remaking of World Order* (New York: Simon & Schuster, 1996).

9. Peter L. Berger, "Four Faces of Global Culture," *The National Interest* (Fall 1997): 24.

10. Thomas L. Friedman, *The Lexus and the Olive Tree: Understanding Globalization* (New York: Farrar, Straus & Giroux, 1999), 195–196.

11. Strange, *The Retreat of the State,* 199.

12. Richard Rosecrance, *The Rise of the Virtual State: Wealth and Power in the Coming Century* (New York: Basic Books, 2000); Rosecrance, "The Rise of the Virtual State," 59–60.

13. Benjamin R. Barber, *Jihad vs. McWorld* (New York: Ballantine Books, 1996).

14. Jon W. Anderson and Dale F. Eickelman (Eds.), *New Media in the Muslim World: The Emerging Public Sphere* (Bloomington: Indiana University Press, 1999).

15. Peter Passell, "U.S. Goals at Odds in a Plan to Sell Off Nuclear Operation," *The New York Times,* July 25, 1995, p. A1.

16. Maryann Cusimano, "James Rosenau and Monica Lewinsky," *PS: Political Science and Politics* (Dec. 1999). Interestingly, Rosenau's thesis explains why President Clinton's approval ratings did not diminish and even improved during his impeachment hearings. The media and conservative thinkers have been at a loss to explain why the US public was not more exercised about President Clinton's extramarital affair, its moral implications, and its effects on the dignity of the presidential office. But if the public judges legitimacy and authority by performance criteria, not by appeals to tradition or moral authority, then breaches of tradition and morality would not affect the public's perception of Clinton's legitimacy or authority. If performance criteria are all that matters, then Clinton's poll ratings make sense given the low unemployment rate and strong performance of the US economy during his administration, especially while European and Asian economic growth rates were simultaneously flat or declining. According to Rosenau, it would seem that political leaders can "get away with" quite a bit as long as it does not poorly affect their record of concrete achievements.

17. Ted Robert Gurr, "Minorities, Nationalists, and Ethnopolitical Conflict," in Chester Crocker, Fen Osler Hampson, and Pamela Aall (Eds.), *Managing Global Chaos* (Washington, DC: US Institute of Peace, 1996), 53–78; David Little, "Religious Militancy," in Crocker et al., *Managing Global Chaos,* 79–92; Ernest Gellner, "Nations and Nationalism," in Richard Betts (Ed.), *Conflict after the Cold War: Arguments on the Causes of War and Peace* (New York: Macmillan, 1994), 280–292; Louis Kriesberg, "Regional Conflicts in the Post–Cold War Era: Causes, Dynamics, and Modes of Resolution," in Michael Klare and Daniel Thomas (Eds.), *World Security: Challenges for*

a New Century (New York: St. Martin's Press, 1994), 155–174; Donald L. Horowitz, "Ethnic and Nationalist Conflict," in Klare and Thomas, *World Security,* 175–187.

18. Robert D. Kaplan, *The Coming Anarchy: Shattering the Dreams of the Post Cold War World* (New York: Vintage Books, 2001); Robert D. Kaplan, *Warrior Politics: Why Leadership Demands a Pagan Ethos* (New York: Random House, 2001); Robert D. Kaplan, *Balkan Ghosts: A Journey through History* (New York: Vintage Books, 1994); Robert D. Kaplan, "The Coming Anarchy," *Atlantic Monthly* (Feb. 1994): 44–76.

19. Susan Woodward, *Balkan Tragedy* (Washington, DC: Brookings Institution, 1995).

20. Michael Brown, *The International Dimensions of Internal Conflict* (Cambridge: MIT Press, 1996), 579.

21. Jong S. Jun and Deil S. Wright, *Globalization and Decentralization: Institutional Contexts, Policy Issues, and Intergovernmental Relations in Japan and the United States* (Washington, DC: Georgetown University Press, 1996), 1.

22. President Clinton declared the era of big government dead, referring to the end of welfare as we knew it and reforms that downsized the federal government to the smallest it had been since the Kennedy administration. Similar downsizing efforts have been under way internationally as privatization and "e-government" spread. Structural adjustment policies trim government spending in developing countries.

23. Jun and Wright, *Globalization and Decentralization,* 3–4.

24. Strange, *The Retreat of the State,* 87.

25. Krasner, "Sovereignty: An Institutional Perspective," 79.

26. Robert E. Bell, *Dictionary of Classical Mythology: Symbols, Attributes and Associations* (Santa Barbara, CA: ABC-Clio, 1982), 207.

27. Rodrick M. Chisholm, *Person and Object: A Metaphysical Study* (LaSalle, IL: Open Court, 1976), 89–92.

28. I. William Zartman, *Collapsed States* (Boulder, CO: Lynne Rienner, 1995), 5.

29. Rosecrance, *The Rise of the Virtual State.*

30. Otto Neurath quoted in A. J. Ayer (Ed.), *Logical Positivism* (Glenco, IL: The Free Press, 1959). This is sometimes referred to as "Neurath's ship."

31. Krasner, "Sovereignty: An Institutional Perspective," 80.

32. Richard E. Neustadt, *Presidential Power and the Modern Presidents: The Politics of Leadership from Roosevelt to Reagan* (New York: The Free Press, 1990).

Date Due